TOLSTOY: THE CRITICAL HERITAGE

THE CRITICAL HERITAGE SERIES

GENERAL EDITOR: B. C. SOUTHAM, M.A., B.LITT. (OXON.)
Formerly Department of English, Westfield College, University of London

---

For a list of books in the series see the back end paper

TOLSTOY

THE CRITICAL HERITAGE

Edited by
A. V. KNOWLES
Lecturer in Russian
University of Liverpool

ROUTLEDGE & KEGAN PAUL
LONDON, HENLEY AND BOSTON

First published in 1978
by Routledge & Kegan Paul Ltd
39 Store Street,
London WC1E 7DD,
Broadway House,
Newtown Road,
Henley-on-Thames,
Oxon RG9 1EN and
9 Park Street,
Boston, Mass. 02108, USA
Printed in Great Britain by
Redwood Burn Ltd
Trowbridge and Esher

British Library Cataloguing in Publication Data

Tolstoy, the critical heritage—(The critical
heritage series).
1. Tolstoy, Leo, Count—Criticism and interpretation
Addresses, essays, lectures
I. Knowles, Antony Vere II. Series
891.7'3'3   PG3410   78-40601

ISBN 0 7100 8947 3

General Editor's Preface

The reception given to a writer by his contemporaries and near-contemporaries is evidence of considerable value to the student of literature. On one side we learn a great deal about the state of criticism at large and in particular about the development of critical attitudes towards a single writer; at the same time, through private comments in letters, journals or marginalia, we gain an insight upon the tastes and literary thought of individual readers of the period. Evidence of this kind helps us to understand the writer's historical situation, the nature of his immediate reading-public, and his response to these pressures.

The separate volumes in the *Critical Heritage Series* present a record of this early criticism. Clearly, for many of the highly productive and lengthily reviewed nineteenth- and twentieth-century writers, there exists an enormous body of material; and in these cases the volume editors have made a selection of the most important views, significant for their intrinsic critical worth or for their representative quality—perhaps even registering incomprehension!

For earlier writers, notably pre-eighteenth century, the materials are much scarcer and the historical period has been extended, sometimes far beyond the writer's lifetime, in order to show the inception and growth of critical views which were initially slow to appear.

In each volume the documents are headed by an Introduction, discussing the material assembled and relating the early stages of the author's reception to what we have come to identify as the critical tradition. The volumes will make available much material which would otherwise be difficult of access and it is hoped that the modern reader will be thereby helped towards an informed understanding of the ways in which literature has been read and judged.

B.C.S.

Contents

After 'Anna Karenina' (1886–1910)

Preface

Much of the contemporary response to Tolstoy's fiction,
especially in his own country, was ephemeral and not
unduly enlightening, some of it was not without interest,
but only a little of it was of any lasting merit. Because
of this, when we read what his contemporaries had to say
about him we learn, ostensibly at least, far more about
the state of nineteenth- and early twentieth-century
literary criticism than we do about Tolstoy the writer.
That is not to say, however, that the seeds of what was to
become the main growth of Tolstoyan criticism are entirely
absent; but many of them are in general so well concealed
by extraneous wrappings, instructions, exhortations,
denunciations and words of caution that they are not
readily exposed to the light of day.
   The amount of critical comment written in Tolstoy's
lifetime is immense; even the early trilogy, 'Childhood',
'Boyhood' and 'Youth', received well over one hundred
reviews and notices; and once he had become well known
all the critics, and indeed everybody who was anybody (and
many more who were not), felt obliged to put pen to paper.
Such a vast amount of criticism presents serious problems
to an editor of a volume in the present series; consequently some sort of fairly arbitrary limitation has had
to be imposed on the selection. In the first place it
would be foolish of me to claim to have read everything
that appeared, and this sets some limitation at the
outset; second, much of it is so lacking in any, even
negative, value that it has been rejected out of hand;
third, a large proportion of it is hardly more than a
recapitulation of the text, or of what fellow-critics
wrote, and this has also been excluded. The final choice
therefore has been restricted primarily to criticism of
Tolstoy's works of imaginative fiction; consequently there
is little comment on his writings of a political, social,

religious, publicistic, or educational nature *per se*, or
his views on art and literature, or on his plays and ideas
about the drama. I have started with a number of opinions
on his early works, as these had their influence on the
reception of the major novels; the main body of the selection is concentrated on the reception of 'War and Peace'
and 'Anna Karenina', and then there is a number of the
later, more general, comments. Within this selection I
have included a few words from some of Tolstoy's fellow-
writers, for in some respects, despite their brevity, they
are among the most perceptive; I have also attempted to
give fair coverage to Tolstoy's reception outside Russia.
Within the obvious limitations of such a scheme, it is to
be hoped that a reasonably well-balanced picture of the
contemporary response will clearly emerge.

Finally I owe Tolstoy an apology. He would without
doubt have hated this book.

Acknowledgments

I would like to thank Professor R.F. Christian (University
of St Andrews) for the initial suggestion that I should
undertake this book; Professor Miriam Allott (University
of Liverpool) for her kind encouragement; the staff of the
Harold Cohen Library (University of Liverpool) for their
assistance on many matters, and especially Miss Joan M.
Lea of the inter-library loan department for her cheerful
optimism and quiet efficiency; the Lenin Library, Moscow,
USSR, for their willingness to make material readily
available to me; the British Library in London and Boston
Spa; my colleague in the Department of Russian, University of Liverpool, Mr R.M. Davison, for his help and
understanding; and Mrs Doris Haughton who typed much of
the manuscript.

Every effort has been made to obtain permission from
the copyright holders to reprint material, and for such
permission I wish to thank the following: the Estate of
Maurice Baring for an extract from his book 'Landmarks in
Russian Literature' (No. 86); William Blackwood & Sons Ltd
for an extract from George Saintsbury's 'The Later Nine-
teenth Century' (No. 100) and for C. Whibley's review of
'Anna Karenina' (No. 84); Miss D.E. Collins for an extract
from G.K. Chesterton's Leo Tolstoy (No. 98); the Editor of
the 'Contemporary Review' for part of J. Wedgwood's Count
Leo Tolstoi (No. 49); the Estate of Edward Garnett for his
Tolstoy's Place in European Literature (No. 95); the
Editor of the 'Guardian' for part of C.H. Herford's Leo
Tolstoy: His Life and Work (No. 104); William Heinemann
Ltd and Dodd, Mead & Co. Inc. for an extract from Count
Lyof Tolstoi in 'Critical Kit-Kats' by Edmund Gosse (No.
89); J.C. Medley and R.G. Medley, the owners of the copy-
right, for an extract from George Moore's Avowals (No.
52); the Editor of the 'New Statesman' for unsigned com-
ments on 'Childhood and Youth' (No. 13), 'War and Peace'

(No. 45), 'Anna Karenina' (No. 80) and 'Resurrection'
(No. 97c); Oxford University Press for extracts from 'The
Life of Tolstoy' by Aylmer Maude (Nos 9 and 53); the
Editor of the 'Spectator' for an unsigned review of 'War
and Peace' (No. 47); and the Society of Authors as the
literary representative of the Estate of Havelock Ellis
for an extract from 'The New Spirit' (No. 91).

Note on the Text

The extracts printed in this volume from commentators who
wrote in English follow the originals in all important
respects; I have not standardized the various versions of
Russian names, as in some ways they have a period charm
of their own. The translations, except for No. 9, are my
own. There is always a certain problem with the trans-
literation of the Cyrillic script, but I hope the system
adopted here strikes the reader as both reasonable and
consistent; in my translations feminine surnames, except
for Karenina, have been masculinized. Quotations from
Tolstoy's works have in general been omitted, although
where they are central to the passage they have been
retained; where the content of an omitted quotation is
not immediately apparent, a short description is appended;
three dots ... , where printed, are in the original, but
four indicate an omission by me. Dates, where they refer
to Russian originals, are in the 'Old Style' or according
to the Julian calendar, which was in operation in Russia
until after the Revolution; it was twelve days behind the
Gregorian in the nineteenth century and thirteen in the
twentieth. Information on Russian literary and historical
references in the text is gathered together in the
Appendix.

Introduction

If one looks at nineteenth-century Russian history and
literature as a whole, there would appear to be a striking
similarity between historiography and literary criticism.
Literature seems to pose the same almost unanswerable
questions to the critics as history does to the historians
and thinkers. The latter asked themselves consistently
and continuously: What is history? What is Russian history? What is Russia's place in history? What is
Russia's historical mission? Is Russian history in general terms similar to that of Western Europe or is it something quite different? Should Russia learn from the West,
or does she have something to teach? Such questions lie
at the basis of all Russian nineteenth-century historiography, and it would scarcely be a distortion of the
facts if, in talking about literature, the words 'history'
and 'historical' in these questions were replaced by
'literature' and 'literary'. To the educated Russians,
living in a country which cocooned its population in numerous regulations and restrictions, where public political
debate was to all intents and purposes impossible, literature was one of the few means through which ideas could be
reasonably freely discussed; consequently literature, and
the written word in general, was far more important a part
of the life of the educated Russians than it was of that
of their contemporaries in Western Europe. This goes some
way towards an explanation of the remarkable zeal and
intensity of many of the critics and the acrimony between
them. Had the social and political conditions been different many of Russia's literary critics might well have
followed other callings, and Russian literature itself
might well have been different.
  Both literature and the criticism of it, however, came

to Russia comparatively late. In the spring of 1825, some
three years before Tolstoy was born, Russia's greatest
poet, Alexander Pushkin, was reading an article by the
novelist A.A. Bestuzhev-Marlinsky, in which the latter
claimed that Russia had plenty of criticism but no literature.(1) Pushkin started to draft a reply: 'We have
criticism? Where is it to be found? What have we critically analysed? Whose literary opinions have been accepted
by the whole nation? Whose criticism can we cite? On
whose authority can we lean?'(2) At the beginning of
June, Pushkin sent a long letter to Bestuzhev-Marlinsky in
which he wrote: *We have criticism but no literature.
Where did you get that idea? On the contrary it is criticism we lack.'(3) The difference of opinion between the
two writers might well be explained by asking what each of
them meant by 'criticism'. It is clear that Bestuzhev-
Marlinsky also bemoans the absence in Russia of those
sorts of critics Pushkin so desired - 'The Addisons, La
Harpes, Schlegels, Sismondi' - on this they were agreed.
Bestuzhev-Marlinsky had continued, though: 'We see plenty
of critics, anti-critics, critics of critics, but few
efficient critics.' Consequently Russia had no literature. Pushkin refutes this last statement; he modestly
declined to quote himself as an example but insisted that
Russia had indeed produced literature, with or without
critics; he mentions Krylov (4) (who is far superior to
La Fontaine) and Derzhavin (5) (who is far superior to
Jean-Baptiste Rousseau) as examples of Russian writers,
but 'we do not have a single commentary, a single book of
criticism. We should rather say: we have some sort of
literature, but no criticism'.(6) Indeed it would be
hard to disagree with Pushkin if one considers that the
first major work of literary criticism was Prince
Vyazemsky's biography of the eighteenth-century dramatist
Fonvizin (written in 1830, published in 1848), and which
Pushkin thought 'well-nigh the most remarkable book to be
written since we began writing books here'.(7)
    Contemporary disagreements apart, there is no doubt
that when Tolstoy began to publish in the early 1850s
Russia had both literature and critics. What had happened
in the intervening twenty years or so? It would be too
simple, however tempting, to reply: 'Belinsky', but he
certainly marks a watershed in the Russian reading
public's attitudes to literature and its opinions about
it.(8) Belinsky has much to answer for, not only on
account of what he insisted literature should be and the
later critics who took up his call, but also for the
opposition he engendered. In short, Belinsky is the orig-
inator of the sociological, or 'civic', school of Russian

literary criticism; he demanded that literature should be
modern, it should be true to life, and, most importantly,
it should be inspired by socially significant ideas. He
is usually seen as the true father of the Russian intelligentsia and 'the embodiment of what remained its spirit
for more than two generations - of social idealism, of the
passion for improving the world, of dis-respect for all
tradition, and of highly strung, disinterested enthusiasm'.(9)   But Belinsky and those who followed him can be
fairly blamed for the contempt for form and workmanship in
literature which had dire effects in the 1860s and 1870s.
If he taught that content was more important than form, he
was equally responsible for the fact that the Russians
tended after him to look for prophecy rather than entertainment in their literature.(10)

With the death of Belinsky in 1848 the critical leadership passed on the one hand to those who followed his
inspiration - the civic critics, honest, radical, 'Wester-
ner' as opposed to 'Slavophile', people like Chernyshevsky, Dobrolyubov and Pisarev - and on the other to the
rather more conservative representatives of the intelligentsia - the non-civic, aesthetic critics for whom
literature was the ultimate expression of ideas, the
writer was to be above such ephemera as the current problems of the day and for whom the ultimate criterion of
literary merit was not content but form, critics like
Annenkov and Druzhinin. Parallel with this development
there was the reaction to it. The rejection of all Western ideas about literature, whether it was a question of
the primacy of form as the aesthetic critics maintained
or that of the social content as the civic critics demanded, led to a new call: that Russian literature should be
Russian. All reliance on Western European norms and concepts should be overcome. Inspired in the early 1850s by
Grigoriev, these new critics formed a cult of Russian
originality, Russian character, Russian spirit. Grigoriev
himself is remembered for his theory of 'organic criticism' which demanded the necessity of literature being an
organic growth from the Russian soil (*pochva*, hence the
untranslatable name of *pochvenniki* for his followers).
Grigoriev admired everything Russian simply because it was
Russian; and the main quality of the Russian character he
saw as its meekness, its submissiveness, as opposed to the
domineering, arrogant nature of Western European man. His
best-known disciple, especially in connection with Tolstoy
and Turgenev, was Strakhov. Such trends continued and
developed, altered and expanded throughout the century
until towards the end there arose new concepts and styles
of criticism, the philosophical and the symbolist,

Leontiev, Rozanov, Shestov, Merezhkovsky, and of course,
later still, marxist.

Thus the critical ground was well prepared for Tolstoy
when he first published in 1852 and critics of all persuasions were to use his works as examples of all that was
right or wrong with Russian literature. It is not surprising that the radical critics should attack him for the
lack of any social content in his stories and novels, that
the 'aesthetic' critics should praise him for the sheer
artistry of his writing, and that the *pochvenniki* should
find in him 'the great writer of the Russian land' and
admire him for the creation of so many 'meek' characters,
the essence of whom reached its apotheosis in the whole
philosophy behind 'War and Peace' as well as being clearly
personified in the characters of Platon Karataev and
Field Marshal Kutuzov.

In general, though, Tolstoy was not well served by contemporary critics, and even when he became well known in
the West from the second half of the 1880s, as will be
seen below, he was received as a fairly typical
nineteenth-century moralist, which did help throw some
light on his writings, but not a lot.

Russian literary journals and the censorship

The usual means of publishing both literature and criticism in Russia was the periodical or, as it was popularly
known, the 'fat journal' (*tolstyy zhurnal*). Russian
periodicals had first appeared in the second half of the
eighteenth century but they were few in number and had a
precarious existence. Even during the reign of Nicholas I
(1825-55) the number of all fat periodicals - political
and social as well as literary - was small, between ten
and twenty. The 'fat journal' came into prominence with
the easing of censorship after Nicholas's death and their
number grew rapidly. In 1855 there were about fifteen, in
1860 about fifty, in 1875 about seventy, in 1880 about 110
and in 1885 about 140.(11) Usually a journal would consist of two parts, one literary, the other more general
(politics, economics, science, sociology and so on); each
journal would have a fairly well-defined political and
philosophic line and would be subscribed to by a distinct
readership. The number of subscribers varied; for example
the most famous of them, the 'Contemporary', had just over
3,000 in 1848 and 6,500 in 1861. It would appear that a
journal could survive healthily on a minimum of some
2,500. Polemics, often couched in indirect language, were
waged between them. In the 1850s and 1860s the leading

radical journal was the 'Contemporary' and when it was
closed down in 1866 its role was taken over by the
'Fatherland Notes' and subsequently by 'Russian Wealth';
the pro-Western, generally liberal, opinion found expression mainly in the 'Messenger of Europe' and in the twentieth century in 'Russian Thought'; the nationalist, patriotic view was in the 'Russian Messenger' which owed its
great popularity largely to the fact that it was here that
Tolstoy, Turgenev, Dostoevsky and many other writers would
be published. As well as these, the leading journals,
there were numerous lesser-known ones.(12) Editors would
vie with one another to attract the leading authors to
their pages; Tolstoy, for example, started with the 'Contemporary', flirted with 'Library for Reading' and
'Fatherland Notes' and published most of 'War and Peace'
and 'Anna Karenina' in the 'Russian Messenger'. Indeed
most nineteenth-century Russian literature first appeared
in one or other of the 'fat journals'.
  Throughout the century the journals always had the
censorship to navigate. Censorship had existed in one
form or another since the introduction of printing into
Russia in the middle of the sixteenth century but was not
officially instituted until the time of Peter the Great at
the start of the eighteenth, and then it was applied
mainly to theological writings. Various vague laws were
formulated under Catherine the Great later in the century
and anti-establishment writers such as N.I. Novikov and
A.N. Radishchev were to suffer from them. The first comprehensive laws were promulgated by Alexander I in 1804.
At first they were not notably restrictive and they were
regarded by contemporaries as a relaxation on previous
practices; they grew, however, progressively harsher and
were at their most severe during the reign of Nicholas I,
especially after the revolutionary year of 1848. A contemporary censor, A.V. Nikitenko, even suggested that the
number of officials engaged in censorship exceeded in any
given year the total of volumes published.(13) On the
whole Russian censorship was negative rather than positive. The various authorities who found themselves in
charge of it were more interested in suppressing what they
considered undesirable than in inculcating into the
readers any officially approved ideas, but it was a censorship on a broad front - religious, political and moral.
However much it might vary in severity it was always there
and was a continuing problem for everyone concerned, not
excluding the censors themselves - they were frequently
found wanting, dismissed and even arrested. Some authors,
however, were prepared to take on the difficult task, the
most notable being the novelist Goncharov, the poet

Tyutchev and the conservative philosopher Leontiev.
After 1865 new 'temporary' laws (they were to last forty
years) were introduced by Alexander II. Their main
objective was to lessen the effects of preventive censorship. Previously all material had had to be submitted
before publication but now original books of more than
ten pages could appear without prior approval. This
meant, though, that the journals were subject to stricter
control than books, but at least authors and publishers
could use their own judgment and risk punishment if it
proved faulty.

Tolstoy and his critics

Tolstoy's attitude to his critics varied from complete
indifference to an almost manic contempt. His wife,
Sonya, wrote in her diary on 24 February 1870: 'We
receive no papers or journals. Lyovochka [affectionate
form of Lev] says he does not want to read any critics.
"Pushkin was troubled by the critics; it's better not to
read them" he told me.'(14) Her brother, Stepan, noted:
'His attitude to journalists and critics was one of no
little contempt... He never read critical reviews of his
works and was not even interested in them.'(15) Tolstoy's
son, Ilya, commented: 'Papa was in general not fond of the
critics and would say that such things occupied only those
who could not do anything else. "The stupid judging the
clever" was his view of professional critics.'(16)
V.F. Lazursky wrote on 27 June 1894: 'Tolstoy said that
Russian critics were all so superficial. Literature in
Russia had always been superior to literary criticism.'
(17)
    Despite the fact that what the critics said about him
had no effect whatsoever on his writings there were two
notable occasions when he did feel the need to state
publicly what he had intended, in connection with 'War and
Peace' and 'The Kreutzer Sonata', but these outbursts were
caused more by what his friends had told him was being
said than by a reaction against what was actually being
written in the journals. None the less, Tolstoy was
always extremely touchy about the views of those people he
liked, and his diaries are full of explanations, rebuttals
and self-justifications. The only professional critic for
whom he had a good word was Strakhov, and this was as much
a result of their friendship as of the fact that Strakhov
was almost invariably enthusiastic about his novels. But
even these personal comments had no effect upon his works.
Criticism, he remarked, is the most boring thing in the

world.(18)   He wrote what he wanted to write, and that was
that.

II

Publication history of Tolstoy's works

Tolstoy began to write his first work, 'Childhood', in
1851 and he had completed it the following summer.   In
July 1852 he sent the manuscript to N.A. Nekrasov, editor
of the leading St Petersburg journal, the 'Contemporary'.
Nekrasov was impressed and agreed to publish it; it
appeared in September, albeit with some changes insisted
upon by the censor and entitled, much to Tolstoy's annoyance, 'A History of my Childhood'.   Tolstoy's next nine
stories also appeared in the 'Contemporary': 'The Raid',
1853, no. 3; 'Boyhood', 1854, no. 9; 'The Memoirs of a
Billiard-marker', 1855, no. 1; 'Sebastopol in December',
1855, no. 6; 'Sebastopol in May' (as 'A Spring Night in
May', much mutilated by the censor who did not like its
critical comments on the Russian high command) and 'The
Woodfelling', which was dedicated to Turgenev, both in
1855, no. 9; 'Sebastopol in August', 1856, no. 1; 'The
Snow Storm', 1856, no. 3 and 'Two Hussars', 1856, no. 5.
'Childhood' and 'The Raid' were signed simply L. N., the
next five L. N. T., but from 'Sebastopol in August' the
author emerged from behind his initials and admitted publicly to being Count L.N. Tolstoy.
   These early stories had all been written while Tolstoy
was in the army and when he returned to St Petersburg from
active service in the Crimean War in December 1855 he was
greeted with acclaim and entered the literary circle of
the capital and of the 'Contemporary' with zest.   So proud
was he of his fame that he offered contributions to other
editors with gay abandon, which explains why 'Meeting a
Moscow Aquaintance in the Detachment' (the clumsy title is
a result of the censor's distaste for the original
'Reduced to the Ranks') appeared in 'Library for Reading'
and 'A Landowner's Morning' in 'Fatherland Notes', both
1856, no. 12.   So popular had Tolstoy become that, even at
this early date, he considered bringing out his collected
works in book form and in September 1856 'The Raid', 'The
Woodfelling' and the three stories of Sebastopol were published together as 'Military Tales' and in October 'Childhood and Boyhood' appeared as a book; by 1897 the latter
had run to ten editions.   The three Sebastopol stories
were issued separately in 1884, both in Moscow in an edition of 6,100 copies (which had reached its sixth

reprinting by 1886) and in St Petersburg with an edition
of 20,000, reprinted in 1890 also in 20,000 copies. The
two books of 1856, however, received little notice (although some of it was of no mean quality) and sold slowly
and this was Tolstoy's first literary disappointment.
When 'Youth' appeared in the 'Contemporary' in January
1857 his star seemed to be on the wane. Discharged from
the army in November 1856 he decided to travel abroad and
for the first seven months of 1857 he was in France,
Switzerland and Germany. During this period he worked
intermittently on various stories. 'Lucerne' appeared in
the 'Contemporary' in September 1857 and 'Albert',
although completed first, in August 1858. Neither of
these two stories made any impression, except to prove to
many people that their belief in Tolstoy's early high
promise had been unjustified; this view was only confirmed
with 'Three Deaths' in 'Library for Reading' in January
1859 (although between 1870 and 1900 the book version of
this tale ran to seven separate editions with more than
77,000 copies in all). Chastened by his apparent loss of
talent Tolstoy worked lethargically on both 'Family Happiness', his first conventional novel, and on 'The
Cossacks'. So dissatisfied was he with the former that
when he read the completed manuscript he thought of publishing it under a pseudonym; it appeared, however, fully
signed, in the 'Russian Messenger' in April 1859. None
the less, Tolstoy began to believe that his literary
career was over and began to devote himself more and more
to a new interest - the education of peasant children.
His pedagogical notes and theories appeared in a special
magazine he published himself called 'Yasnaya Polyana',
named after his estate on which he established his school.
Twelve numbers appeared between February 1862 and March
1863. The only literary works of this period (which was
interrupted by his second trip abroad when he visited
France, Germany and England to examine the school systems
there) were, first, 'The Cossacks', which he had started
some ten years before while in the Caucasus and was forced
to complete in 1862 to pay off some gambling debts and
which appeared in the 'Russian Messenger' in January 1863,
and, second, 'Polikushka' which came out the following
month. In 1864 the Moscow publisher Stellovsky brought
out a two-volume edition of Tolstoy's collected works.(19)
     On 23 September 1863 Tolstoy married Sonya Behrs, the
eighteen-year-old daughter of a neighbouring family he had
known for years, and there began the period of his life in
which, he stated, he lived a correct, honourable family
life. The fruit of this early settled happiness was 'War
and Peace'. It took six years to complete and went

through many changes; it was not until March 1867 that he
finally decided upon its title. It began to appear, entitled '1805' in the 'Russian Messenger' in 1865, nos 1
and 2, and was continued the following year in the February, March and April editions. In June all these sections
were published separately as a book, still called '1805'.
Towards the end of 1867 it was reprinted with some additional material and given the title 'War and Peace'. In
March 1868 the fourth volume was published separately in
Moscow, the fifth a year later and the sixth and last in
December 1869. On the whole it was a literary sensation
and quickly went into a second edition.

After completing 'War and Peace' Tolstoy devoted himself once again to education and wrote numerous stories in
simple language with the aim of helping children to learn
to read. Two of these appeared separately in 1872: 'The
Prisoner of the Caucasus' in 'Dawn', no. 2, and 'God Sees
the Truth, but Waits' in 'Conversation', no. 3. Between
1883 and 1901 there were at least twenty-four editions of
the latter story with some 250,000 copies. All the other
stories of this nature appeared in four 'Readers' which
ran to innumerable editions; they were later to be adopted
throughout the Russian educational system; there was also
his 'ABC Book' of 1872 which contained a complete curricu-
lum for the initial teaching of children. Also in 1872 an
eight-volume collection of his works began to appear in an
edition of 3,600 copies per volume. From this time onwards his 'Collected Works' continued to appear, increasing in size with each year and in the numbers of copies
printed; for example, the fourth edition of 1880 had
eleven volumes of 5,000 copies, the sixth, 1886-7, twelve
of 6,000, the eighth, 1889-91, thirteen of 10,000 and the
tenth, 1897, fourteen of 16,000 copies each.

Tolstoy began to work on 'Anna Karenina' in March 1873
but his life was full of problems - religious, educational, family and personal - and his work on the new
novel was often interrupted; also his passion for writing
fiction had considerably lessened. In December 1874 he
sold the serial rights to Katkov, the editor of the
'Russian Messenger', for the quite remarkable sum of
20,000 roubles and 'Anna Karenina' started to appear in
the first four numbers for 1875; further instalments were
published the following year, nos 1-4 and 12, and the next
year, 1877, nos 1-4. Katkov refused to print the final,
eighth, part because of Tolstoy's adverse comments on the
Russian volunteers (of whom Vronsky was one) who were then
leaving Russia to help the Serbs in their fight to rid
their country of Turkish domination. Part VIII was printed separately. The whole novel, revised with the

assistance of his friend, the critic Strakhov, appeared as a book in 1878.

While at work on 'Anna Karenina' Tolstoy became increasingly concerned with the metaphysical torments which he was to describe in 'Confession' (banned by the censor in 1882). Following his rejection of the Orthodox Church and his adoption of the rational elements of the Sermon on the Mount, he devoted the rest of his life to philosophical, religious, social and political problems, both practical and theoretical, rejected all his imaginative literature as worthless, and wrote comparatively little fiction afterwards which did not bear a didactic message of one sort or another. 'The Death of Ivan Ilich' (1886), 'Strider' (1888), 'The Kreutzer Sonata' (banned 1890), 'Master and Man' (1895, and more copies of which were printed in Tolstoy's lifetime than any other of his works) and 'Resurrection' (1899) are the most 'literary' of his later works and in many respects show no falling off of his artistic talents whatsoever. 'Hadji Murad', which he completed in 1904 but which was not published until after his death, is pure literature as it were, with no 'message' at all; Tolstoy was even a little ashamed to be writing it when there were so many more serious matters to attend to. But by this time Tolstoy was so famous, not only in Russia, but internationally as well, that everything he wrote sold in enormous quantities; this was helped by the fact that in 1891 in accordance with his new principles he had renounced the copyright on all his writings, and publishers the world over were not slow in taking advantage.

III

The critical reception

(a) Before 'War and Peace'

In 1865 the April number of the 'Contemporary' carried a valedictory notice on Tolstoy written by the critic Pyatkovsky. The year before a two-volume edition of Tolstoy's collected works had appeared in Moscow shortly after 'The Cossacks' had been given a mixed reception; Tolstoy had fallen silent, or was, as far as the public was concerned, still pursuing his interests in educating the children of the peasants on his estate at Yasnaya Polyana; to the outside world he had stopped writing fiction altogether and apparently for good. Consequently Pyatkovsky thought it not amiss to attempt to evaluate what Tolstoy had given to

Russian literature and at the same time take a few shots
at 'Family Happiness' and 'Lucerne' (see No. 20). Tolstoy
was clearly talented, had notable powers of observation
and was capable of acute psychological analysis; he was
truthful and straightforward; he did not strain after
literary effect. None the less his works did suffer from
a certain idealization and some occasional tendentiousness, although he was a wonderful portrait painter and
landscape artist, if somewhat old-fashioned in his style
and general outlook on life. Such was Pyatkovsky's view;
it is not unbalanced or untypical; it does summarize much
of what was usual in contemporary criticism of Tolstoy,
but not everything; other critics had noticed further aspects, both positive and negative. The early views of
Tolstoy's fellow-countrymen are intructive because they
were to colour much of the later criticism, especially
of 'War and Peace' and 'Anna Karenina'.

The early fiction, from 'Childhood' in 1852 to 'Sebastopol in August' in 1856, was met by general acclaim and
in some cases with great enthusiasm; not for Tolstoy an
early struggle for recognition, indeed he was to find it
difficult to live up to his early fame. Some of the
favourable opinion on his first works was to affect what
was said about 'The Snow Storm' (1856) but by the end of
the decade his stories passed all but unnoticed, and
when 'The Cossacks', which Turgenev as late as 1874 still
thought Tolstoy's best work, appeared in 1863 it did
little to enhance his reputation. The reasons for the
change in critical opinion is explained partly by the fact
that the stories after 'Sebastopol' were less artistically
successful, partly because everyone knew Tolstoy had
turned himself into a pedagogue, and partly because the
attitude of the critics to Tolstoy the man was having too
great an influence over their opinions of Tolstoy the
writer. The literary set of the 1850s in St Petersburg
was an inward-looking and small group, writers doubled as
critics and vice versa, and everyone knew everyone else.
Their activities tended to centre on the 'Contemporary'
with its editors Nekrasov and the less-talented Panaev,
and their outlook was in general terms radical, especially
after the accession of the 'reforming tsar', Alexander II,
in 1855. There were, however, varying shades of opinion
within the circle which in time coalesced into two distinct camps; on the one hand were the generally younger,
non-noble people like Chernyshevsky and Dobrolyubov with
their insistence on the social purpose of literature, and
on the other the aristocratic liberals such as Turgenev
and the 'art for art's sake' critics like Annenkov and
Druzhinin. When Tolstoy arrived in the capital he was

courted by both sides, something which flattered his
vanity no end. The 'aristocrats' took his support for
granted; he was a count, would naturally gravitate towards
them and join the attack on the likes of Chernyshevsky and
Dobrolyubov (the snake and the rattlesnake, as Turgenev
called them).(20) The younger element expected 'the lion
of Sebastopol',(21) with his clear anti-establishment
opinions, to lend them his support. Tolstoy, though, was
to disappoint both sides; psychologically and socially
antagonistic to the younger group and even daring at one
point to attack their oracle Alexander Herzen, he was
equally scathing of aristocrats attempting to be liberals;
Turgenev's democratic pretensions he found particularly
distasteful and it is from this time that their long love-
hate relationship dates. Everyone in St Petersburg came
to the conclusion that his was a great literary talent but
that he was also his own man. He was always to remain so.
Indeed something of the cool reception afforded to 'Two
Hussars', 'Lucerne', 'Albert', 'Family Happiness' and 'The
Cossacks' must be attributed to the reaction of the critics
he had earlier offended.
    'Childhood', however, was an immediate success, with
the readers, the critics and his friends. Nekrasov had
earlier written to Tolstoy with encouragement (see No. 1a)
and he had ordered Turgenev to read it, telling him that
they had found a new and possibly great talent.(22)
Turgenev replied with his congratulations.(23) In one
of the earliest reviews of the story Dudyshkin praised it
for its feeling, nobility and sympathy with reality;(24)
an anonymous critic commented favourably on its verve and
charm;(25) B.N. Almazov commented on the warmth of its
descriptions:(26) Turgenev wrote to a friend about his
enthusiasm and tells the story of Panaev being shunned by
his friends on the street for fear they would be button-
holed into listening to him reading whole passages out
loud;(27) and Dostoevsky from exile in Siberia was to
admit liking the story although he did not think the
author would write much more, hastily adding that he might
be wrong.(28) Almost alone in not being totally favourable were F.A. Koni, who, while finding it an amusing
little tale, said it was quite without inspiration,(29)
and A.A. Grigoriev who wondered if it was only some psychological exercise, and he became the first in a long
line of critics to accuse Tolstoy of having no plot in his
works.(30) Nine years later, however, Grigoriev was to
write some of the most original criticism on Tolstoy of
the whole century (see below).
    When Tolstoy's second story, 'The Raid', appeared it
was received as warmly as 'Childhood', even though it had

suffered at the hands of the censor. Nekrasov wrote to
Tolstoy (6 April 1853) telling him not to be discouraged
by this sort of thing as it was the fate of all great
authors, and Dudyshkin (see No. 3) was full of praise,
seeing the way Tolstoy described ordinary soldiers as
something quite new in that they appeared as real living
people and not some relics of the past in the style of the
jingoistic Bestuzhev-Marlinsky. The reaction to 'Boyhood'
was the same; Annenkov (see No. 2) congratulated Tolstoy
on avoiding the usual pitfalls of the first person narrative form and commended his penetrating analysis of feeling and the successful manner in which he had depicted the
awakening of reason in a young boy. Nekrasov spoke of its
general success with the public (see No. 1c) and both
Dudyshkin (31) and Almazov (32) continued where they had
left off with 'Childhood'.

'The Memoirs of a Billiard-marker', although Nekrasov
thought it weak because of the poor language Tolstoy had
used (see No. 1b), and 'The Woodfelling', which Tolstoy
had dedicated to Turgenev, only furthered his reputation.
Turgenev wrote: 'Nothing in my literary career has ever
flattered my self-esteem so much', but he added: 'the
military life is not for you. Your weapon is the pen not
the sword.'(33)

However, using his experiences with the latter as ink
for the former, Tolstoy wrote three stories about the life
of the Russian army during the siege of Sebastopol during
the Crimean War, and it is these that mark the unambiguous
peak of his early fame.

On 19 May 1855, soon after the first of them, 'Sebastopol in December', had appeared, Panaev wrote to Tolstoy
that so good was it that 'all of us who love Russian
literature are praying God may spare you'. Turgenev wrote
to Panaev (10 July 1855) that the story was wonderful and
he cried when he read it, and the novelist and playwright
Pisemsky commented on 'Sebastopol in May' that its pitiless honesty made it hard to read.(34) The critics were
as enthusiastic as his friends. 'Nowhere does the author
express his admiration, but he forces us to admire. We
are astonished at every turn.'(35) 'Sebastopol is the
work of a master; there is vigour and concision' and Tolstoy's chief value was his severe truth.(36) It was rum-
oured that Tsar Nicholas I was so impressed with the first
story that he ordered it to be translated into French, and
it did indeed appear in 'Le Nord', a French-language Russian newspaper published in Brussels.(37) 'Sebastopol in
May' had alarmed the censor and once again the editor of
the 'Contemporary', who had been told to print the story
with its changes, had to write to Tolstoy telling him it

was what had to be expected in the circumstances.(38)
The 'St Petersburg News' found it full of sincerity,
warmth and lyrical characters (39) and 'Fatherland Notes'
praised its vividness, feeling and sheer poetry.(40)
Nekrasov told Tolstoy that the truth of what he was writing was exactly what Russia needed (see (No. 1d) and commented that 'Sebastopol in August' showed accurate powers
of observation, a deep penetration into the heart of
things, a wealth of poetry and the rare ability to touch
the readers' hearts (see No. 1e). Other critics suggested
it was by far the best thing written on the last days of
the siege especially because the soldiers were so well
drawn, their conversations and their jokes were so full of
the very stuff of life.(41) Druzhinin while admitting,
for example, that Russell's dispatches to the London
'Times' were obviously the work of a talented author
claimed they could not be spoken of in the same breath as
Tolstoy's stories.(42) Adverse comments were few and far
between. An anonymous critic (see No. 5) seemed determined to swim against the general tide and attacked Tolstoy for writing less and less well, the more serious the
events he was describing became; looking at the three
stories together he accuses Tolstoy of simply painting
pictures and his main fault is that there is no action.
    When 'Childhood and Boyhood' and 'The Military Tales'
appeared in book form they drew from Chernyshevsky a remarkable essay (see No. 6a); it is without a shadow of a
doubt the best piece of literary criticism to come from
his pen and was to influence much subsequent Tolstoyan
criticism. Chernyshevsky summarizes what other critics
have seen in Tolstoy but accuses them of failing to differentiate what makes Tolstoy remarkable; everything they
have seen in him is certainly there but so is it in many
of his illustrious predecessors. What really marked Tolstoy's originality was his successful and idiosyncratic
use of 'interior monologue' and his ability in his psychological analysis to get through to the psychic process
itself, which Chernyshevsky termed 'the dialectic of the
soul'.
    Tolstoy's next three stories show the first signs of
some reaction in the critics to their earlier fulsome
praise. 'The Snow Storm' was certainly seen by the early
reviewers as more poetry than prose in its tonalities and
structure and Turgenev was as usual carried away.(43)
S.T. Aksakov agreed, attempting to capture some of Tolstoy's glory; after all he had been caught in snow storms
too and knew exactly what they were like.(44) Herzen
called it a marvel (45) and Druzhinin thought there had
been nothing better since the days of Pushkin and

Gogol.(46)   The praise for 'Two Hussars' and 'A Landowner's Morning' was, however, more muted. Younger people
saw the former with its contrast of two generations as an
attack upon them (and this was not the last time Tolstoy
was to be accused of favouring the old over the new;
indeed he can be seen as looking askance at everything in
Russia which post-dates Peter the Great), although Druzhinin ('Library for Reading', 1856, no. 139) defends the
author from such comment, and 'A Landowner's Morning'
which is a semi-autobiographical description of an attempt
to improve the peasants' lot was hardly liked at all; even
Turgenev, while praising the language, complained of the
awful picture of Russia which it gave (see No. 8a).

It was 'Youth', the sequel to 'Childhood' and 'Boyhood',
which really marked the change in Tolstoy's reputation.
Druzhinin (see No. 4) wrote that it was good and Tolstoy
should not pay any attention to people saying it was weaker
than the previous two parts; but some of the chapters were
too long, he must guard against excessive analysis, and he
must look to his style which was heavy and often ungrammatical. Panaev told Tolstoy (letter, 5 December 1856):
'your phrases are too long and the same words keep recurring', and to Turgenev (letter, 6 December 1856) he was
less restrained: 'Tolstoy simply does not know how to
write. His sentences are all two yards long. The thought
is admirable but its expression is quite obscure.' The
'Fatherland Son' complained that it was over-long and in
places carelessly written, although the portraits of the
students were excellent as was the description of the
awakening of intellectual development;(47) Chernyshevsky
lost patience and accused Tolstoy of simply preening himself like a peacock (see No. 6b) and Bastrov said that to
present the hero as typical of all Russian youth was an
insult not only upon the young but upon the whole of Russian society.(48)   In a general review of Tolstoy's works
K.S. Aksakov found time to praise 'Youth' but warned him
to beware of excessive detailization, of putting certain
facets of the soul under a microscope, thus making them
out of proportion to everything else (see No. 7).

A visit to St Petersburg in the autumn of 1857 added to
Tolstoy's dejection. Talking to Nekrasov and other
writers on the 'Contemporary' he persuaded himself that
his talent was declining. His latest stories had not been
bad but they were certainly a disappointment to the admirers of 'Sebastopol'. Tolstoy wrote to Botkin on 1 November 1857: 'I must say that as a result of the new trend in
literature most of our old friends, including myself, no
longer know where we stand.' His bewilderment might be
partially explained by Nekrasov's attitude to 'Albert'

which led to Tolstoy's final break with the 'Contemporary'. Nekrasov had returned the manuscript to Tolstoy
suggesting that he should not bother to publish it; he
pointed out the tendentiousness and banality of the story
and said that the morally sick and drunken hero needed a
doctor rather than the sympathy and understanding of
society. Tolstoy changed it a little but it was hardly
noticed.(49) Perhaps the didactic nature of the discussion of the true essence of Art was not to the taste of
the literary critics at the end of the 1850s, a time when
Russia was embroiled in the turmoil leading up to the
Emancipation of the Peasants in 1861. 'Lucerne' was
greeted coolly in the 'St Petersburg News';(50) it was
thought by another critic only to show the sick mood of
the author, and Turgenev, Botkin, Annenkov and Panaev all
disliked its overt moralizing and attacks on Western civilization.(51) Pisarev, as was to be expected, poured scorn
upon it in his long article, Downfall of Unripe Thought,
although he did find some ironic praise for the fact that
never had the type of its philosophizing hero been drawn
in such a wonderfully ridiculous and sad light. His ironic
style took on a gentler hue when reviewing 'Three Deaths'
for the lady subscribers of the magazine 'Daybreak' (see
No. 10) and indeed he was not antagonistic although Turgenev was not the only reader who could find no connection
between the death of the oak tree and the other two.(52)
Everyone was sure Tolstoy had said all he had in him to
say.
     In 1858 Tolstoy was working on 'Family Happiness' and,
true to his mood of the time, as soon as he had finished
it he became convinced that it was worthless, but on the
insistence of Botkin he sold it to the 'Russian Messenger'. Botkin read the proofs and wrote to Tolstoy (15 May
1859):

     To my amazement the result was entirely different from
     what I had expected. Not only did I like the second
     part but I found it all beautiful. In the first place
     it has dramatic appeal; in the second it is an excel-
     lent psychological study; the descriptions are very
     life-like; in a word the whole thing is admirable, full
     of meaning, and talented.

On the whole very few critics bothered with it, but those
who did concurred with Botkin's opinion. 'Northern
Flower' hailed the story of a young woman's marriage to an
older husband and ultimate happiness as a poetic idyll,
(53) the 'St Petersburg News' put it on a par with 'Childhood' (54) and the 'Fatherland Son' declared that the

psychology was extremely accurate and that the author was
clearly a connoisseur of the human heart.(55)
Despite this relative success Tolstoy continued to be
dissatisfied with it and returned to 'The Cossacks' which
he had started six years before, but he did not really believe he would ever finish it. Druzhinin had written
asking for a story for the 'Library for Reading' and Tolstoy replied (9 October 1859):

I'm not much use as a writer any more. I've written
nothing since 'Family Happiness' and I do not think I
shall write again. Life is too short for me to fritter
it away making up books like the ones I write which are
a source of embarrassment to me afterwards.

Even Khomyakov's public praise for him (see No. 9) failed
to excite him and he took himself abroad for the last time
in his life.
During the three weeks he spent in Brussels on this
trip he wrote 'Polikushka' which went unnoticed except by
his friends; they were unenthusiastic (see No. 8c).
In 1862 the perceptive and original critic Grigoriev
wrote two articles on Tolstoy for Dostoevsky's journal
'Time' (see No. 11). What he had to say was to prove as
seminal as Chernyshevsky's earlier review, if not more so.
Much of what Grigoriev wrote has been taken up (usually
without too much acknowledgment) by later critics. He
takes the theme that Tolstoy accepts nothing on trust,
everything is examined by a profound analysis; but so profound is that analysis that Tolstoy is lead to denying
everything and seems to be heading for an absolute intellectual nihilism. This even applies to those phenomena
in Russian society of which he most obviously approves; by
concentrating on their negative sides in order to accentuate the positive the latter are in danger of being swamped.
Grigoriev, who put forward theories of 'organic' literature, literature that had its roots deep in the Russian
soil, down to which the best authors dug, and Tolstoy
deeper than most, analyses the traditions of the 'meek'
personality as opposed to the 'domineering' one. Tolstoy
clearly favours the former, in his simplicity, his submission to life and his gentleness. Those who recall
Platon Karataev in 'War and Peace' and Tolstoy's idealization of him will surely take Grigoriev's point.
The last story of the period before his first great
novel was 'The Cossacks'. It had a mixed reception.
Countess Alexandra Tolstoy wrote: 'My friends were en-
chanted; others criticized it for a certain crudeness
which they say inhibits the aesthetic response' (56) and

Tolstoy was not disposed to disagree. Turgenev (see No.
8b) disliked the hero Olenin, but Fet wrote (letter to
Tolstoy, 4 April 1863),

> How many times I hugged you from afar as I read 'The
> Cossacks' and how many times I laughed at your dero-
> gatory remarks about it. You may write other books
> that are just as good but it is a sort of *chef
> d'oeuvre*.

But the poet Tyutchev was terse (see No. 14) and the critics were dubious. Polonsky praised Tolstoy for capturing
the very breath of the Caucasus but thought Olenin only a
pale copy of characters of Pushkin's day and complained
that several of the episodes were just stories within a
story.(57) Golovachov in the 'Contemporary' thought he
was a good storyteller but no thinker at all;(58)
Evgeniya Tur (see No. 16) expressed her indignation at
Tolstoy for daring to romanticize drunkenness, piracy,
theft and blood lust and allowing Olenin 'the representative of civilized society' to be debased, degraded and
defeated; but on the other hand what could be expected
from a character like Olenin?
     Annenkov (see No. 17) declared the work one of the best
achievements of all Russian literature and said that it
told you more about the Caucasus than a score of ethno-
graphical articles, while Edelson wrote that Tolstoy was
contrasting civilization with unspoilt Nature to the
apparent disadvantage of the former (see No. 15); Markov
thought Tolstoy had described the various types found in
the area remarkably well (see No. 19). The public by one
account was, however, raving about it although it had been
thought by some indecent and impossible to give to young
girls to read.(59) All in all, though, the novel was
thought to be somewhat old-fashioned; but whatever its
contemporaries thought about it, it still manages to cast
its spell: even Ernest Hemingway has admitted to its
attractions.
     Thus the critical battle-lines for the reception of
'War and Peace' were drawn up. On the one hand Tolstoy
was known for his great ability as a painter of pictures,
the charm, vigour, concision and poetry of his style, his
great powers of observation and the capacity to use them,
his extremely acute psychological analysis, his honesty
and straightforwardness and scorn for literary effects for
their own sake and for the fact that he wrote about people
and events as they really were; on the other hand he was
accused of being old-fashioned, tendentious and didactic,
he often took his psychological analysis to perverse

lengths, his outlook on life tended to be purely negative,
he suffered from an over-detailization, his stories had no
plot or action and his use of the Russian language left
much to be desired. All in all, both sides were to find
further evidence for their case in his subsequent works.

(b) 'War and Peace'

Tolstoy began writing 'War and Peace' without a clear idea
of what exactly the finished work would be. He first
though of a novel about the Decembrist Revolt of 1825, but
his examination of the reasons behind it led him back to
the war against Napoleon in 1812, and in looking at that
he was driven further back, to the beginning of the century. He decided to write a sort of historical novel
about upper-class life, and with this rather vague plan in
mind he wrote the first two parts which appeared under the
title '1805'.(60) Tolstoy was excited about the book's
publication and was particularly anxious about the reactions of his friends, but supposed that it would in general
pass unnoticed.(61) He was right, for reviews only began
to appear in the second half of 1866, some fifteen months
after the start of the serialization in the 'Russian
Messenger'. His friends, however, immediately began writing to each other with their opinions, and continued to do
so for years to come. It was to be expected that they
would be generally sympathetic in their reactions and
essentially they were; yet in praising its good points,
they found it rather slow-moving, too digressive, weighed
down by excessive detail and having a superfluity of
French. The critic Botkin wrote to Fet (see No. 21) about
how subtly Tolstoy described the inner movements of the
soul, but that, although he had read more than half of
it, he could not find the main thread; he saw a mass of
details and assumed they formed the background for what
was coming but there were certainly too many of them;
Tolstoy also, he thought, was still a little careless
with his Russian. Turgenev wrote to Botkin (25 March
1866): 'The second part of "1805" is weak. Where are the
traits of the time? The historical colour? There is no
background at all.' So both Botkin and Turgenev saw too
many details, while the former saw them all as background
and the latter could not even see that. Soon afterwards
Turgenev complained to Fet (letter, 8 June 1866): 'The
novel is bad because Tolstoy has not studied anything; he
does not know anything, and under the name of Kutuzov and
Bagration he describes modern generals.' When he had read
the fourth volume, he found parts of it wonderful and

others unbearable. On the whole he preferred the third
volume which he thought 'almost all a chef d'oeuvre' (see
No. 36b). Botkin informed Fet (letter, 26 March 1866) that
everyone was reading the book, they were in ecstasies over
it, although he was not unaware that the professional critics and the army men were finding fault: 'The latter
especially say Borodino was not the way Tolstoy describes
it at all.' Turgenev told the critic Annenkov that he
found parts of the novel marvellous but that the 'historical addition' was a 'puppet comedy' (see No. 36a); yet
when Tolstoy forgets his philosophizing and gets back to
basics he is incomparable.(62) By the time the last part
appeared Botkin was enthusing that everything in the marvellous novel aroused the deepest interest, even Tolstoy's
ideas about war. He called it a real *Russian* book.(63)
Pogodin, editor and publisher and the centre of literary
Moscow, told Tolstoy (letter, 3 April 1868) that when he
read it he melted, wept, rejoiced, and on the following
day he continued: 'You've done for me. You've turned me
in my dotage into - Natasha. And Pushkin not here to see
it! How he would have applauded, how happy he would have
been, how he would have rubbed his hands with glee.' A
few months later, however, he wrote in the journal
'Russia':(64)

> What the novelist absolutely cannot be forgiven is his
> offhand treatment of such figures as Bagration, Sper-
> ansky, Rostopchin and Ermolov who belong to history.
> To study their lives and then judge them on the basis
> of the evidence is all well and good, but to present
> them without any reason as ignoble or even repellent,
> the mere outlines and silhouettes of men, is in my
> opinion an act of unpardonable irresponsibility and
> provocation, even in an author of great talent.

Suvorin, the founder of the paper 'New Time', was at something of a loss and he could not explain why; there was
nothing spectacular or strained and the 'gifted author'
had not resorted to any tricks. He gave up trying to
write a criticism of the work by stating that it was a
smooth-flowing epic by a painter-poet.(65) Leskov, the
short-story writer and novelist, wrote some unsigned reviews for the 'Stock Exchange News' in 1869-70; of 'War
and Peace' he wrote:(66)

> Long periods elapse between the publication of each
> volume in the series during which, as the saying goes,
> reeds are broken on the author's back; he is called
> this and that, a fatalist, an idiot, a madman, a

> realist, a troll; and he, in the following instalment,
> remains what he is and what he intends to be... He
> paces along, a massive charger borne up by solid legs
> and iron-shod.

The novelist Goncharov yawned to Turgenev: 'You speak of
the appearance of "Peace and War"' (Goncharov took delight
in such mistakes - Dostoevsky's novel was retitled 'Crimes
and Punishments'); not surprisingly he admitted to not
having read it 'but those who have say the author has colossal power'.(67)

The professional critics, though, were in general less
tolerant than Tolstoy's friends and fellow-writers; they
admired his great skill as a writer but they expressed a
distaste for his philosophizing and many of his ideas and
ideals. Although there was some praise for Tolstoy from
them the majority showered him with abuse and denigration.
The political views of the critics were taking increasing
precedence at this time over their literary judgments.
The right wing extolled Tolstoy for his artistry, the
left wing attacked him for his failure to deal with contemporary problems. Indeed some people have seen ample
justification for the truth of the former in the vehemence
of the latter: so well did Tolstoy write that the attacks
on what he said just had to be violent. So beautiful was
the form that the unsuspecting would not notice the vile-
ness of the content; consequently both the novel's philosophy and its artistic presentation came in for equal
shares of negative comment.

Despite the fact that there were hundreds of critical
reviews and articles on 'War and Peace' most, if not all,
the critics were at a loss when dealing with the work.
The immense physical size, the scope of its events, the
multitude of characters, the ideas, the philosophy of war,
the glorification of the family, the idealization of the
peasant, all proved rather too much. So bemused were they
that they began to ask themselves what exactly Tolstoy was
trying to write. 'What is "War and Peace"?' became as
much a 'question of the day' as the position of the peasantry, the reorganization of local government, the reforms
of the legal system and the place of women in society. A
brief notice in 'Voice' inquired: 'What is this? To which
literary genre can we ascribe it? What is it? Fiction,
pure creation, or reality?'(68) In 1866 the anonymous
critic of the 'Book Messenger' (see No. 22) found it impossible to fit into any accepted genre; 'it is not a
novel; it is not a story; it is rather an attempt at a
military and aristocratic chronicle of the past, wonderful
in places, but in others dry and tedious'. The following

year Akhsharumov found himself in similar perplexity (see
No. 23); 'It is neither a chronicle nor an historical
novel', he wrote; it was an essay on Russian society some
sixty years before. The anonymous critic of the 'Affair'
(see No. 27) could not make up his mind whether the novel,
or whatever it was, had even actually started, but whatever Tolstoy was trying to do, he had failed.

In reply to such widespread confusion Tolstoy made one
of his rare public statements about his writings and tried
to explain what he was doing in 'War and Peace' (see No.
26). His article, A Few Words about the Book 'War and
Peace', is a poor defence against the criticisms being
levelled against it. · Quite simply it is 'what the author
wanted to and could express in the form in which it was
expressed'. His comments on historians do not bear scru-
tiny and his suggestion that most 'novels' from Gogol to
Dostoevsky were difficult to fit into the genre is at best
extremely dubious. In a discarded foreword to the work
Tolstoy said that Western European literary forms were unsuitable for expressing artistically the Russian mind, and
consequently he had to find new ones.(69) But what these
were no one seemed quite sure. Even Annenkov, who wrote
what was probably the best contemporary critique of the
artistic side of the book (see No. 24), failed to understand it fully. He spoke of its naturalness and simplicity; Tolstoy had done well to concentrate on *petite
histoire,* the details of which gave him the right background for his ideas in the form of personified and drama-
tized documents; he found there was poetry and imagination
and a wonderful grasp of life and the depiction of it; but
on the other hand he discerned a lack of any dramatic
development, of any 'intrigue', and in Annenkov's opinion
Tolstoy had erred in making the historical facts not the
backdrop to his story but the very foreground; he also
found many of Prince Andrey's opinions uniquely ahead of
their time.

In his dealings with the aristocracy Tolstoy was accused of a certain idealization. Pisarev in his unfinished
article, The Old Landed Gentry (see No. 25), stated this
criticism in no uncertain terms and stressed his point by
dealing with two of the less important heroes, Boris Drubetskoy and Nikolay Rostov. The satirical writer
Saltykov-Shchedrin found the whole philosophy distasteful
because Tolstoy had praised elements of the so-called
highest society.(70) Tolstoy was especially fiercely
attacked for his depiction of the Russian aristocracy and
the emotive year of 1812 by people from the more reactionary sections of the nobility and by military historians.
In their opinion Tolstoy was misrepresenting the facts and

denigrating the unwavering patriotism of past generations.
Norov (see No. 30), who had served in the army towards the
end of the campaign and had later been minister of education, said the novel was in fact painful to read and that
the nobility, the Guards' officers and the Russian generals just were not as Tolstoy had depicted them. Vyazemsky
was no less pained.(71) Like Norov, he had participated in
1812 and in the 1820s and 1830s he had been a liberal but
had grown increasingly conservative with the years. He
saw 'War and Peace' as a 'protest against 1812'; he particularly disliked Tolstoy's portrayal of the empty lives of
the nobility in their salons or on their estates and their
apparent indifference to the fate of their country.
Tolstoy had found only Famusovs and Bobchinskys (72) in
society and like Griboedov had seen fit to satirize the
upper classes. Vyazemsky felt obliged to defend Tsar
Alexander and Rostopchin from Tolstoy's portrayal of them,
and Rostopchin's son wrote to the journal which published
Vyazemsky's article with his thanks for putting the record
straight about his father.(73) General Dragomirov, who
wrote by far the most searching analysis of the novel from
a military viewpoint (see No. 32), although deprecating
Tolstoy's philosophy of war, was generous enough to give
the author his due as a writer of immense talent; indeed
'War and Peace' could form a useful part of any soldier's
training. And Liprandi (see No. 31), another participant
in and historian of the campaign, admitted that it was
difficult for any one man to come to any conclusions about
the period (even though, of course, Tolstoy had) but that
if Tolstoy had sinned against history 'then it was no bad
thing'. Liprandi was in some respects justified, for
although Tolstoy had to bear much criticism of this nature
from the conservatives (who were really suffering from
hurt pride) he was attacking only the false patriotism of
certain elements in the society of the period; the patriotism of the ordinary people, as Soviet critics will never
tire of pointing out, is not satirized at all and indeed it
is quite the contrary, for everything that is praiseworthy
in the Russian character is personified in Platon Karataev.
    If he found little support from conservative circles,
Tolstoy found even less from the radicals. In their view
he failed on two main counts - in idealizing the nobility
he had not depicted the intelligentsia and in praising the
landowners he had not attacked serfdom. Bervi-Flerovsky,
a politico-sociologist of no mean influence, in reducing
Prince Andrey's father to size (see No. 29), said that if
he really was one of the best men of the time it must have
been because of his success in managing to make tens of
thousands of peasants unhappy. A woman critic (see No.

28), M.K. Tsebrikova, sees the fact that Prince Andrey is the hero only as proof of the poor social position of women, for all the three women in his life - Princess Liza, Princess Maria and Natasha - play a markedly secondary role in his affairs, and the family life, which Tolstoy so extols and which is based upon the devotion of the mother, is but further proof. Shelgunov (see No. 35) accused Tolstoy of being socially and politically reactionary and of propounding a philosophy of Eastern fatalism as the only answer to Russia's many problems, while Skabichevsky (see No. 37) sees Tolstoy going the way of Gogol in that he appears to be paying less attention to literature and is descending into a hopeless mysticism and a desire to change the world in line with his own rather obvious misconceptions.

In some ways the radicals were not so much pouring their scorn upon Tolstoy as upon their political opponents, especially the neo-Slavophiles. The views of the latter group are best expressed by Tolstoy's friend and correspondent over many years, Nikolay Strakhov, who wrote two long articles on 'War and Peace' for the journal 'Dawn' in 1869 (see No. 33). He saw the book as the best possible expression of the *pochvenniki*'s 'meek Russian personality' beloved of Grigoriev (see No. 11), Tolstoy is given boundless praise (and the minor faults which Strakhov finds pale into insignificance), but it is ultimately for the most conservative elements in the novel. Even Dostoevsky (see No. 34) could not bear (or understand) Tolstoy's historical fatalism, and in some ways he found what Tolstoy was saying old-fashioned and second-hand.

Most of the contemporary comments on 'War and Peace' in Russia do have their justification but they seem in retrospect to have been made from false premises. Tolstoy is indeed a writer of the first rank; he is indeed in many ways conservative, even on occasion reactionary; he does indeed prefer the gentry and their foils, the peasants, to the intelligentsia; and he does tend to denigrate all innovations in Russian life and society; and it is no difficult matter to take Tolstoy's ideal in 'War and Peace' to be the landowning aristocracy who can run their estates efficiently and humanely and base their lives on strong family ties and a general Christian ethic - his whole philosophy of history and human free will leads to this conclusion. But that is not the whole story, although his contemporaries had their reasons for thinking it was.

In a word 'War and Peace' was not understood; its critics were ill-equipped to deal with it, and that is something which applies equally, if not more so, to 'Anna Karenina'.

(c) 'Anna Karenina'

'Anna Karenina' deals with many problems - the question of
love and marriage, the attitude of parents to their children, the effects of the breakdown of marriage on the
parents, the place of women in society, the question of
the land and the peasantry, and the more usual Russian
preoccupations with man's purpose in life; it is certainly
much more than the commonplace Soviet criticism of it as
dealing primarily with the contradictions in Russian society caused by incipient capitalism, although Tolstoy's own
attitude to the latter's manifestations is clear and unam-
biguously negative - but for reasons diametrically opposed
to those of critics in Russia since 1917. Contemporary
critics, however, were at a loss when faced with the novel.
'War and Peace' might have caused them difficulties and
argument but 'Anna Karenina' aroused in most writers only
non-comprehension. It evoked far more political and ideo-
logical criticism than literary. Every side used it to
support their own particular viewpoint. Conservative critics can always find more to their taste in Tolstoy than
can radicals but 'Anna Karenina' proved even more problem-
atical than 'War and Peace'. Furthermore Tolstoy's own
conservatism, snobbism and puritanism stand out far more
clearly here than in his earlier masterpiece. 'Anna
Karenina' was poorly served by contemporary critics in
Russia because the vast majority of them dealt with it
politically or socially - and even abroad it was not fully
appreciated because of its critics' concentration on questions of morality. Neither approach managed to explain
why it should still be read with pleasure and interest
today when the political, social and moral climates are
very different from those in Russia in the 1860s and
1870s.
    The reading public, however, was by all reports exceed-
ingly enthusiastic. Strakhov, who was to be slightly less
ecstatic in his own review (see No. 70) than he was about
'War and Peace', sent Tolstoy a series of encouraging
letters throughout the novel's serialization. 'It is
nothing less than delirium. I have seen solemn old men
jumping up and down in admiration' (13 February 1875).
'Excitement keeps mounting' (21 March 1875). 'There is a
roar of satisfaction as if you were throwing food to
starving men' (5 March 1876). 'Everyone is taken up with
your novel. It's incredible how many people are reading
it. Only Gogol and Pushkin have ever been read like this'
(February 1877). Confirmation came from Countess Alexandra Tolstoy; on 13 June 1877 she wrote that society was in
uproar and that there was no end to the comments, praise,

gossip and arguments. Everyone seemed to be affected
personally. Fet declared that Tolstoy was beyond peer;
'What artistic daring in the description of the childbirth. Nobody has done anything like it before, and
nobody will ever do it again' (letter, April 1877).

But not all Tolstoy's acquaintances and fellow-writers
were as pleased. Saltykov-Shchedrin, who described its
atmosphere as genito-urinary (which was even more offensive than Skabichevsky's saying it was full of the fragrance of babies' nappies (see No. 58)), wrote to Annenkov
(9 March 1875) that 'Anna Karenina' saw the conservatives
in Russian life clearly triumphant; the novel had become
their political flag. He considered concocting a satire
to be called 'The Enamoured Bull', which is a theme taken
up by Tkachov (see No. 56). Nekrasov, who had been the
first person to appreciate Tolstoy's artistic qualities in
the early 1850s, thought its 'message' was simply that
married women should not take lovers (see No. 60), and
Suvorin agreed: it had no social significance and was
basically concerned with a description of Anna's love
affair.(74) Even Turgenev, although relations between him
and Tolstoy were at one of their frequent low ebbs, was
luke-warm. Tolstoy, he thought, had taken the wrong road;
the book was burdened by the influence of Moscow, the
Slavophiles, aristocrats and old spinsters, and lacked real
artistic freedom. Despite the fact that, he admitted,
parts of it were quite wonderful - the race, the mowing,
the hunt - Tolstoy had sunk in the bog of high society.
(75) Dostoevsky (see No. 64) was hesitant, yet it is not
untypical of him to see the best qualities of the book in
the atmosphere of love and forgiveness that surrounds the
'death-bed' scene after Anna had given birth to Vronsky's
daughter.

But what of the professional critics? Why was their
response in the main so hostile? Some of the adverse comments are explained by the length of time between the
appearance of the various instalments. Reviews were published after each part came out but the long gaps when the
'Russian Messenger' had nothing further from Tolstoy led
some to suggest endings of their own, most of which were
of ironic scabrousness; others grew tired of waiting and
expressed their irritation in satire and general denigration and one critic even suggested that Tolstoy was in
cahoots with Katkov, the editor of the 'Russian Messenger', and was stringing the narrative out simply to fill
the journal's empty pages and earn himself some extra
money (see No. 58); not for Skabichevsky an ironic ending:
no, Tolstoy could go on writing it for ever; after all,
was he not a past master at psychological analysis and the

depiction of numerous superfluous details?

The one overriding reason for the low level of critical response to 'Anna Karenina' in Russia is that the novel's publication coincided with one of the more vehement manifestations of the continuing discord between the various journals.(76) There were three principal camps, differentiated in the main politically. Conservative writers and critics tended to appear in the 'Russian Messenger', liberals in the 'Messenger of Europe', 'Voice' and the 'Northern Messenger', and the radicals in 'Fatherland Notes' and the Affair'. The vast majority of critics tried to see in 'Anna Karenina' what they wanted to see or regretted what was missing. It is not without significance that most of the novel appeared in the 'Russian Messenger' or that most of the very few laudatory notices should be printed on its pages. As a generalization, the conservatives liked the novel, the liberals liked most of the form but little of the content, and the radicals were antagonistic towards the whole thing.

Of the conservatives, Avseenko (see No. 57) saw the novel as a protest of the best elements of the upper classes against the inroads being made into society by the new middle and professional classes. Although he bemoaned the fact that the theme was banal and that there was neither plot nor character development, Avseenko believed that the readers would not object because Tolstoy possessed that great ability to depict feelings. This opinion was supported by the anonymous critic of the 'Citizen' (see No. 62) who added that the 'Levin' story would probably be of more lasting interest than that dealing with Anna. The 'Russian News' (see No. 61) agreed with Avseenko in that in some ways it was a pity that a marvellously talented author like Tolstoy should waste his time on such petty subject matter as the love of a society lady for an army dandy, but the psychological analysis of even these characters was so penetrating that the reader is won over. Such critics generally saw Tolstoy as a 'pure artist' and consequently right not to concern himself with current social and political questions. This view has echoes of the earlier 'art for art's sake' critics like Dudyshkin, Druzhinin and to some extent Annenkov; consequently the fact that Tolstoy did not deal with such questions was a positive point in his favour. When Tolstoy did deign to be contemporary such critics were at best bemused, at worst horrified. After all Katkov, the editor of the 'Russian Messenger', did refuse to print part VIII with its adverse comments on the Serbs and the Russians who were rushing off to give them assistance against the Turks.

Liberal critics, on the other hand, complained that the novel was notable for a marked absence of elements from the intelligentsia and that the latter therefore would find it quite without interest.(77)   Tolstoy was attacked for the lack of intellectual content and also for his mis- representation of the upper classes whom he portrayed, in their eyes, as only vulgar and petty.   'War and Peace' had earlier shown that he knew better.   Tolstoy's powers of psychological analysis received praise equal to that which the conservatives gave, yet, just as in 'War and Peace', his preoccupation with a mass of apparently useless detail was again regretted.   The 'Northern Messenger' praised Tolstoy for disdaining current obsessions and dealing with the more general questions which concerned mankind; his solutions, however, were not well received: how could he allow Levin to place more trust in the beliefs of the simple Russian peasants than in the writings of the great philosophers?   It was pure affectation on his part.(78) Other critics, including Chekhov (see No. 94a), saw no solutions at all.   E. Markov accused Tolstoy of writing about life without any ideal,(79) and the 'Odessan Messen- ger' agreed, in that it saw 'Anna Karenina' as the culmi- nation of what happens with an author completely devoid of ideology.(80)   One of the more gentle of the liberal cri- tics was Chuyko (see No. 54); in comparing Tolstoy with Stendhal, to the former's advantage in that Stendhal begins with a psychological theory and builds his charac- ters around it, whereas Tolstoy introduces psychological traits in succession which ultimately form a theory, Chuyko did find the development of the action rather slow. Tolstoy also had to overcome the fact that there was little or no interest to be found in the affairs (and more particularly the *affaires*) of aristocratic characters, but Chuyko does say that the very choice of a milieu where social problems play no part whatsoever in people's lives actually works to Tolstoy's advantage in that it provides a neutral background against which psychological problems can be successfully examined and solved - and even in the empty Vronsky, he adds, there are indeed psychic processes worthy of our attention.   The writer and journalist Bobo- rykin, whom his enemies on both sides saw as a typical liberal in that he never seemed to agree with them on any- thing, wrote that 'Anna Karenina' dealt with all kinds of problems, not only social, but moral and political ones too; the novel had its foundations in reality and was clearly didactic; nevertheless both Tolstoy's treatment of his subject matter and his conclusions were one-sided. (81)   Vsevolod Solovyov, a brother of the philosopher, wrote a series of reviews on the novel as each part appeared and his opinion of it changed from favourable to antagonistic (see No. 55). He began praising it for its sublime ordinariness, something it took a writer of genius to fashion into a work of art - we all recognize Stiva Oblonsky as someone we know, and like - and Tolstoy obviously writes about all his characters with love. But then Solovyov suggests that the more of the novel you read, the more you become convinced that you have read it all before - and you have, in 'War and Peace'. He sees all the leading characters as but younger versions of those in the earlier work, Kitty of Natasha, Levin of Pierre, Vronsky of Anatole, Stiva Oblonsky of Count Rostov. Furthermore he finds Anna boring (Dolly is far more alive) and accuses Tolstoy of having written himself out: he was just going through the motions. The famous art critic Stasov, however, saw 'Anna Karenina' as a definite development of Tolstoy's talent and claimed that it was a novel with which Russians could at long last stand side by side with their European counterparts without a shadow of any feeling of inferiority.(82)

Tolstoy's wife, Sonya, wrote in her diary (3 March 1877) that Tolstoy had told her that as in 'War and Peace' he loved the idea of his country, so in 'Anna Karenina' he loved that of the family. The novel can indeed be seen as supporting the sanctity of the family as the only stable social unit, but V. Markov (see No. 67) thinks the morality as expressed is not only old-fashioned but also outlived; to propound the idea through a heroine as empty-headed and frivolous as Anna casts serious doubts on the validity of the argument; in his view the whole tone of the novel is quite squalid. On the other hand Stankevich (see No. 66) asserts that Tolstoy is quite right to deal with such questions, the position of the family in society is, after all, extremely important; nevertheless Stankevich is not pleased with Tolstoy's solutions. In being one of the first critics to see the novel as really two - one about Anna, the other about Levin - which are poorly integrated (despite Tolstoy's own pride in its construction (see No. 65)) and in defending Karenin from attacks on his emotional coldness and bureaucratic formalism, Stankevich is one of the more original of the contemporary commentators; but he is still of his time in that he complains of Tolstoy's concentration on detailization, something which he sees as a purely aristocratic pursuit. And Veynberg (see No. 63) when ostensibly defending Tolstoy from his critics agrees with this view, but because Tolstoy is writing a novel and not a pamphlet this is no real criticism.

In receiving praise from the conservatives - largely for the wrong reasons - and a mixed reception from the

liberals, whose views betrayed a widespread misconception
of what the novel is actually about, Tolstoy was to suffer
the most abuse from the radicals. Tkachov (see No. 56)
attacked his idealization of the submissive and passive
characteristics of the Russian people - a dull family life
and an egotistic satisfaction of sexual desires was no
answer to Russia's deep-rooted and serious problems; Levin
is no hero, he is a typical Russian 'philosophizer'; Oblonsky and Vronsky are nothing but 'idle skivers' and Tolstoy
has lost his artistic balance because he puts love for a
woman and love for horses on an equal level and devotes
equal care and attention to the description of both. In
reviewing the novel before its completion, Tkachov suggests to Tolstoy that a suitable ending would be to have
Levin fall in love with his cow and then Kitty could die
of jealousy. What an opportunity for Tolstoy to display
his huge talents at depicting the most fleeting of feelings and psychological nuances! Skabichevsky took up the
theme (see No. 58); so full of praise was Tolstoy for
everything Russian that it was surprising that he had
omitted to comment on the wonderful Russian bath-houses:
his powers of description would be put to their full use
by telling us how Vronsky took a bath after his fall in
the steeplechase and his notable use of contrast as an
artistic device would be seen in his comparison between the
heat of the bath-house and that of Vronsky's passion for
Anna; and that could be contrasted with a description of
Anna taking a bath herself when we could be treated to a
portrait of her in rather more detail than that of
Hélène's shoulders.... And the notorious scene of Kitty's
examination by the doctors is seen by Skabichevsky as further evidence of Tolstoy's anti-Europeanism - it is
clearly an attack on doctors and medicine, and they, of
course, were introduced into Russia by the Germans.

M. Antonovich attacked the novel for its actual lack of
tendentiousness but more particularly for its quietist
philosophy.(83) Views such as these were typical of those
who, even if they admitted to Tolstoy's powers as a writer,
nevertheless accused him of being a poor thinker. Mikhaylovsky, the Populist writer and publicist, wrote three
articles in a general series, 'Notes of an Ignoramus',
entitled the Left Hand and the Right Hand of Count Tolstoy (see No. 59), where he refutes this view. He begins
by defending Tolstoy from the conservative critics who
merely wish to include him in their number; in fact, says
Mikhaylovsky, Tolstoy is the enemy of the reactionary camp
as can be clearly seen in 'Anna Karenina' which is an
attack on high society. The essence, though, of Mikhaylovsky's articles is that Tolstoy writes his works of

fiction with his left hand, that his right hand, through
which his thoughts are expressed, is the one to which
attention ought to be paid; the confusion of the critics
is rooted in their lack of comprehension of this fact.(84)

The most detailed and analytical contemporary treatment
of 'Anna Karenina' was written by Gromeka in 1883-4 (see
No. 69), although, like many critics, he had some harsh
things to say about the meaning to be attached to the epigraph 'Vengeance is mine; I shall repay'. In defending
Anna, Gromeka states that she is superior to the society
in which she lives because she lacks its spiritual emptiness; her love for Vronsky is sincere. However shallow
Vronsky might be, Anna is not to blame that he possessed
the very qualities she missed in her husband. Karenin
might be a good man, but he is no good for Anna. But it
is not a divine justice which enacts its revenge, but
society's; *its* rules have been broken by the honesty of
the liaison, by its openness. God's commandments might be
flouted, common morality discarded and even Tolstoy's own
ethical code disregarded, but all such transgressions are
secondary. If society's, albeit hypocritical, morality
had been observed all would have been well (and this view
is supported by the attitude of Vronsky's mother to the
relationship); but Anna is incapable of observing it
simply because she refuses to be hypocritical, and therein
lies her tragedy. Gromeka's opinion was reinforced some
twenty years later by Prince Kropotkin (see No. 85) who
placed the blame for Anna's suicide entirely on the
shoulders of Princess Betsy and her ilk. Karenin might
find asylum in their company, but he has the support of
an accommodating religion, a higher version of which
Bulgakov (see No. 73) saw as the way out of the impasse of
Russia's historical situation.

The contemporary response to 'Anna Karenina' in Russia
highlights a problem which is as old as literary criticism
itself. The critics attacked it from many standpoints yet
the author had said what he wished to say in manner he
considered best suited to the subject - and the readers
loved it.

(d) After 'Anna Karenina'

Tolstoy's spiritual crisis is usually dated in the second
half of the 1880s. As one critic writes:(85)

At the height of his fame and creative power, a wealthy
and successful man with a large and growing family, he
became the victim of growing moodiness and depression

and sought in earnest for the answer to the meaning and
purpose of life in a religious faith which could pre-
scribe rules of behaviour without requiring him to
engage in practices, or to subscribe to beliefs, which
his reason found repugnant.

It used to be considered that Tolstoy's change of direction was a sudden reversal of previous patterns, but
latterly the roots of what was to grow and flower in the
last thirty years of his life have been seen right from
the early days of 'Childhood'. Tolstoy has himself described the process in his 'Confession' which can be seen
to follow quite logically from the last part of 'Anna
Karenina', and with one or two notable exceptions, like
'Strider' and 'Hadji Murad', all his writings after 'Anna
Karenina' are an illustration in varying degrees of his
new beliefs. Shestov (see No. 93), writing in 1900 is
more explicit: 'All Tolstoy's works of the last few years,
even the fictional ones, have but one object: to make the
philosophy of life which was worked out in them, compulsory for everyone.' However that may be, the first of
these later works, 'Confession', contained enough of the
objectionable for the censor to refuse to assume that it
was either compulsory for him or for anyone else - he
banned its publication. But, following Russian tradition,
this did not prevent it from being read. Manuscript
copies were much in evidence. One of the first to read
one was Turgenev and he reacted in a way that was predic-
table. He wrote to D.V. Grigorovich, 31 October 1882,
that he had read 'Confession' with great interest; 'it is
remarkable for its sincerity, truthfulness, and strength
of conviction. But it is built on false premises and
ultimately leads to the most sombre denials of all human
life. This, too, in its way, is a kind of nihilism'. Yet
for an understanding of the later Tolstoy, 'Confession'
remains invaluable.
   Furthermore the 'new' Tolstoy also had his influence on
the manner in which his later works were reviewed. He was
at least writing about subjects which could readily be
related to contemporary life, yet, ironically, many of the
critics of the later nineteenth century were in some ways
less concerned with this question than their predecessors.
Moral and aesthetic matters became more important than
social and political ones.
   The more readily definable 'literary' works after 'Anna
Karenina' include 'The Death of Ivan Ilich', 'The Kreutzer
Sonata', 'Master and Man' and 'Resurrection'. Stasov told
Tolstoy (letter, 28 April 1886) that 'The Death of Ivan
Ilich' was the most outstanding work written in any

language, and which convinced the composer Tchaikovsky
that Tolstoy was the greatest 'author-painter' of all.(86)
'The Kreutzer Sonata', with its attacks on sexual intercourse as the root of all human evil, caused the most controversy of all Tolstoy's books and led him to suffer the
most virulent attacks from all sides.   In response to
these he came to his own public defence with the 'After-
word', which in its way was as ineffectual an explanation
of what he was doing as his essay on 'War and Peace' had
been some twenty years earlier.   Tsar Alexander III
thought it was directed explicitly at the institution of
marriage and more particularly the family and refused to
allow it to be published separately, but after the personal supplication of Tolstoy's wife he did permit it to
appear in an edition of Tolstoy's collected works.(87)
The Archbishop of Kherson was so disturbed by the force of
the way in which Tolstoy had expressed his ideas that he
preached about the dangers of 'this wolf in sheep's
clothing';(88) and Isabel F. Hapgood, Tolstoy's American
translator, at first refused to read it, let alone translate it; 'I have never read anything like it,' she said,
'and I hope I never shall again'.(89)   When it did appear
it found itself banned from transmission through the
American postal service.   'Master and Man' on the other
hand proved extremely popular and was taken by the majority of readers as an allegory on the death of Christ and
its meaning for humanity.   But it was 'Resurrection' which
caused the most interest among the critics and widespread
excitement among the readers.   Stasov told Tolstoy that
no one could wait for Fridays (the day on which 'Niva', in
which it was being serialized, appeared).   Fridays, he
wrote, have turned into Sundays,(90) a reference to the
fact that in Russian the word for Sunday and Resurrection
is the same.   The story of the publication of 'Resurrection' is too well known to repeat here;(91) but it sold in
vast quantities and was received by the critics with as
much variation of comment as any of his previous works.
Russian critics did, of course, have much on which to
write, but it is not without interest that hardly any of
them chose to judge it on the basis of what Tolstoy had
recently written on literature in 'What is Art?'.   That
was left to a later generation.   The conservative critic
P.N. Krasnov bemoaned the fact that the heroine, Katyusha
Maslov, came from the lower classes, but as the morality
expressed by the novel was praiseworthy, perhaps Tolstoy
could be excused this lack of taste, and he was being
truthful and not idealistic about his subject-matter;
naturalist writers, he concluded, should present life as
it is, and this was what Tolstoy had done.(92)   The same

Tolstoy, one might add, who was cited in France as the
shining example of all the qualities the naturalist school
so manifestly lacked.   Sementkovsky looked at the hero,
Nekhlyudov, and took him as a warning to the Russian
intelligentsia.   In tracing his ancestry back to Chatsky
in Griboedov's 'Woe from Wit' in the 1820s, he saw Tolstoy's message to be that the time had come to stop thinking about what to do and actually get down to doing something; he none the less played down the social value of
the novel and Tolstoy's attacks on contemporary society,
declaring that the main interest was in the relations between Katyusha and Nekhlyudov.(93)   M.A. Protopopov returned to some of the arguments over 'War and Peace' by
wondering first of all whether it was really a novel.   Who
is resurrected? he asked.   Where is Tolstoy's famous
psychological analysis?   What sort of people are Katyusha
and Nekhlyudov supposed to be?   They are characteristic
of nothing; they are typical of no one; they are but puppets made to act out Tolstoy's retribution upon Russian
society.   And what is the practical use of the idealistic
ending?   Protopopov's dislike of 'Resurecction' is aptly
summed up in the title of his review: Not of this World.
(94)   But Bogdanovich still saw all the old Tolstoy with
his wonderful grasp of life, his simplicity and sincerity,
in taking the readers so effortlessly and to so much point
from the salons of the capital to the wastes of Siberia,
from the prisons and law courts to the Russian countryside; there was no trace of any artificiality or 'fic-
tionalizing'; everything was just as it is in life itself;
it was as if life opened up before the reader in all its
infinite variety; and the hero and heroine were as realistic as any of Tolstoy's creations - there were hundreds of
Katyushas and Nekhlyudovs in Russia.(95)   Solovyov also
reacted positively to the novel; he saw it as a plea for
humanity and its positive values of love, sincerity and
honesty.(96)   The theatre director and entrepreneur
Nemirovich-Danchenko wrote to Tolstoy (10 July 1899) that
the novel was more than literature; he felt that he was
not reading but walking about, actually seeing the people,
the cells, the rooms, the piano, the roads.   Chekhov (see
No. 94) thought it a remarkable work of art, although he
was not much taken with the characters of Katyusha and
Nekhlyudov - but all the others were wonderful.   He found
the ending 'theological' and quite false in technique, yet
Tolstoy's transparent sincerity was an inspiration to
everyone.   Although the style left a little to be desired,
if 'you read between the lines you see an eagle soaring in
the sky and the last thing in the world he cares about is
the beauty of his feathers'.(97)   M. Moskal, however, was

not prepared to see an eagle in flight, more a viper in
the bosom; in 'Resurrection', he wrote, 'tendentiousness
has replaced artistic creation' and four fifths of the
novel consisted in negating or ridiculing the existing
order of things in all its manifestations.(98) Moskal can
be seen as typical of those conservative critics who were
not opposed to tendentiousness in art in general, quite
the reverse, but they insisted on its value only when it
was directed to the support of Russia's existing institutions rather than to undermining them.(99) And 'Resurrection' with its attacks upon the legal system, the Orthodox Church and the influential sections of Russian society,
and with its overt propagandizing for a 'new Christianity'
did nothing at all to give comfort to Russia's hard-pressed
reactionaries. That Tolstoy's excommunication from the
Orthodox Church should follow hard on the publication of
'Resurrection' is no surprise; what is, perhaps, is that
it did not happen sooner.

The last thirty years of Tolstoy's life did, however, see
the appearance of some criticism of his works of fiction
that was to prove of more than passing interest. In particular, the philosopher Shestov (see No. 93), taking up a
point made by Akhsharumov some thirty years before, suggested that Tolstoy was not at all objective about his
characters; but if he disapproved of them then all of them
were to be punished in one way or another - by death, by
illness, by unhappiness, or what you will. In Shestov's
eyes Tolstoy lacked the virtue of compassion for anyone
who did not match up to his own high ideals - be it
Napoleon or Anna Karenina, Speransky or Olenin. In an
oblique way Tolstoy reduces everything to a display of
human egoism, but none the less manages to accept life as
it is as far as he himself is concerned. Konstantin
Leontiev (see No. 90), while accusing Tolstoy, as he had
often been accused before, of excessive detailization,
still found him to be unwaveringly accurate and perceptive
in the psychological sphere. It was the novelist and
critic Dmitriy Merezhkovsky (see No. 96) who was to write
one of the most influential essays on Tolstoy. His book
'Tolstoy as Man and Artist' of 1902 was widely read and
soon translated into English and was to have what was
later to be seen as a rather doleful effect on Tolstoy
criticism in the West. To Merezhkovsky Tolstoy was the
supreme master at describing the human body; his special
glory lay in that he was the first to discover new ways,
unexhausted and inexhaustible, of describing the most
subtle and complex of physical and mental sensations and
to make the reader look at phenomena in a different way

from before - what later critics were to refer to as 'making it strange' - and in Tolstoy's works nothing was extraordinary because everything was equally important.

In sum, if one looks at the development of Russian nineteenth-century literary criticism through what it had to say about Tolstoy over a period of sixty years, and remembers what Pushkin had written in the 1820s, it would not be unjust to say that Russia had certainly produced an independent, indigenous literature of great quality and originality but that it still had to wait, with one or two exceptions, for some critics worthy of it.

(e) International recognition

Tolstoy was virtually unknown outside Russia before the middle of the 1880s. There had been an English translation, quite competent, of 'Childhood and Youth' in 1862, parts of which were translated into French as 'Nicolenka' in 1866. The English version occasioned a few comments but they showed no marked enthusiasm (see Nos 12, 13). An American edition of 'The Cossacks' appeared in 1878, translated with an introduction by a former US consul in St Petersburg, Eugene Schuyler; it had the misfortune to be called 'dry and matter-of-fact' by Turgenev. It was he who was the first of the great Russian novelists to be known in the West; he lived in Europe for much of his adult life and was considered almost a European man of letters. In 1855 an edition of the 'Sportsman's Sketches' appeared in France, a year after Prosper Mérimée had published an article on its author. Mérimée was responsible for any early appreciation of Russian literature in France and acted as a counterweight to the likes of Balzac who had complained in 'Le Cousin Pons' in 1847 of the creation in Paris of university chairs in Slav, Manchu and literature as little fit to be professed as the literatures of the north, which instead of giving lessons to others ought to be receiving them. Mérimée, though, was of a different opinion; he translated Gogol's 'The Government Inspector', four of Pushkin's stories, including 'The Queen of Spades', and wrote brief articles on Turgenev, Pushkin and Gogol. (100) In 1876 Turgenev arranged for Tolstoy's Sebastopol stories to be published in 'Le Temps' and five years later Dostoevsky's 'House of the Dead' came out in English as 'Buried Alive: Ten Years Penal Servitude in Siberia'. But all of these editions were isolated events. It might well be asked why the Russian masters in general and Tolstoy in particular were slow to be appreciated outside Russia. The following reasons might help towards an

answer: very few people could read Russian, it was a difficult language to learn, and the early translations were
poor, English ones tending to be worse as they more often
than not came from the French or German; there was little
general interest in Russia - even an international event
like the Crimean War failed to arouse more than a brief
acquaintance; there was no academic interest worth speaking of; there was the opinion, especially in France, that
all educated Russians spoke French and consequently there
was probably little native literature of any note; and,
there was a strong home-grown literary tradition and the
reading public was generally conservative in its taste and
unadventurous in its demands.

However the Franco-Prussian war of 1870 changed things
a little. France looked towards Russia for a possible
ally; popular theatres put on plays, and novels were
written, with Russian characters. Five years later a
chair of Russian was established at the École des Langues
Orientales Vivantes and in the same year Courrière published his 'Histoire de la littérature contemporaine en
Russie' (see No. 38) which contains the first French comment on Tolstoy of any length. In Courrière's opinion
Russian literature was good because of its realism and its
preference for the didactic and socially instructive.
Tolstoy is treated briefly and the intrusion of philosophy
and Tolstoy's own special brand of fatalism are both de-
plored. E. de Cyon pulished his Lev Tolstoi: un pessi-
miste russe in the 'Nouvelle Revue' in 1883 where he
pointed at Tolstoy's circumstantial narrative, minute descriptions, realism and subtle psychology (see No. 41).
However, despite these two works Tolstoy remained little
known in France. It was left to Eugène Melchior de Vogüé
to set Tolstoy on his way to lasting European literary
fame. Between October 1883 and June 1886 he published in
the 'Revue des deux mondes' a series of six articles on
Russian literature, which later became a book entitled
'Le Roman Russe'. De Vogüé was secretary at the French
Embassy in St Petersburg from 1876 to 1881, met many Russian literary figures and corresponded with Tolstoy. He
uses Russian literature to counterbalance the influence of
the Naturalist school, especially Zola; Flaubert is criticized for his impassiveness and lack of pity, neither of
which was apparent in the Russians; if France were to
adopt the Russians' humanity and charity, then the French
— novel would improve. De Vogüé's comments on Tolstoy (see
No. 87) are a landmark in Tolstoy's European reception.

Soon after the appearance of his book Hachette brought
out a translation of 'War and Peace'; this was the same
one that had been published in St Petersburg in 1879 where

it had, not surprisingly, sold poorly. 'Anna Karenina'
appeared in 1885 and 'The Cossacks' and 'Sebastopol' were
printed together in 1886. After this date various translations of Tolstoy's works appeared with increasing fre-
quency. Parallel with this interest by the reading public
there was an increase in critical appreciation. Soon
after de Vogüé there were studies by Barine (see No. 72),
Sarcey and Dupuy (see No. 71). Barine's is somewhat shallow, Sarcey's not without some originality, and Dupuy's
is a fairly straightforward popularization. There was
some reaction to the popularity of Russian writers but in
general they kept their reputations, such as they were,
intact. Later, contemporary French commentators concentrated more on the non-literary aspects of Tolstoy which
was something they had in common with critics in other
countries.

The explosion of Tolstoy's popularity in France was
paralleled in England and America and the two events are
not unconnected. The studies by de Vogüé and Dupuy were
available; there was a mild war scare caused by English
fears of Russian encroachment in India; Tolstoy's non-
literary fame as a religious and social reformer had
spread; and Russia refused to sign the Berne Convention
which enabled translations to be made without copyright
problems. Just as Tolstoy had been fortunate in France
with de Vogüé so was he with influential critics in England and America - Matthew Arnold (see No. 82), E. Gosse
(see No. 89) and W.D. Howells (see No. 79), and it was
these three in particular who set the trends for Tolstoy
criticism for a number of years. The main points in
Anglo-American criticism may be summarized as: Tolstoy's
realism is based upon a moral and religious interpretation of life; although his novels are exceedingly long,
they are composed from an amalgamation of detail; his
work is marked by a fidelity to life as it is; he had an
ability to create fictional characters who seem to be
more life-like than actual people; he possessed great
powers as a psychologist; and he had a complete disregard
for such matters as plot, structure and style. These
ideas were reflected in and developed by later English-
speaking critics, however much Gosse, Saintsbury (see No.
100) or Henry James (see No. 103) might have been antagonistic to the sheer size and scope of Tolstoy's major
novels. All in all, though, it was man's soul that such
critics saw reflected in his fiction. The publication of
Merezhkovsky's book, with its insistence upon Tolstoy's
supremacy at describing the body, changed this tendency a
little, but Western critics nevertheless still insisted
(and did not Tolstoy's own later years support them?)

that Tolstoy was a moralist and preacher, and consequently
by definition was less concerned with man's body as such.
    Although writing specifically about Tolstoy in France,
T.S. Lindström well summarizes how he was received everywhere outside Russia with the words:(101)

> Tolstoy's activities, in centering upon the burning
> actuality of the times, greatly enhanced his moral
> importance; this crystallized around the problem which
> preoccupied the West at the end of the century: the
> problem of the survival of the human personality in a
> society becoming more and more that of the materialist
> and statist.

Indeed, by his death in 1910, despite being the most
famous man in the world, Tolstoy, the writer of works of
fiction of almost incomparable quality, was in danger of
being overshadowed. Happily, this danger was averted.

IV

Tolstoy's reputation since 1910

If contemporary preoccupations prevented Tolstoy's fiction
from receiving in his lifetime a proper appreciation, not
only in Russia but also abroad, then posterity has made
ample amends.
    Tolstoy died seven years before the Revolution of 1917,
the revolution of which, in Lenin's words (see No. 102),
he was the mirror. Lenin's influence in the Soviet Union
as a literary critic is greater than what is contained in
the relatively little he wrote on Tolstoy would perhaps
warrant - and, for example, the marxist critic Plekhanov,
who wrote much less, is rather better (see No. 101) - but
Soviet critics have, for obvious reasons, leant heavily on
his advice; yet bearing that in mind, Soviet scholarship
on Tolstoy has been second to none. Although Soviet
writers keep Tolstoy the writer of fiction quite separate
from Tolstoy the religious reformer, this has not prevented them from making great progress in the appreciation of
the man who is without doubt in their eyes only second to
Pushkin as Russia's greatest writer of the nineteenth century. If only more of the Soviet criticism were translated, which seems a vain hope, or more people studied
Russian, which seems an even vainer one, much valuable
criticism would not be overlooked and non-Russian readers
would have more to rely on than, for instance, Gleb
Struve's somewhat carping article in the 'Russian Review'

of April 1960; having paid due homage to Lenin, the best
Soviet critics do not find the demands of Socialist realism placing as severe limitations upon them as he suggests; one need go no further than the work of Viktor
Shklovsky for this to become apparent. If one excuses
Struve as being a captive of his times then perhaps he
would himself change his mind now with the book by
Zaydenshnur on 'War and Peace' (1966) and the more general
appraisals of Kupreyanova on Tolstoy's aesthetics (1966)
or Khrapchenko on Tolstoy as an artist (1963).(102)

Soon after the Revolution a flood of memoirs and biographical material was published in the Soviet Union, but
it is the ninety-volume 'Complete Collected Works', written over a period of thirty years, which will be the lasting monument to Tolstoy scholarship, a work almost unparalleled of its kind; it has been supplemented by various numbers of the generally prestigious 'Literary Heritage' series, (103) and by the biographical material
gathered together by N.N. Gusev.(104) Soviet criticism of
Tolstoy showed the quality of which it was capable soon
after the Revolution when one of the members of the Formalist school, Boris Eykhenbaum, began his three-volume
study, only the first of which has been translated into
English.(105) Although finding his Formalist criteria
unsatisfactory for dealing with the two major novels,
Eykhenbaum's ideas have none the less had a marked influence (often unacknowledged) on subsequent Tolstoy criticism both in the Soviet Union and abroad.

As for Tolstoy's reputation outside the Soviet Union,
it has done nothing but grow, if spasmodically. In the
second decade of this century there was a 'Russian fever'
in both England and America. Although interest at that
time was centred more on Dostoevsky than Tolstoy (Middle-
ton Murry's book on Dostoevsky of 1916 being the fever's
most notable immediate result) it none the less led to
further interest in the latter. One thinks of the comments that were to come from D.H. Lawrence, with his
praise for the writer but his deep disgust about the
moralist; for example, Lawrence seems to suggest that
Tolstoy's dislike for Vronsky stems from Tolstoy's jealousy of Vronsky's sexual prowess. Others followed in
the traditions of Henry James in being unable to grasp the
physical size and intellectual scope of a Tolstoy novel -
Percy Lubbock accused Tolstoy of wasting material and confusing his readers in that none of them could understand
what, for instance, 'War and Peace' was actually about;
in preferring cameos to panoramas he paradoxically prefers generalities to details. Virginia Woolf, although
she could not cope with the scale of the novels, felt he

was somehow the greatest Russian writer of all, and she
suggested that it had something to do with the mixture of
pleasure and pain that one received from him. On the
other hand someone like E.M. Forster could praise Tolstoy
precisely because he introduced for the first time to the
novel the sense of *space*.(106) Appreciation of Tolstoy
was also helped by the fact that reliable and good translations of his fiction soon appeared. Constance Garnett
was the instigator, but it was Aylmer Maude in his Centenary Edition (1928-37) who ensured that Tolstoy was readily,
readably and accurately available to English-speaking
readers, and although there is perhaps a need for a new
edition of the major fiction based on the definitive
'Complete Collected Works', there is little argument that
Maude's versions are still by and large the best in
English.

The amount of academic comment on Tolstoy in the West
was relatively small before the 1950s, although E.J. Simmons had first published his life and works in 1946.
Since then, though, Tolstoy has received some perceptive
comments from commentators the world over, and as a subject for critical analysis he is by no means exhausted;
controversy still exists; 'War and Peace' and 'Anna Karenina' still lend themselves to various interpretations, let
alone the more obvious thorns of 'Resurrection' and 'The
Kreutzer Sonata'. If reasoned argument and the possibility of reinterpretation by succeeding generations are
but two of the hallmarks of a great writer then Tolstoy's
fame is assured. It is only ironic, something which he
himself would surely have appreciated, that he is
remembered today for those of his writings he considered
worthless. Often idiosyncratic in his literary judgments,
he was no different when he looked at his own work, but,
as he told his diary in 1853, he was a writer. Nor had he
then, as G.K. Chesterton would have said, succumbed to his
tendency to madness. Aylmer Maude's hopes that it would
be Tolstoy's literary works that would ultimately be the
most important seem to have been realized, and although
for different reasons this is the case both in his own
country and abroad.

NOTES

1 A Survey of Russian Literature in 1824 and the Beginning of 1825, 'The Pole Star', 1825.
2 Quoted by T. Wolff, 'Pushkin on Literature', London,
   1973, p. 126.
3 Ibid., p. 146.

4   I.A. Krylov (1769-1844), journalist, dramatist and
    poet, but best known as a fabulist.
5   G.R. Derzhavin (1743-1816) was the first Russian poet
    of any great originality. His most famous works are
    the philosophic ode 'God' (1784), and 'Felitsa'
    (1782), written in honour of Catherine the Great.
6   Wolff, op. cit., p. 147.
7   A.S. Pushkin, letter to P.A. Pletnyov, 11 April 1831.
8   To those Russians who recalled Boileau's 'Art Poét-
    ique' it was: 'Enfin Belinsky vint.'
9   D.S. Mirsky, 'A History of Russian Literature', London,
    1949, p. 167.
10 J.H. Billington, 'The Icon and the Axe', London, 1966,
    p. 353.
11 'Entsiklopedicheskiy slovar'' ('Encyclopaedic Diction-
    ary'), Brokgauz i Efron, St Petersburg, 1899, vol.
    XVII(a), pp. 416-17.
12 These journals also played a unique role in the
    development of Russian public opinion, as they spread
    ideas over the whole Russian Empire and thus managed
    to link like-minded people who did not happen to live
    in Moscow or St Petersburg. The speed with which
    political parties emerged at the beginning of this
    century is due in no small way to the existence of
    these journals. Lenin, the leader of the Russian
    Revolution, was well aware of their great influence -
    he closed them all down within a year of taking power.
13 R. Hingley, 'Russian Writers and Society, 1825-1904',
    London, 1967, p. 228.
14 'L.N. Tolstoy v vospominaniyakh sovremennikov' ('L.N.
    Tolstoy as Remembered by his Contemporaries'), ed.
    N.N. Gusev, Moscow, 1960, vol. 1, p. 144.
15 Ibid., p. 160.
16 Ibid., p. 188.
17 Ibid., vol. 2, p. 12.
18 Tolstoy, letter to N.N. Strakhov, 9 April 1876.
19 The first volume contained 'Childhood', 'Boyhood',
    'Youth', 'A Landowner's Morning', 'The Memoirs of a
    Billiard-marker' and 'Three Deaths', while the second
    had 'The Raid', 'The Woodfelling', the three Sebasto-
    pol stories, 'The Snow Storm', 'Family Happiness',
    'The Cossacks', 'Polikushka', and various pedagogical
    articles.
20 E.J. Simmons, 'Leo Tolstoy', New York, 1960, vol. 1,
    p. 142.
21 Tolstoy was often dubbed 'the lion of...'. This is
    explained by the fact that his first name, Lev, is
    also the Russian for 'lion'.
22 N.A. Nekrasov, letter to I.S. Turgenev, 21 October
    1852.

23   I.S. Turgenev, letter to N.A. Nekrasov, 28 October
     1852.
24   'Fatherland Notes', 1852, no. 10.
25   'Fatherland Notes', 1853, no. 1.
26   'Muscovite', 1852, no. 19.
27   A. Maude, 'The Life of Tolstoy', Oxford, 1953, vol. 1,
     p. 84.
28   F.M. Dostoevsky, letter to A.N. Maykov, 18 January
     1856.
29   'Pantheon', 1853, no. 10.
30   'Muscovite', 1853, no. 1.
31   'Fatherland Notes', 1854, no. 11.
32   'Muscovite', 1854, no. 23.
33   L.N. Tolstoy, 'Sobraniye sochineniy v 12-i tomakh'
     ('Collected Works in 12 Volumes'), Moscow, 1973, vol.
     2, p. 385.
34   A.F. Pisemsky, letter to A.N. Ostrovsky, 26 July 1855.
35   'Fatherland Notes', 1855, no. 7.
36   'Muscovite', 1855, nos 15-16.
37   H. Troyat, 'Tolstoy', Harmondsworth, 1970, p. 176.
38   I.I. Panaev, letter to Tolstoy, 29 August 1855.
39   'St Petersburg News', 1856, no. 21.
40   'Fatherland Notes', 1855, no. 10.
41   'St Petersburg News', 1856, no. 2.
42   'Library for Reading', 1856, no. 139.
43   I.S. Turgenev, letter to S.T. Aksakov, 27 February
     1856.
44   'Russian Review', 1894, no. 12.
45   A.I. Herzen, letter to M.K. Reykhel, 18 June 1856.
46   'Library for Reading', 1856, no. 139.
47   'Fatherland Son', 1857, no. 6
48   'St Petersburg News', 1857, no. 46.
49   There were brief comments in 'Northern Flower',
     1858, no. 10, 'Fatherland Son', 1859, no. 8, and the
     Moscow literary almanac 'Morning', 1859.
50   'St Petersburg News', 1857, no. 210.
51   Tolstoy, op. cit., 'Sobraniye sochineniy', vol. 3,
     p. 404.
52   I.S. Turgenev, letter to Tolstoy, 11 February 1859.
53   'Northern Flower', 1859, no. 22.
54   'St Petersburg News', 1859, no. 155.
55   Troyat, op. cit., p. 270.
56   Ibid., p. 378.
57   Ibid., p. 378.
58   'Contemporary', 1863, no. 7.
59   Simmons, op. cit., vol. 1, p. 293.
60   For a discussion of the genesis of 'War and Peace'
     see R.F. Christian, 'Tolstoy's "War and Peace": a
     Study', Oxford, 1962.

61   Tolstoy, letter to A.A. Fet, 23 January 1865.
62   I.S. Turgenev, letter to P.V. Annenkov, 13 April 1868.
63   V.P. Botkin, letter to A.A. Fet, June 1869.
64   Troyat, op. cit., p. 419.
65   Ibid., p. 422.
66   Ibid.
67   I.A. Goncharov, letter to I.S. Turgenev, 22 February
     1868.
68   'Voice', 1865, no. 93.
69   S.P. Bychkov, 'L.N. Tolstoy v russkoy kritike' ('L.N.
     Tolstoy in Russian Criticism'), Moscow, 1960, p. 19.
70   T.A. Kuzminskaya, 'Moya zhizn' doma i v Yasnoy
     Polyane' ('My Life at Home and at Yasnaya Polyana'),
     Moscow, 1928, part III, p. 42.
71   P.A. Vyazemsky, Vospominaniya o 1812 gode (Reminisc-
     ences of 1812), 'Russian Archive', 1869, no. 1.
72   See Appendix.
73   'Russian Archive', 1869, no. 1.
74   A.S. Suvorin, 'New Time', 1877, no. 432.
75   I.S. Turgenev, letters to A.S. Suvorin, 14 March 1875;
     Ya.P. Polonsky, 14 March 1875; A.V. Toporov, 20 April
     1875.
76   For a Soviet view of these arguments see I.E.
     Grinyova, Russkaya zhurnal'naya kritika 70-kh godov
     XIX veka o romane L.N. Tolstogo 'Anna Karenina',
     'Uchoniye zapiski moskovskogo oblastnogo pedagogi-
     cheskogo instituta imeni N.K. Krupskoy' (Criticism
     of Tolstoy's Novel 'Anna Karenina' in the Russian
     Journals in the 1870s, 'Papers of the N.K. Krupskaya
     Moscow Regional Pedagogical Institute'), vol. CXXII,
     1963, pp. 129-47.
77   Literature and Journalism, 'Rumour', 1876.
78   'Northern Messenger', 1877, no. 92.
79   E. Markov, 'Voice', 1877, no. 3.
80   'Odessan Messenger', 1875, no. 88.
81   P.D. Boborykin, 'Word', 1878, no. 6.
82   V.V. Stasov, 'New Time', 1877, no. 433.
83   'Word', 1878, no. 1.
84   For a development of Mikhaylovsky's arguments see I.
     Berlin, Tolstoy and Enlightenment, 'Mightier than the
     Sword', London, 1964.
85   R.F. Christian, 'Tolstoy, a Critical Introduction',
     Cambridge, 1969, p. 212.
86   Quoted by Troyat, op. cit., p. 641.
87   Maude, op. cit., vol. 2, p. 288.
88   Simmons, op. cit., vol. 2, p. 131.
89   'Review of Reviews', April 1890.
90   Simmons, op. cit., vol. 2, pp. 281-2.
91   See, for example A. Maude, How 'Resurrection' was

written, 'Tolstoy and his Problems', London, 1905, or
the 'Bookman' (New York), June 1900.

92 P.N. Krasnov, 'Books of the Week', 1900, no. 1.
93 R. Sementkovsky, 'Niva', 1899, no. 10.
94 M.A. Protopopov, 'Russian Thought', 1900, no. 6.
95 A. Bogdanovich, 'Religious World', 1900, no. 2.
96 V.S. Solovyov, 'Life', 1900, no. 2.
97 Troyat, op. cit., p. 763.
98 M. Moskal, 'Rebirth or Fall?', Moscow, 1900.
99 Bychkov, op. cit., p. 37.
100 For a discussion of the reception and influence of
    Russian literature in France see F.W.J. Hemmings, 'The
    Russian Novel in France, 1884-1914', Oxford, 1950.
101 T.S. Lindström, 'Tolstoi en France (1886-1910)',
    Paris, 1952, p. 152; quoted by E.J. Simmons, 'Tol-
    stoy', London, 1973, p. 227.
102 V.B. Shklovsky, 'Material i stil' v romane L'va
    Tolstogo "Voyna i mir"' ('Material and Style in Tol-
    stoy's "War and Peace"'), Moscow, 1928; E.E. Zayden-
    shnur, '"Voyna i mir" L.N. Tolstogo. Sozdaniye
    velikoy knigi' ('Tolstoy's "War and Peace". The
    Creation of a Masterpiece'), Moscow, 1966; E.N.
    Kupreyanova, 'Estetika L.N. Tolstogo' ('Tolstoy's
    Aesthetics'), Moscow/Leningrad, 1966; M.B. Khrap-
    chenko, "Lev Tolstoy kak khudozhnik' ('Tolstoy as
    an Artist'), Moscow, 1963.
103 'Literaturnoye nasledstvo' ('Literary Heritage'),
    vols 35-6, 37-8, Moscow, 1939; 69 (two volumes),
    Moscow, 1961; and 75 (two volumes), Moscow, 1965.
104 N.N. Gusev, 'Lev Nikolaevich Tolstoy: Materialy k
    biografii' ('Materials towards a Biography'):
    '1828-55', Moscow, 1957; '1855-69', Moscow, 1957;
    '1870-81', Moscow, 1963; and '1881-5', Moscow,
    1970.
105 B.M. Eykhenbaum, 'Lev Tolstoy, kniga pervaya, 50-e
    gody' ('Leo Tolstoy, I, the fifties'), Leningrad,
    1928 (translated into English as 'The Young Tolstoi',
    Ann Arbor, Mich., 1972); 'Lev Tolstoy, kniga
    vtoraya, 60-e gody' ('Leo Tolstoy, II, the sixties'),
    Moscow, 1931; 'Lev Tolstoy, semidesyatiye gody' ('Leo
    Tolstoy, the seventies'), Leningrad, 1960.
106 D.H. Lawrence, 'Introduction to "Cavalleria Rusti-
    cana"', London, 1928; Percy Lubbock, 'The Craft of
    Fiction', London, 1921; Virginia Woolf, The Russian
    Point of View, 'Collected Essays', vol. I, London,
    1966; E.M. Forster, 'Aspects of the Novel', London,
    1927.

Before 'War and Peace' 1852-65

1. NEKRASOV ON SOME EARLY WORKS

1852, 1854, 1855, 1856

(a) On 'Childhood'
In 1848 N.A. Nekrasov (1821-77), poet and radical, bought
the 'Contemporary', a journal which had been founded ten
years before by Pushkin, and under his editorship it became the leading literary journal of its day. Tolstoy
had sent the manuscript of 'Childhood', signed only with
his initials, L.N., to Nekrasov on 3 July 1852, explaining
that it was the first part of a planned tetralogy to be
called 'Four Periods of Growth'. Nekrasov replied by
letter in the middle of August 1852.

I have read your manuscript ('Childhood'). It contains so
much of interest that I am publishing it. Without knowing
how it goes on, I cannot speak with any certainty, but I
think the author has talent. In any case the author's
manner and the simplicity and reality of the content form
the undoubted value of the work. If in the following
parts, as is to be expected, there is more liveliness and
action then it will be a good novel. Please send me the
sequel. Both your novel and your talent have caught my
interest.

(b) On 'The Memoirs of a Billiard-marker'
After publishing 'Childhood' in September 1852 and 'The
Raid' in March 1853, Nekrasov was anxious for the promised
sequel to the former. Tolstoy sent him 'The Memoirs of a

Billiard-marker instead; this might be part of the explanation of Nekrasov's cool reception. This extract is taken
from a letter from Nekrasov to Tolstoy, 6 February 1854.

'The Memoirs of a Billiard-marker' is very good in conception but very weak in execution; the reason for this is
the style you have chosen: the language of your Marker
has nothing distinctive about it - it is quite run-of-the-
mill, the sort used a thousand times in our stories when
an author introduces someone of low calling. And because
you chose this form you have quite needlessly hampered
yourself; the story has turned out rough and the good
things in it disappear.

(c) On 'Boyhood'
From a letter to Tolstoy, 17 February 1855.

Your 'Boyhood' .... had what is called an effect, that is
people in Petersburg are all talking about it. As for
the literary circles, all honest people are unanimous in
finding it full of poetry, original and artistically
written.... My friends Turgenev and Annenkov are delighted with it, as am I.

(d) On 'Sebastopol in May'
From a letter to Tolstoy, 2 September 1855. The problems
referred to here by Nekrasov concern the activities of
the censor; not only had Tolstoy's second story of the
siege of Sebastopol been severely cut but it had been
personally corrected by the censor, Musin-Pushkin, himself. It was however published, as 'A Spring Night in
May', along with 'The Woodfelling', in the September number of the 'Contemporary'; the author was given as L.N.T.)

I arrived in Petersburg in the middle of August when the
'Contemporary' was in the direst straits. This disgraceful state of affairs into which your piece ('Sebastopol in
May') was brought really upset me. Even now I cannot
think about it without anguish and rage. Your work will
not, of course, be lost .... it will always bear witness
to someone who had the strength to keep his capacity for
such profound and searching truths in circumstances when

not everyone would have done so. I do not wish to say how
highly I value your story and the tenor of your talent and
how it is generally impressive and new. This is just what
Russian society now needs - the truth, the kind of truth
so little of which has remained in Russian literature
since the death of Gogol. You are right, this is the most
valuable of all your gifts. This truth, in the way you
bring it into our literature, is something completely new
for us. I know of no other writer who could make one love
and sympathize with him as you can. But one thing I fear
- that time and the filth of reality, the deafness and
dumbness of the surroundings, will do to you what it has
done to most of us: kill in you that energy without which
there can be no writer, at least no writer of the sort
that Russia now needs.... You have started your career
in such a way that you have forced even the most circum-
spect people to hold out the highest hopes for you.

(e) On 'The Woodfelling' and 'Sebastopol in August'
The first passage is from Notes on the Journals for
September 1855, the 'Contemporary', 1855, no. 10, and the
second from Notes on the Journals for December 1855 and
January 1856, the 'Contemporary', 1856, no. 2.

The sensible, as it were practical, direction taken by our
literature in the last fifteen or twenty years and which
consists in the aspiration to a study of its own national
life - in all its manifestations and conditions - has
scarcely touched upon the military. Since the days of
the phrase-mongering stories of Marlinsky, in which both
officers and men appeared in the uncharacteristic uniforms
of medieval warriors, we have heard nothing of Russian
soldiers. But now an author has appeared who takes us
into a completely new world. Like Turgenev, who nine
years ago began his essays on national characters and
gradually placed before us a series of original, living
and real people, so Count L.N.T. in his 'The Woodfelling'
presents us with several types of Russian soldier, types
who can serve as the key to a comprehension of the spirit,
ideas, customs and the general component parts of military
life. A few more such essays and the life of the military
will cease being a dim puzzle. The mastery of the story,
the complete knowledge of what he is writing about, the
deep truth of the understanding and depiction of the
characters, the comments full of a quiet but penetrating
mind - these are the qualities of Count L.N.T.'s story.

['Sebastopol in August'], both in its qualities and faults,
finally proves that the author is graced with an unusual
talent. Its faults, besides a certain carelessness of
presentation, are a lack of a strict plan of campaign
whereby the parts are reduced to the general and the unified, thus presenting a proportioned and tidy whole; from
this we have a somewhat incomplete impression, arising
mainly from the very title of the story, which prepared
the reader to expect a vast picture of the destruction of
the besieged town, a picture whose general depiction was
no part of the author's plan and this is not something we
regret. As a sincere artist, the author understood that
such a picture was hardly possible; the imagination of the
reader, accustomed over a whole year to the terrible reality, would hardly attune to even the widest and most masterly depiction. The merits of the story are first-class:
accurate and original powers of observation, a deep
penetration into the heart of things and characters, a
strict truth yielding to nothing, an abundance of fleeting
impressions which sparkle with intelligence and surprise
and the sharpness of eye, the wealth of poetry, ever free,
suddenly bursting into flame, yet ever measured, and
finally power, a power overflowing everywhere, whose presence is felt in every line and heard in every carelessly
dropped word - these are the merits of the story. In the
very idea of presenting the feel of the last few days of
Sebastopol and of showing them to the reader through the
prism of a young and noble mind which still retains the
beauty of youth and is still uncluttered by the debris
of life, we see that poetic tact which is granted only to
artists.

2. ANNENKOV ON 'CHILDHOOD' AND 'BOYHOOD'

1855

P.V. Annenkov (1812-87) was a leading art and literary
critic who began in the 'civic' traditions of Russia's
first critic of note, Belinsky (see Introduction), but
later turned to the advocacy of theories of 'art for
art's sake'. The extract below is from his Notes on the
Latest Works of Turgenev and L.N.T. which appeared in the
'Contemporary', 1855, no. 1; it begins with a discussion
of the advantages for a young author of the first person

narrative form, and then deals with Turgenev.

Count L.N.T.'s stories have a strict form of expression
and in this lies the secret of the impression they make
upon the reader. With unusual attention he follows the
impressions which are born in first a boy and then an adolescent and his every word is full of respect both for the
task he has given himself and for that time of life which
has so many more unanswered questions, moral lapses and
turning-points than any other. All of this must have consequences. Fulness of expression in the characters and
objects, profound psychological analysis, and finally a
picture of the morals of a certain upper-class and strictly
proper milieu, a picture painted with such a delicate
touch, the like of which we have not seen for a long time
in descriptions of high society, all are the fruits of a
deep understanding by the author of his subject-matter.
On top of this the depiction of the first waverings of the
will and the recognition of thoughts by the boy are raised
by the author, thanks to that same quality, to a history
of all children of a particular place and time, and like a
history written by a poet it includes, together with
grounds for aesthetic pleasure, abundant food for every
thinking man....
    Now to look closely at the actual application of his
psychological analysis to the matter in hand. No sooner
does he recall some sensation experienced by the child or
some early attempts at thinking by the boy than he presents immediately the effect of this thought upon the
character of the young man in the chain of events and
happenings called forth by the thought; in other words he
clothes it with the forms of art, gives it flesh and an
actual existence within the bounds of literature. In what
true relations these results are to the original cause
which gave them birth the reader may ascertain from Count
L.N.T.'s stories. Rare are the writers who are as logically consistent, as strictly true to their ideas and as
strongly convinced of the unity of thought and action, as
he is. All this shows, in the first place, a proper conception of the essence of autobiography and in the second
his deep understanding of the very nature of that time of
life of which he has become the chronicler. In this
lively and artistic representation of childhood there is
one characteristic of the author which displays in a purely
poetic way his capacity for understanding his subject-
matter, namely that he believes in the living activity of
his organism and with the true feeling of the poet catches

that moment when nature, of her own accord, with no help
from outside, gives the flash of an idea, the first sign
of feeling and the first inclination.

He then follows their journey, in every twist of their
flight, through the multiplicity of sensations and events
which they colour with their light. As the author behaves
in relation to himself, to his inner history, so does he
behave in relation to the external circumstances, which
fate has determined for him.

He does not discuss the milieu into which he has been
put and which, not very deeply or seriously understanding
things, retains only an external appearance of worth and
nobility: he describes it. This milieu serves as a framework for the author, where the narrative revolves around
the travels of his child's thoughts, continually arising
according to the law of their own productivity. The relation between the milieu and the young observer trying to
work it out and experiencing its influence upon him forms
a chronicle filled with entertaining reversals of fortune
and catastrophes, all of which to the surprise of the
reader grip his attention in the same way as the reversals
and catastrophes which occur to dramatic heroes, and thus
out of the presentation of the parallel existence of actual
events and psychological processes his story is formed,
full of thought and completely artistic. It goes without
saying that if this is the general impression of his
stories then all the details of them are distinguished in
the same way.

With our writer there are almost no external factors of
little importance with the characters, no insignificant
details with the events. On the contrary every characteristic of the one or the other is given such meaning, such
intelligence, we dare to say, that it hits the eye even of
those who by being used to the dark are little capable of
making things out. Because of this we have a remarkable
clarity of both characters and events. The author leads
the reader with relentless verification of everything he
meets to the conviction that man's soul can be seen in a
single gesture, an unimportant mannerism or a careless
word and that such things often disclose the personality
of a character as truly and certainly as his most obvious
and unambiguous actions. Both parts of the story are full
of similar expressions of the role of secondary and ter-
tiary signs in a person's life, but this is especially
expressed through the presence of thought which fills with
substance everything it touches in the chapters of the
second story, 'Boyhood'. In one of them, for instance,
he describes two young girls, Lyubochka and Katenka, and
without saying a word about the differences in their

characters he opens up the moral essence of the two - in
the way they walk, hold their heads, fold their arms, talk
to others and look at someone approaching, and in this way
he elevates unconsidered external factors to truly profound psychological testimony.

The events in the story have exactly the same importance: always the translation of thought into action, into
something material. Every minute part of spiritual, moral
life is reflected by the author in the same good, gentle
but grandiose and true way. The truth of both the first
impulse and its result is especially affirmed in Count
L.N.T.'s story by the fact that there is not a trace of
anachronism or any chronological confusion of events. The
impressions and events of childhood are simple, more naive,
more graceful than those of boyhood, which becomes more
complicated, confused, rational and therefore more dramatic. That is why thoughts and their framework in the
realm of art, i.e. the characters and events, are fused
together in our author and present a unified whole, powerfully and beneficially affecting the reader.

3. DUDYSHKIN: REVIEW OF 'THE RAID' AND 'THE WOODFELLING'

1855

From a review published in 'Fatherland Notes', 1855, no.
12; this journal had been the leading organ of the West-
erners in the 1840s (Belinsky had been its literary critic
for a time) and would become that of the Populists in the
1870s. S.S. Dudyshkin (1820-66) was a liberal critic and
one of the first to write a notice on Tolstoy - in 1852
on 'Childhood'; although belonging to none of the groupings, he was nearer to the 'pure art' critics than to the
'civic' ones.

In ['The Raid'] we involuntarily turn our attention to
Captain Khlopov. It appears that the author has showered
all his love onto this captain; he is the hero of the
story and also an innovation. To define this character,
however, was extremely difficult for the author because he
has nothing out of the ordinary about him. 'He had one of
those gentle Russian faces which pleasantly and lightly

looks you straight in the eye.' That is all that can be
said about Captain Khlopov. He is not Lermontov's Maksim
Maksimych, but he is a little akin to him; in the same way
that Lieutenant Rozenkrantz is neither Pechorin nor Mulla-
Nur, albeit looking like the latter. Captain Khlopov is
not like Captain Mironov in Pushkin's 'The Captain's
Daughter', but he is akin to him....

From this story we go on to another, published two
years later, 'The Woodfelling'. Both the place of the
action and the action itself are the same in the two. The
same Russian detachment has set off into the Caucasian
mountains, in the first story to punish some unruly warriors and destroy their village, in the second to cut some
wood. The very descriptions in the two stories are the
same; but the characters are different although the idea
expressed is not. Here the main character, although not
obviously so, is a Russian soldier, many of whose characteristic traits are rather well caught. In contrast to
this simple soldier a certain Captain Bolkhov is introduced, just as in the previous story the contrast was made
through Rozenkrantz. This Captain Bolkhov for God knows
what motives has turned up in the Caucasus. To look at he
is nothing like Mulla-Nur, but spiritually there is something of Pechorin in him and consequently he is able to
influence his surroundings. One cannot but assume that he
is a great destroyer of female hearts; he has apparently
experienced everything and considers it his duty to find
boredom everywhere. Just as in 'The Raid' Rozenkrantz is
exposed and Captain Khlopov brought out in good light so
here all the pomposity and trumpery of Captain Bolkhov is
routed in a similar scene.

[Quotation omitted.]

Any sincere glance at events which breathes the truth
is the more fruitful in art when it instantaneously turns
into a multiplicity of characters and all these characters
seem as alive as the truth which warms them. Let the
studied mask, the same for everyone, but fall from the
heroes' faces which are all made up too monotonously and
unnaturally and suddenly all of them show their faces,
characteristic and real as they always had been. So in
the same story the author has depicted many characters
typical of military circles, and although all of them are
touched on by the author only slightly - as he has done up
till now in all his military stories - these characters
somehow feel familiar. Here we sense again the influence
of the contemporary Russian short story on Count L.N.T.'s
military tales.

If the first element of their influence can be called
the unmasking of tawdriness and precociousness which
earlier had been worn by the Rozenkrantzes and the Bol-
khovs and the desire to contrast them with simple characters as, for example, Captain Khlopov, Trosenko and similar characters, then the second element, borrowed from
contemporary literature, we must call a striving for typical characters from the mass of the people. In our literature before - running through the best stories - the type
of Russian soldier found was always the same. Count
L.N.T. does not work this way. Where he speaks as a
thinking man his Russian soldier is distinctive, as is his
characterization; where he presents us with characters as
an artist each of them has his own individuality. These
differing characters give him the means of noticing characteristic traits and creating types. This we suggest is
the second reason for Count L.N.T.'s success....

When Count L.N.T. goes from general descriptions of
types to the particular, when Maksimov, Antonov and Valen-
chuk the recruit appear on the scene, we find before us
the author's *subtle* powers of observation, in which
humour, kindness, cheerfulness and a direct look at things
are so marvellously blended, and also that many-sided
talent of the author with which so few are blessed. Picture follows picture again and again, each one better and
more poetic than the one before. But unfortunately we
cannot now go into details, the details in which there is
so much poetry - as there is in both 'Childhood' and
'Boyhood', works taken from a completely different social
milieu. From the one conversation between the soldiers
over the campfire we could develop a multi-volumed novel.
These five pages are imbued with such genuine poetry that
one can read them time and time again.

4. DRUZHININ ON THE BAD STYLE OF 'YOUTH'

1856

From a letter to Tolstoy, 6 October 1856. A.V. Druzhinin
(1824-64), critic and novelist (his 'Polinka Sachs' of
1847 was one of the most popular novels of its period -
even Tolstoy liked it), was one of the first people Tolstoy met when he arrived in St Petersburg in 1855, and
once he had overcome his feelings of awe before the famous

writer Tolstoy decided he did not like him much. In his
literary criticism Druzhinin was one of the first men in
Russia in his day to deny that literature should have any
social purpose; consequently his great idol was not Gogol,
as was usual at the time, but Pushkin.

Your task was a terribly difficult one and you have carried it out very well. None of our current writers could
have so seized and depicted the agitated and confused
period of youth. For people who are developed your 'Youth'
will provide immense pleasure, and if anyone tells you it
is inferior to 'Childhood' and 'Boyhood' you can spit in
his eye. There is no limit to the poetry in it - all the
first chapters are wonderful, only the introduction is
dry, until we have the description of spring, when the
framework of the story is established. The description of
the arrival in the country is excellent; so is that of the
Nekhlyudov family and the father's explanation of why he
is getting married and the chapters entitled New Friends
and I Fail my Examinations. In many chapters one feels
the poetry of old Moscow, which no one has yet reproduced
properly. The drinking party at Baron Z's is marvellous.
But its faults are .... some chapters are dry and long,
for instance all the conversations with Dmitriy Nekhlyudov, the depiction of all the various feelings towards
Varenka and the chapter dealing with the family's 'understanding' of itself. Grap's visit with Ilinka is also
long and Semyonov's conscription will never pass the
censor.
  Do not be afraid of your reflections, they are all
clever and original. But you have a tendency for over-
subtle analysis, which might grow into a great defect.
You are sometimes about to say: 'So-and-so's thighs indicated that he wanted to travel about India'. You must
curb this tendency, but do not on any account extinguish
it altogether. All your work on your talent should be of
the same kind. All your defects have their share of
strength and beauty, and almost all your qualities bear
within them the seed of a defect.
  Your style fully supports this conclusion: you are most
ungrammatical, sometimes with the lack of grammar of an
innovator and powerful poet who reshapes the language to
his own ends - and for ever; but sometimes it is with the
lack of grammar of an officer sitting in a dug-out and
writing to a friend. One can say with certainty that all
the passages you have written with love are wonderful; but
as soon as you grow cold your words get mixed up and

diabolical turns of phrase appear. Therefore the parts
written coldly should be looked at again and corrected.
I tried to correct some parts myself but gave it up; only
you can do it and you must. To give you a sensible system
I shall say only - above all avoid long sentences. Cut
them up into two or three; do not be grudging with full
stops; do not stand on ceremony with particles; and cross
out by the dozen the words *which, who* and *that*. If you
are in difficulties, take a sentence and imagine that you
want to say it to someone in the most conversational way.

5.   UNSIGNED REVIEW OF 'SEBASTOPOL IN AUGUST'

1856

'Fatherland Notes', 1856, no. 11. This review which deals
primarily with Tolstoy's five 'military' tales starts with
a statement that Tolstoy is well known for his vivid
characterization, masterly and typical use of language,
and great powers of description, portraiture and psychological analysis, all of which the author approves; he
then illustrates these qualities with examples from various stories.

'Sebastopol in August' .... is weaker than the first
Sebastopol stories and of course the author felt this
himself too because he ended his military stories with
this one....
    The weakness in the story is explained in two ways,
both important and both mistakes.
    In the first place all the interest is focused on the
young boy Volodya Kozeltsov, who has just left cadet
school to fight on the redoubts of Sebastopol. This young
boy is the complete embodiment of that ignorance and
inexperience which a man who has seen nothing of the world
should have. The feelings he experiences on seeing the
firing, shells, bombs, and his comrades who are used to
firing, shells and bombs - these feelings are not new to
us. We know them from the author's earlier stories, from
'The Woodfelling', 'The Raid', and 'Sebastopol in December'; and furthermore these same feelings could be aroused
by any battle, by any 'raid', and not only by such a

terrible picture as 'Sebastopol in August'.

This is the first mistake. The second consists in the
very nature of Count Tolstoy's talent; his stories have no
action, they contain simply pictures and portraits. The
portraits of the characters, mainly soldiers, had already
been painted by the author in the first story where we
discovered that coldblooded firmness and that carelessness
of danger which was the strength of the defenders of
Sebastopol. In the succeeding stories, once the portraits
had been excellently painted, we awaited the action and
thirsted after stories about the events, but Count Tolstoy,
in the following parts 'Sebastopol in May' and 'Sebastopol
in August' appears as the same observer and psychologist
who does not omit the smallest detail. The details have
certainly not been missed, but the general picture has
vanished, is lost; there is no general picture. At Sebastopol, as in the simple commonplace raid on the mountain
tribesmen, the author has again thought of riveting us to
his observations on the psychological phenomena of the
young man's soul! Is it possible to make such a blunder?
The events taking place are remarkable, while we sit with
the young man in a corner and look not at a general picture of the assault, the battle and the retreat; no, we
see how the feelings of fear, pride and despairing bravery switch in the young man's soul! The author should
have called his story 'Ensign Volodya Kozeltsov' and not
'Sebastopol in August' and then Volodya Kozeltsov would
have been one more wonderful portrait from the hand of
the talented author; we would have been satisfied with him
while now we are cross at him for distracting our attention from the terrible and shattering picture. Evidently
the author is not in control of this picture in which
there is a mixture of feelings of personal bravery and
national pride which excited not only young men but also
the aged leaders. Everyone experienced their own special
feelings: where are they? Where is that masterly brush-
stroke which in two or three words describes what would
normally need many pages to describe?

> On the banks of the deserted waves
> He stood, full of great thoughts,
> And looked into the distance. Before him wide
> Stretched the river...
>   And he thought...
> Here the city will be laid out...(1)

Do you think that a whole volume of history would better
explain the grandeur of that moment when Peter chose the
place for his new capital? This is what is called a truly

poetic ability, letting us feel in a few words the pictures and events which an untalented man would need whole
volumes to describe - and still fail. Such an ability,
such a choice of time and place was needed also for that
decisive day when finally it was decided to abandon the
southern part of Sebastopol.

   It is no drawback that in such a great picture one does
not know which elements to describe; all the force of art
is concentrated on the ability to fix the point at which
creative fantasy can suddenly look over the picture and
allow it to be felt in the heart of the reader, trembling
in amazement. Here we do not need accurate powers of
observation, here we need the flapping of the eagle's
wings.

Note

1   From 'The Bronze Horseman' (1833) by A.S. Pushkin.
    (Ed.)

6. CHERNYSHEVSKY ON TOLSTOY

1856, 1857

(a) From a review of 'Childhood', 'Boyhood' and 'The
Military Tales', the 'Contemporary', 1856, no. 12, and
occasioned by the appearance in book form of 'Childhood'
and 'Boyhood' in one volume and of 'The Raid', 'The Woodfelling' and the three Sebastopol stories in another under
the title 'The Military Tales', both St Petersburg, 1856.
   N.G. Chernyshevsky (1828-89) was a leading radical
literary critic and socialist political thinker; he is
best remembered for his somewhat uninspired but influential social novel 'What is to be Done?' written in 1863
while he was imprisoned in the Peter and Paul Fortress in
St Petersburg, and for his political and philosophical
ideas which were immensely influential on both the Nihilists and more especially the Populists of the 1860s and
1870s.

'Exceptional powers of observation, delicate analysis of
the psychological processes, precision and poetry in describing nature, and elegant simplicity - these are the
distinguishing features of Count Tolstoy's talent.'   Such
is the opinion you will hear from everyone who follows
literature.   The critics have repeated this evaluation
suggested by the general consensus and have, in so doing,
been completely true to the facts of the matter.

But can one limit oneself to this judgment, having
noticed, it is true, the characteristics that distinguish
Count Tolstoy's talent, and yet not show the special way
in which these qualities appear in the works of the
author of 'Childhood', 'Boyhood', 'The Memoirs of a
Billiard-marker', 'The Snow Storm', 'Two Hussars' and
'The Military Tales'?   Powers of observation, delicacy of
psychological analysis, poetry in the description of
nature, simplicity and elegance - you will find all of
these in Pushkin, Lermontov and Mr Turgenev.   To define
the talent of each of these authors only by these epithets would be just, but completely inadequate to distinguish the one author from the other; and to repeat the
very same things about Count Tolstoy is hardly to catch
the distinguishing characteristics of his talent or show
how his remarkable talent differs from many other equally
remarkable talents.   It has to be characterized more
accurately....

Count Tolstoy's attention is more than anything directed to how some feelings and thoughts develop out of
others.   He is interested in observing how a feeling
immediately arising out of a given circumstance or impression and then, subjected to the influence of memory and
the powers of association in the imagination, turns into
different feelings and returns to its former starting
point and again and again sets out and changes along the
whole chain of memory; how a thought, born of an original
sensation, leads to other thoughts, is carried further
and further away, blends reverie with real sensations,
dreams of the future with reflections on the present.
Psychological analysis may take different directions; one
poet is primarily occupied with outlining characters,
another with the influence of social relationships and the
conflicts of life on his characters, a third with the connection between feelings and actions, a fourth with the
analysis of passions; Count Tolstoy is most of all concerned with the psychic process itself, its forms, its
laws, with, to express it precisely, the dialectic of the
soul.

Of our other remarkable poets this sort of psychological analysis is most developed in Lermontov; but even with

him it none the less plays too much of a secondary role,
is found rarely and even then it is completely subordinate
to the analysis of feeling. It is seen most clearly and
surely most remarkably in those pages which we all remember when Pechorin is thinking about his relations with
Princess Mary, when he notices that she has fallen for him
completely and has given up flirting with Grushnitsky in
favour of a serious passion....

[Omitted: quotation from 'A Hero of our Time'.]

Here more than anywhere else Lermontov has caught the
psychic process of the origin of thought, but it does not
bear the slightest resemblance to those descriptions of
the course of feelings and thoughts in the heads of those
characters of whom Count Tolstoy is so fond. It is not at
all the same as the half-dreaming, half-reflective con-
junctions of concepts and feelings which grow, move and
change before our eyes when we read a story by Count Tolstoy; it does not bear the slightest resemblance to his
descriptions of pictures and scenes, of expectations and
fears that go through the minds of his characters; Pechorin's thought processes are observed from a completely
different point of view from that of those various moments of psychic life in Count Tolstoy's characters. As
an example of this there is the description of what a
man experiences in the moment just before a blow which
he expects to be fatal and then at the time of the final
shattering of his nerve when the blow comes.

[Omitted: quotation from 'Sebastopol in May'.]

This description of interior monologue must be called,
without exaggeration, amazing. In none of our other
writers will you find psychological scenes written from
this viewpoint. In our opinion, this aspect of Count
Tolstoy's talent, which enables him to catch these psychological monologues, gives to his talent a special force
which only he possesses....
This special characteristic of Count Tolstoy's talent
which we have been discussing is so original that one must
examine it with great care and only then will we catch all
its importance for the artistic merit of his works.
Psycholgoical analysis is almost the most essential of the
qualities for powerful creative talent. But it usually
has, if one may put it thus, a descriptive character; it
takes a determined, unchanging feeling and breaks it down
into its component parts and gives us, if one may put it
thus, an anatomical table. In the works of great writers

we notice, besides this facet, another tendency, the
appearance of which acts extremely positively on the
reader or spectator and that is the catching of the dramatic transitions of one feeling into another, one thought
into another. But usually we are presented only with the
two end links in the chain, only the beginning and end of
the psychic process; this is because the majority of
writers who have the dramatic element in their talent are
concerned primarily with the results, the phenomena of the
inner life, the conflicts between people, and with action,
but not with the secret process by means of which the
thought or feeling is worked out; even monologues, which
evidently more often than not should serve as the expression of this process, nearly always express the conflict
of feelings, and the noise of this conflict distracts our
attention from the laws and transitions responsible for
the association of ideas - we are concerned with their
contrasts and not the forms of their origins; monologues
almost always, if they contain more than the simple ana-
tomizing of a stable feeling, differ from dialogues only
externally. In his famous meditations Hamlet as it were
splits into two and argues with himself; his monologues,
in essence, belong to the same sort of scene as the dialogues between Faust and Mephistopheles or the arguments
between the Marquis of Posa and Don Carlos. Count Tolstoy's special talent lies in the fact that he does not
limit himself to a description of the results of the psychic process; he is interested in the process itself, and
the scarcely perceptible manifestations of this inner
life, changing from one into another with great speed and
an inexhaustible variety, are described by Count Tolstoy
in masterly fashion. There are painters who are famous
for their art in capturing the flickering reflection of
the sun's rays on the fast-rolling waves, the shimmering
light on rustling leaves and the play of colours on the
changing shape of clouds, it is generally said of them
that they can catch the life of nature. Count Tolstoy
does something similar with the secret movements of the
psychic life. It seems to us that it is in this that the
completely original character of his talent consists.

(b) On 'Youth'
From a letter to I.S. Turgenev, 20 January 1857. Chernyshevsky, who had been extremely fair to Tolstoy in his
recent review (see previous extract) was becoming increasingly convinced that both Turgenev and Tolstoy were being
too influenced by the critics of the 'art for art's sake'

school with whom he profoundly disagreed - hence this
outburst.

Just read 'Youth' and you will see it is wishy-washy nonsense (save for a couple of chapters). These are the
fruits of Aristarchus's advice. Our local Aristarches go
into ecstasies over this verbiage, nine tenths of which is
just vulgarity, senselessness, and the boasting of a
stupid peacock about his tail - which just reveals his
vulgar arse; and it reveals it simply because the peacock
displays his feathers in this conceited way. It is a
pity, because the man does have some talent.

7. K.S. AKSAKOV ON TOLSTOY'S POWERS OF ANALYSIS

1857

From a general article published in 'Russian Conversation',
1857, no. 1. Aksakov (1817-60), the son of the writer
S.T. Aksakov, was one of the younger leading Slavophiles.
In general in his literary criticism he accused Russian
writers of being divorced from the mass of the people. He
had met Tolstoy and did not take to him; he found him
'unsettled' and 'lacking a centre'.

Stories of another sort, the personal ones, have a special
meaning, more psychological; here the story is about himself. This does not mean that the author has told us
about himself exactly; we do not have the right to suggest
this, and it is not the point anyway; it is sufficient to
say that an 'I' talks about itself, that we have a personal story. To this group of personal stories belong
'Childhood', 'Boyhood' and 'Youth'. In these from the
very outset, besides beautiful pictures of the outside
world - and by the way the description of the outside
world is sometimes taken to unbearable, cloying lengths
with its every little detail - we see an analysis of the
self. In 'Childhood' and 'Boyhood' the analysis has a
somewhat objective nature for the author is examining an
unformed personality, but in 'Youth' the analysis takes on
the character of a confession, a pitiless exposure of

everything stirring in a man's soul. This self-exposure
is bold and decisive, it has no waverings, nor forced
attempts at apologizing for its inner movements. No, the
author reacts severely to the inner world of the soul,
deals with himself pitilessly and firmly and one sees that
he wants one thing only - *truth*. The inner analysis of
Mr Turgenev has nothing sickly or weak in it, nor anything
indefinite, while that of Count Tolstoy is bold and inexorable. He has noticed much that is true in the convolu-
tions of the human soul and this firm desire to reveal
himself in the cause of truth is in itself a service and
leaves a fine impression. But we must however make a few
comments. Count Tolstoy's analysis often notices trivia,
not worthy of attention, which pass across the soul like
a small cloud, leaving no trace; once noticed and analysed
they take on a meaning greater than they really have and
hence become unreal. Analysis here becomes a microscope.
Microscopic manifestations certainly occur in the soul but
if they are magnified under a microscope and you leave
them there while everything else remains its natural size,
then their relationship to other things is destroyed, and
being truly magnified they become decidedly false, for
they are given a false size and the true relationships of
life, their relationship one to the other, are destroyed -
and it is that which leads to truth....

Here is the danger of analysis. By magnifying with all
accuracy the trivia of the soul under a microscope it
presents them in a false light for they have a *disproportionate* size. Furthermore, it can give a justifiability
which they do not have to fleeting sensations passing
through the soul like a puff of smoke (sometimes they are
even contradictory to the man's basic character). Finally
analysis can find in a man even something which is not
there at all; an anxiously directed glance at oneself
often sees apparitions which distort one's actual soul.
One must be occupied less with oneself and deal with God's
wide world, bright and full of light, think of one's
brothers and love them, and then, without losing one's
consciousness of the self, one will begin to see oneself
and to feel things in their true proportions and real
light. This is the danger of analysing the soul, and in
Count Tolstoy's stories, of which we think very highly,
there are many traces of these properties of analysis.

8. TURGENEV ON THE EARLY TOLSTOY

1857, 1863, 1864

I.S. Turgenev (1818-83) was the first Russian writer to
gain an international reputation and it was primarily
through his efforts that Tolstoy's works were to be introduced to Western Europe. His friendship with Tolstoy was
marked by constant quarrels and constant reconciliations,
but whatever his attitude to Tolstoy the man, he was
usually a great admirer of his writing, although not
blindly so.

(a) On 'A Landowner's Morning'. From a letter to A.V.
Druzhinin, 25 January 1857.

I have read 'A Landowner's Morning' which I liked very
much for its sincerity and almost complete freedom of
outlook; I say almost because in the manner in which he
has set out the problem there is hidden (perhaps unbeknown to him) some prejudice. The main moral (I shall
not mention the artistic) impression consists in that
while serfdom exists there is no possibility of the two
sides drawing together and understanding each other despite the most disinterested readiness so to do - and this
impression is good and proper; but along with it runs
another, secondary, idea - namely that in general to
enlighten the peasant and improve his lot leads nowhere,
and this impression is unpleasant. But the mastery of the
language of the story is characteristically great.

(b) On 'The Cossacks'. From a letter to A.A. Fet, 7 April
1863. Fet (real name Shenshin, 1820-92), poet of the
'pure art' school, was a correspondent and friend of many
of the contemporary literary figures; he was often in the
embarrassing position of being friends with both Tolstoy
and Turgenev.
    Eleven years later Turgenev was still convinced that
'The Cossacks' was one of the masterpieces of Russian
literature.

I read 'The Cossacks' and went into ecstasies over it (so
did Botkin). Only the personality of Olenin spoils the
generally marvellous impression. To contrast civilization
with fresh primeval nature there was no need to introduce
again that tedious, unhealthy figure, always preoccupied
with himself. Why does Tolstoy not rid himself of that
nightmare?

(c) On 'Polikushka'. From a letter to Fet, 25 January
1864.

After you had gone I read Tolstoy's 'Polikushka' and marvelled at the power of his great talent. Only an awful
lot of material is wasted and there was no need for him to
have drowned the son. It's terrible enough without that.
But there are some truly wonderful pages. It even induces
shivers up my spine, which with me as you know is thick
and insensitive. A master, a master!

9.   KHOMYAKOV ON TOLSTOY'S VIEW OF ART AND LITERATURE

1859

Tolstoy was elected to membership of the Moscow Society of
the Lovers of Russian Literature on 4 February 1859 and
made a speech entitled The Supremacy of the Artistic
Element in Literature in which he defended the theory of
'art for art's sake' and attacked those who propounded
ideas of the social role of literature; these views of
Tolstoy's were diametrically opposed to those he was to
state some forty years later in 'What is Art?' A.S.
Khomyakov (1804-60), poet, theologian, philosopher and
one of the founders of Slavophilism, presided over the
meeting.
     (From 'The Life of Tolstoy' by Aylmer Maude, published
by Oxford University Press. Reprinted by permission.)

That which is always right, that which is always beautiful, that which is as unalterable as the most fundamental
laws of the soul, undoubtedly holds and should hold the

first place in the thoughts, the impulses, and therefore in the speech, of man. It and it alone will be handed on by generation to generation, and by nation to nation, as a precious inheritance. But on the other hand, in the nature of man and of society there is a continual need of self-indictment. There are moments, moments important in history, when such self-indictment acquires a special and indefensible right....

So the writer, the servant of pure art, sometimes even unconsciously and despite his own will, becomes an accuser. I will let myself cite you, Count, as an example. You consciously follow a definite road faithfully and undeviatingly, but are you quite alien to the literature of indictment? If only in the picture of a consumptive post-boy dying on a stove amid comrades apparently indifferent to his sufferings ['Three Deaths'] have you not indicated some social disease, some evil? When describing that death, is it possible that you did not suffer from the callous indifference of good but unawakened human souls? Yes, you too have been, and will be, an involuntary accuser!

10. PISAREV ON WHAT TO LOOK FOR IN TOLSTOY'S WRITING

1859

D.I. Pisarev (1840-68) was a utilitarian political thinker and critic. Arrested in 1862 for publishing radical propaganda, he spent the next four years in prison, where most of his political and literary articles were written. He was the inspiration of the Russian Nihilists in the 1860s and in his writings he usually considered art a somewhat dubious activity - he valued a tragedy by Shakespeare less than a pair of boots and did much to demolish any idea that Pushkin had any social value as a poet. Herzen, the founder of Russian Populism and the leading publicist of the time, albeit from exile in Europe, wrote of him: 'he writes in a lively manner on everything, and sometimes even on things he knows something about'. This extract is taken from a long review of 'Three Deaths' which was printed in the women's magazine 'Daybreak', 1859, no. 12.

Pictures of nature, breathing with life and distinguished
by a marked freshness, the depiction of characters taken
straight from reality, a boldness of the general outlines
and the crucial importance of the ideas placed at the
basis of an artistic work - all these are those general
qualities which are the property of all our best writers
and which are reflected in the most mature works of our
literature. But besides these general qualities Count
Tolstoy has personal idiosyncratic traits. No one has
taken psychological analysis further than he, no one has
looked more deeply into the human soul, no one has dis-
closed the most secret motives, the most fleeting and
evidently accidental of the movements of the soul with
such close attention and such inexorable consistency. How
thoughts develop and gradually form themselves in the mind
of man, through what changes they pass, how a feeling
swells in the breast, how the imagination plays, drawing a
man from the real world into a world of fantasy, how in
the very midst of his dreams reality rudely and materially
reminds him of its existence, and the first impression
made on a man by this rude collision of two different
worlds - these are the motifs which Count Tolstoy has used
with especial love and brilliant success....
    Whatever scene we think of, we meet everywhere either
a subtle analysis of the mutual relationship between the
characters or an abstract psychological treatise which
retains in its abstractions a fresh and complete liveliness, or finally the tracing of the most mysterious and
darkest movements of the soul, scarcely realized nor fully
understood even by the man who experiences them, but which
are expressed in words and yet still retain their
mystery....
    He who expects to find in Count Tolstoy's tales and
stories a romantic plot and interesting events will in
the first place be disappointed and in the second in
following the thread of the action he will lose sight of
what is the chief delight and most lasting quality of
these stories; he will lost sight of the depth and subtlety
of the psychological analysis. When reading Count Tolstoy
one has to look at the particular, stop on the separate
details and check these details against the feelings and
impressions one has experienced oneself; one has to ponder, and only then will the reading enrich the store of
one's thoughts and give the reader knowledge of human
nature, thus providing him with a complete, fruitful and
aesthetic pleasure.

11.   GRIGORIEV ON TOLSTOY'S NEGATION AND PRAISE FOR THE 'SUBMISSIVE' TYPE OF PERSONALITY

1862

A.A. Grigoriev (1822-64) is arguably the most original nineteenth-century Russian literary critic. He held that art should be 'organic' and intuitive, and that Russian literature should be 'rooted in the soil' of Russian life. He was the first to treat seriously and theoretically the polarization of Russian literary characters into the 'submissive', meek and generally passive personality on the one hand, and the 'arrogant', domineering, falsely brilliant, passionate and active one on the other; the former, and preferable, type was more to be found in Rus-sia, while the latter was more often than not over-influenced by the traditions, customs and way of life of Western Europe, thus having lost his Russian roots.

    This extract is taken from the second of two articles Grigoriev wrote on Tolstoy, published in Dostoevsky's journal 'Time', 1862, no. 2.

The basic characteristic which struck everyone in the psychic process shown in Count Tolstoy's works was an unusually new and bold analysis, an analysis of spiritual movements which no one had analysed before. He did not unmask 'the vulgarity of the vulgar man' like Gogol; he did not laugh the sick laugh of the Hamlet of Shchigrov Province at the bankruptcy of the so-called advanced man like Turgenev; he did not contrast, like Pisemsky, a healthy, albeit rough and somewhat base, view of life with tawdry, conventional or warmed-up feelings; he did not, like Goncharov, relate to idealism in the name of a narrow practicality, or to empty thought in the name of a narrow or conventional idea - yet everyone felt he had something in common with all the aspirations of our time, that he - of course half consciously, half unconsciously like every artistic talent - was working on the same con-temporary problems as the other writers I have named. He is close to Turgenev in his poetic tenderness of feeling and deep sympathy with nature, but completely opposed to him in the sobriety of his gaze, pitiless to all sensa-tions in the slightest degree out of the ordinary, and in his hostility to everything false, however brilliant it might appear - and in this respect he could well be

closest of all to Pisemsky, if his realism, that is, was
native to him and not *born of* analysis. In his externally
hostile and mistrustful relationship to idealism he could
be compared to Goncharov if the conventional image was
presented as an ideal in practice. On the other hand with
his mercilessness to the vulgarity lurking not only in the
vulgar man but in everyone he as it were develops Gogol's
theme, but he does not weep over any fallen idol or any
conventionally beautiful person. He has only one thing in
common with the methods of our time - negation. But negation of what? Of everything borrowed and assumed in our
false development. Cut off from his native soil by birth
and upbringing, he tries through negation to dig down to
his roots, the simple bases, the primary causes. Everyone
does this but he is different in that he digs deeper. He
is not content like Turgenev with looking reverentially
from afar at the soil and bowing down before it with the
rapture of Moses beholding the Promised Land. It is not
enough for him (for clarity I allow myself to give an
example) just to sense the black-earth strength in Uvar
Ivanych - he prefers to discover and raise up in himself
this innate strength. Having stripped away the layers of
false idealism, he cannot take for reality, like Goncharov, the equally alien but far more dirty layers of practicality and formalism. Neither does he stop at the evidently similar, but in essence coarsened, layers on which
Pisemsky stands firm-footed; he is also little capable of
sympathizing, we suggest, with say Zador-Manovsky or even
Pavel Beshmetev, with either Elchaninov or Bakhtyarov, or
even less with the hypochondriac Durnopechin or his aunty,
Solomonida. He is even less capable of accepting any
ideals in the air, any creation from above rather than
from below, or that which destroyed morally, and even
physically, Gogol himself. He digs to the depths, con-
scientiously, directed by his extraordinary analysis, but
not having dug far enough he ends up with the pantheistic
grief of 'Lucerne', grief over life and ideals, despair
for everything in any way at all artistic or coming from
the human soul, a despair evident in 'Three Deaths' in
which the most straightforward death is that of the oak
tree, and with a bitter submission to fate which has no
mercy on the flower of human feeling in 'Family Happiness', and lastly in apathy - no doubt temporary and
passing....
    The roots of this negating process, to which Count
Tolstoy along with others is a contemporary sacrifice,
lie not in Gogol but in Pushkin. Gogol and others took
the task set by Pushkin to certain limits, although Gogol
took it further than others. But in speaking of Count

Tolstoy as one of the most important representatives of
this negating process one cannot escape a certain repeti-
tion of what I have often said about the beginnings, about
the starting-point of this process.

[Omitted: section dealing with Pushkin and more particularly with his 'Tales of Belkin' and the comparison of
the 'meek' type of person with the 'passionate' or 'arrogant'.]

   This type of the simple and humble man, first brought
artistically onto the scene by Pushkin in Belkin, has
appeared since in various forms in our literature: in the
shape of the simple and humble but brave and honourable
(albeit a little limited in human nature) Maksim Maksimych
of Lermontov; in the shape of the man, hounded by fate,
continually giving way to the 'arrogant' and brilliant
character in Turgenev; in the shape of the same simple yet
passionate man, endowed with a strong but undeveloped
nature who also gives way in his life to an externally
brilliant but inwardly empty man in Pisemsky; in the shape
of the man, finally, whose profound analysis has led to a
consciousness of the exceptional legitimacy of the type of
the simple man before the brilliant one but one who is
constantly walking about on moral stilts, even to a lack
of belief in the possibility of the real existence of such
a pompous man in Count Tolstoy.... Pushkin's Belkin still
believes in the existence of the gloomy self-centred
Silvio; Lermontov still ironically sympathizes with his
Maksim Maksimych and, unfortunately, still believes in his
Pechorin; Turgenev, deeply and morbidly sympathizing with
his hounded hero, not only believes in brilliant and passionate people but is himself attracted by them; Pisemsky
is patently indignant at the triumph of the 'arrogant'
man over the 'meek' and ingenuous. Count Tolstoy, though,
analyses and through his analysis arrives at a positive
disbelief in all feelings in any way 'elevated'. His disbelief by the way is not the rather crude prosaism of
Pisemsky, nor is it on the other hand that artificial
practicality which makes Goncharov prefer Stolz to the
romantic Oblomov. Count Tolstoy's disbelief is the
result of a deep analysis, often taken to extreme limits,
often destroying its own foundations, but almost never
being carried away by any particular sympathies or anti-
pathies....
   Count Tolstoy's analysis has reached the deepest disbelief in all 'elevated' and 'out of the ordinary' feelings in the human soul. In this lies its most important
facet and also its one-sidedness. His analysis has

destroyed in us prepared, formed and only partially alien
ideals of power, passion and energy. In Russian life he
sees like everyone else only the negative type of the
simple and meek man but embraces him with all his heart.
He follows everywhere the ideal of simplicity in spiritual
matters....

But in the first place, in spite of his deep sincerity
and perhaps as a result of the problems posed by sincere
analysis, Count Tolstoy sometimes goes too far in his
severity on all 'elevated' feelings. Not many people, for
example, will agree with him about the great depth of the
nanny's grief compared with that of the old countess. In
the second place this analysis which reaches love for the
'meek' type, primarily because of his disbelief in the
'arrogant' type, leads in the end, because it is not
rooted in a soil which gives both types equally, to a sort
of pantheistic despair which is evident in 'Lucerne' and
'Albert' and also in the earlier 'The Memoirs of a
Billiard-marker'. In the third place this analysis turns
into something with no content, into analysis of analysis,
which through its lack of content leads to scepticism and
an undermining of any spiritual feelings. The key to the
ultimate destination of this analysis is the death of the
oak tree in 'Three Deaths' which is presented on a level
of consciousness superior to that of the sophisticated
landowner's wife and that of the simple peasant. From
this there is surely but one step to Nihilism.

12.   UNSIGNED REVIEW OF 'CHILDHOOD AND YOUTH'

1862

This notice, published in the 'Saturday Review', 29 March
1862, is probably the first on Tolstoy to be printed in
English after Tolstoy's stories had been translated by
Malwida von Meysenbug and published in London early that
year; the author was called Count Nicola Tolstoi, thus
transferring to Western Europe the suspicion which was
current in Russia on the first appearance of 'Childhood'
that the author was perhaps Tolstoy's older brother
Nikolay.

'Whoever,' says the translator of this work in the preface, 'likes to come out into the fresh air of a fine day
in spring, when all is fragrant, blooming, and promising,
will enjoy reading this, the reflection of a youthful
soul full of noble tendencies and earnest aspirations.'
Possibly it may be ignorance of Russian that makes the
pleasure actually experienced fall short of the hopes held
out, but certainly, so far as the translation goes, we
much prefer the ordinary spring morning. Count Tolstoi
does not come near it. Nor is it, as it appears to us,
anything more than a figure of speech to say that this
little volume reflects a youthful soul of noble tendencies
and earnest aspirations. It is at the best a very thin
narration of the early life of an affectionate and sensitive boy placed under such circumstances as must be very
common in his class and country. To us in England it may
be some little amusement to know how a Russian nobleman
brings up his children, and this adds to the faint interest the book would otherwise excite. Count Tolstoi is
also highly praised by the few Russians whose voices are
heard in Western Europe, and we naturally wish to know
what a creditable Russian is like. But the translator,
although possessing a very fair command of the English
language, knows very little of English tastes, or of the
English standard of taste, when she announces to us that
Count Tolstoi reveals himself to us as a poet and a
philosopher. There is nothing to blame in the book. The
incidents recorded are very trivial, and therefore, probably, true, and the whole production is insipid, unless
we force an interest in it by reminding ourselves that it
is improving to know how Russians write. But as a record
of childhood it has its merits. It is not sickly or pre-
tentious. Its merits are, however, mostly negative, and
few compositions have less claim to philosophy. Perhaps,
in the original, the language may be poetical, and there
is an amiable tenderness of character shown in the childish history recorded, but that is the end of the poetry.
The translator, as a matter of business, is quite right
to try to make the public look through her spectacles at
the book on which she has bestowed her labour. But not
all the big sentiments that ever filled the biggest mind
of a German translator can put poetry and philosophy in an
original where they do not exist, and 'Childhood and
Youth' is at most a pleasing story of childhood, with the
accidental advantage of teaching us a few foreign customs.
    If a poet is to be poetical about his childhood at all,
or a philosopher to philosophize about early affections,
one would think it natural that the special subject to
draw them out would be the tale of their first love. We

take this instance, therefore, as a favourable one, and as
calculated, if any, to produce on us the impression that
we are gathering violets and primroses on a fine April
morning. This is how the story is told.

[Relation of the episode and quotation omitted.]

This is simple and natural. It is like the love of
children - like their curiously sensitive and yet physical
affection. If a man is to record at all how, when he was
a little boy, he felt when looking at a caterpillar with a
little girl, it is much better that he should tell us what
really happened than that he should invent a faded coun-
terpart of maturer love in order to make us think how forward he was. But at the same time nothing can be more
bald than the manner in which the little incident is nar-
rated. The odour of the fine spring morning we were promised does not seem to come particularly near it.
This is said to be a true history of Count Tolstoi's
childhood, and the people introduced into it are real
people. We are unable to say whether there is any disguise of names; but whether there is or not, it must be
obvious to all Count Tolstoi's circle who is meant. As
he is still a young man, most of those mentioned as companions of his childhood must be living. We are glad to
find people in Russia are so patient, and can endure to
hear plain unvarnished opinions on their physical and
mental defects given to the world. We hope, for example,
that the family of Prince Kornakoff is pleased with this
May-morning effusion.

[Quotations omitted.]

No good-natured friend could be more candid. Nor is
the account of Etienne's subsequent behaviour much more
to his credit, although perhaps he did nothing more than
every Russian boy is accustomed to do to his serfs. The
most curious part of the narrative consists in the revela-
tions it gives of the attitude assumed by Russians to
their inferiors. It only needs a very little scratching
for the Tartar to appear in this respect beneath the sham
skin. At the same time the serfs are represented as ven-
turing on a tone of familiarity mixed with cringing, which
is not unlike the affectionate insolence of the model
'nigger'.

[Quotations omitted.]

Count Tolstoi seems to have been very fortunate in his

mother, and her death was the great sorrow of his childhood. He relates, with his usual honesty, what passed in
his mind at the time, and is easily able, with the experience of later life, to detect the insincerity which
mingles so largely even with the sincerest grief of the
young, and from which no grief is, perhaps, wholly exempt.
That is, no grief, or scarcely any, is what in imagination
we picture grief to be. It is liable to be distracted.
Passing events demand a passing attention, and if a
theory denies this, and an attempt is made to have a grief
that is wholly absorbing, there is doubtless what may be
called insincerity. There are, however, traits in the
character of others which it is better not to analyse; and
it appears to us by no means desirable that sons should
publish to the world the shortcomings they may perceive in
the demeanour or conduct of their parents on solemn occasions. Count Tolstoi tells us that his father was, in his
opinion, too theatrical on the occasion of his mother's
funeral. The bereaved husband did all that was proper,
and that Russian custom enjoined; but he rather overdid
it.

[Quotation omitted.]

   In another passage he expresses himself more fully
about his father, and tells us that, in spite of being a
model of deportment, he was addicted to many very serious
weaknesses. We do not like this. It makes no difference
whether a writer is a Russian, or a German, or an Englishman - whether he is or is not like a spring morning, or
what may be his noble tendencies. He is not, we think,
justified in telling his family history in this way, and
in probing the failings of parents in order that he may
have the satisfaction of sketching his own childhood. It
is no excuse to say that, unless he puts in the dark
shades, the picture cannot be truthful. There is no
reason why he should draw the picture at all. The world
can get on very well without criticisms written by a son
on the behaviour of his father at his mother's funeral.
It would destroy all family confidence if we were all of
us liable to be sacrificed in this way to the exigencies
of literary art; and if this is the style in which sons
who are like spring mornings write, most fathers would
devoutly wish their own offspring should be like autumn
evenings.

13. UNSIGNED NOTICE OF 'CHILDHOOD AND YOUTH', 'ATHENAEUM'

16 August 1862, no. 1816

Reprinted by permission.

This is a very clever and life-like story of childhood and
boyhood. The Russian dress does not disguise the truth of
the human nature. It gives a well-described picture of
Russian daily life. Story it can scarcely be called, for
it is the rambling recollections of a child and youth; but
it gives an insight into the thoughts, perverseness and
sorrows of a child. The translation is that of a
foreigner, and the stiff, peculiar English gives it an
originality that is rather quaint and pleasant.

14. TYUTCHEV: VERSE ON 'THE COSSACKS'

1863

F.I. Tyutchev (1803-73), one of Russia's greatest poets,
was first published in the 'Contemporary' in 1836 but was
not appreciated for many years and only received full recognition at the end of the century. This verse, written
in February 1863, was occasioned by the appearance of
'The Cossacks' the month before.

The conceit of this story
We may determine thus:
Our dirty Russian pigsty
Has been moved to the peaks of the Caucasus.

15.   EDELSON: REVIEW OF 'THE COSSACKS'

1863

E.N. Edelson (1824-68) was a writer and critic of the 'art for art's sake' school. His extensive review of 'The Cossacks', the conclusion of which follows, appeared in the 'Library for Reading', 1863, no. 3.

The main fundamental idea behind this new tale by Count Tolstoy is clear. It is the clash of a good soul, but one broken by an artificial civilization, with a crude but fresh way of life, one that is integral and settled. The victory lies of course with the latter.... We are almost positive that there will be critics who will be ready to see in Count Tolstoy's tale a fabricated preference for a crude but natural way of life over that of civilization. But it is hardly worth refuting such a narrow and one-sided understanding of the real tasks of artistic works. The inner sense, i.e. the strictly immediate content of Count Tolstoy's tale, is a highly interesting episode in the life of a man with fine innate qualities, with a serious approach to life and attitudes to people but some-what dreamy, weak-willed, not very practical, and who cannot find true interests in the society he finds himself in....
     The artistic service of Count Tolstoy's new tale lies in the fact that for not particularly commonplace events, and having as we have shown a profound general sense, he has found a very happy setting and at the same time one which is to a high degree natural. The author's task, i.e. the analysis of one of those states of mind which being legitimate and natural rarely finds expression under normal conditions with complete sincerity and clarity, this task was capable of being expressed only through the clash of two well-known factors. But take each of these clashing sides separately - they are both depicted with such depth and truth as if the author had in view only the most conscientious and exact reproduction of them. The psychological analysis of all the twists and turns going on in Olenin's soul up to and including the meeting with Caucasian life and Mariana is a task in itself worthy of the artist's pen. On the other hand the life of the Caucasus, its nature, the various Cossack and enemy types and the series of pictures poetically depicted with love

are an accomplishment which would be an honour for any
writer. The idea, of which we have spoken above, is as it
were an added bonus for the reader and something about
which the author possibly did not think directly, but
which of itself enters the head of the man used to thinking about what he has lived through, seen or read.

We have said that the general idea which we have ex-
pounded above might not have been a direct task of the
author, but that it is easily seen in his work. Just as
easily other thoughts might be occasioned by Count Tolstoy's tale. Strictly speaking L.N. Tolstoy has depicted
for us with a masterly brush a completely personal event:
the struggle of feelings, passions, doubts, in a word part
of the inner life of one young civilized man amid crude,
savage, alien but attractive surroundings. If only because of its profound, true analysis and the clarity of
every little scene the tale demands our complete attention; but it has for us yet another point of interest, and
that is the proximity of Olenin to us all, the proximity
of that milieu which gave birth to him and from which he
ran away. It is no wonder that the tale should give rise
to so many thoughts.

16.   EVGENIYA TUR ATTACKS OLENIN

1863

From a long review of 'The Cossacks' in 'Fatherland
Notes', 1863, no. 6. Evgeniya Tur (1815-92), writer,
especially of stories for children, and critic was the
pseudonym of E.V. Salias de Tournemir; she was the sister
of the dramatist A.V. Sukhovo-Kobylin.

A man aged twenty-four who has never completed any formal
education, never occupied himself seriously in anything,
who has succeeded in squandering half his inheritance
before reaching the age of twenty-five, who feels the
approach of hard work or a struggle and hurries away, in
the author's words, to defend his freedom, or in our
words, more simply to escape hard work and struggles, who
has neither faith nor fatherland - such is a person all
we Russians know well. Olenin .... is bored, half-

educated, lazy; he idles his life away; he is a mother's
boy, a 'landowner's little son'; he is an empty, vain
dandy, half-drunkard, half-rake (not from a surplus of
energy but from idleness and dissipation), and a spend-
thrift whose acquaintances are no different. These
acquaintances pass their evenings in drawing-rooms and
their nights with a bottle of champagne at Chevalier's,
Amalia's, Louise's or similar filthy places where vulgar
flirtations and escapades are carried on. As for the
embellishments with which the author has adorned his hero,
we just cannot accept them as being true, and even if we
did decide to take them into consideration they would turn
out to be mere tinsel, and it only takes a moment to realize that. The desire to dedicate himself to music or to
loving a woman (and what it is to dedicate oneself to
loving a woman God only knows) or to science or to something else is quite senseless in someone like Olenin. We
do not doubt that on occasion he said all this, but we are
not obliged to take anything he says into account....

The author then goes on to explain that up to the start
of the story Olenin loved only himself. We do not doubt
it. People like Olenin are not grown-up enough to know
how to love others and can only love themselves; they are
empty, petty and insignificant. The author tries to explain why Olenin loved only himself: he adds that he
'could not help loving himself because he expected the
best from himself'. Very true but on what grounds?
'Because', says the author, 'he had not become disillusioned in himself.' Also very true but how could he have
been? To become disillusioned one has to have some high
ideal, one has to aspire to something. To what can an
ignoramus, a drawing-room dandy and a restaurant boozer
aspire? He only knew how to run after young ladies but
ran away as soon as love (on their part, not on his)
threatened to become serious. Olenin is so petty that he
fears strong feelings in others. Then again he is a past
master at getting others to pay his dinner bills....

One must however add that having thus presented Olenin
to us just as he is the author attempts to justify his
hero, almost treats him seriously and from time to time
wishes to present him in a good light, to make him appear
poetically seductive. For our part we categorically deny
the presence of anything serious in people like Olenin.
The author does not tell us why his hero decided to leave
the drawing-rooms, the restaurants, the gipsies, the
ladies, the Sashkas or the parties - in a word so honourable a life - and decamp to the Caucasus as a young army
officer. We guess it was partly laziness which can cast
a man aimlessly hither and thither, partly a desire to see

something new, partly to gain military honours or a title,
and partly to go drinking somewhere else and where he
could avoid paying his debts which had grown rather too
large. There is also the thought that people will talk
about him, will follow his exploits, will feel sorry for
him and sigh after him. All this is flattering and he
will be able to pose, to put on airs and generally play a
part. In short not life but a carnival. Olenin says his
good-byes without settling his debts (very characteristically) and leaves for the Caucasus, telling us (or rather
the author tells us) that earlier he had not wished to
live *correctly* but that now a new life is beginning for
him in which there will be no mistakes, no despair, and
only happiness. As well as these elevated thoughts
Olenin has others more fitting and characteristic of him.
He thinks that if he were to marry that rich young lady
who likes him then he would have no debts. But let not
the reader be misled. It does not follow from this that
Olenin and people like him will not marry for money. They
will, but not until it is absolutely necessary for it is
stupid to sacrifice one's freedom and restrict one's life
by marriage, especially one for which one has no enthusiasm, not even sensual, when one still has one's youth and
strength, one's way to make in the world, and while one's
debts do not concern overmuch and especially as they do
not have to be paid anyway. It is another question when
one's standing has been squandered and one's youth is
past - then it would be stupid not to marry for money.
But for the moment he will wait....

We do not need further characteristics, these will
suffice. Depravity, the inevitable condition of a dis-
ordered life among petty, empty and grubby little people,
is grafted onto his shallow nature. He is no longer 'a
nice young chap' but 'a good-for-nothing adult'. What
else can we call a man of twenty-four who is like Olenin?

It is a great pity that Count Tolstoy casts the pearls
of his poetry before Olenin.

17.   ANNENKOV ON OLENIN AND 'CIVILIZATION'

1863

From a review in the 'St Petersburg News', 1863, nos
144-5, under the title Contemporary Fiction. Count L.N.

Tolstoy: 'The Cossacks, a Tale of the Caucasus, 1852'.

Contrary to the opinion which the public has of Olenin,
we consider this character as deeply thought out and as
excellently depicted as all the other characters and parts
of this wonderful novel. True, this type has already had
his day and passed into history, but around his roots, as
we see it, little shoots have appeared which justify every
new dalliance by the critic with their progenitor. In
accordance with the dramatic denouement and artistic aims
of the novel Count Tolstoy had to contrast the real world
of the Cossacks he depicted with a civilized Russian man,
with the condition of course that this civilized man be
also real, was taken from reality and contemporary life
like his fellow-countryman from a lower, more spontaneous
way of life. To get away with this in abstract characters
like Aleko or Pechorin there was no possibility - first,
because they would have introduced a discordant note into
the general tone and character of the novel and, second,
because they are contrary to the general nature of the
artistic complexion which Count Tolstoy has. What has he
hit on? Possibly the most intrusive side of the novel
lies in the fact that the author could not find in civilized society a true representative of Russian civilization who could show how the national spirit and national
elements unite with a highly moral, political and scientific upbringing. The writer who all his life throughout
his career has sought life's truth was forced in creating
an artistic contrast to present instead of someone approx-
imating at all to the idea of a civilized Russian -
Olenin....
   Olenin has travelled to the Caucasus to recover from
civilization, to acquire through a health cure everything
which it had left unfinished, like other people go there
to recover from the physical ailments left by a dissolute
life. One cannot say that civilization has completely
ruined Olenin, it has given him a salutary agitation of
mind and feeling and many noble aspirations, but has shown
him no serious purpose in existence and removed the means
to attaining anything concrete because he did not ask it
for any. Olenin had the misfortune - which even today
threatens many people - to take for the true aims of education all that elegant, vain, empty and frivolous life of
the upper classes which was developed in his youth. He
had hardly put a foot in the Caucasus when with all his
heart he stretched out towards the magnificence of its
countryside and even more to its free inhabitants, to the

clarity of their thoughts, the obviousness and comprehen-
sibility of their aims. It must happen in this way with a
man who is not protected from any of the seductions of a
truly national civilization. On the contrary they triumphantly and with dignity defended before the inferior
tribes their lofty educative concept of their fatherland.
It is not like this with Olenin. Having fallen in love
with Mariana, which does not need explaining because love
and passion often have their basis in inaccessible psychological mysteries, Olenin wanted to become a Cossack, to
destroy in himself his instinctive moral origins and all
that spiritual life given to him by his education, whatever it might have been. In a moral sense this was tan-
tamount to that crawling about on all fours, to that
ridiculous return to nature which several of our landowning philosophers tried to accomplish in the eighteenth
century after reading too much Rousseau with too little
understanding. And when after the heroic death of
Lukashka in hand-to-hand fighting after an ambush by the
mountain tribesmen, Mariana with hate spurns Olenin's
repellent love, the poor junker goes away accompanied by
the scorn of all the village not excluding that of his
friend Eroshka, whose regret is also of a rather suspi-
cious nature. And Olenin fully deserved these results of
his own dissoluteness, his lack of moral force which only
a practical education would have furnished him with if he
had had one. The village too would have submitted to this
force because if it scorns everyone it sees from Russia,
both soldiers and civilians, then it scorns them for the
same reason: it does not feel they have any original
character or will and considers them only representatives
of certain regulations....

This profoundly true characteristic is noticed by that
same Olenin who turned out to be just as bankrupt before
the village as he had before educated society. It reminds
us that Olenin, being a generally confused and vacillating
character, is at the same time an extremely keen observer
of life, a most receptive fellow to the poetic qualities
of natural phenomena and the most subtle psychologist
towards himself and others. The contradictions marvellously delineating his nature and behaviour patterns were
formed of course by his upbringing.

In this poetic and artistic form appears the obsessive
idea of Count Tolstoy in this novel written, if we are not
mistaken, ten years ago. However you react to this idea,
to whatever visions and conclusions it might draw you, the
work based on it, thanks to the participation of real creative power in its writing, remains all the same a model
in its strict truth of form, the honesty and warmth of its

colouring and the freshness, beauty and reality of all its details.... But the last word on the works of Count Tolstoy must point to the complete negation of the natural, spontaneous way of life which is contained in the novel itself, in spite of all its charm, and to which the author was brought against his will possibly solely by the fact that it is achieved by a wonderful author, by faithfulness to his chosen subject, and the artistic fulfilment of his task.

18.   TOLSTOY ON 'POLIKUSHKA' AND 'THE COSSACKS'

1863

On 11 April 1863 Fet wrote to Tolstoy that 'in "Polikushka" everything is crumbling, putrid, poverty-stricken, sick. It is all accurate and truthful, but so much the worse for that. It smells of its corrupted environment. It's like the backwoods of yesteryear'. Tolstoy replied on 1 May 1863.

....I am living in a world so remote from literature and its critics that on receiving such a letter as yours my first feeling was one of astonishment. Who was it who wrote 'The Cossacks' and 'Polikushka'? And what is there to discuss about them? Paper endures anything and editors pay for and print anything. However, that is only my first impression; but then one enters into the meaning of what you say, rummages about in one's head and finds somewhere in a corner of it, among long-forgotten rubbish, something indefinite labelled 'Art'.... You are right.... 'Polikushka' is the chatter of a man who 'wields a pen' on the first thing that comes to hand; but 'The Cossacks' does have something in it, although poor.

19.   E. MARKOV ON MARYANKA, HEROINE OF 'THE COSSACKS'

1865

'Fatherland Notes', 1865, nos 1 and 2.   E.L. Markov
(1835-1903) was a writer, publicist and critic.   His long
review of 'The Cossacks' is entitled National Types in our
Literature; it deals basically with Olenin, Uncle Eroshka
and the Cossack girl Maryanka, all three of whom Markov
considers extremely typical of the sort of 'Russian' they
represent.

In the type represented by Maryanka not the slightest detail is missing; she is so clear that one can almost reach
out and touch her.   She is healthy, beautiful, young and
belongs as much to her surroundings as a buffalo does to
its.   Note with what eyes she looks upon her own beauty
and her relationship with Lukashka.   Life has taught her
that all young men like the girls, that they flirt with
them and demand kisses and promises from all of them.
There cannot be anything at all special or flattering in
Lukashka's attitude to her.   He wants his own way with her
for his own good not hers.   He will beat her when they are
married but will fawn upon her from time to time until she
is his.   She well knows that she is not alone in attracting him and that he comes to her from another sweetheart.
Consequently one can understand her rather indifferent,
reserved and somewhat severe behaviour towards him.   It
cannot be said that she does not love him; out of all the
Cossacks it is he whom she would most like to marry.
Lukashka is a splendid fellow and the leading brave in the
eyes of the whole village.   Also she is one of its most
striking girls; everyone tells her so, and she knows it
herself; consequently it is obvious that they should be
man and wife.   And that is not the only reason: physical
passion too is seen in her strong young body .... but
common sense and an innate decorum lead her to restrain
the impatience of the young Cossack.   She has nothing
against their kissing and she allows him to caress her and
listens with immense pleasure to his declarations of love,
she is aflame in his embrace, but every strong demand by
Lukashka is firmly and severely declined because the serious side of life as Maryanka sees it takes precedence over
the attractions of love.   Love is fine but is none the
less a luxury and life has already shown her that before

luxury one must comply with much else of importance.
These unavoidable and constant conditions limit her
thoughts and stop her from giving in to a transient passion, the delights of which would be incomparably great....

Count Tolstoy's Maryanka is thus a woman of her own
background and race, i.e. she is calculating and material-
istic and places the dictates of common sense above all
the passions. Everything which cannot be based on the way
ordinary people behave is incomprehensible and even improbable to her. She considers the tender words and reck-
less impatience of her admirers stupid and self-indulgent.
According to her moral ideals all this is *bourgeois* in the
most insulting sense that has been given to this word; and
in the manner in which her opinions manifest themselves,
it is all one can expect from a *muzhik*....

It is impossible not to marvel at that feeling for
truth and artistry so rare in our literature which re-
strains the author from the slightest tendency to give his
heroine a gentler colouring. Similar tendencies usually
seduce even highly talented authors like Dickens. But
they are very understandable.... Furthermore how many
by-ways and sidetracks there are in Count Tolstoy's novel
down which a less sincere writer, one less in command of
his artistic talents would not fail to turn. How many
excuses for idyllic pictures, dramatic effects, poetic
dialogues and psychological fantasies! Count Tolstoy has
negotiated these reefs with the skill and self-confidence
of an experienced pilot, and nowhere does he lose sight
of his objective or his main ideas.

20. PYATKOVSKY SUMS UP TOLSTOY'S CAREER

1865

From an essay in the 'Contemporary', 1865, no. 4.
A.Ya. Pyatkovsky (1840-1904), editor and critic, wrote
this valedictory notice on the occasion of the publication
of Tolstoy's 'collected works', which came out in two
volumes in 1864 and convinced him that Tolstoy's literary
career was over.

Count Tolstoy's literary talent, his powers of observation

and his acute psychological analysis were all sufficiently
expressed in his first work 'Childhood and Boyhood'; it
was because of these qualities that several of his works
received their undoubted success with the majority of the
reading public. On those occasions when Count Tolstoy
does not propose some preconceived idea and does not
strain to produce something new and startling to the whole
universe he completely satisfies his readers with the
accuracy of his observations and the masterly strokes he
uses in the portrayal of his fictional characters. In a
word the more humble the task and the further the author
removes himself from any sly cleverness and deliberate
manipulations of his artistic creations the better it is
both for him and his public. To the number of works which
present a truthful and unartificial combination of various
facts from our lives belong 'Childhood and Boyhood', the
memoirs of Sebastopol, the stories of the Caucasus ('The
Raid' and 'The Woodfelling'), 'The Memoirs of a Billiard-
marker' and the tale of 'Polikushka'. We would have
included 'Family Happiness' had it not shown some ulterior
motive in its idealization of a certain social class of
an extremely bourgeois nature.... The story 'Lucerne' and
the novel 'The Cossacks' suffered even more from tendentiousness and lyrical interpolations. The main character
in 'Lucerne' is Prince Dmitriy Nekhlyudov who first
appeared in 'Boyhood' and 'Youth'. It is true that this
Nekhlyudov has developed somewhat since the time he was
the guest of Ivan Yakovlevich Koreysha and was glad of the
opportunity to make the acquaintance of that remarkable
man. His development, though, is not of a very deep
nature and the Schweizerhof hotel shelters the same
spirit that in earlier days wandered the hills. Prince
Nekhlyudov, walking along the shores of Lake Lucerne,
comes across a poor singer who had been performing beneath
the windows of the hotel without receiving a reward of
even a franc for his pains from the starched lords and
ladies staying there. Nekhlyudov who from his youth has
made it a rule to 'sympathize with everything beautiful
and lofty' loses his temper at this and causes the most
stupid of scandals in which the personality of the singer
is used as a battering ram against English stand-
offishness and arrogance. The singer, as one would
expect, does not thank the Russian prince for his well-
meant demonstration and Nekhlyudov directs his anger at
the whole canton of Lucerne, the whole Swiss republic and
at all republics in the world where singers can die from
hunger and only unskilled labourers with horny hands can
find a living. Serious questions occur to Nekhlyudov;
they grow to a crescendo and are finally resolved in

amazing politico-moral maxims.

[Quotation omitted.]

This rhetoric, this lyrical tirade perplexes and confuses
the reader; but he must never forget that Count Tolstoy is
very bad at abstract questions and is here out of his
depth. All this philosophical cleverness is simply only
quietism and through it he has nothing with which to
acquaint the public. 'I do not know', he says, 'what is
good and what is bad; perhaps there is no difference.'
As the reader will see, these subtleties are not far
removed from the philosophy of the Russian rough diamond
and prophet Koreysha before whom Prince Nekhlyudov made
obeisance in his youth. Only everything is enveloped in
flowery phrases which only befog the short-sighted reader.
Furthermore the whole trouble in this stems from the fact
that Count Tolstoy did not confine himself to the depiction of Prince Nekhlyudov - the repentant nobleman - but
tried to elevate him into some all-Russian type and to
give him some important concerns which could not conceivably have entered his narrow skull. When he was talking
of Nekhlyudov's life in Moscow, Count Tolstoy was true to
his talent; he described very accurately his hero's young
love and his friendship with Irtenev, a similar degenerate
of serfdom and Moscow society. But then Nekhlyudov grew
up and wished to figure in life, he felt stifled in the
classroom or lecture theatre and wanted to take a more
open road. This is why we find him in Lucerne attacking
republican ways of life and also in the country ('A Landowner's Morning') like some virtuous caliph going round
all the peasants' huts and doing good to the poor while
they - out of stupidity, of course - value his goodness
not one whit. In both these last two examples Count
Tolstoy could have dealt with his subject matter humor-
ously but it is evident he loves his hero too much to let
him be insulted by the reader. To prove his mental powers
Nekhlyudov removes from himself all the youthful nonsense
that we mentioned above.

[Omitted: Pyatkovsky's attacks on various other critics.]

'The Cossacks' has the same virtues and faults as the
stories in which Nekhlyudov appears. The pictures of
nature and the descriptions of Cossack life are wonderful
in their artistry; the impressions which the hero gains
as he arrives in this half-savage country are accurately
depicted; but the character of Olenin is indescribably
weak and the central idea of the novel is even worse. As

far as the latter is concerned the novel is no better than
the 'Byronic' stories in our literature where our civilized Europeans set off to seek rest and oblivion in the
countryside.

[Quotation omitted.]

But what was attractive and contemporary in the 1820s
smells of anachronism in the 1860s. It is a little late
for Count Tolstoy to restore ancient pictures. Furthermore he would seem to share Nekhlyudov's opinion that
'civilization is not a blessing nor is barbarism an evil',
and that, given the opportunity, should one not exchange
one for the other?

'War and Peace' 1865-9

21. BOTKIN, FROM A LETTER TO A.A. FET

1865

---

14 February 1865. V.P. Botkin (1811-69) was a critic and
publicist of the 'art for art's sake' school. A friend
and correspondent of Tolstoy's, it was he who talked
Tolstoy into publishing 'Family Happiness' in 1859 after
Tolstoy had decided it was worthless. Botkin's view of
'War and Peace' changed after he had read it all; it was
'a work, exceptional from every point of view'.

I have started to read Tolstoy's new novel. The most
striking thing is how subtly he describes the various
inner movements of the soul. In spite of the fact that I
have read more than half of it, the thread is still not
at all clear; this is because of the predominance of
detail. Besides this, why is there all that conversation
in French? It is enough to say that the conversation
takes place in French. It is all quite superfluous and
has an unpleasant effect. And he is rather careless with
his Russian. This is evidently the introduction, the
background for the future picture. However marvellously
he may depict the merest detail, though, it must be said
that this background takes up too large a place.

22.   UNSIGNED REVIEW OF '1805'

1866

The 'Book Messenger', 1866, nos 16-17.
   The first parts of 'War and Peace' were originally entitled '1805' (see Introduction).

In the same volume before us at the moment we have the
first two parts of '1805', which first appeared in the
'Russian Messenger', but we have just read them for the
first time, and not without pleasure. Several pages
remind us in their freshness of this author's best works
and several of the characters (e.g. Prince Vasiliy, Princess Drubetskoy and Captain Tushin) are depicted in masterly fashion. In general, though, '1805' seems strange
and indeterminate. Evidently the author himself does not
know what it is he is writing: the title merely says
'"1805" by Count Lev Tolstoy', and indeed it is neither a
novel nor a novella; it is rather some sort of attempt at
a military and aristocratic chronicle of the past, wonderful in places, but in others dry and tedious. When
one is reading these two parts one just cannot make out
either the basic idea behind the work or why and for whom
the author brings in all those poor little Nikolenkas,
Natashas, Mimis and Borises, on whom it is impossible to
focus one's attention amid all the descriptions of military actions and a kind of fictional relating of the times
in which it seems the work's main interest lies. One does
not even know whether these characters figure as heroes or
whether in their individual insignificance they form but
the background. The character of Prince Andrey is more
successful but leads one to the same questions and perplexities; the author has also been unsuccessful with the
phantoms from the aristocracy of a former age, with the
exception of the afore-mentioned Prince Vasiliy, Princess
Drubetskoy and the old Rostov, and what is more, besides
these, many more are introduced and some of them (Anatole
Kuragin, Dolokhov, etc.) appear to be the main personages
in the story; because of their multiplicity the opening of
the story becomes a little fragmented and the unsatisfied
interest of the reader flags. From reading these two
parts one is also unsure of whether the end has been
reached or are they but the prologue for some huge epic,
for something original albeit somewhat tedious and a

little tendentious? The language in which '1805' is
written is good, as in all the author's works; but for
some unexplained whim half his characters speak in French
and all their correspondence is in the same language, so
that a good third of the work is written in French and
whole pages are covered in it (albeit with a translation
at the bottom). This original innovation also strikes the
reader as something odd and one just cannot understand why
the author needed it all. If he wanted through these
words to prove that our aristocratic ancestors at the
start of this century, these various Bolkonskys and Dru-
betskoys, spoke a pure and good French, then all that was
needed was for one or two phrases to appear and then we
would all have believed him willingly, scarcely anyone
would have doubted his word; but to read a book which has
this mixture of French and Russian without the slightest
need for it is indeed neither pleasant nor comforting; it
might be all very well on the aristocratic pages of the
'Russian Messenger' but in a separate edition the French
texts should have been left out.

23. AKHSHARUMOV, REVIEW OF '1805'

1867

_____

'Universal Labour', 1867, no. 6. N.D. Akhsharumov (1819-
93) was a critic and minor novelist.

_____

....We cannot place this work categorically in any of the
usual literary genres. It is neither a chronicle nor an
historical novel. Although in form it is fairly close to
the latter, in content it lacks any dramatic unity; the
action has no central point; an opening, an intrigue, and
a denouement are all missing; also it is clearly unfinished; but its general sense does not suffer in any way
from these faults, and which we therefore cannot call
faults. On the contrary it seems to us that a more strict
framework would have been inhibiting and in order to be
complete would have demanded things which the author
neither had nor should have had in mind. His object was
to write about Russian *society sixty years ago,* and we
must admit to the correctness of the taste with which he

rejected all superfluous decoration and every attempt at effect, sacrificing all to the demands of strict historical truth. The story has lost very little because of this, and has gained much.

[Omitted: discussion of the previous fifty years of Russian history.]

In this progressive development a period such as 1805 is of great interest. It was a time of golden childhood in which the child's character had already formed and his personality was already present. If we look at the story from this point of view all the members of society depicted by Count Tolstoy seem to be children. Their attitude to life is naive and ingenuous; they have made no compromises with their position nor have they yet chosen any path for themselves; they are unacquainted with that demoralising mental activity which forces so many of us to stand in perplexity before a problem for many years, grumbling, looking askance at it and being unable to do anything. They all believe in something whole-heartedly, one in the heroes of his fatherland, another in Napoleon or Jean-Jacques Rousseau and a third unthinkingly in his Sonya or his Natasha; some believe in military glory or in their own witticisms, others in their great daring and strength; and lastly there are those who might be the greatest of all, those who believe in the possibility of living for ever as they live now, on the income from their patrimonial estates amid endless feasts and carefree leisure in the lap of the limitless hospitality of the Russian land.

Let us look more closely at these children. Most of them are so nice that it is a pleasure to look upon them and in many of them we can see characteristics we recognize. In one we can see the rounded youthful portrait of a father or an uncle; another reminds us distantly and vaguely of a future Chatsky or Onegin. We cannot see enough of that young girl with the thin, round little face and bright fiery eyes and something tells us that we have met her more than once since, in her maturity, or at least someone very much like her, someone who belongs to us.

But let us go up to these children and look more attentively at them.

The story begins in the Winter Palace at an evening reception given by one of the dowager empress's ladies-in-waiting. The most brilliant members of society are gathered there and rumours of the coming war with France form the background for all the conversations which, by the

way, do not all have the mark of patriotism. Almost all
of them are in French with the rare dash of an untrans-
lated Russian word. But this mixture which today sounds
passé and incurably childish to our old ears had in those
days its childlike, naive comicality and very understandable justification. We recall that we are in Petersburg
and at court and that for more than a century all of
Europe, in the form of its upper classes, had been under
the sway of the glitter of the court of France, her glory
and enlightenment, and that the echo of the time of Louis
XIV had not died away like the fires of revolution, and
that right after the Revolution the great deeds of a new
Caesar had taken their place. Our own Russian society and
especially that part of it which was gently pushing us
towards Europe, the highest circle in Petersburg and the
court, all of this was at that tender stage of growth
where independence is unthinkable and the force of impressions from outside is not counterbalanced by any internal
convictions. To demand that at that time we should have
had our own originality is as unreasonable as to expect a
clean sheet of paper in a press not to receive the imprint of the letters. The irritating inclinations of
children are well known. Their imaginations are filled
with what surrounds them daily, with what shines the most
brightly and sounds the most loudly. They try to be like
adults, copy their tone and mannerisms and instinctively
parody them in their games. For this simple reason the
tone of our high society in Petersburg at that time could
of course be no other than an echo of the external, superficial side of things outside Russia, more rarely of Bona-
partism and more rarely still of those liberal ideas which
at the very start of the revolution were held by the best
sections of French aristocratic youth. All these nuances
and all that superficial, naive and purely childish affectation is expressed in masterly fashion in the first few
chapters of the book. You will see at once that this
small collection of people have not yet developed their
own distinctive physiognomy. They are neither Russians
nor Frenchmen, but naughty children who play a minor role
with an air of amusing importance. They are all saturated
with the arrogance of the most refined taste and irreproachable respectability, but it has not occurred to any
of them to be respectable in their own way and not according to the traditions of the Faubourg St Germain. These
traditions and even the gossip are known to them by heart
as something it would be shameful not to know and they
behave with the amusing enthusiasm of schoolboys vying with
each other to show that they have learnt their lessons
well. In order further to establish the plausability of

the game a real live Frenchman, and not simply anyone but
one of the best, Vicomte Mortemart (allié aux Montmorencys
par les Rohans, tout ce qu'il y a de plus Faubourg St
Germain), is served up by the considerate hostess for her
guests as something supernaturally refined, as a real live
model of the way one should act in society; and our children play their small parts before this paragon as they
would before a real expert and connoisseur with such a
lively childlike zest that one just cannot be cross with
them for their pranks. The parts are not distributed but
simply and enthusiastically taken; by some unspoken
agreement each takes one on without asking himself which
he would prefer or which would suit him best. There is
the mournful, disenchanted society lion and salon clown, a
fool with his hair done à la Titus with his *cuisse de
nymphe effrayée* coloured pantaloons and a lorgnette; there
is the pretty princess who behaves as if everything that
she had done had been *partie de plaisir* for her and for
everyone else, the princess about whom the vicomte said
indulgently that she was 'bien, mais très bien et tout à
fait Française', and so on. Comedies of this nature have
been endlessly repeated since then and have been not in-
frequently successful, the only difference being that in
those days they were fresh and natural while today they
have aged, lost any meaning and have become distasteful to
all of us who have ever thought about them. There were
even then, though, some clever children who disliked them.
Although playing at Frenchmen in their drawing-rooms and
imitating from an early age all their external mannerisms,
they none the less realized that it was all a childish
game and that it was high time to cease, because a more
serious affair awaited them and to act as children in the
face of it would be quite shameful. The fact of the matter is that neither they nor those surrounding them had
ever been French nor could they ever become so. An open,
adaptable attitude to external forms, the ability to
forget their own and adopt the alien but just as quickly
and easily to reject it all, in short the very fact that
they were so capable of adopting foreign ways is what differentiated them from foreigners and from the French in
particular. Not one of them, however he might have
appeared from the outside to be alien to everything Russian, however attracted he might have been to current
fashions, could ever identify himself with his role to
such a degree that it would be difficult for him to cast
it off at a moment's notice and appear as a completely
different person. This fleeting and natural appearance of
the slightly rough but energetic Russian face showing beneath its tight-fitting and scrupulously correct mask has

been subtly grasped by the author and spread throughout the
the whole book. But in places the actors take off their
masks themselves. No sooner have the guests managed to
disperse from Anna Scherer's reception than we see from
two different sides a protest against that characteristic
of contemporary life which the author has depicted in the
reception. On the one hand the sincere and serious confession of Prince Andrey, full of proud consciousness of
his own worth; and on the other that wild explosion of
youthful strength and whole-hearted daring at the flat of
the young Kuragin after cards and an evening's drinking.
Here there is nothing of the spirit of St Germain correctness and *bon ton*; it has rather the odour of the fire of
Moscow and that unexpected, discourteous welcome, far
removed from any conceptions of European decorum, with
which we greet our guests seven years later.

From Petersburg the action moves to Moscow; but the
move is hardly felt. Princess Anna Mikhaylovna Drubetskoy, a persistent suppliant who had at Anna Scherer's
reception dragged from Prince Kuragin a promise to arrange
the transfer of her son into the Guards, returns after
this victory to Moscow and the family of her friends the
Rostovs and we go with her to be the guests of Count
Rostov. There is a completely different atmosphere here,
as everywhere in Moscow, from Petersburg. People live
without straining every muscle to be like others or worrying about how one ought to behave. It is possible to
define this even more accurately but this would take too
much time and would anyway be superfluous because it is
better to feel it than define it. and in the story one
feels it extremely strongly. Rumours about the coming war
are the subject of conversation here too but they have a
completely different character. In Petersburg it is a
piece of court news and provides the setting for beautiful
French phrases but here it is part of the domestic scene
going hand in hand with other cares and interests - with
visits, gossip, meetings and dinner parties. The troops
have been moved abroad; the young men have given up their
studies and enlisted - the son has left; but in the family
there is a name day and so the house is full of visitors
and best wishes, the mistress is almost rushed off her
feet and in the marble hall a long table is laid out for
twenty people and the father of the house has his mind
full of some grouse sauté au madère or the value of his
serf cook for whom he has paid a thousand roubles. How
our modern preachers would have thundered about this! How
they would have attacked poor Count Rostov and his good
lady the Countess with all their offspring, the members of
their household, their guests, their serf maids, grouse

sauces and 'la santé à maman' and 'la comtesse Apraksine' and all this nonsense of Moscow's idle life! But times change and when we read Count Tolstoy's story about the past we travel back sixty years and understand the people to such a degree that we neither hate them nor feel repugnance for their lives. We say: tout compte, they were all good people, warm-hearted people and no worse than you, inexorable censor and preacher. And the main reason why we cannot judge them in any other way is that they are children. This time, though, among the grown-up children we have before us some real children and they are drawn by the author with such fascinating delight that we cannot see enough of them. They also play their parts, parodying their elders but their parody is gentler and simpler. They fall in love and are jealous of each other and before parting they give each other vows of faithfulness even unto the grave. Here we have no vicomtes, no prattle of a passé aristocracy, none of that nauseating affectation of French *bon ton*; here we have simply pranks, but they are so charming, so natural and open-hearted that they only need time to ripen and enter fully into real life.... And then as we are feasting our eyes upon them, the picture again slightly changes and moves into a different sphere.

From the gossip of a name day in the Rostov household we discover that the illegitimate son of Count Bezukhov, Pierre, whom we met in Petersburg at Anna Scherer's reception and in Prince Andrey's study, has been expelled for some misdemeanour he committed after a drunken party. The position of this young man in society is insecure and ambiguous and his life is evidently ruined; but fate is preparing a surprise for him. His father Count Bezukhov, one of those important people during the reign of Catherine the Great who managed one way or another to make their way from darkness and ignorance to the heights of wealth and power, lies at death's door and the problem is who should inherit his huge fortune after his death. An intrigue is afoot around the dying man's bed. A relation of his, another person the reader met in Petersburg, Prince Vasiliy Kuragin, whose nieces, the Mamonovs, live with the count, is explaining to one of them that in the count's will everything is left to his illegitimate son Pierre and that there is a letter to the tsar requesting the legitimization of his son and that if what is in these documents is set in motion then everything will go to Pierre and no one else will get a penny. Pierre is there himself but Pierre is a ninny, brought up abroad, in Paris; he is captivated by the glory of Napoleon and dreams of his conquest of England at the very moment when his inheritance is about to be taken from under his nose. He suspects

nothing, but happiness is decidedly to be his. That same
persistent suppliant and distant relative of his father's,
whom we already know, Anna Mikhaylovna Drubetskoy, bursts
into the dying man's house with his godson, her son Boris,
who lacks an inheritance himself. Fired with maternal
concern she hopes to get a few crumbs from the legacy for
her Boris and, seeing no means to achieve her aim other
than joining forces with the good-hearted Pierre, she
rushes to his defence. With an inimitable combination of
cunning and dexterity she worms herself into the circle of
the relations, divines all their plots and destroys them
in favour of her protégé. All of this together forms the
only dramatic episode in the story. But it is carried
through to perfection. It is haute comédie, comedy of the
highest type. In spite of its fragmentary and condensed
nature, the characters of those participating in it stand
out against the action and these characters are conceived
so deeply and drawn so successfully that we can see right
through them. The role of the prince and the old princess, their explanations to each other about the will and
the role of Pierre and Anna Mikhaylovna are all things
that once you have read them remain in the memory for
ever as examples of a first-class talent.

[Quotation omitted.]

No less wonderful but completely different in character
is the scene which follows. From Moscow the picture
moves to the estates of old Prince Bolkonsky. Prince
Andrey is taking his pregnant wife there to stay with his
father while he goes to join his regiment. Just as in
Moscow we see no foreign influence here, except for a
French companion and the superficial signs of a French
upbringing. The way of life, the people, their relation-.
ships one with the other, all have a clear Russian nature.
Their full lives, the typical faces of the Bolkonskys,
father and son, and the deep sympathy and interest they
arouse in the reader all make us sigh deeply. Where have
such people gone? Why do we not see them in our midst
today? Especially Prince Andrey: his sharp, clear mind
which is taken in by nothing, the unspotted purity of his
soul, that ability to see things not as he would like to
see them but as they really are with nothing obscuring
their true sense. This is all possibly an ideal, of
course, but it may well be that the model standing before
the author was rather inferior to the portrait, that he
improved him a little, made him more good-looking, and
that the true metal really existing in the character has
been even more cleansed by art of accidental admixtures

which do not belong to it; but this is unimportant. What
is important is the fact that this character is not invented, that it is a truly native, Russian type and that the
breed of men of that stamp, if they still exist today,
could be of immense service to us. This again forces us
to repeat the question: Where have such people gone? Why
are there no longer people like them around? Was the
school of life antipathetic to their natures and did it
slowly and irretrievably pervert and degenerate them? Or
was it possibly life's struggles which destroyed them? It
is possible because such people cannot calmly lay down
their arms and withdraw or strike shameful bargains. They
would fight in the front line and they must be victorious
or lose their lives. Either our Andreys have degenerated
into Onegins and Pechorins or they have perished without
changing; but the outcome is the same. We have lost them,
and for ever. We thank the author that he has saved at
least the characteristics from oblivion. They are dear to
us as the ideal of our youth, expiating in our memories if
not our sins then at least those of our fathers.

The second half of '1805' is not so interesting, but is
necessary for the whole. In it we see our fathers on the
battlefield, covered in glory. We see the same people who
seven years later saved their fatherland and whom we can
never forget. The story is lively, the colours bright and
the scenes of military life are painted with the same
sharp brush which acquainted us with the defence of Sebastopol and they breathe the same truth. The review of the
infantry at Braunau, the high command, the hussars' camp
at Zalzeneck, the crossing of the Enns, the Austrian court
at Brünn and the battle of Schöngraben - all of this reads
well and easily. Several of the historical figures, Mack,
Bagration and Kutuzov, and the military types of the past
like Denisov, give the story the appearance of historical
accuracy; the rest is rather general and could have taken
place in any war at any time. The gift of the proper
selection from the limitless mass of details of what is
really interesting and which describes the events in their
typicality is possessed by the author to such a degree
that he can choose whatever he likes as the subject of his
story, although it all happened a long time ago, and be
certain that he will never bore us. After the masterly
and complete pictures of the first part we wander through
various camps, headquarters and crossings a little sorry
that the scene changes, and not becoming bored once, and
at the end our only regret is that there is no more to
come. We would have served to the end of the war as willingly and then returned home to our friends and acquaintances. We repeat the author's method is almost

irreproachable. The only thing that strikes us as always being the same and which is somewhat wearying in its monotonous impression is the eternal patch of shade, slowly following, always in its own way, always separately, every bright side of the description. This gives the impression that the author is afraid that the personages he has created will fly away into some abstract ideal and so he quickly weighs them down a little. It seems to us that there is no danger of this happening and the huge credit which the author enjoys with the mass of his readers could save him from the worry of paying with the small change of satire for every spark of poetry and every sign of beauty appearing in his portraits.

Having read the story to the end and trying to free ourselves from the multitude of colours in the various parts in order to get a true impression of the whole and to evaluate to what degree it corresponds with the thought that inspired it, we cannot find a false note anywhere. The work could, of course, have been conceived differently, the separate groupings and scenes could have had a stronger connection if in the foreground and at the centre of the action there had been one important historical figure; then we would have had a drama or a novel. But hardly a quarter of the rich material that the author had at his disposal could be used within the narrow framework of the story and we cannot accuse him of deciding not to make the sacrifice; we see only too well how much we would have lost. There is a reproach of a different nature which is no more crucial but equally possible. We could complain that the author describes almost exclusively the upper classes and that beyond the tight circle of counts, princes and princesses all talking in French we see not only none of the common people but no other classes either. As a result of this exclusiveness we could add that we see a far from complete picture of the epoch but rather something like the memoirs of a homespun Faubourg St Germain; and in this there is a certain truth. But one must be completely just. One must understand that the choice of actors and events did not depend on the personal whim of the author or his class sympathies, that he was naturally limited by the accidental store of stories, memoirs and letters grouped around a certain family chronicle or private diary which survived, luckily for us, over half a century and that without this ground even the imagination of Shakespeare would not have been able to create such a clear and true story.

24.   ANNENKOV ON 'WAR AND PEACE'

1868

'Messenger of Europe', 1868, no. 2.   From an extensive
review entitled Historical and Aesthetic Questions in
Count L.N. Tolstoy's Novel 'War and Peace'.

....The mind of the reviewer who would like to follow this
complex work through all its obvious and hidden movements
must certainly become confused at the sight of the huge
mass of different events taking place and the immense
crowd of people who pass across the scene and at the unceasing movement of the story which gives to each part of
it as much time as is needed to explain its significance,
and then immediately removes it from the scene before recalling it after a more or less long interval by which
time it has already taken on new forms and has become as
it were renewed. The clearest evidence of the complexity
of the huge construction is the fact that only in the
second half of the third volume does something approaching
a plot begin to emerge, and only then do we find whom we
must consider as the novel's main heroes. These characters, three in number, are the serious but humane young
Bezukhov, a type similar to Oblomov, if Oblomov had been
immensely wealthy and the illegitimate son of one of the
leading figures of the reign of Catherine the Great; the
poetical young countess Natasha Rostov who has received no
moral education at home, which has made her susceptible to
all the temptations of her own organism and troubled
thoughts and causing her even from childhood to fall in
love on all sides and finally compelling her to exchange
her fiancé Prince Bolkonsky for the handsome, heartless
and debauched Prince Kuragin; the last and most important
of this triad is the young Prince Bolkonsky whom we mentioned earlier. It is this severe, serious character who
must solemnly represent in himself the idea expressed by
the novel, extracting it from the chaos of its details,
and thus justify the author's choice of the scene of the
action and his choice of contents and give it all its
sense and meaning. Such characters are usually formed by
their authors with great care. What part Prince Bolkonsky
and his two companions play in the plot of the novel we
shall know when their portraits are completed in the
novel's fourth part. We shall just repeat here that it is

only in the second half of the third part that they appear as the main heroes and the motivators of the action. But what do we have at the moment?

We have a truly marvellous pageant. A vast diorama stretches out before us full of colour, light and the dark mass of a nation at war with various shapes marked out on it. We pass from the diplomatic salons of Fraülein Scherer to the fashionable orgies of the guards officers, to Moscow society where we are present during the last hours of the dying notable, the old Prince Bezukhov, father of one of the novel's heroes, magnificent and some-how menacing in the agony of death. We watch the cupidity of his heirs and the machinations, worthy of the pettiest little clerk, of the old Prince Kuragin, a minister of state, who is looking everywhere to pick up a fortune for the setting up of his disgraceful son. From the home of the dying notable we move into the peaceful yet active Rostov household, populated with young people, and where its head, the old Count Rostov, a pillar of the English Club, considers it his duty to bring up his children by means of endless parties which in the first place are bringing him to the point of ruin and in the second turn Natasha Rostov into someone who is later to be so disil-lusioned in herself. On the way we meet the ageing Prin-cess Drubetskoy who comes from an impoverished noble back-ground and is trying to place her worthy son with enough energy, practical sense, mental agility and readiness for any useful treachery to amaze the world with some great political crime were she in different surroundings. Around the princess swarm various characters, each bearing a strong family resemblance and on the point of developing an original physiognomy. From here we are carried ever onward. We are now in the village of the old, stern Prince Bolkonsky, the father of another of the novel's heroes, and we enter the atmosphere of the petty tyranny of the old grandees which has nothing in common at all with the dissipations of life in Moscow. The whole house is in order and all-a-tremble. The prince writes his memoirs, works at his lathe, studies the Napoleonic cam-paigns, teaches his terrified daughter Princess Maria mathematics, and is engrossed in convulsive activity in his study from which he rarely emerges but from where he is all-seeing and all-knowing concerning what is happening in the house and, through his old connections and former service, everything that is going on in the state adminis-tration. He has no pity on either, confident in his own lack of sin and the religion of veneration and respect before his own person which he has created for himself. The quiet, reserved meetings, full of thought and feeling,

between the ridiculous old man and his son Prince
Andrey, who is on his way to active service in the army
and who has brought his pregnant and repellent wife to
stay, take place before our eyes. But hardly have we
begun to look at the relations between these two original
and independent characters when we find ourselves in the
very midst of the Russian armies and on the battlefields
of the years 1805-7. One after the other pictures start
to pass before us, pictures of the movements of Russian
troops, their skirmishes with the enemy, the disorderly
retreat and the despairing efforts, after every defeat, to
reform the broken and helpless units. The skill of the
author in depicting scenes of military life reaches its
apogee. The plans for the battles and the places where
they take place hit the eye like the engravings on English
keepsakes, and the main moments of the battles tower above
all the details in which they are described and assembled.
Nothing can compare with the description of that moment
when Bagration leads two battalions against an enemy
column, rising to meet them out of the depression at
Schöngraben, and when both forces meet and fall in fire
and smoke; it is as accurate as the incomparable description of the misty day of the battle of Austerlitz, the
foreboding and weariness of the troops on the day before,
the general bustle when the first rays of the sun show the
proximity of the enemy and light up the instantaneous
massacre of the Russian army. Even amid the brilliance of
the scenes there are pages which are the most striking of
all in showing that special skill of the author in vividly
describing the general feeling of a huge mass of people
and every individual feeling which has grown in it as in
its native soil; scenes such as that of the military
transport retreating in disarray and having lost in its
terror, panic and fear not only all sense of discipline
but also all sense of the most elementary conditions of
self-preservation; and that of our troops crossing the
bridge at Enns when an advancing enemy battery threatens
to overtake them, and even more the crossing of the weir
near Austerlitz when all the force of the enemy artillery
is directed at this point and sweeps away all the people
and horses crowded upon it like specks of dust. And
again in the midst of all this movement all sorts of military types pass before us, boldly drawn and then at once
deserted; they pass alternately with silhouettes and descriptions of historical characters, Kutuzov and his officers, the Emperor Francis and his camp at Olmütz, Tsar
Alexander at the review and in battle and so on. Along
with these we meet those young people we already know from
the society circles of Moscow and Petersburg. To all

these things which grip our attention and rouse our
curiosity there is added something new: we observe which
aspects of the characters of each of them are brought out
by their contact with world events, with the fight for
existence and the nearness of death; how each of them
meets the hurricane of history going on around him, which
way he bends, and what he thinks at the time. We see the
wounded Rostov running from the sabre of a French dragoon,
and Prince Bolkonsky left for dead on the field of Austerlitz; but both of them succeed in telling us something of
their thoughts and feelings at this fateful hour when they
belong both to life and to death. Tired, almost completely exhausted, from the different impressions we
finally reach the marvellous description of the meeting
at Tilsit which is prefaced like a report by a description
of a typhus hospital with wounded Russians with whom both
the doctors and the directorate refuse to deal and, a
little before this, the scene where the corrupt diplomat
laughs at the 'Orthodox believers' (as he calls the
Russian troops) in his attempt to combat the giant of the
century. Peace is concluded. Everything returns to its
former usual ordinariness; only the young Bolkonsky, who
has lost his wife between the time of Austerlitz and
Tilsit and, having recovered from his enthusiasm for
Napoleon, associates out of a thirst for activity with the
stars of the then administration who shed some of their
flickering and dubious rays on him, while his friend,
young Bezukhov, gets married without knowing how to Princess Kuragin, a born libertine, and seeks comfort, activity and peace of mind in the intense religion of the
feelings and in the society of the masons who introduce
him and us to all their secrets. Let us pause here and
ask: surely this is all marvellous from start to finish?
     Indeed it is; yet whatever has taken place the novel,
in the strict meaning of the word, has not moved at all
or, if it has, only with incredible apathy and slowness.
The big wheel of the novel's mechanism has scarcely
changed its position; it has not put any real part into
action and has merely let the small wheels move with
inscrutable speed through their extraneous work. The big
wheel of the novel in our opinion can only be the plot and
the central idea of the work which is inextricably connected with it. The plot is nowhere to be seen, not even
in the scenes of political and social life however remarkable they might be. One may suggest that we will not be
alone after the intoxicating impressions of the novel in
asking: Where is it, this novel, what has it done with its
main business - the development of its 'inner sequence',
its 'fable' and its 'intrigue'? For without these,

whatever the novel is about, it will appear empty and one
to which its own real interests are extraneous. There is
no doubt that one could take whatever manifestations of
life or history one liked as the plot of the novel, as
its, in other words, central idea, but only if this central idea is not overwhelmed by the number and diversity
of the manifestations, for if they are the result will
always prove far more harmful than useful to the work. Of
course there is no more melancholy sight than watching an
author reduce the importance of the serious character of
the historical and social facts, removing their essential
sense in order that they may stand on a par with his own
ideas without being ashamed of their presence; but on the
other hand there is something approaching betrayal when a
novel as it were lives out of doors. The danger facing
it, as it does every moral creature, begins from the
moment it goes against its own nature or ceases to recognize it. It is not difficult to prove mathematically on
the basis of the laws of perspective that in any novel
great historical facts must not stand in the foreground;
only then is it possible to present them in some fulness
and completeness. Only by removing them from the position
that must be exclusively occupied by the main characters
in the novel will the conditions for their proximity to
actual history be preserved. This proximity will be the
more destroyed the more the author moves them forward by
tearing them out of the background where they allow him
the most necessary space. It might happen that once they
have reached the final stage of their movement forward
they will not appear to the reader in the full expression
of their content but only in those few aspects of it which
remain after the journey and which falling under a strong,
accidental or even artificial light will appear clearly
and distinctly in an excessive and false size. The worst
thing in this is that the real and legitimate occupiers of
the foreground of a novel - its heroes and the events
connected with them - will be crowded out by this invasion
of a strong element against which it is impossible to
fight. The novel withers away like the plants of a
country trampled over by the feet and horses of an invad-
ing tribe. We are not saying that this is what has happened with L. Tolstoy's novel; he still keeps the historical part at a proper although dangerous distance from his
heroes. He defends the latter with incredible care from
the unnecessary risks of over-contact with the power of
the historical element which seems about to swallow them
up, but even so the general state of affairs is reflected
unpleasantly on them. To his heroes and their private
lives he gives as much space, light and air as is

necessary only for the support of their existence. This
meagre ration, this *le strict nécessaire*, which gives them
life amid the luxury and wealth of the condition of everything else, affects the reader unpleasantly and he guesses
in the end that the real shortcoming in the whole creation, in spite of its complexity, mass of scenes, its
brilliance and elegance, is the lack of any *development in
the plot*.

The novel does not move, as we have said, and moreover
almost no character or situation in the novel develops
before the second half of the third volume. They only
change or present new sides with every turn of the picture
as it catches them, but they do not develop. It could not
be otherwise. The depiction of the movement of scenes in
order to explain some phenomenon or make a close inspec-
tion of the psychological changes taking place in a man is
not possible with a mass of characters and events, all
taking their turn to appear on the scene. The new scene
takes all its characters already prepared to appear on the
stage and we recognize the new traits which they introduce
or the new events which alter their inner world and mood
only when the author treats his characters with the deep
analysis of which he is capable. The reader is not present at the birth of the changes which occur to the characters and events between the scenes nor through the
course of their development; the changes have taken place
in the depths of the author's imagination to which no one
is admitted. We see the faces and the forms when the process of the change has already taken place. It is true
that these changes have sufficient foundations and stem
from signs and indications already present in the characters and events; nowhere are sharp contradictions visible, nowhere is there anything forced or arbitrary in
the additional characteristics; it was possible always to.
expect exactly this order of events and this new side of
the character; but the absolute necessity for the changes
suffered by them both is nowhere shown. If there had
been no connection between their old and their new selves
everything could have occurred without them. A brilliant
scene full of effect, psychological analysis and wonderful
touches would immediately redeem the unexpectedness or
artificiality of any nuance, would immediately make one
forget about everything that is a little dubious or unjustified in its origin. We shall not again turn the
burning pages of this remarkable novel in order to convince the reader that many of the characters - both Bolkonskys, for example, Bezukhov, Natasha, Princess Maria
and others - have acquired in the interval between their
first, second and third appearances in the novel real

physiological and moral traits the explanation for which
must be sought only in the blind passage of time between
one period of their development and the next. The events
are shown to us just as precisely only when they noisily
flow into a new channel which has been dug for them while
the work which they have done in changing their course,
overcoming difficulties and destroying impediments
occurred mainly with the lone and voiceless witness of
time. How else can one explain, for example, how the
dissolute wife of Pierre Bezukhov turns from a notoriously
empty and stupid woman into someone having the reputation
for unusual intelligence when she suddenly appears as the
focal point of the upper-class intelligentsia presiding
over a salon where people gather to listen, learn and
sparkle. Generally almost as many changes take place
outside the novel as do within it. The reader, it is
true, is never forced to reject any detail as being
absolutely impossible but he does not arrive at the conviction as often as he should that a thing could not have
happened in any way different from the way it did.
Instead of such a conviction the author drags from the
public that sort of semi-agreement and unwilling support
which in the language of politics is called the acceptance
of the accomplished fact. The fact is legitimized by this
acceptance but the possibility remains to each of the
judges to think to himself that the fact might not have
come to life in the form which it apparently did. This is
usually the way with works suffering, as a consequence of
the special nature of their construction, from the absence
of any development.

We do not hide from ourselves that it might be said in
response to all these points: what have your comments on
the lack of any development to do with it when the novel
in the form in which it appears achieves all its aims and
intentions? With the help of the various scenes the
characters achieve typicality which basically is all that
is needed. A picture of the epoch, even when split up
into a multiplicity of scenes, is none the less a complete
picture giving everyone a full and incontrovertible impression of its veracity. Also the author's descriptions
are dressed in such a poetic cloth, drawn with such a
strong dramatic element and subtle analysis using the
varied methods of both the thinker and the artist, that
to think here of development is only for the man unsuscep-
tible to these qualities. It is also possible that the
labour of creating development in the novel would harm the
work's unfettered appearance; it is further possible that
the demand itself for development belongs to the weaponry
of an old *aesthetic* routine which is incapable of

understanding new creative forms which arise in the
artist along with new tasks. What development is capable
of replacing, for example, those two truly bewitching
scenes, two especially remarkable pearls from the many
scattered throughout the novel? We are speaking of the
two scenes describing the arrival of the half-ruined
Rostovs at their country estate. In the first of them
Natasha Rostov, worried by an excess of physical and
mental strength, appears at the wolf-hunt, is upset by all
her sensations and passes part of the evening in the house
of the simple landowner Ilagin who treats her to all the
riches of his as yet untouched Russian open-heartedness,
his servant to whom he acts as an equal, his balalaika
which strikes the cultivated ear of his guests strangely
and, finally, of his Russian singing which brings them to
tears. In the other scene the same Natasha organizes the
dressing-up for the Shrove-tide festivities and having
thrilled her friends, maids and everyone else, rushes
through the night in a dashing troika in the moonlight
past the forest and along the snowy wastes to her relative
on the neighbouring estate. In this all of Russian nature
is expressed without any development together with national Russian actions and motifs which deaden, cover up or
heal the sufferings of even an *educated* Russian soul
better than anything else. What development of the plot
could have brought the author to such poetry and such dis-
coveries, a development which by its very nature prefers
the long, sickly study of the thoughts of two or three
characters, the wearisome descriptions of the changes in
their inner worlds and the tedious justification of their
egoistic imprisonment within themselves to scenes from
history, politics and daily life?
        As for the historical part, we intend here to develop
in somewhat greater detail the view we expressed earlier.
Whatever place the historical side might have had in the
novel, at the beginning, in the middle or at the end, it
would be subject to exactly the same laws of artistic
existence as the fictional part: it must prove its right
to express what it expresses. It is well known that the
whole of the historical part of Count Tolstoy's novel is
based on documents and the witness of so-called *petite
histoire* without which, we hasten to add, there is hardly
the possibility of real scholarly history. The works of
Schlosser, Ranke, Gervinus and others have been followed
naturally by a host of more modest labours, private ex-
posures, secret memoirs - in a word all the business of
petite histoire to which they often refer and which are
particularly respected when a certain society feels the
need for self-determination. Up to now society has been

well satisfied with official, scholarly and traditional
history; but with the first gleams of critical thought
desiring to check the present against the past the services of this *petite histoire* are invaluable and are
accepted with great and fully deserved gratitude.   It
helps to bring down the political figures from the misty
heights where they have lived peacefully up to now, like
the gods of Olympus, to the level of human beings; and it
does even more.   In dispersing the haloes and glitter
given them by superstition or political calculation, it
helps to see their real faces and finds in them characteristics general to people of their times.   And its services
are not limited to just this; it reveals the presence and
influence of forces and causes in great historical events,
present even today in the sight of everyone, which all
helps in people's political education.   Hence the success
with the public of those respected publications which have
become the organs of that *petite histoire*, and also in
part the success of Count Tolstoy's book which is based on
it and which provided the greater part of the author's
reading.   But in this it cannot avoid an extremely unwel-
come factor which does not exist for the collections and
publications which also use it.   The latter leave all the
documents with very few exceptions as open questions
patiently awaiting the advent of a really scientific history which will resolve them, and if they sometimes try to
affirm from the documents a certain view of their own then
these attempts belong usually not to the most essential,
even the most brilliant side of these publications.   A
novelist is put in a different position.   For example,
Count Tolstoy always speaks with conviction and indeed has
to speak in this way for no other way is possible.   The
slightest doubt before the documents would be a denial of
the novel itself or rather of its historical side.   Firm,
decisive and brave words must always and everywhere be
heard from literature for in literature we are dealing
with the language of *images* and the slightest hesitations
must lead to confusion and lack of clarity in the images,
which is the same as removing people's tongues or making
them dumb.   From this it can be concluded that the *petite
histoire* which forms the basis of the images suddenly
shows a proud pretence at giving the final verdict on the
characters and events, as if the whole essence of the subject had been completely exhausted by it.   Justice is
thereby dispensed by a not completely legal or competent
judge and the more decisive and effective his judgments
through the means of images and pictures the more the imposture is made clear.   It would be a different matter if
the ideas and opinions of such a judge were based on all

the documents which he has at his disposal, but the conditions of a novel do not permit him to make anything like
a full study of his material. On account of its internal
order and the necessity for economy the novel forces him
to limit himself more often than not to a single trait, a
single meagre trait, in order that after exaggerating and
expanding it to incredible limits he, this unsummoned
judge, can include in it the bases, grounds and causes of
his verdict on people and events. Hence when *petite histoire* turns itself into a novel it resolves the question
of the figure of Kutuzov on the basis of a few words said
by him here and there and the expression on his face at
the time; of Speransky on that of his artificial laugh and
his programmes for conversations at table; of the loss of
the battle of Austerlitz on that of the influence of the
favourite generals surrounding Tsar Alexander and the betrayal of their duty by the others which would have been
worth Alexander's attention, and so on. There is equally
no development here either; the scenes are always strikingly precise on that particular moment they are depicting
and much of what would justify their appearance lies once
again outside the novel in the empty and dumb space between the scenes. It is all made the more melancholy by
the fact that the extremely apt and vivid comments and
thoughts of the author force one to think that he knows
far more about any given topic than his characters. But
when the *petite histoire* withdraws into the background,
pictures of undoubted skill rise before us revealing in
the author an unusual talent for writing about war and
history in an artistic manner. Such are the depictions of
the mass of the army, which is presented to us as a single
huge entity, living its own life, having its own passions
and sympathies and even thinking for itself and complaining about erroneous or wrong dispositions; such are all
the descriptions of the administration, the military headquarters, the stupid and narrowly egoistic Austrian conception of people and events which is expressed on every
face at the court which bear the stamp of stubborn incompetence but in the end always win the game; such especially are the descriptions of the dust, catastrophes and
emotions of battle, etc., etc.
   The domestic side of the novel raises a question no
less important than the one we have just been discussing
in connection with the political section. This part contains the personification of the morals, conceptions and
general culture of upper-class society at the beginning of
this century and is fully, widely and freely developed
thanks to several types who cast several bright rays of
light on the whole of the class to which they belong in

spite of being mere silhouettes or sketches. There is no
place here for the reproaches about the glorification of
ignorance and barbarity which several critics laid at the
author's door in connection with his best work, 'The
Cossacks'. Here, on the contrary, we find ourselves in
the midst of the most refined, civilized company, replete
with elegance, French dialects and the unceasing analysis
of the author which tells us the real meaning of almost
every movement he has his characters make, their every
look, word and even their clothes because in this peculiar
world people express themselves far more through elusive
signs, hints and all sorts of little ways than through
simple human speech, behaviour or the natural play of expression on the face. One must provide oneself with a
special key to understand their relationships one with the
other and one must be initiated into the secret meaning
of the hieroglyphs, with which they deceive each other, in
order to know their real thoughts and intentions. The
author belongs to the initiated. He knows their language
and uses it to discover the depths of the frivolity, insignificance, craftiness and sometimes the completely
crude, uncivilized and base pretensions, beneath all the
forms of social behaviour. One example is particularly
remarkable. The members of this circle seem to be ruled
by some unkind fate which condemns them to severe retribution - never to achieve any of their objectives, plans
or aspirations. As if hounded by some unknown evil force
they rush past the objectives they have set themselves
and if they reach something it is never what they expected. The only exceptions to this are their least significant and most ordinary plans and calculations: nothing
that is the slightest bit serious is allowed them. In
following the masterful depictions of the author it is
possible to think that there is some special Nemesis
specifically constructed for them which strikes them with
impotence half way through any enterprise and constantly
leaves them with powder and dust instead of the desired
benefits. They succeed in nothing and everything breaks
in their hands. Even the most normal human feelings and
thoughts either produce different fruits from those one
usually receives or in a short period of time result in
something approaching parody or self-caricature. The
young Pierre Bezukhov, who is capable of understanding
good and moral worth, marries a society beauty who is as
dissolute as she is stupid. Prince Bolkonsky, with all
the instincts of a serious mind and development, chooses
for a wife a nice little empty-headed society doll who
brings him only unhappiness, although he has no cause to
complain about her; his sister Princess Maria escapes from

the yoke of the despotic ways of her father and the continually lonely country life into a warm and bright religion which ends in her associating with itinerant priests
and so on. This sad story occurs so often to the best
people in the society being described that in the end, at
every scene which starts with young fresh life, at every
story of some happy event promising a serious or instructive outcome, the reader suffers from fear and doubt: no,
no, all their hopes will founder, they will betray their
substance and turn into the impenetrable sands of emptiness and vulgarity where they will perish. And the reader
is hardly ever mistaken; they all do turn and perish.
But, it is asked, what pitiless hand has laid this fate on
them all, and for what sins? What has happened?
Evidently nothing out of the ordinary. Society continues
calmly to live on the basis of serfdom as did its fore-
bears; the doors to the winning of fortune or to ruin in
civil or military service are as open as ever to those who
have the right to go through them; the State Loan Banks
are still operating for their benefit; and finally no new
figures crossing their path or confusing their thoughts
are to be seen in Count Tolstoy's novel. How is it then
that this society which at the end of the last century
still firmly believed in itself, its members as strong as
a castle and dealing with life light-heartedly, could now,
according to the author, do nothing it wanted to, col-
lapsed on all sides, almost despising itself and afflicted
with a feebleness which prevented its best people from
defining both themselves and any clear objectives for
spiritual activity? Remember that between 1796 (1) when
Tolstoy's novel begins and 1805 only nine years have
passed. How was it possible for such a marked change to
take place in such a short space of time? The thought
involuntarily occurs to the reader that Tolstoy has perhaps erred in one of two respects: either, left without
any reliable witness, he has seen some powerful new force
which appeared in Russian life and which managed unnoticed
in the course of ten or fifteen years to undermine the
faith of a society in the foundations on which it had
lived peacefully up to then; or that the picture of the
insolvency of this society in the first ten years of this
century, and especially its moral sufferings expressed
mainly through Prince Andrey Bolkonsky, are a little exaggerated and a little anachronistic. We think for our part
that the novel partly deserves this reproach not from just
one of these points but from them both.

[Discussion of Russian attitudes to Napoleon omitted.]

Of course there were also enthusiastic admirers of
Napoleon in this un-unified society even though they
adored their tsar, as everyone adored him, for his youth,
good looks, gentleness of heart and moderation in the use
of his rights. The author shows us such admirers of Napoleon, who place the foundation of their protest against
contemporary life in something similar to considerations
of a higher order, in Pierre Bezukhov and the young Prince
Andrey Bolkonsky. One could say of both of them, but
especially of Prince Bolkonsky, that by the nature of
their convictions they belong only nominally to that
society where fate has caused them to be born. The latter
especially - the real hero of Count Tolstoy's novel as far
as one can judge from the sketchy and unfinished portrait
of this character - seems to us to be of the same stamp
and leanings as young advisers with whom Alexander surrounded himself at the start of his reign. The same confidence in himself; the same boldness in his plans and
designs, constructed, without the help of experience, on
his own completely untested ideas; the same noble and
human attitude to the lower classes in society even though
he feels himself their superior; and finally the same contempt for Russian life which does not satisfy in any way
the political ideals which are paraded before his eyes.
Andrey Bolkonsky has not experienced the brilliant and
respectable life of those like himself; hence his dissatisfaction with life and the order of things which is connected with the griefs and disappointments of his own life
and understood as some obscure entity which he finds missing in the circles in which he lives. Every time he comes
out of these circles he carries the stamp and cast of mind
of an idle minister, an unrecognized but natural counsellor to the crown. In this apparently lies the tragic side
to his life, that he is not recognized, and when he speaks
with despair of the impossibility of any sort of state
service in Russia we already know that he considers serious work to be only that which is carried out in the very
highest positions in the country - no other work is serious.
    He is ambitious but languishes in being only a good,
stable, useful citizen. The author has selected him to be
the representative of that dissatisfaction which, in distinction from that ordinary blind and mercenary opposition
of the majority, is based on an understanding of the true
conditions of the political development of society. Here
we meet the slight exaggeration and the partial anachronism we have mentioned. Prince Andrey Bolkonsy introduces
into his criticism of current events and in his views
generally on his contemporaries ideas and concepts which

apply to our view of them. He has the gift of seeing into
the future without any difficulty; he has the ability to
stand above his times. He thinks and judges wisely not
with the wisdom of his own times but with that of another,
later period which the kind-hearted author has revealed to
him. He was able to rid himself of all the real but tedious and annoying characteristics of his contemporaries
about whom he speaks and among whom he lives. He cannot
be entranced by or come under the influence of any of the
remarkable figures of his times because he already knows
the biographical details and all the anecdotes about all
of them, which have been collected together only recently.
He also makes no mistakes except for those made by the
sources from which he drew his supernatural insights. We
need no further proof of his acquaintance with the books
and researches of the recent past than the fact that he is
ashamed of his work with the commission on the
re-codification of the laws where he happens to become the
head of a section. His fellow workers, to whom one can
deny neither knowledge nor intelligence, understood the
impossibility of simply applying the French code to
Russian conditions only after a series of unsuccessful
experiments, but Bolkonsky realized it at once. He surpasses them by the inspired insight of opinions being
expressed in historical literature *today*. In general,
judgments occur to him that would never have occurred to
his contemporaries at the time of Alexander; but Bolkonsky is a special contemporary, one to whom is known
what is discovered later. His thoughts are not those of
his contemporaries but those of our present day dilettan-
tes dealing with the new history of Russia and from them
he gets his scepticism, his cold and sober attitude to
the government measures and the phenomena which so
troubled and upset those poor people who had the misfortune to belong only to their own times. We even
think that the role of the social critic who has lost
faith in official innovations of whatever nature is in
itself an anachronism. It is well known that it was only
in 1815-16, after three years abroad fighting, that there
appeared in Russia a group of young men who found life in
Russia inexpressibly empty and idle compared with the
action which accompanied the movements of people before and
the social phenomena which had grown on European soil in
their wake. It was only then that real scepticism was
born in us with respect to the ability and goodwill of the
administration to respond to the needs and demands of
society. Up till then it is almost impossible to imagine
a man who would react with majestic indifference to such
facts and measures as the institution of the State

Council, the promise of public accountability in respect
of the state's financial affairs, the establishment of new
schools and universities, the laws allowing the peasantry
to become free farmers, the orders about the examinations
for attaining certain ranks, etc., etc. History has not
suggested the possibility of such a relationship between
government and society at that time; but Bolkonsky who
knows far later ideas, knew even that one which was comparatively closer to him and made use of it as he did all
the others. This is how we see, at the moment, the hero
of the novel in his role as a leading figure of his times;
but of his noble character, the depths of his psychological make-up and his melancholy role in life we shall speak
at another time.

Note

1 Date of the death of Catherine the Great. (Ed.)

25. PISAREV ON NIKOLAY ROSTOV

1868

'Fatherland Notes', 1868, no. 2. Pisarev's article, which
is written in more forthright style than, for example, his
earlier review of 'Three Deaths' (see No. 10), is entitled
The Old Landed Gentry and appeared after the publication
of the first three volumes of 'War and Peace'. It starts
off with a discussion of Boris Drubetskoy whom Pisarev
then compares with the young Rostov.

Nikolay Rostov is the complete antithesis of Boris.
Drubetskoy is careful, reserved and cautious, measures up
and weighs every decision and does everything to a prepared and carefully worked out plan. Rostov on the other
hand is headstrong and impulsive, he is neither capable of
nor disposed to thinking, he always acts without concern
for the consequences, always gives himself over completely
to whatever he is doing and even feels a certain contempt
for people who can counteract perceived impressions by re-
working them in their minds.

Without doubt Boris is more intelligent and has a
deeper character than Rostov. Rostov for his part is more
gifted, responsive and versatile. In Boris there is a far
greater capacity to observe attentively and to make sensible generalizations about surrounding phenomena. In
Rostov there is a predominance of the capacity to react
with his whole being to everything which demands (and even
to those things which have no right to demand) a response
from the heart. With the proper development of his talents Boris would make a good investigator while Rostov
with the same proper development of his would make in all
probability an exceptional artist, poet, musician or
painter.

The essential difference between these two young men is
apparent from the moment they step out into the world.
Boris, who has nothing to live on, manages to get himself
into a guards' regiment by dint of the bootlicking efforts
of his mother, and lives there, at others' expense, only
to be seen and to associate more frequently with people in
influential positions. Rostov, who gets ten thousand a
year from his father and could live in the guards on a par
with other officers, goes into the cavalry full of martial
and patriotic fervour in order to see action as quickly as
possible, to prance around on a spirited horse and to
amaze himself and others with deeds of daring horseman-
ship. Boris seeks for solid and tangible benefits. Rostov wants more than anything, and come what may, bustle,
glamour, strong sensations, effective scenes and bright
pictures. The image of the hussar as he speeds into the
attack, waving his sword, flashing his eyes, trampling on
the cringing enemy with the iron hooves of his indomit-
able steed, the image of the hussar as he feasts gaily and
noisily with his dashing comrades, surrounded by the
smoke of battle, the image of the hussar as he curls his
long moustache, rattles his spurs, glistens with the gold
lace of his jacket and sows alarm and confusion in the
hearts of beautiful young maidens, all these various
images combined into one confused, entrancing impression
settle the fate of the young and ardent Rostov and inspire
him to give up the university where he would doubtless
have found little to attract him anyway and plunge head-
long into the life of the hussars.

Boris enlists in his regiment calmly and coldbloodedly
and behaves himself properly at all times; but in the
regiment generally and among his fellow-officers in particular he establishes no deep or intimate relations.
Rostov literally throws himself into the embrace of the
Pavlograd Regiment of Hussars, takes to it as a new
family, immediately begins to value its honour as his own

and out of enthusiasm and love for that honour commits
some hasty acts, puts himself in an embarrassing position,
quarrels with the regimental commander, repents of his
foolishness before a council of senior officers and with
all his touchiness and youthful sensitivity to reproach
submissively listens to the comments of the friendly older
men who are teaching him some common sense and the basic
morality of the Pavlograd Regiment of Hussars. Boris
tries to leave the regiment as quickly as possible and
become an adjutant. Rostov considers being an adjutant a
kind of betrayal of his beloved Pavlograd Regiment. For
him it is the same as rejecting the woman you love and
marrying a rich young girl simply for her money. All
adjutants, all 'little boys on the staff' as he scornfully
calls them, are in his eyes soulless and unworthy re-
creants who sell their brothers in arms for a mess of
pottage. Influenced by his scorn and for no good reason
(and much to Boris's horror) he has an argument in Boris's
flat with Bolkonsky, who actually is an adjutant; the
argument is without serious consequence only thanks to
Bolkonsky's firmness and cool self-control....

With the servility of a little schoolboy Boris does not
stand up to anybody; he is always ready delicately and
politely to flatter anyone whom he imagines will be able
to be of any help to him; he is always ready to adapt himself and acquire and master any new skill which might
bring him success in society or advancement in his career;
but he is quite incapable of selfless and open-hearted
affection for anyone or anything; he can strive only for
advantage and never for an ideal; he can only envy and
imitate people who are ahead of him in his career or who
are leaving him far behind but he cannot revere them as
one might revere a beautiful and bright embodiment of an
ideal. With Rostov, on the other hand, ideals, idols and
authorities spring out of the ground like mushrooms at
every step. For him Denisov is an ideal, Dolokhov an idol
and Captain Kirsten an authority. To believe and love
blindly, passionately and boundlessly, to persecute with
the hate of a fanatic those who do not genuflect before
the idols he has raised - such is the undying need of his
passionate nature. This need is seen especially in his
enraptured gazing at his tsar.

[Quotations and commentary omitted.]

The excitement which grips Rostov when he sees the tsar
and draws near to him removes from him the ability to
think and consider his position. On the day of the battle
of Austerlitz when he is sent with a commission, which he

is not obliged, but at least has the right and even the
power, to give directly to the tsar, Rostov meets the tsar
at that very moment when the battle has been decisively
and irreversibly lost. Seeing the tsar, Rostov, as usual,
feels himself utterly happy partly because he is seeing
him and partly and more importantly because he can certify
with his own eyes the rumour that has been circulating
about the tsar's being wounded. Rostov knows that he can
and even must deal directly with the tsar and hand over to
him what he had been given. But the excitement which
surges over him removes the chance of making up his mind
in time.

[Quotation omitted.]

    Being unable to decide on what he wanted most of all in
the whole wide world Rostov rides off and at that very
minute sees that another officer has seen the tsar, rides
straight up to him, offers to be of service and helps him
across a ditch. From a distance Rostov with envy and
regret sees this officer talk long and heatedly with the
tsar and the tsar shaking the officer by the hand. Then
when the opportunity has passed Rostov imagines another
thousand new reasons why it would have been pleasant,
polite and even necessary to ride up to the tsar. He
thinks to himself that he, Rostov, could have been in that
officer's place, that the tsar might have shaken his hand,
that his own shameful weakness had prevented him and that
he had lost his only chance of expressing to the tsar his
undying devotion. He turns his horse and gallops to the
place where the tsar had been - but there is no one there.
He leaves in utter despair and in this despair, however
subtly and closely we may analyse it, there is nothing
approaching a thought of the influence which a conversation with the tsar could have had on the future course of
his career. It is the simple and disinterested despair of
a young man in love, in which expressions of respectable
passion have been seething inside and have long remained
unsaid because of his own bashfulness.
    Rostov himself is not capable of analysing his own
feeling; he cannot ask himself the question: 'Why do I
experience this feeling?' He cannot because in the first
place he is unaccustomed to enter into psychological examinations and give himself a more or less clear account
of his feelings, and in the second because in the question
itself he quite justifiably feels the dangerous embryo of
some demoralizing doubt. To ask why this or that feeling
is experienced means to think about the causes and foundations on which the feeling is based, to measure, weigh

and evaluate these causes and foundations and then to
submit to the verdict which, after mature reflection, will
be pronounced over them by the voice of one's own reason.
He who asks himself 'Why?' must evidently feel the necessity of pointing out for his passions certain boundaries
at which they must stop in order not to harm the interests
of the whole. He who asks himself 'Why?' must already
recognize the existence of those interests which for him
are more important and more dear than his feeling and in
whose name and from whose point of view an account of its
provenance is demanded from this feeling. He who asks
'Why?' already has the ability to a certain extent to renounce his feeling and to look at it from the side like a
phenomenon from the outside world; between feelings which
are not submitted to this operation and those which we
even for a moment look at from aside with the eye of the
trained observer there exists a tremendous difference....
But Rostov never asks himself 'Why?' He neither knows why
nor wishes to know. He understands instinctively that the
whole force of his feelings lies in their complete spontaneity and that this spontaneity is sustained by his continual readiness to see an insult to the object of his
worship (or whatever might be connected with it) in any
attempt by himself or others to react to it in any calm
or unemotional way. 'I'. said St Louis, 'shall never for
any reason argue with the heretic; I shall simply go up
to him and cut open his stomach with my sword.' This is
exactly how Rostov thinks and feels. He is extremely
prickly about everything which in any way is removed from
a tone of enraptured reverence.

[Quotation of Denisov's joking about his love for the
tsar omitted.]

It is impossible to suspect Denisov of being a Jacobin.
He is in this respect above all doubt and Rostov knows it
but with his prickly nature he cannot refrain from an
outburst when Denisov allows himself a kind-hearted,
friendly joke. In this joke Rostov senses the ability,
albiet for a brief moment, to react quietly and coldbloodedly to the object of his enraptured adoration. This
is quite sufficient to call forth on his part an outburst
of disapproval. Replace the dashing Pavlograd hussar
and good friend Denisov with some stranger and replace the
kind-hearted friendly words with others expressing real
doubt and you will get as the obvious result not the outburst from Rostov but some serious and violent reaction
recalling the programme suggested by St Louis.
Two years pass. The second campaign against Napoleon

ends with the defeat of our troops at Friedland and the
meeting of the two emperors at Tilsit. The many events he
has seen take place, both political and otherwise, the
mass of perceived impressions, both strong and weak, all
provide Rostov with some troubling mental labour which is
beyond his strength and which arouse in him a swarm of
serious doubts with which he cannot cope.

Joining his regiment in the spring of 1807 Rostov finds
himself in the position where the horses, disgracefully
thin, are eating the thatch from the houses and the people
who have received no provisions are filling their stomachs
with the sweet roots of some plant similar to asparagus
and of which their hands, legs and faces smell. In its
battles with the enemy the Pavlograd Regiment has lost
only two wounded, but hunger and disease has taken almost
half of them. If a soldier was taken to hospital then
death was certain, and the troops, sick from fever and
swollen limbs, carried on and dragged themselves to the
front simply to avoid being taken to hospital and to a
certain and painful death.

Among the officers there is the certain conviction that
these evils are caused by the colossal incompetence of the
quartermasters; and this conviction is supported by the
fact that all the provisions that do arrive are of the
lowest quality. The awful, repulsive condition of the
hospitals and the disorder in the provisions' supply
cannot be explained by any natural disasters independent
of human will.

[Discussion of Denisov's raid on the provisions' transport omitted.]

At Tilsit, Rostov sees happy faces, sparkling uniforms,
gleaming smiles, and bright scenes of peace, surplus and
luxury - the sharpest possible contrast to everything that
he has seen his own Pavolgrad Regiment suffering both on
the battlefield and in the hospital where Denisov lay
injured.

This contrast confuses him, causes a whirlwind of un-
invited thoughts in his head and arouses clouds of un-
precedented doubts in his soul. Boris immediately and
without the slightest difficulty recognized General Bonaparte as the Emperor Napoleon and a great man, and even
tried to arrange things in such a way that his prepared-
ness and diligence in this matter was noticed by the commanders and regarded as something worthy. Boris just as
easily and with the same pleasant smile would have recognized the convicted thief Telyanin as the most honourable
of men and the greatest of patriots if in so doing it

would have pleased the commanders. Without a doubt Boris
would not have allowed himself the dastardly attack on his
own Russian transports in order to obtain dinner and
supper for the starving soldiers in his company. Boris
would, of course, not have attacked so violently the
person of a Russian civil servant however much the past of
this civil servant was filled with ambiguous actions. It
goes without saying that Boris would have more willingly
stretched out his hand to Telyanin whom the commanders
thought an honest citizen than to Denisov whom the court
martial was forced to punish as a thief and brawler.

If Rostov were capable of adopting the shameless and
undaunted flexibility of Boris, if he could once and for
all push to one side his wish to love that which he served
and start serving that which he loved then of course all
the glitter of the scenes at Tilsit would have made the
most pleasant impression upon him, the hospital miasma
would have only forced him to hold his nose even tighter,
and the Denisov affair would have led him to honourable
thoughts about how harmful it was to a man not to know
how to control his passions. He would not have become
confused by contrasts and contradictions; satisfied with
the truth that what exists exists and that for the
successful persuance of a career one needs to study the
demands of reality and adapt oneself to them, he would not
have persistently wished that life was well organized,
sensible and beautiful.

But Rostov does not see and does not understand for
what great services General Bonaparte was promoted to
Emperor Napoleon; he does not see and he does not understand why he, Rostov, must today be polite to those
French with whom yesterday he clashed swords; why Denisov
for his love for his men whom he was obliged to protect
and cherish, and for his hatred for thieves whom no one
ordered him to love, should have to be shot or at best
reduced to the ranks; why people after bravely fighting
and honourably carrying out their duty should die slow
deaths under the supervision of medical attendants and
army doctors in a leper hospital where it was even dangerous for a healthy man to enter; why scoundrels like the
dismissed officer Telyanin should have a big and active
influence on the fate of the Russian army.

In Rostov's place an experienced man would have found
refuge in the thought that absolute perfection is unattainable, that human powers are not limitless and that mistakes and inner contradictions are the inevitable accom-
paniment of all human actions. But experience is bought
at the price of disappointment and the first disappointment, the first cruel collision of brilliant boyhood

illusions with the dirty and unpleasant facts of real
life, usually marks the decisive turning-point in the
history of the man who experiences it.

After this initial collision the complete faith of
childhood in the simple, inevitable and lasting triumph
of good and truth, the faith flowing from an ignorance of
evil and lies, is destroyed; man sees himself among
dangerous ruins; he tries to cling to the fragments of
that building in which he had hoped safely to pass the
rest of his life; he seeks in the pile of shattered illusions for something firm and stable; out of the surviving
fragments he attempts to build himself a new building,
more modest but then more solid than the first one; this
attempt ends in failure and leads to further disillusion.
The ruins collapse on their own component parts; the fragments shatter into little pieces and turn into thick dust
in the hands of the man sincerely trying to hold them
together. Passing from disillusion to disillusion the
man comes finally to the conviction that all his thoughts
and feelings, whose birth he is unaware of and which grow
as he grew, need the most careful and thorough examination. This conviction becomes the starting-point of that
process of development which can bring a man to a more or
less clear and intelligible understanding of the world
around him.

Not everyone is able manfully to bear the first disillusionment. One of these is Rostov himself. Instead of
looking at the facts which have destroyed his youthful
illusions he screws up his eyes with cowardly obstinacy
and faint-hearted bitterness and chases his thoughts away
as soon as they begin to take on too unaccustomed a form.
Rostov not only shuts his own eyes but also with a fana-
tical zeal tries to shut those of others too.

Having suffered failure in the Denisov affair and seen
too much of the general glitter of Tilsit which had been
thrust upon him, Rostov chooses the better part which
never deserts the poor in spirit or the rich in ready
money. He drowns his doubts in a couple of bottles of
wine and taking his hussar's spirit to appropriate limits
begins to shout at two officers who are expressing their
dissatisfaction at the Peace of Tilsit.

[Quotation omitted.]

In due course the two bottles he drank reward the young
Count Rostov with an efficient medicine against all disillusion and doubt and every conceivable painful inner
collapse and breakdown. Whoever was lucky enough in his
first mental torments to discover the formula 'It is not

for us to think', and found consolation in it even for a
minute, even with the assistance of a couple of bottles of
wine, will in all probability always run to the protection
of this formula as soon as unpleasant doubts start to disturb him and the alarming call to independent action begins to overtake him. 'It is not for us to think' is such
an unassailable position that it cannot be destroyed by
any evidence coming from experience and before which all
proof remains powerless. Freedom of thought has nowhere
to berth and has no possibility of tying up at a bank
where such a stronghold is built. The formula will cut it
loose at its first appearance. As soon as a man senses
the need to weigh and compare his perceptions, as soon as
he notices in himself the intention of thinking and
generalizing involuntarily about the facts he has gathered, he will immediately, using his formula and recalling
that wonderful peace of mind which it brought him, say to
himself that it is a sin, a diabolical delusion, an illness, and will cure himself with wine, shouting, gipsies,
hunting and generally that multifarious shift of strong
sensations with which a strongly-built and substantial
Russian nobleman can provide himself.

If you should think of proving to such a firmly established man that his formula is senseless then your evidence is wasted. In this respect too the formula shows
itself indestructible. The most valuable of its qualities
lies precisely in the fact that it needs no reasoned foundations and even excludes the possibility of them. Indeed, in order to prove the sense or nonsense of the formula, to attack or defend it, one must believe that because 'it is not for us to think' any proof in itself
independent of the objectives it may have must be recognized as superfluous and reprehensible.

Rostov remains constantly true to the rule he discovered in the bar at Tilsit under the influence of the
bottles of wine. Doubts never again destroy his spiritual
calm. He knows and only wants to know his service life
and noble recreations, suitable for a rich landowner and
dashing hussar. His mind refuses any activity, even the
activity necessary to save his family estates from the
swindling machinations of the little-educated bailiff,
Mitinka.

With the greatest force he shouts at Mitinka and very
skilfully pushes him in the backside with his leg and
knee, but after this turbulent scene Mitinka still remains
the all-powerful overseer of the whole estate and things
continue just as they did before.

Incapable of putting his financial affairs in order or
of dismissing the domestic thief, Rostov is even less

capable of giving his life over to any activity demanding
any complicated and concerted mental effort (and does not
even wish to). Books evidently do not exist for him.
Reading apparently occupies no place in his life, not even
as a way of killing time. Even fashionable society in
Moscow presents itself to him as too confused and complicated, too full of difficult conventions and senseless
subtleties. He is fully satisfied only by life in the
regiment where all is defined and orderly, where all is
clear and simple, where there is no need to think decisively about anything and where there is no place for hesitation or freedom of choice. He likes regimental life and
a quiet life precisely because they are quite unbearable
to a man who has any capacity at all for independent
thought; he likes it for its calm lack of activity, its
unruffled routine, its sleepy monotony, and the fetters it
lays on all manifestations of personal initiative and
originality.

On such a superficial observer Rostov in all probability makes a charming impression; he likes Rostov just as
no doubt many readers like him and even, perhaps, just as
the author does himself. It will never occur to the
superficial observer that Rostov lacks precisely that in
which the most essential and deeply touching charm of
healthy and fresh youth lies.

Because the world of thought is closed to Rostov, in
the twentieth year of his life he appears fully developed.
By twenty all that life has to offer has been exhausted;
all that is left for him is first to grow coarse and stupid
and then to become decrepit and rot away. This lack of a
future, this fatal sterility and inevitable fading, are
hidden from the eyes of the superficial observer by the
appearance of freshness, strength and responsiveness.
Looking at Rostov the superficial observer will say with
satisfaction: How much fire and energy there is in this
young man! How courageously and cheerfully he looks at
life! How much unspoiled and unspent youth there is in
him!

On such a superficial observer Rostov in all probability makes a charming impression; he likes Rostov just as
no doubt many readers like him and even, perhaps, just as
the author does himself. It will never occur to the
superficial observer that Rostov lacks precisely that in
which the most essential and deeply touching charm of
healthy and fresh youth lies.

When we look at a strong and young being we are delighted to see the joyful hope, to see that his powers are
growing, developing, being put to some use, taking an
active part in life's great struggle, increasing albeit
slightly the sum of human happiness existing on the earth
and destroying albeit only fractionally the piles of nonsense, disorder and suffering. We still do not know the
bounds for the development of such powers and this ignorance forms in our eyes the greatest fascination of a
young being. 'Who knows,' we think, 'perhaps something
extremely great is developing here before us, something

pure, bright, powerful and indestructible.' A young
being, full of life and energy, presents to us an extremely
interesting puzzle and this puzzlement gives it a special
attraction.

It is precisely this puzzling fascination which Rostov
lacks and only the superficial observer on looking at him
can possibly retain some vague hope that his unspent force
will concentrate on something good and be used on something
useful. Only the superficial observer in envying his
vitality and passion can push to one side the question of
whether this vitality and passion will be put to good use.

The superficial observer capable of being attracted by
Rostov's youthful ardour, for example during the hunt when
he prays to God that the wolf will appear before him; when
he says, almost beside himself with excitement, 'What will
it cost you to do this for me? I know that you are great
and that it is a sin to ask you for this; but for Heaven's
sake let a grown wolf appear and may Karay in the sight of
the old man who is looking from over there latch on to him
in a fatal grip round his throat'; when he goes from a
boundless joy to a dismal disappointment during the hunt,
with a wild lament calls to his old dog Karay and finally
feels himself happy seeing the wolf being surrounded and
torn apart by the dogs.

Whoever pauses on the cheerful exterior of what is described, the vivid and lively scene of the hunt, will experience the most melancholy of thoughts. If such a
trifle, such tawdry rubbish as the fight of a wolf with
several dogs can provide a man with a full complement of
strong sensations - from frenzies of despair to ecstatic
delight with all the intervening semi-tones and modula-
tions - then why should such a man concern himself with
deepening or broadening his experience of life? Why should
he seek work to do? Why should he find interests in the
vast and stormy seas of social life? Why, when the
stables, kennels and the nearby forest will more than
satisfy all the demands of his nervous system?

26. TOLSTOY DEFENDS 'WAR AND PEACE'

1868

Article entitled A Few Words about the Book 'War and

Peace', 'Russian Archive', 1868, no. 3.   (See Introduction.)

In publishing a work on which I have spent five years of
uninterrupted and exclusive labour in the best conditions
possible, I wanted in the foreword to set out my idea of
what it is and thus avert those misunderstandings which
might arise in readers. I wanted the reader neither to
see nor to seek in it what I did not wish to or could not
express but to turn his attention to what I wanted to say,
but because of the conditions of writing I did not think
it convenient to do so. I had neither the time nor the
ability fully to do what I intended and I am using the
hospitality of this journal to set out albeit incompletely
and briefly my ideas on the work for those readers who
might be interested.

 1 What is 'War and Peace'? It is not a novel, nor is
it a poem, still less an historical chronicle. 'War and
Peace' is what the author wanted and could express in the
form in which it was expressed. Such a declaration of
disregard by the author for the conventional forms of
prose fiction might have seemed over-confident had it not
been deliberate and had there not been precedents. The
history of Russian literature since Pushkin not only provides many examples of such a departure from European
forms but also gives no example of the opposite. In the
modern period of Russian literature from Gogol's 'Dead
Souls' to Dostoevsky's 'House of the Dead' there is not a
single prose work of fiction which rises even a little
above the ordinary which falls completely into the form
of the novel, poem or short story.

 2 The character of the times, as several readers
pointed out to me when the first part of the work appeared, is insufficiently defined. In answer to this reproach I would say I know which characteristics of the
time did not enter my novel - the horrors of serfdom, the
immolation of wives, the flogging of adult sons, Salty-
chikha and so on. These characteristics which live on in
our memories I did not think correct and did not wish to
write about them. When I studied the letters, diaries and
legends I did not find these horrors in any greater number
than I do today or at any other period. In those times
people loved, envied, sought the truth and virtue and got
carried away by the passions; there was the same complex
moral and intellectual life in the upper class, if not even
more refined than today. If we have formed the opinion
that they were times of violence and brutality it is only

because all the legends, memoirs, stories and novels that
we have contain the most obvious occurrences of violence
and brutality. To conclude from this that the predominant
characteristic of the times was therefore brutality is as
sensible as a man who looks down from a hill and sees the
tops of trees concluding that there is nothing there
except trees. There is a character to that time (just as
there is a character to any age) which comes from the
greater alienation of the upper class from all the other
sections of the community, from the rule of philosophy,
from a particular upbringing, from the custom of using
French and so on. It was this character that I wished as
far as I could to express.

3 The use of French in a Russian work. Why in my work
do both the French and the Russians talk partly in French
and partly in Russian? The reproach that the characters
speak and write in French in a Russian book is like that
which a man makes when he looks at a picture and notices
in it black spots (shadows) which are not there in reality.
The painter is not to blame if the shadow he has put on the
face of the picture looks like a black spot, but only if he
has painted it inaccurately or roughly. When I was studying the beginning of this century and depicting the Russian characters of a certain class and Napoleon and the
French who played such a direct part in the life of the
times, I was involuntarily carried away by the form of
expression of that French style of thought more than was
necessary. Therefore, without denying that the shadows I
painted were probably inaccurate and rough, I would wish
only that those to whom it seems funny that Napoleon should
speak now in French and now in Russian should realize that
it seems funny to them only because they are like a man
looking at a portrait and seeing not the face with its
light and shadows but a black spot under the nose.

4 The names of my characters, Bolkonsky, Drubetskoy,
Bilibin, Kuragin and others remind one of certain Russian
names. In confronting the non-historical characters with
the other historical ones I found it awkward on the ear to
make Count Rostopchin talk to Prince Bronsky or Strelsky
or to any other princes or counts with invented double or
single surnames. Bolkonsky or Drubetskoy, although they
are not Volkonsky or Trubetskoy, sound familiar and natural in Russian aristocratic circles. I could not invent
names for all the characters which would not have sounded
false to the ear, like Bezukhov or Rostov, and could not
get round this difficulty other than by taking at random
those names which sound most familiar to a Russian ear and
then changing one or two letters. I am very sorry if the
nearness of the invented names to real ones has made anyone

think that I wished to describe this or that real person, especially because the literary activity which concerns itself with writing about real people, living or dead, is not what I was engaged in.

M.D. Akhrosimova and Denisov are the only two characters to whom I involuntarily and unthinkingly gave names closely approaching two very characteristic and charming real people of the society of the time. This was my mistake and it came from the particular personalities of those two people but my mistake in this respect is limited only to their introduction and the readers will probably agree that nothing similar to reality happened to my two characters. All the other characters are completely invented and do not have even for me any prototypes in tradition or reality.

5 The difference between my description of historical events and that of historians. It is not accidental but unavoidable. The historian and the artist when they describe an historical epoch have two completely different subjects. As the historian will be wrong if he tries to represent the historical figure in all his entirety, in all the complexity of his relations to all sides of life, so will the artist not do his job if he represents a person in his full historical significance. Kutuzov did not always ride a white horse while looking at the enemy through a telescope. Rostopchin did not always go about with a torch setting fire to the Voronovsky house (he never even did that), and Empress Maria Fyodorovna did not always stand dressed in an ermine cloak leaning with one hand on the code of laws; but this is how the popular imagination sees them.

For the historian there are heroes in the sense of people who help attain some purpose, but for the artist there cannot and must not be heroes but people in the sense of their correspondence with all sides of life.

The historian is sometimes obliged to bend the truth by fitting all the actions of the historical figure into the one idea to which he has given the figure. The artist on the other hand sees an incompatibility with his task in the very individuality of this idea and tries only to understand and show not a certain figure, but a man.

In the description of the events themselves the difference is even clearer and more important. The historian deals with the results of the event, the artist with the facts of it. In describing a battle, the historian says: 'The left flank of such and such an army was moved against such and such a village, defeated the enemy but was forced to retreat; then the cavalry was sent into the attack and overran...' and so on. The historian cannot speak

otherwise. And yet these words have no sense for the
artist and do not even touch upon the event itself. The
artist draws his own idea of the way the event happened
either from his own experience or from letters, memoirs
and stories, and very often (as in the case of a battle)
the conclusion about the actions of such and such armies
which the historian allows himself to draw turn out to be
the very opposite of the conclusion drawn by the artist.
The difference between the results obtained is explained
also by the sources from which they derive their information. For the historian (we continue the example of the
battle) the main source lies in the reports of the private
commanders and the commander-in-chief. The artist can
derive nothing from such sources, they tell him nothing,
nor do they explain anything. What is more the artist
turns away from them, seeing in them a necessary lie.
There is also the fact that the opposing forces in every
battle almost always describe the events in totally different ways. In every description of a battle there is
the necessity of lying stemming from the demand to describe in a few words the actions of thousands of people
spread out over several miles and acting under the strongest moral incitement influenced by fear, shame and death.

In the descriptions of battles it is usually written
that such and such troops were ordered to attack such and
such a position and then commanded to withdraw and so on
as if proposing that the discipline which subjugates
tens of thousands to the will of one man on the parade-
ground will have the same effect when it is a matter of
life or death. Everyone who has been to war knows how
untrue that is; and yet the reports are based on this proposition and consequently the military descriptions.
(After the first part of my book was published with its
description of the battle of Schöngraben I was told of
what Nikolay Nikolaevich Muravyov-Karsky had said about
my description of the battle and this confirmed me in my
convictions. N.N. Muravyov-Karsky, the commander-in-
chief, declared that he had never read a more accurate
description of a battle and that from his own experience
he was convinced that it was impossible to carry out the
orders of the commander-in-chief during a battle.)

Go round all the troops immediately after the battle,
even on the following day, or the day after that, before
the reports are written, and ask every soldier and every
officer of whatever rank how the battle went and you will
be told what all these people experienced and what they
saw and you will form a majestic, complex, infinitely
varied, heavy and indistinct impression, and from none of
them, least of all from the commander-in-chief, will you

find out how the battle went. But in two or three days
they begin to bring in reports, the chatterers begin to
tell how what they did not see actually happened, and
finally the general report is put together and from this
report the general opinion of the army is formed. It is
a relief for everyone to exchange his doubts and questions
for this lying but ever clear and flattering representation. Question a man who took part in the battle a month
or two later and you will not feel in his story the vivid
raw material which was there before and he will answer you
according to the reports. Thus was I told about the battle
of Borodino by many active and intelligent participants in
that affair. They told me one and the same thing and all
in accordance with the incorrect description by
Mikhaylovsky-Danilevsky, or by Glinka or others; even the
details which they told me, even though the narrators were
several miles away from one another, were exactly the same.

After the loss of Sebastopol the commander of the artillery, Kryzhanovsky, sent me the reports of the artillery
commanders of all the bastions and asked me to make a
general report from them - there were more than twenty of
them. I regret that I did not copy out these reports.
They are the best example of that naive, necessary military lie from which reports are composed. I suppose that
many of those friends of mine who wrote those reports will
laugh as they read these lines at the memory of how they
on the orders of the commanders wrote that they could not
have known. All those who have experienced war know how
capably Russians carry out their duties in war and how
incapable they are of describing it with the necessary
boastful lie. Everyone knows that the duty of writing
reports in our armies is carried out in the main by non-
Russians.

I say all this in order to show the inevitability of the
lie in military descriptions which serve as material for
military historians and therefore to show the inevitability
of frequent disagreements between the artist and the historian in their understanding of historical events. But
besides the inevitability of a lack of truth in the exposition of historical events in the historians of the period
I was studying I came across (probably as a result of the
habit of grouping events, of expressing them briefly and
being aware of the tragic tone of the events) that special
stamp of bombastic phrasing in which the lie and the distortion often pass not only to the events but to the
understanding of them. In studying the two main historical
works of the period, Thiers and Mikhaylovsky-Danilevsky,
I was often perplexed at how these books could have been
printed or read. Forgetting the fact that these historians

were describing the same events in a serious and significant tone with reference to the material, and yet were
diametrically opposed to each other, I came across descriptions at which one does not know whether to laugh or
cry when one remembers that both these books are the only
ones from the period and have millions of readers. I shall
give but one example from the book by the famous historian
Thiers. Having described how Napoleon brought false bank-
notes with him, he says:

> Relevant l'emploi de ces moyens par un acte de bein-
> faisance digne de lui et de l'armée française, il fit
> distribuer des secours aux incendiés. Mais les vivres
> étant trop précieux pour être donnés longtemps à des
> étrangers, la plupart ennemis, Napoléon aima mieux
> leur fournier de l'argent et il leur fit distribuer des
> roubles papier.

(Regarding the use of these means as an act of charity
worthy of him and the French army, he ordered their
distribution to those who had been burnt out. But as
the provisions were too precious to be given for long
to strangers who were for the most part hostile, Napoleon preferred to give them money and so paper roubles
were distributed among them.)

By itself this passage is striking in its stunning, I
shall not say immorality, but simply stupidity; but in the
book as a whole it is not striking at all because it fully
corresponds with the general bombastic tone of the work
and has no direct sense.

Thus the tasks of the artist and the historian are
completely at variance and the disagreements with the historian in the description of events and characters in my
book should not strike the reader. But the artist must not
forget that the representation of historical figures and
events formed among the people is based not on fantasy but
on historical documents so far as the historians have been
able to group them, and consequently the artist, although
he understands and represents these events and figures differently, must none the less be guided by the historical
materials.

Wherever historical figures speak and act in my novel I
have not invented anything but have made use of materials
which during the course of my work have grown into a
veritable library, the books which I see no need to name
here but to which I can always refer.

6 Finally the sixth and for me most important consideration concerns the small significance which in my view is

to be given to the so-called great men in history.

When I was studying this period, so tragic, so rich in the grandeur of its events, so near to us and about which there are so many varied traditions, I arrived at the obvious fact that the causes of the historical events are not accessible to our minds.

To state (which seems to everyone very simple) that the causes of the events of 1812 consist in Napoleon's spirit of conquest and Tsar Alexander's patriotic firmness is as silly as saying that the causes of the fall of the Roman empire were that such and such a barbarian led his people into the west and such and such a Roman emperor directed the affairs of state badly, or that an immense hill which is being removed finally fell because the last labourer struck it with his spade. An event where millions of people kill each other (and in all half a million were killed) cannot have as its cause the will of one man; just as one man could not have undermined the hill, so one man could not have caused the deaths of five hundred thousand. But what are the causes? Some historians say it was the spirit of conquest in the French and Russia's patriotism, others talk of the democratic element which Napoleon's hosts spread abroad and of the necessity for Russia to form an alliance with Europe, etc. But how did millions of people start killing each other? Who ordered them to? It is clear to everyone that from this event no one is going to be better off and everyone will be the worse for it; so why, then, did they do it? It is possible to draw (and indeed people do) an endless number of conclusions in retrospect about the causes of this senseless event; but the vast number of these explanations and their coincidence with a single purpose only goes to show that the number of explanations is vast and no one of them can be called the cause. Why did millions of people kill each other when it has been known since the creation of the world that it is physically and morally wrong? Because it was inevitably necessary and in so doing people were obeying that elemental zoological law which the bees obey when they destroy each other in the autumn and when male animals kill each other. There is no other answer one may give to this terrible question. This truth is not only obvious but is so innate in man that it would not be worth proving except for the fact there is another feeling, another consciousness, in man which convinces him that he is free every time he carries out some action.

When we look at history from a general viewpoint we are indubitably convinced of the eternal law which governs how events take place; but when we look at it from a personal viewpoint we are convinced of the opposite. A man who kills another, Napoleon who gives the order to cross the Niemen, you and I handing in a petition about going into government service, raising and dropping our arms, are all absolutely convinced that our every act has at its base rational causes and free will and that it depended on us whether we acted in one way or another, and this conviction is so innate in us and so valued by all of us that despite all the arguments of history and the statistics of crimes (which convince us of the lack of free will in the actions of others) we extend the consciousness of our freedom to all our actions.

The contradiction seems insoluble. In doing something, I am convinced that I do it according to my will; but if I look at it in the sense of its participation in the general life of humanity (in its historical significance) then I am convinced that what I have done was predetermined and inevitable. Where is the error? The psychological observations about a man's capability retrospectively to fabricate on the spur of the moment a whole series of imaginary free rationalizations (I intend to expound this in greater detail at another time) confirms the supposition that man's consciousness of freedom in the performance of a certain kind of action is erroneous. But the same psychological observations prove that there is another kind of action in which the consciousness of freedom is not retrospective but instantaneous and unquestionable. Whatever the materialist may say, I can unquestionably by the use of my will alone and without outside interference transport myself in my imagination to America or to any mathematical problem. I can, testing my freedom, raise and forcibly drop my hand through the air. I have just done it. But near me stands a child and I raise my hand above him and want to drop it on the child with the same force. I just cannot do it. A dog makes for the child and I cannot but raise my arm against the dog. I am standing at the battle-front and I cannot but follow the movements of the regiment. In a battle I cannot but move into the attack with my regiment or flee when all around me are fleeing. When I stand in a court in the defence of the defendant I cannot stop speaking or knowing what I am going to say. I cannot help blinking when a blow is directed against my eye.

Thus there are two kinds of act. Some are dependent and others independent of my will. And the error causing the contradiction comes only from the fact that consciousness of freedom (legitimately accompanying everything referring to my ego, up to the highest abstractions of my existence) is transferred to my actions which are performed in conjunction with other men and depend on the conjunction of the wills of others with my own. It is extremely difficult to determine the boundary between freedom and dependence and the determination of this boundary is the essential and only task for psychology; but observing the manifestations of our greatest freedom and our greatest dependence it is impossible not to see that the more abstract and consequently less connected with the actions of other people are our own actions, the more they are free; and conversely the more our actions are connected with other people, the less they are free.

The strongest, most indissoluble, serious and constant connection with other people is the so-called power over others which in its true meaning is but the greatest dependence upon others.

Whether this is erroneous or not I became fully convinced of it during the course of my work and in describing the events of 1805, 1807 and especially those of 1812 in which this law of predetermination is most clearly present.(1)   I naturally could not ascribe any significance to those people who thought they were directing the events but who less than all the other participants in the events introduced into them free human activity.   The activity of these people was interesting to me only in the sense of an illustration of that law of predetermination which I am convinced guides history and of that psychological law which forces man in performing the least free action to fabricate mentally a whole series of retrospective rationalizations whose only purpose is to prove to him his own freedom.

Note

1   It is worthy of note that almost everyone who has written about 1812 has seen in it something special and fateful. [Tolstoy's note.]

27. UNSIGNED REVIEW, 'AFFAIR'

1868, no. 4

Before the publication of the last volume of Count Tolstoy's novel we do not propose to look in detail at either the essence of the main idea behind it (if indeed such an idea exists) or at the personalities of its characters.

We can only acquaint the reader relatively with the first
impressions which we have of the first four volumes and of
those possibly exceptional parts which can in some small
way characterize the virtues and the shortcomings of this
war story.

The dramatic period chosen for the novel, the inner
life of society, the salons of Moscow and Petersburg, the
campaigns and battles of the Russian army, Austerlitz, the
meeting of Napoleon and Alexander, the masonic lodges and
finally all the leading figures of the time, including
Arakcheev and Speransky, will all interest the reader as
history presented not in any dogmatic form but in a series
of pictures and vivid characters. These pictures and
characters are not united by any controlling idea or anything which would give an inner life or a logic to the
events: everything is mixed up into a general mass where
one can see neither the reasons for nor the consequences
of the events or the appearance of heroes or facts. As in
an ancient tragedy where fate directed the will and mind
of the characters so Count Tolstoy's novel has its own
fate and its own predestination which treats events and
people as puppets.

The first two volumes are predominantly concerned with
pictures of fighting, life during the campaign and only
half way through the third volume does his novel (if 'War
and Peace' is a novel and then if it is but one novel and
not two or three joined together) stand on purely fictional soil and enter the everyday framework of the novel
where the characters are drawn more sharply and fully, the
plot is developed and the historical element withdraws
into the background and becomes the threshold, the necessary beginning or first word of some idea, some objective
which he intends to implement but which it must be said is
nowhere expressed nor is even one word said about it; this
undefined secrecy of thought awakes the interest of the
reader and causes the most lively discussion. Some think
the author wishes to take his novel up to the twenties and
show the origins of those thinking people who were created
by our intercourse with Europe; others suggest he will
only show the impossibility of conceiving of the appearance or existence of any new ideas whatsoever among the
landowning classes, will show the sores and the evil which
locked them away and cut them off for centuries from anything alive and fresh; several dwell on the details and
ask themselves: how will the author resolve the fate of
his heroes? What will happen at the end to Prince Bolkonsky, Count Bezukhov, Natasha and Princess Drubetskoy?
Whom will he choose for some future intelligent action?
How will the plot develop? Will one of the characters be

chosen to carry the affair on or will the author introduce
yet newer and fresher ones? Will the novel finally end
with just their appearance? And so on. These are the
sort of questions and ideas which are being expressed by
those readers seeking above all in the novel its main
central purpose and not wanting at all to get from it only
an historical story or something like Danilevsky's '1812'
or an artistic collection of anecdotes characterizing the
lives of our landowners.

   However, in speaking of the first impression which the
novel has made on us we see it no more than in an interesting condition, on the point of giving birth to something but not actually having given birth or in the process
of so doing. The historical side of the novel in its descriptive form is not connected with anything and just
presents a number of lively pictures; the other side of the
novel, the intrigues, ambition, dissipation and debauchery,
in short all those aspects of our upper classes that we
have known for a long time, are also presented by the
author with great insight and extremely clearly.

   These intrigues of ambitious courtiers which are described during the description of the battle of Austerlitz
in whose honour thousands of people are thrown into battle
lead the reader as it were towards an idea and make a
serious impression upon him. The picture of the battle at
Austerlitz after the salon games, the description of the
carefree, idle and dissolute life of the Moscow and
Petersburg drawing-rooms somehow stops the reader in his
tracks, stunned by the horrors of the ragged, hungry
crowd of soldiers hounded in their thousands like a flock
of sheep from place to place, and then to the description
of the hospital where at the very entrance the doctor explains to Rostov that it is a leper hospital and whoever
enters will die, and then to another picture of the meeting at Tilsit, the festivities and illuminations, the
eating and the drinking, the serene, solemn faces of the
over-dressed chamberlains, all after you have collected
yourselves after the impression of the leper hospital, all
is artistically described.

[Quotation omitted.]

   But all these scenes and many others contrasted with
them, it must be said, are no more than true to the reality
of the subject they describe, but we can see in them no
unity, nothing definite which would tell us a little of
the novel's idea or objectives. The first three volumes
give us only material, a series of well-described scenes,
a series of different motifs - but nothing else. We

notice that several of the scenes and characters, as for
example the portraits of Alexander and Speransky, are
painted as it were in passing, briefly, so that several
points in Speransky's portrait are indefinite and unclear,
and furthermore with the historical side of the novel in
mind two such contrasting and strong personalities as
Speransky and Arakcheev side by side with Alexander surely
should have caught the author's attention. But perhaps all
this is premature and perhaps what is now indefinite will
become clear later and all the apparent lack of content
will later be filled and so we shall leave a full review
of the novel until the final part is published. But looking at the fourth volume one may dare say that the rest
will be just the same - that is they will have the same
lack of content and the same lone virtue of describing
military life. The fourth volume to come out with its
description of the battle of Borodino, the crossing of
the Niemen, the taking of Smolensk has not added a thing
to the previous three except for these new descriptions
and the extremely un-new and curious philosphy of the
author himself. From the very first pages of the fourth
volume Count Tolstoy enters into explanations for the
reader (which he did not do in the first volumes) about
history which make everyone involuntarily wonder whether
the count is joking; but from the explanations which
appeared right after the fourth volume in the 'Russian
Archive' it is clear that he is not, and that he 'spent
five years of uninterrupted and exclusive labour' on the
work; I, says the count, 'arrived at the obvious fact that
the causes of historical events are not accessible to our
minds' and that 'looking at history from a general point
of view we (that is Count Tolstoy) became absolutely convinced of the eternal law which governs how events take
place' and that 'almost everyone who has written about
1812 has seen in it something special and fateful'. And
to those people thinking about the laws of predestination
Count Tolstoy adds himself. This explanation of predestination is expressed by the author in the novel through
various ifs, if onlies and buts as for example 'if a
soldier did not want to fight nor did another and another
so that there became too few people in Napoleon's army,
then the war would not have taken place'. From these ifs
and buts Count Tolstoy draws the old philosophic and
mystic conclusion that 'fatalism is necessary in history
to explain the senselessness of facts' (that is, the
author adds, the sense of facts we cannot understand), and
that 'the more we (i.e. Count Tolstoy) try to explain these
facts sensibly the more senseless and incomprehensible they
become'. After deductions such as these worthy of the

most faithful disciple of Kaydanov, we will look only at
one further paragraph from the thoughts of Count Tolstoy,
the one where he states: 'I wanted the reader neither to
see nor seek in my book what I did not wish to or could
not express but to turn his attention to what I wanted to
say but because of the conditions of writing I did not
think convenient so to do.' What is this 'wanted to but
could not because of the conditions of writing' when the
conditions are defined thus: '"War and Peace" is not a
novel, a poem or an historical chronicle but is what the
author wanted to and could express in form in which it is
expressed'?...

Not wishing to detain the reader by further even more
curious explanations by the author, we shall in concluding
our brief review reply to Count Tolstoy on his attempt to
express the character of the epoch he was describing with
his own answer, that he 'tried but could not'.

28.   TSEBRIKOVA ON NATASHA ROSTOV

1868

'Fatherland Notes', 1868, no. 6.   This review, written by
a woman, is entitled Our Grandmothers: on the Women
Characters in 'War and Peace'; it begins with a general
look at the heroines of Russian literature and the secondary roles they are forced to play; however regrettable
this might be, it is none the less a reflection of reality.
The author then deals with Natasha, Princess Liza, and
Princess Maria, the fiancée, wife, and sister respectively
of Prince Andrey.   The whole piece is basically an attack
on him.

M.K. Tsebrikova (1835-1917), niece of the Decembrist,
was a noted critic and writer.   Her 'American Women in the
Eighteenth Century' (1871) and 'The Childhood of Dickens'
(1877) were very popular in their day.   Taking up the
'women's cause' and Populism, she wrote extensively on
both; her short story, Grandpa Egor, was widely distributed among the workers and peasants in the years before the
'Movement to the People' in 1874.   Exiled in 1891 for
anti-tsarist activities, she lived in Geneva where she
continued writing articles attacking the policies and
actions of the Russian government.

Natasha Rostov is no small force; hers is a rich, energetic and gifted nature, from which at a different time
and in different circumstances a truly exceptional woman
could have developed, but the fateful conditions of a
woman's life hang over her and she lives fruitlessly and
almost perishes from an excess of her own undirected
strengths. The author paints with a special love this
lively, charming girl at that period when she is no
longer a child but not yet a woman, with her playful,
childish escapades in which the future woman is seen.
Natasha does not know what it is to feel shy or embarrassed; at a great dinner she decides to be playful and surprises everyone with the affrontery of her dealings with
the terrifying Mme Akhrosimov, who is not without justification in calling Natasha a Cossack; she burns her finger
with a red-hot iron as a sign of eternal friendship; all
this is childish, but the other children do not dare do it
and can only say: 'Oh, how could you do such a thing?'
Natasha grows up like a happy, free little bird, the
favourite child in a good kind family of Moscow nobles
over which a continuous atmosphere of love reigns. The
descriptions of the quiet family joys, the children's
games, the reunions after being parted and the loving relations of every member of the family to one another
(which for the most part come over rather cloyingly) are
filled by the author with feelings of warmth and sincerity
and win the reader over, for he is ready to love these
nice, affectionate and good people, until, that is, he
looks a little closer and sees that their goodness is a
little cheap, that it is nothing other than the feeling of
well-being after a good dinner. And indeed, have they any
reason not to be good? They had no need to worry about
every penny or keep a constant check on things; they had
no need to feel that any of them was taking anyone else's
place in life or that they put a constraint on anyone in
even the most usual daily habits and behaviour; they all
had full scope and could live the way they liked; they
could even affect generosity on occasion. The countess
gives a friend of hers several hundred roubles to buy army
uniform for her son; Nikolay makes his mother shed tears of
emotion when he nobly tears up the promissory note from
Boris Drubetskoy who, having made his career, does not wish
to know his benefactors; but that same countess squanders
thousands and that same Nikolay bets ten thousand at cards.
It is true that they are without doubt better people than
many others; they are satisfied with their substantial
dinners and will not stoop to the trouble of adding new
dishes to them unlike many who have even more substantial
fare. But in these substantial meals lies their whole

life. Take them away from them and then good-bye to that
well-being which we all so admire. The first threat to
their substantial dinners is the argument between the
mother and her son whom she adores but wishes to marry to
a girl older than he and whom he finds ridiculous and
repellent; in order to guarantee him his substantial meals
she is forced to insult a generous benefactress and up-
braid her orphaned niece, whom she loves as a daughter, for
daring to be loved by her son when she cannot provide him
with his substantial meals. These nice, good people adore
their children but can give them no other idea of life or
prepare them for anything in the world other than the enjoyment of large meals. The old Count Rostov, who finds
everything for the best in the best of all possible worlds
and weeps gently at every opportunity, knows only how to
pour out thousands on tutors for his children and to give
them complete freedom, because worrying about children,
giving advice and correction only destroy his feeling of
well-being. At the beginning the countess had tried to be
clever with her elder daughter and bring her up a perfect
lady who could talk and behave impeccably; but she turns
out cold and callous in everything and has an unpleasant
effect on everyone; she is a fitting wife for the philistine Berg; for her, life is the opportunity to wear a
pearl necklace like a countess and organize receptions as
they do in the highest society. But she does not try to
be clever with Natasha. Her young powers developed without constraint, and she took from life what would satisfy
her need for happiness, pleasure and love. Her upbringing
was what would prepare her for this life. Like all young
girls Natasha was taught languages, i.e. she knew extracts
from poetry and prose by heart without knowing what they
meant or the connection between them, dancing, singing and
music - all of them necessary to a young lady to make her
pleasing; in a word everything which arouses the imagination and stirs the feelings. Natasha gives herself over to
these studies with all the zest of her being; she dreams of
being a dancer; at fourteen she sings and her listeners'
hearts miss a beat in admiration and her mother is appre-
hensive of the expression and passion in her singing.
'Will she be happy?' the countess wonders as she senses
the youthful passion within her daughter. The countess has
not lived in the world so long for nothing. She has seen
that the only happy people in the world are those like her
daughter Vera with her Berg, Boris Drubetskoy, Anatole and
Hélène Kuragin, and that suffering is the fate of all those
who try to stand above such little people. She cannot
understand why this is so and can only note the unavoidable fact and fear for Natasha's future....

Natasha grows into a charming girl; a young and happy
life throbs in her laughter and expression, in every word
and movement; there is nothing artificial or calculating
in her; there is none of that affected nature of young
ladies; her every thought and idea is reflected in her
shining eyes. She is all outburst and enthusiasm; she
captivates everyone. Denisov writes poetry to the young
enchantress when she is all of fifteen; the generous Boris
forgets his plans for a career and falls in love with a
poor young girl; Prince Andrey, despite his earlier bitter
experiences, when he sees her at a ball decides she will
be his wife; the mason Pierre Bezukhov refreshes himself
after the torments of his thoughts about life in his love
for her. In order to have such a captivating influence on
people with such differing characters more than just external beauty is required. The marvellous Hélène does not
possess it; beneath the external beauty there needs to be
strength and life, what Prince Andrey calls Natasha's
'beautiful soul'. Natasha also has this influence over
all the members of the household; her brother Petya obeys
her every word without question; even the most morose and
querulous servants joyfully rush to carry out her orders
even though she pesters them and sends them off on errands
for no apparent reason. Natasha is aware of her powers
and likes to exercise them. She is flirtatious, but not
in the usual playful way of nice young ladies, or with the
childish grimaces, pouting and making eyes like the young
princess, or in the unimaginative fashion of young ladies
who are trying to catch a husband; nor is it the calculating coquetry of the experienced society beauty coldbloodedly trapping in her net further sacrifices to her
vanity. Natasha's flirtatious behaviour is utterly involuntary, natural, and is part and parcel of her personality.
From her childhood she has been used to the admiration of
everyone and is happy at it, just as she is happy at a
beautiful summer's night, her own singing, her nice little
brother, and her own prettiness. 'I am who I am,' she
says, admiring her own attractiveness, and adds: 'I am
just that... Admire me.' In Natasha this is all part of
that young strength which boils within her, her need for
the joys of life and its pleasures. It is made even more
irresistible by the fact that Natasha has a sensitive heart
(which is considered an excellent facet of the female
nature and is something which, in the opinion of many, may
be a complete substitute in a woman for mind, experience
and knowledge of life). That women have this quality is
an undisputed fact, but it develops only with the complete
inactivity of the mind; the mind, unconcerned by more
serious matters, naturally concentrates on trifles; the

ability to understand and catch the most subtle nuances in
the voice or a glance and the slightest expression on the
face is extremely refined; it is extremely difficult to
notice these trifles, for thoughts and feelings keep bursting in which one would prefer to conceal, but on the basis
of these very elusive trifles women can often devine
people's characters and draw amazingly accurate conclusions; this sensitivity can serve as an excellent guide in
the drawing-room or in friendly or family circles but as
soon as a woman goes out into the big,wide world or has to
take an important decision this sensitivity shows itself
completely bankrupt. However, Natasha is possessed of
native wit; in all her arguments with her brother Nikolay
she invariably comes out on top; she very quickly sees
what sort of a man Boris is and says he is 'narrow' and
'grey' - these are just the sort of impressions produced
by people like Boris who are incapable of any real base-
ness or evil but who employ narrow and petty means to
follow their narrow road to their petty objectives. But
all of this flashes in Natasha like a spark but dies down
without catching fire; there is only one feeling in her -
passion, the thirst for love. As a thirteen-year-old girl
she falls in love with Boris, promising to be his wife.
She dreams of love, sings about it, falls in love with her
singing teacher, then with Pierre, and again with Boris,
the same Boris she called narrow and grey, and discusses
it all with Sonya. She falls in love with Prince Andrey
at the ball and feels that this love is nothing at all
like her previous fleeting attractions. 'Here it is,' she
says, that real love about which she had dreamed and which
will bring her happiness. Natasha intuitively realizes
the superiority of Prince Andrey over everyone else and
this spoilt, wilful young girl conquers him completely.
'What is he looking for in me? What if he does not find
in me what he seeks?' she asks herself in alarm. A
thought is about to awaken within her. If Prince Andrey
had understood the forces within her he would have has-
tened to unite himself with her rich nature, but Prince
Andrey was seeking nothing out of the ordinary in her and
only wished to find out if she were the same sort of little
doll his first wife was and he remains fully satisfied with
Natasha as she is: with the purity of her beautiful soul
and her responsiveness to every feeling. Prince Andrey,
fearing Natasha's youth, wants to give her time to test her
feelings for him; but more than that he is obeying his
failing father who thinks a union of a Bolkonsky with a
Rostov degrading, and so Prince Andrey goes away for a
year, postponing the wedding. Natasha is offended and
cannot understand how love can be sacrificed to anything;

she languishes. 'As well as the absence of the man she
loved Natasha was frightened persistently by the thought
that the time she spent on her love for him would all be
wasted.' With these words the author catches extremely
well what love is for women. For a man love is happiness,
rest, pleasure; for a woman, in the social conditions she
finds herself in, it is a matter of life and death. Without love life is wasted and a woman lives not for herself
but for others. 'It offended her to think', continues the
author, 'that while she lived on thoughts of him, he was
living a real life and seeing new places and new people
whom she did not know.' What woman in love has not had
these thoughts? That while the man she loves is everything to her, he has his own special life, a real life,
in which she has no place. In narrow, egotistic creatures
like Natasha who are also passionate it is thoughts like
these which make those unbearably tender wives, who,
because there is nothing in their lives besides the man
they love, demand that he should have no other interest
but her and torment him for every minute he does not spend
with her and for every thought which is not of her. In
Natasha this was the first glimmer of that consciousness
which awakes in a woman of her own pitiable condition and
the inequality of life when she compares herself with a
man, a consciousness which was to be fully expressed a
whole generation later. Prince Andrey makes no attempt to
introduce Natasha into his real life and she is depressed
for a while; she soon cheers up, however, because her
healthy nature is not capable of sighing and pining for
years. With renewed vigour she gives herself over to all
the distractions of country life. Horse-riding, hunting,
Russian dancing and singing all arouse her; under the
influence of these sensations Natasha feels that the
period of calm, maidenly life with its bright joys has
passed for ever. With her organism and upbringing the
period of passions arrives too early. She does not wish
to wait any longer for happiness; she needs it now, at
this very minute; with tears in her eyes she throws herself on her mother's neck and begs: 'Give him to me now,
Mama, give him to me!' But Prince Andrey is far away and
her unsatisfied love throws her into the arms of Anatole
Kuragin. Natasha has met a devil-may-care philanderer,
well used to conquests and capable of feeling for women
only animal lust. He behaves impertinently and aggres-
sively and confuses the inexperienced girl with his looks.
'She felt with horror that between him and her there were
no moral boundaries, and that she was as close to him as
she had been to anyone.' She looks to her father, seeking
an explanation for this worrying feeling, but old Count

Rostov is capable of comforting his children or getting
distressed over them only when they are ill and is incapable of understanding what is happening to his daughter.
This incomprehensible power over her by a stranger is terrible for Natasha; she does not know whom she loves and
berates herself for betraying Prince Andrey. She does not
know whom to turn to for advice. There is Sonya, but
because of her love for her wonderful Nikolay she will not
understand Natasha. She is so virtuous, says Natasha, not
realizing that Sonya's virtue comes from a nature which is
completely satisfied with making lace until her wonderful
Nikolay makes her his wife. It never occurs to Natasha to
seek advice from her mother who has the marvellous conviction that her children never hide anything from her. The
power which parents have over their growing children interferes with their moral influence; standing perplexed before
a decisive step, we are not going to ask the advice of
people who can stop that step being taken, and all the
experience of parents which could help their children
avoid many bitter mistakes is wasted because it is often
thrust upon the children who do not wish to hear of it.
Furthermore, from the example of Sonya and Nikolay,
Natasha knows that the most important thing in life for
her parents is a substantial meal and they are happy to
provide one for all their children even at the cost of
their own happiness. But the kiss which Anatole roughly
takes from her settles all her doubts. This is love, she
decides, and does not hesitate for a moment; she will
write herself, without anyone's advice, to her fiancé and
turn him down - an act of will in a girl unheard of at
that period; she agrees to elope with Anatole and all but
perishes as a sacrifice to that ignorance of life in
which it is thought necessary to bring up young girls in
order to preserve their innocence and purity. If Natasha
has known what sort of feeling it was which had drawn her
to Anatole she would have realized that it was hardly
proper even for a woman like Hélène - that *superb animal,*
as Napoleon had called her - and quite unworthy of any
self-respecting woman; she would not have given the grand
title of love to a feeling of which she was secretly
ashamed; and if she felt any conscious shame the feeling,
after stirring for a moment, would have sunk without trace.
As soon as something is given its proper name it loses its
imagined power. But ignorance and youth which had lived
exclusively on dreams of love, and the romantic spirit of
the times, all fanned an unclean spark into fire. A
simple, heartless rake was turned into the best, the most
noble and the most generous man in the whole world. To
sacrifice everything for him, family, friends, the future,

became the greatest possible happiness imaginable.

The elopement is discovered. The virtuous anger of her godmother rains down upon her. Disgusting creature, shameless hussy, and so on; the epithets are lavished upon the distraught girl. O wise leaders of the young! You throw the ardent but inexperienced child into the maelstrom of life without having taught him anything at all and you accuse him of the crime of his unavoidable mistake; you, you who yourself admired all his youthful strength and could point to no other useful purpose for it except pleasure and happiness; and then when this strength bursts from the framework you have given it you turn your anger and scorn upon him without pity. Natasha becomes the subject of gossip throughout Moscow. Prince Andrey accepts her refusal of his proposal. Pierre tries in vain to talk him into forgiving her by reminding him of the wonderful things he said to him when he broke from Hélène. Prince Andrey replies with pitiful evasion, saying: 'I said that one should forgive, not that I was capable of forgiving.' From an ordinary man one does not have the right to demand great generosity but from one of the best people of his time we have an absolute right to expect his words to accord with his deeds. And then, what a difference in the two! He found that he ought to forgive a dissolute woman without a spark of human feeling in her body, a woman who had bought her weak-willed husband, whom she despised, with the magnificence of that body, a woman who, thanks to her connections and lack of shame, could always maintain her position in society; and then he could not forgive an inexperienced young girl her one mistake, when he himself had left her as a sacrifice to every temptation, when he knew that a renewed proposal would re-establish the girl in the eyes of society, a girl who sincerely and passionately loved him and still felt joined to him because, more than by shame or sorrow about her ruined life, she was tormented by the thought that she had caused him suffering. It is not offended love that speaks in Prince Andrey, it is hurt pride; he cannot pick up what Anatole Kuragin has left behind - *je ne puis marcher sur les brisées de ce monsieur*. This is why one of the best men of his time shows such a discrepancy between his words and his deeds; in this discrepancy is seen the eternal egotism of a man who thinks that women exist for him alone and that once having given themselves to him they must remain his possession for ever.

One cannot help asking that if this was how the best man of the period behaved what must the rest have been like?

29.   BERVI-FLEROVSKY ON THE BOLKONSKYS

1868

From a review in 'Affair', 1868, no. 6, entitled An
Elegant Novelist and his Elegant Critics, written under
the pseudonym of S. Navalikhin. V.V. Bervi-Flerovsky
(1829-1918) was a Populist economist and publicist; his
best-known work is 'The Position of the Working Class in
Russia' (1869).

When Count L.N. Tolstoy's novel 'War and Peace' was published there was no reason to comment on it; the name of
Tolstoy was scarcely remembered by most people and his
failures in the field of his pedagogic fantasies were more
famous than his works of literature. Why this novel made
any impression at all and precisely what impression was
completely unknown. But then from all sides prolific
reviews poured out; our elegant critics were so overjoyed
at the novel's appearance that they all praised it in
different ways just as if Count Tolstoy had discovered
America. The 'Messenger of Europe' reacted to it with
deference, bowing down before its magnificence; it is not
for us to teach a great artist, it proclaimed and slavishly
touched its forelock to the elegant and mannered life it
portrayed....
     In bringing on to the scene Tsar Alexander, Kutuzov,
Speransky, Arakcheev and others Count Tolstoy clearly
wants to show us that he is introducing us to the highest
and most influential sections of Russian society at the
beginning of the nineteenth century. The same intention
is seen in the fact that most of his heroes are rich and
high-born people; his Count Bezukhov, for example, has an
income of half a million a year; the author uses names
which by their sound remind us of the names of very famous
aristocratic families, for example Prince Bolkonsky and
Prince Kuragin; even those characters who are looked down
upon in this society bear names which are also reminiscent
of no less famous people, for instance the princes
Trubetskoy. There is no doubt that Count Tolstoy wished
to take us into the most lofty areas of Alexandrine
society and the critic of the 'Messenger of Europe'
assures us that in this society we shall find examples of
truly elegant life. But where is the elegance? Surely
not in the art of dressing, or decorating one's flat and

concocting tasty meals; Count Tolstoy could not describe
all this dilettantism of designers, interior decorators and
cooks and nor did he. He depicts only actions, thoughts
and feelings, and consequently it is in these that one must
seek that elegance which the elegant critic of the 'Messenger of Europe' found. As a start I shall take a scene in
which Prince Bolkonsky appears; he is better than all the
other characters in the novel and is shown as even the
best among the best.

[Omitted: quotation concerning Prince Bolkonsky's anger at
a servant's unintentional rudeness.]

A person at all accustomed to thinking who reads this
scene would be justified in thinking that Prince Bolkonsky
had never actually seen elegant society and had spent all
his life among crude bushmen, because only the crudest
bushman would have reacted so rudely to a man who wished
to help him and do what he did. Prince Bolkonsky, we are
assured by the author, was one of the richest men of his
time; he was not as rich as Count Bezukhov who possessed
160,000 serfs but he was none the less very rich. Let us
suppose that Prince Bolkonsky possessed not 160,000 serfs
but half as many, i.e. 80,000 in all; no one will dispute
that to make 80,000 living people unhappy is not at all
elegant; on the contrary it is disgraceful and criminal.
Is it possible to call a man civilized who is at such a
low mental and moral level that he cannot even understand
that in having the fate of tens of thousands of people in
his hands he has a heavy and great responsibility towards
them? But the author himself hardly understands it,
evidently attracted by the elegance of his hero. Prince
Bolkonsky behaves no better towards his daughter. The
scenes with her remind us of an already probably forgotten character in Dickens's 'Oliver Twist', the thief
William, who taunts his mistress as he might a domestic
animal. Bolkonsky treats his daughter in almost the same
way; in the course of the whole of his life described in
the novel he never, even unintentionally, expressed a
human feeling towards his own daughter; on the contrary
he continually and consciously rains insults upon her and
she bears them with endless patience. And in spite of
this the elegant novelist tries to assure us that Prince
Bolkonsky was one of the most enlightened men of his time,
and as if fearing that we shall not believe him he attempts
to assure us with the authority of the whole of Russian
society.

[Omitted: quotation describing Moscow's tributes to him on

his name-day.]

   Having presented in this way one of the most remarkable
men of his time as the author expresses it, Count Tolstoy
introduced another one, Andrey, Prince Bolkonsky's son.
When he went to Moscow the old Bolkonsky immediately became
the leader of Moscow society and his son became an associate of Speransky and wrote, as his father said, a whole
volume of laws. The same young prince was also a hero of
the battle of Austerlitz and the benefactor of his peasants. Prince Andrey Bolkonsky talks with Count Pierre
Bezukhov who tells him how he wounded Dolokhov in a duel.
He challenged Dolokhov to a duel for no reason other than
that he suspected him of an illicit relationship with his
wife. This relationship was not proved at all.

[Quotation omitted.]

   From the story of Austerlitz which preceded this conversation it is clear, by the way, what life was for
Prince Andrey; along with other Russians and Germans
Prince Andrey tried to kill as many Frenchmen as possible
while the French were trying to kill as many Russians and
Germans as possible. Prince Andrey might have expressed
things better if he had said that he lived to kill others
rather than lived for himself. He is so obtuse and limited as a personality that he failed to understand that in
wartime those people who live for others are those who try
to lessen the bloodshed and bring peace and not those who
try to set one man against another and from vanity kill as
many innocent people as possible. He says the war destroyed his own life; actually he killed not only his own
life but the lives of many others as well without a
thought about the true relationship of a man with his
fellows.

[Quotation omitted.]

   With his low level of intellectual ability and his
despicable view of life and people the prince could not,
of course, understand that a peasant has exactly the same
feelings as every other human being and just like other
human beings he has the capacity to love, feel affection,
suffer deeply the privations of his family, to endure hard
work and deprivation for the sake of others and sometimes
sacrifice his own happiness and even his life for them;
like all short-sighted and mentally impoverished people he
is in the same condition as a semi-savage and imagines that
only he and his friends have the ability to feel any moral

requirements and that everyone else is but a machine.

[Quotation omitted concerning Count Pierre Bezukhov's attempts to help his peasants.]

Count Tolstoy thinks that the speeches made by Prince Andrey are of equal importance to the humane intentions the author gives him in respect of his peasants; but they are not. It is evident that the author does not understand people who do good to others, especially a great good. At whatever time and under whatever conditions this type of person might have lived he usually had a highly developed social sense. Besides personal and narrowly egotistical objectives they had other, superior, ones which came from the deeply human conviction that the happiness of the individual only occurs in conditions of the general happiness of a given society. All that these people did stemmed from this and all their aspirations and interests were directed towards achieving it. Humane feelings and a deep love and humility before others were the distinguishing characteristics of these people; and these ideas did not stem from sentimentality but from a highly developed intellect which led to a complete harmony between the inner world of thoughts and feelings and the outside one of practical activity. This is what Count Tolstoy evidently wished to show in Prince Andrey. He is the best character in the novel, he became famous throughout all Russia for what he was doing for his peasants and attracted the attention of Speransky. A man who is ahead of his time understands only too well all the harm which can be done by cynical and heartless speeches and cannot but see that his moral and intellectual development places him above the ordinary and the vulgar; he is well aware that to speak means to act. But is this Prince Andrey? From everything that he says and does it is clear that he is a grubby, crude and heartless robot who does not possess a single truly human feeling or aspiration. And in this respect Count Tolstoy did not dare to hide all the inner vulgarity of the Bolkonskys. Of all the heroes of the novel they stand out particularly clearly; they could form a model for the others. What is masked in others under weakness of character, pettiness or, as in the case of Pierre, good nature and carelessness is drawn in the Bolkonskys in sharply defined lines. After this the comment of the elegant critic of the 'Messenger of Europe' on the elegance of Tolstoy's heroes can only make one shrug one's shoulders. Such a comment produces a depressing and repulsive impression on even the slightest live moral feeling. It is clear that both the elegant novelist and

his elegant critic do not have the slightest idea of the
true character of a man capable of doing good to others.
For them the elegant and the humane mean the upper class
and the wealthy and this external gloss they take for real
human worth.   Both of them look up to the heroes in the
novel and their reverence, like a mist, clouds everything
before them.   Through this mist they do not see what is
actually there but a mirage created by their idle fantasy.
The critic of the 'Messenger of Europe', thinking that the
upper class should lead an elegant life and could not possibly lead any other, found such a life in the characters
Count Tolstoy has created, although not one of them ever
showed the slightest elegance and all of them behaved in-
differently or crudely and grubbily like wild bushmen.

30.   NOROV ON TOLSTOY'S FALSIFICATION OF HISTORY

1868

A.S. Norov (1795-1869) is typical of those conservative
Russians, politicians, historians and soldiers who were
upset by Tolstoy's portrayal of the Napoleonic campaign,
not so much for its eccentric view of the events as for
the slurs it cast on Russian upper-class society and the
Russian high command.   This extract is from a long article,
'War and Peace' from an Historical Point of View, printed
in the 'Military Almanac', 1868, no. 11.   Norov's views
also appeared as a book the same year.

Under the title 'War and Peace' there has appeared a work
by Count Tolstoy in which he presents in the form of a
novel not just a single episode from our military and
social life but a rather long epoch covering both peace
and war.   The novel opens with the Austerlitz campaign
which is something which still calls forth a deep response
in the heart of every Russian, and has so far reached the
battle of Borodino.   The readers, most of whom, like the
author himself, were not born until after the time of the
events being described but acquainted with them from
childhood through stories they had read or been told, were
struck first of all by a melancholy impression of the
petty-minded and almost immoral members of high society in

the capital, although these same people were influential in
the government; second, by the lack of any sense in the
military events, and, third, by the almost complete absence
of that military prowess of which our army has always been
justly proud. Reading these melancholy pages and charmed
by their beautiful and artistic style, you hope that the
coming brilliance of the 1812 period will erase this early
melancholy impression; but how great is your disappointment
when you see that the glorious year of 1812, glorious both
in military and civilian life, is presented as a mere soap-
bubble; that the whole phalanx of our generals, whose
military glory is clearly seen in all the documents and
whose names have been passed by word of mouth from generation to generation, is shown as being but the untalented
and blind instruments of chance; they are shown as being
occasionally successful but this is only mentioned in passing and sometimes, even ironically. I have often been
asked whether our army and Russian society were really like
that. Had Count Tolstoy's novel been written by a foreigner then people might well have said that it had been based
only on personal accounts; but it is written by a Russian
and consequently cannot be regarded in that way by its
readers even though they have neither the time nor the
opportunity to check what is written in the novel against
official documents or talk with the few remaining eye-
witnesses of those great events in our fatherland. Being
one of the latter I cannot read this novel which purports
to be historical without feeling my patriotism deeply
insulted.

It is not difficult to show from the writings of our
honourable historians that only the scandalous anecdotes
of the time find a place in the novel.... If it is suggested that Russian writers or contemporaries are more or
less prejudiced, I shall cite but one example: Chambray's
'Histoire de l'expédition de Russie', where the glorious
qualities of the Russian troops are given much more acknowledgment than in Count Tolstoy's novel. I do not demand
from a novel written *for effect* what I demand from a history book, but as this novel portrays historical characters
then I must compare what is described with what I personally know and remember.

None of us who were in Petersburg society in the years
1805 to 1812 recognized the salon of the famous Mme
Scherer, the confidante of the Empress Maria Fyodorovna,
which fact enabled her to attract the leading members of
society and the diplomatic corps to her house, and
although one may guess who she really was we do not have
the right to name her. From my youth, from the time I
became a junker in a Guards' Regiment of Artillery until I

received my commission and was mobilized in March 1812, I
lived in Princess V.V. Golitsyn's house; she was the wife
of General Prince S.F. Golitsyn who was then in command of
our troops in Galicia and both of them were close friends
of my parents. Their son, Prince F.S. Golitsyn, and his
wife, the daughter of Field Marshal Prince Prozorovsky,
also lived there at that time. The members of the house
were in constant contact with the aristocracy of the
capital; consequently I can name all the houses where the
highest Petersburg society gathered and into which I was
also accepted. These were: Count and Countess Stroganov,
the Counts Rumyantsev (these two houses received mainly
scholars and writers - Countess S.V. Stroganov had actually
translated the whole of Dante's 'Divine Comedy'), Princess
Catherine Dolgoruky, Princess Elena Vyazemsky, Prince and
Princess Kochubey, Natalya Zagryazhsky, Count and Countess
Litta, Prince and Princess Yusupov, Count and Countess
Guriev, Count and Countess Lavalle, Prince and Princess
Lieven, Count N.A. Tolstoy, Alexander and Dmitriy Narysh-
kin, Sophia Tutolmin and Sophia Svechin and many more it
is needless to mention; their salons all put that of Mme
Scherer firmly in the shade. All these houses were marked
by a delicacy of behaviour or a luxuriousness of hospitality, and I do not think that in any of them would you have
heard Napoleon being called the Antichrist or any other
comments of that nature. Not one of these salons bears
the slightest resemblance to that described by Count Tolstoy.

Also the guards' officers (and this time was their
Golden Age) consisted in the main of people from the old
aristocratic families and they were well brought up and
educated.... Naturally there was some prankish behaviour,
I even participated in a little myself, but nothing like
that described by Count Tolstoy which just could not have
happened in the company of the guards' officers of the
time.

As for the Austerlitz campaign, many of my old friends
took part in it, as they did in the Prussian one, and I
have heard many fresh reminiscences about both. It is
extremely unpleasant for Russians to recall those sad
events, but it is even more so to read about them in the
story concocted by the artless pen of our soldier-author.

[Omitted, relation of Norov's version of Austerlitz,
Tilsit and Borodino, based on his own reminiscences and
especially those of General Ermolov.]

The author of our novel has preferred to concern himself with Mr Bezukhov and tell us how this *barin* took the

French by the scruffs of their necks. And indeed, for him
the real hero of Borodino is Count Bezukhov!

31. LIPRANDI, NOTE ON THE BATTLE OF BORODINO, 'VOICE'

1868, no. 129

I.P. Liprandi (1790-1880) was a soldier and military historian who had participated in the 1812 campaign, and was
later to write about it and various other Russian campaigns.

In 'Voice', no. 83, there is a review of 'War and Peace'.
In speaking of the battle of Borodino the honourable
writer quotes the following from Volume IV: 'in giving and
accepting battle at Borodino both Napoleon and Kutuzov
acted involuntarily and unconsciously', and then adds

> to describe accurately the course of the battle is some-
> thing which if not impossible is extremely difficult,
> and the proof of this is General Liprandi who has writ-
> ten whole volumes of critical articles about the war of
> 1812 and Borodino; he has devoted lengthy research to
> this battle in his 'Historical Readings' of 1866 and
> *still was unable to give a clear idea of the general
> course of the battle.*

In this there is at best a misunderstanding. I never
thought I could expound on the *general course of the battle*
and have always thought, along with the honourable writer,
that to do so would be 'if not impossible then extremely
difficult', and he can confirm this in my earlier 'Materials on 1812' where I said:

> an accurate description of [the battle] is like the maze
> of Daedalus on Crete where more than one scholar will
> lose his way, if he did not himself participate in the
> battle, and dreams of defining some moments during it in
> order to point out clearly their influence on the gener-
> al course of the battle and its outcome.

I thought that a clear exposition of this battle of the

giants, as Napoleon called it, could only be achieved by society at large and not by one man, and certainly not by me.

[Quotations omitted.]

   Finally as Tolstoy's 'War and Peace' has occasioned all the misunderstandings I have mentioned, I think it fitting that I should say a few words about this in my opinion remarkable work. I shall take the episode dealing with Borodino.... The count is reproached, among other things, for the fact that many of the things he says are not historically accurate. But for history in the strictest sense of the word it is perhaps still too early to give an accurate assessment of many of the personalities (and there are, of course, many such assessments in 'War and Peace') who have a lot to say in the novel - and this can go a long way to explaining a lot too. It is not my place here, being a participant in the epoch being described, to deal critically with what is set out in the novel, but I think that if in the event the novel has indeed sinned against history then it is no bad thing.

32. DRAGOMIROV ON PRINCE ANDREY AND THE ART OF WAR

1868, 1869

M.I. Dragomirov (1830-1905), soldier and military historian, wrote a number of articles devoted to Tolstoy's novel, entitled 'War and Peace' from a Military Point of View, which were published in 'Weapons Miscellany' in 1868-70. They came out as a book in 1870. Dragomirov was rare among the military commentators on the novel in that his criticisms of Tolstoy's philosophy did not blind him to the merits of Tolstoy as a novelist. The first extract is from 'Weapons Miscellany', 1868, no. 4, the second, 1869, no. 1.

Count Tolstoy's novel is interesting for a soldier in two ways - by the description of battle scenes and army life and by his attempt to draw certain conclusions concerning the theory of military affairs. The first, the scenes of

military life, are inimitable and it is our firm belief
that they could form one of the most useful additions to
any course on the theory of war; the second, the conclusions, will not stand up to even the humblest criticism
that they are one-sided, although they are interesting as
the first step in the development of the author's ideas
about military affairs....

Count Tolstoy's battle scenes are no less instructive:
all the internal side of a battle, unknown to the majority
of military theoreticians and peacetime military practi-
tioners but none the less leading to success or failure, is
brought right into the foreground in splendidly sharp pictures. The difference between his descriptions of battles
and those of the historians is like that between a landscape and a topographical plan: the first gives less and
from a single viewpoint but gives it in a way more accessible to the human eye and heart; the second gives every
local object from a large number of viewpoints, and it
shows the locality for miles around, but everything is
conventional and has nothing in common, to the human eye,
with the objects depicted; thus everything on it is dead,
lifeless even to the prepared eye. Thus in the majority
of historical descriptions of battles you know the movements of divisions, sometimes of regiments, rarely of
battalions; 'they advanced despite the heavy fire, they
broke through and repulsed the enemy, or were repulsed,
they were supported by reserves', etc. The moral physiognomy of those in charge and their struggle with themselves and those around them, which precedes every decision, all disappears and from something made up of a
thousand human lives there remains only something like a
badly worn coin - the outlines are there, but of whose
head? The most knowledgeable numismatist is unable to
say. Of course there are exceptions but they are extremely
rare and in any case do not bring events to life before
your eyes anywhere nearly as well as the landscape picture, i.e. by representing something which at a given time
and from one particular viewpoint could have been seen by
one observant man.

It might be said that these Tushins and Timokhins and
so on are no more than fictions, that they never really
existed, that they lived only in the author's head. We
might well agree; but it must also be agreed that even in
historical descriptions not everything is true by a long
way, and that these characters who never actually existed
illumine that internal side of the battle better than the
majority of multi-tomed descriptions of wars in which
faceless characters pass fleetingly by and instead of
names like Napoleon, Davout, Ney and so on you might just

as well insert numbers or letters without any great loss.
These fictional characters live and act before you in such
a way that invaluable practical lessons may be learnt from
their activity by anyone who has decided to devote himself
to military affairs and who does not forget in peacetime
for what he is preparing himself. These lessons are such
that we may confidently place them beside those of Marshal
Saxe, Suvorov, Bugeaud and finally Trochu. If you also
remember that they appear in Count Tolstoy's story not as
generalized abstract ideas but as living persons who put
them into practice and are presented in such a way that you
can follow their every gesture, look and word, then if you
take all this into account the tremendous importance for
any soldier who takes his profession seriously will become
as clear as day....

....The author of 'War and Peace' does not restrict himself
simply to the depiction of scenes of battle or military
types but enters also into discussions of questions like,
for example: Is any theory of the art of war possible?
What is the role of the commander-in-chief? What were the
causes of the events on the world stage in 1812? Answers
to these questions are given sometimes by the author himself and sometimes through the hero of the novel, Prince
Andrey. In reviewing the various views about such questions one is forced into repeating oneself as one and the
same idea is often repeated several times in the novel too,
although in varying ways.
     Although there is much in common between the views of
the author and those of Prince Andrey one must differentiate between them; Prince Andrey, both because of the man
he is and considering the times he lived in, could not look
on certain things other than in the way the author makes
him. In this the author becomes a painter; Prince Andrey
had ambitions of becoming a man of action; because of this
the one-sided discussions of this or that question are
explained in extremely variable ways and one has to take
this into account. What in Prince Andrey appears as the
consequences of his failures in life appears in the author
as nothing other than enthusiasm, unavoidable in an author
who steps beyond the limits of the art-form suitable to
his talent.
     Prince Andrey belongs to that group of people whom one
meets often enough who through some strange whim of nature
present a combination of enormous ambitions with the lack
of strength to carry them out. Count Tolstoy has reproduced this type both artistically and accurately; despite
all his sympathy for Prince Andrey he has presented him as
hastily resolving problems, often extremely complicated

ones, straight from the shoulder, as someone capable at everything but good at nothing. He does not flatter him and deals with him as a true artist; taking the known factors of his character he develops them pitilessly to their ultimate conclusion. We would ask you to recall Prince Andrey's first appearance: in society he narrows his eyes, scarcely responds when spoken to and treats everything and everyone in an extremely superior fashion; before you is a man who is making every effort not *to be* but *to appear,* who is playing a part, who is not a force but only a pretence at one. Realizing the emptiness of the environment to which he belongs Prince Andrey regarded all this as a special merit in himself or else he would not have made himself out to be so scornful or tried to be so with such effect.

War breaks out in 1805 and Prince Andrey, not hesitating to take advantage of the privileges offered by the milieu he so despises, becomes adjutant to Kutuzov and dreams of finding his 'Toulon' on the battlefield or in other words of becoming a Napoleon. While awaiting his Toulon Prince Andrey the adjutant picks up extremely easily and quickly the habits of the leading commanders by putting into practice the 'unwritten' ranking table. Furthermore, as a person highly gifted in his own estimation, he considers it unnecessary for him to enter into a hard and long apprenticeship which alone produces master craftsmen: without ever having met war face to face he does so with a complete set of ready-made opinions about how it should be fought.

Having skimmed through half a dozen books he imagines he knows so much about military matters that when he puts things into practice he can teach everyone else and has himself nothing to learn.

By a happy chance he obtains an advantageous position and receives the chance to follow step by step such pupils of the Suvorov school as Kutuzov and Bagration. What could be better? Look, learn and adapt your own theories from the greatest book there is - the book of life. But it was not to be; like the most died-in-the-wool doctrinaire he could not admit the possibility that he could be wrong; no, it had to be life that was false.

And so he is amazed when Bagration does nothing, and is ready to give his advice on how the Austerlitz campaign should be fought when he is at the council not by right but because he is attached to Kutuzov. And the facts then take their course showing the insolvency of both Prince Andrey's military opinions and his pretensions. After this it is not surprising that, learning from bitter experience how difficult it is to become a Napoleon in one fell swoop, he should begin to preach that Napoleon is

nonsense and that his wonderful achievements were equally
nonsensical.

This just had to be: Prince Andrey was so sure of his
own talents and infallibility that when he saw the insolvency of his own theories he had inevitably to reach the
conclusion that there could be no theories at all concerning military matters. To seek and twenty times to fall
and twenty times to rise again, passing through all the
torment of doubt and disappointment is not in Prince
Andrey's nature. God alone knows why he should have
imagined that everything should come easily to him. He
says himself, albeit in another connection, that he is not
capable of forgiving; so how could he forgive the theory
of military art? Which is why he so bitterly dismisses it.

It is a pity; an honourable man, up to a certain point,
even capable and possessing character, but empty when it
comes to action. He seeks his *métier* everywhere but does
not find it; he can find nowhere, as it were, to plant his
roots - in a word, he is a little great man, capable of
anything but achieving nothing.

True he was a living reproach to Kutuzov in Bucharest
by his actions and he brought in many practical innovations on his estates, but the author writes this himself
and shows not one scene where Prince Andrey was actually
doing either of these things.

In our opinion this is a sign of great artistic feeling
on the part of the author; scenes in which Prince Andrey
appeared as a creative, practical man would have been dis-
sonant with the general outlines of his character, and so
the author left them out.

We would like to think that we have added nothing to
this description of Prince Andrey but have looked only at
what Count Tolstoy wrote; we have merely thrown some light
on those sides of it which Count Tolstoy left in the shade
out of a completely understandable sympathy for his hero.

That said, it becomes clear why Prince Andrey reacts
to something in which he had no luck with a prejudiced
although probably unwitting and therefore quite sincere
one-sidedness. He had either to admit to there being an
art of war about which he was quite ignorant or remain
with the faith in his own great capabilities and then deny
the existence of any such art and consequently of all
military genius. He chose naturally the latter. This is
fully confirmed by two places in Part IV where he expresses his views on the matter.

[Quotations omitted.]

Confusing knowledge and theory Prince Andrey tries to

prove that in military matters there is neither knowledge
nor theory and consequently (!) there can be no such thing
as military genius; this is another example of Prince
Andrey's inability to follow a line of thought consecu-
tively without any illogicalities. In the first place
knowledge and theory are not at all the same thing (in
the sense that all knowledge leads to theory but all
theories do not lead to knowledge) because theory is possible and necessary in any art whereas knowledge has
little to do with it. Second, the more difficult something is then the less often will there be masters at it
and the more likely they will belong to that category of
exceptional people whom we call geniuses.

At the present time no one would dream of suggesting
that there could be such a thing as the science of war;
it is as unthinkable as the possibility of there being a
science of poetry, music or painting; but this does not at
all mean that there cannot be theories of the art of war
just as there are theories about all the arts. Theory in
the art-forms I have just mentioned does not give us
Goethes, Beethovens or Raphaels but it does give them
certain techniques without which they would never have
risen to the heights they did. The theory of the art of
war does not pretend to prepare either Napoleons or even
Timokhins; it points to models of the ways things can be
done and consequently eases the path of the man who is
naturally gifted in military affairs.

If we add to this that in all sincerity it admits its
powerlessness to help in the most terrible of military
considerations - that of chance; that it is unable to give
a man the skill to act as he ought; then it appears that
the art of war has a very serious nature but also it does
not allow a man to rest assured that he knows all about it
when he only knows a part; military theory will not tell
you how to fight any particular battle but it will show
models of great campaigns for military man to study in the
same way that a painter, a musician or a poet will study
the great works in his own speciality not simply to reproduce them but to become imbued with their spirit.

It will probably be said that this is a very modern
view and consequently Prince Andrey could not have held
it; but this is a view which has been held in all times by
those who not only made war but also thought about it.

33. STRAKHOV, REVIEW OF 'WAR AND PEACE'

1870

From a long review in 'Dawn', 1870, no. 1. N.N. Strakhov (1828-96), Slavophile, writer and critic, was a close friend and correspondent of Tolstoy's. In his writing, as can be seen here, he usually stressed the value of every-thing Russian as opposed to Western European. Tolstoy was delighted with this review, as he often was with people who praised him and whom he liked.

....Finally, the great work is finished. Finally it lies before us, it is ours for ever, and all our worries are over. During the time Tolstoy seemed to be lingering over finishing his labours, we unwillingly suffered from terror and hope. The artist, as we now see, quietly and confid-ently continued his work; with a firm hand he completed the last part, while we, mere mortals, with our hearts unwillingly missing a beat, awaited the completion of the secret affair. We marvelled and were amazed at how the creative power, not weakening for a moment, could function on such a huge a canvas, and furthermore, not being able to grasp the magnitude of the power which opened out before us nor managing to accustom ourselves to this magnitude, we feared in our weakness for the completion of the great and invaluable labour. The most frightening dangers occurred to us.

But, finally, the picture is ready and lies completed before us. Its beauty opens out with a new and striking force. Only now do all the details fall into place, the centre stands out clearly, the colouring of the separate parts clearly appears, and taking in the picture at one look, we can see distinctly its general lighting, the connection between all its figures and the irresistible idea which forms the soul of the whole work and gives it its perfect unity and life. Look into it, read it and try to survey the story as a whole and the impression will strengthen and grow in proportion to your attention and study.

What size and what harmony! We can think of nothing comparable in all literature. Thousands of characters, thousands of scenes, every conceivable scene of public and private life, history, war, every horror on earth, all the passions and all the moments of human life, from the cry

of a newly born baby to the last outburst of feeling in a
dying old man, all the joys and griefs of man, every conceivable mood of the soul from the feelings of a thief
taking a few roubles from a friend to the supreme actions
of heroism and thoughts of inner lucidity - everything is
in the picture. Furthermore not a single figure is placed
in the shade by any other, not one scene, not one impression interferes with any other, everything is in its place,
everything is clear, everything is distinct, everything is
in harmony with itself and the whole. The world has never
seen such a marvel in the realms of art and, what is more,
a marvel achieved with such simple methods. This simple
but at the same time unimaginably artistic grouping is not
a matter of external imaginings and adjustings; it could
only be the result of a genius's insight, which in one
brief and clear-sighted glance takes in and penetrates all
the multifarious flow of life.

We jealously examine this our treasure, this unexpected
wealth in our literature, the honour and beauty of our
times: Are there no shortcomings in it? Are there no gaps
or contradictions? Are there not significant imperfections
in the work for which we would be abundantly compensated
by the strengths of 'War and Peace' although at which it
would still be painful to look? No, there is nothing that
could interfere with the complete joy, nothing that might
destroy our delight. All the characters are sustained,
every side of the matter is caught and the writer even to
the final scene has not departed from his immeasurably
broad plan, has not left out a single essential moment and
has completed his labour without a sign of change in tone,
in viewpoint, in the methods and power of his creation.
The whole thing is truly remarkable!

For the sake of clarity we shall attempt to write
briefly on the final two volumes.

Volume V contains the taking of Moscow by the French
and their stay there; Volume VI their retreat and the epilogue, the denouement of all the events, both public and
private. Over the fifth volume terror reigns, while over
the sixth, in spite of all its pictures of gloom, one
feels the atmosphere of peace, it is already clear that
everything is becoming quiet and the battle is over and
soon the normal flow of life will begin again.

Volume V, beginning with the conference at Fili, at
which it was decided to surrender Moscow, and ending with
the scene where Kutuzov receives news of the French retreat from the capital, is striking in its depiction of
that terrible blow which was given to Russian hearts by
the loss of Moscow. People feel lost, go mad, and panic
from that cruel shock. Rostopchin, Pierre, the clientele

of the restaurant on Varvarka all lose their heads, all
feel and act under the pressure of indescribable horror.
Kutuzov himself believing to the end, and not once waver-
ing, ponders as he had never pondered before. The main
character of Volume V, Pierre, in whom the moral process
going on in Russian hearts is more and more clearly reflected by his escapades, all the better depicts the feelings
which controlled everyone at the time. His flight from
his palace, his disguise, his attempt to kill Napoleon and
so on all bear witness to the deep spiritual shock, to the
passionate desire one way or another to share in the disaster of the fatherland and to suffer where everyone is
suffering. He finally has his way and calms down once he
is captured. As a prisoner he is united with the mass of
the common people and among them meets the man who all the
more clearly, all the more profoundly, shows him the
strength and beauty of the Russian people - Platon
Karataev. Escaping from the battlefield at Borodino,
Pierre thinks: 'How terribly frightened I was and how
shamefully I surrendered to the feeling. While they ...
they were steadfast and calm right to the very end.'
They in Pierre's mind were the soldiers, those who were
on the battery, those who fed him and who prayed to the
icon. '*They were those strange people whom he had not
understood, whom he had not known up till then and they
were clearly and sharply separated from other people in
his mind*.' Then he dreams of the philanthropic mason
talking of good and of the possibility of being as *they*
were.

[Quotation omitted.]

Thus an image of the people is impressed indelibly on
Pierre's soul at Borodino. This impression, however, is
repeated for Pierre with greater force and in more concrete forms in captivity surrounded by great suffering
when he was the most susceptible to accepting it.

[Quotation omitted.]

In the character of Karataev Pierre saw how the Russian
people think and feel in the direst conditions and what
great faith lives on in their simple hearts. Karataev's
spiritual beauty is striking and superior to any praise.
We recall how long our literature has been concerned with
the common people and how many attempts it has made to
catch its spirit and strength, and how many attempts
Tolstoy himself has made. All this literature, all these
attempts, have been surpassed and overshadowed by the

incomparable figure of Karataev who shows how well the
writer has mastered the most difficult of tasks which
have aroused a whole literary epoch including himself and
others.

Thus the inner sense of Volume V is concentrated on
Pierre and Karataev as figures who, suffering alongside
everyone else but finding themselves with nothing to do,
had the opportunity of thinking about and bearing in their
hearts an impression of the general great disaster. For
Pierre, the profound spiritual process ends in moral rebirth; Natasha says that Pierre has washed himself morally,
that captivity was for him a moral bath. Karataev had
nothing to learn; in word and deed he taught others, and
he died, bequeathing his spirit to Pierre.

Beside these events of inner spiritual life there stands
a whole series of exterior happenings: from the Rostov's
departure, Rostopchin's activities and efforts and the
murder of Vereshchagin to Captain Ramballe and his
stories, Michaud telling the tsar of the taking of Moscow
and the shooting of the Russian incendiaries and so on.
All these scenes picture for us with amazing liveliness
the course of the whole affair at this dark time in the
life of Moscow and of Russia and people from the tsar to
the most insignificant soldier.

Our writer's creation, though, reaches its highest
point where it is concerned with the eternal, intransient
interests of the human soul. The participation of Prince
Andrey in the story ends at Borodino where he is mortally
wounded. He is left with only private concerns now, his
meeting with Natasha, and death. The depiction of this
meeting and the inner enlightenment experienced by Prince
Andrey just before his death are the peak of artistic
perfection, an actual opening out of the secrets of the
human heart and shaking us with its immeasurable profundity. Another episode is no less striking; we are told how
in the middle of all the general calamity love grows between Nikolay Rostov and Princess Maria. The purity and
tenderness of their relations are inexpressible and
eternal. One is involuntarily amazed at the simplicity
and purity of these two people, and at what a clear light
can shine in the most ordinary of people. And so, Prince
Andrey dies, Nikolay Rostov falls in love with his future
wife, and Pierre suffers - once again the whole gamut of
human life is run by the author in Volume V.

Volume VI is the denouement, the end of the terrible
events and the start of a new life. The character of the
retreat of the French army and the form of the actions of
our troops are shown with the same clarity and accuracy as
were the scenes at Borodino and the meaning of the fall of

Moscow both for us and the French. Events occur quickly
but nothing necessary for the completeness of the picture
is omitted. The partisan war is described, the condition
of the retreating French, the cruelty of some Russians and
the magnanimity of others, the feeling of a magnificent
triumph united with sorrow for the enemy and the consciousness of our own rightness, as the author puts it.
Finally Kutuzov, as in Volume V, appears at the beginning
'when it had already become clear that the enemy had been
put to flight' and at the end when he listens to the
tsar's speech at Vilnius.

We also see our young men perishing (the death of Petya
Rostov), girls grieving for their boyfriends and sisters
for their brothers (Natasha and Princess Maria over Prince
Andrey) and mothers in despair over their sons (Countess
Rostov over Petya). Once the war is over we see meetings
in Moscow between those people separated by war, we have
stories and inquiries, new relationships are established
and new lives begin.

The inner sense of the chronicle ends with the final
homilies given to Pierre by his personal suffering and the
words of Karataev before his death and by his death
itself. The writer depicts vividly and profoundly
Pierre's rebirth. And in his rebirth is personified that
of the whole of Russia, that discovery of spiritual
strengths which ought to follow trials and struggles. For
Pierre, as for Russia, a new, better period has begun.
Cleansed, strengthened and enlightened by suffering Pierre
earns Natasha's love and experiences all the happiness of
which he is capable.

Here the artist enters again the area of human life's
eternal intransient interests and again scales the heights
in amazing and incomparable fashion. He draws for us two
families, two new families, formed under the influence of
all the events described and forming as it were the consummation of the affair, as it were the fruit on one of
the numerous branches of a tree which has endured a bene-
ficial storm - Russia. Never before has the world seen a
comparable description of married life, because there has
never been a description of a Russian family, i.e. the
very best of all families in the world. The love between
husband and wife in the full blossoming of their powers -
pure, tender, firm, unshakeably profound - is depicted for
the first time in all its great strength and without a
single embellishment.

The picture of the two new families ends the chronicle
strikingly harmoniously. When the story began we saw
before us two families, already long established - the
Bolkonskys where there were an adult son and daughter and

the Rostovs, where Nikolay was still a student and Natasha
a twelve-year-old girl. Fifteen years later (this is the
period of time covered by the story) we have before us two
young families with young children. With his sense of
proportion the artist of genius began his family chronicle
with people adult enough to hold our interest and ended it
with pictures in which even babies at the breast seem
charming to us because they belong to families to whom
we have grown accustomed and become linked during the
telling of the story.

A complete picture of human life.

A complete picture of Russia at that time.

A complete picture of what is called History and the
struggle between nations.

A complete picture of everything in which people find
their happiness and their grandeur, their grief and their
humiliation.

But what then is the sense of the work? It is all but
impossible to express in a few words the significant
thoughts developed in this huge epic, to point to its soul,
of which all the details of the story form only the
embodiment and not the essence.

It is a difficult matter. We shall say here a few
words in this connection in order to illuminate some of
the misunderstandings.

'War and Peace' has suffered the fate of everything
truly great. The truly great is often not recognized by
people at all; sometimes it fascinates them and overcomes
them with its power but almost without exception it is
not understood. The usual course of events is that
people *feel* its greatness, but do not *understand* it. So
was it with Pushkin during the last period of his literary
activity, and it has continued up to now, in spite of the
tremendous progress we have made; this is what happened,
and had to happen, with 'War and Peace'. The inexpressible charm of the story struck everyone and overcame
them; but there was at the same time a general bewilderment caused by the inability to grasp what the work was
all about. One could say that 'War and Peace' is the
least understood of all the works in Russian literature,
as little understood in fact as Pushkin himself.

But what is surprising in this, how could it have been
otherwise? The greater an event is in itself, the more
difficult it is to understand. With respect to 'War and
Peace' one cannot even put all the blame on to the dire
condition of Russian literature and our readers. The
chief cause of the lack of understanding is the heights
scaled by Tolstoy which are unattainable for the majority.

Indeed 'War and Peace' reaches the highest peaks of

human thought and feeling, peaks not usually climbed by
man. Indeed Tolstoy is a poet in the ancient and best
sense of the word; he bears within himself those most profound of questions, which only man is capable of asking.
He sees clearly into and discovers for us the most secret
mysteries of life and death. How do you expect him to be
understood by people for whom such questions do not exist
and who are so stupid, or, if you like, so clever, that
they can find no mysteries either in themselves or around
them? The sense of history, the strength of nations, the
mystery of death, the essence of love and family life and
so on - these surely are the subject matter of Tolstoy's
novel. And so? Are all these and similar topics such
simple things that they are understood at once by the
first person to come across them? Is there not something
surprising in the fact that many, many people do not have
sufficient breadth of mind or experience of life to understand them?

[Omitted: an attack on the poor state of criticism.]

What, then, is the sense of 'War and Peace'?
The sense, we think, is most clearly expressed where
the author says: 'There is no greatness without *simplicity, good and truth*.'
The aim of the writer was to depict true greatness, as
he understands it, and to contrast it with false greatness which he rejects. This aim was expressed not only in
the contrast between Kutuzov and Napoleon but also in the
tiniest details of the struggle waged by the whole of
Russia in the form of the thoughts and feelings of every
soldier, in the whole moral world of the Russian people,
in their customs, in all the manifestations of their life,
in their way of living, suffering and dying. The writer
has depicted in all clarity in what Russians place the
value of human life, in what that ideal of greatness
lies, that ideal which is present even in the weakest
heart and which does not desert the strong even at times
of confusion and moral lapse. This ideal exists, in the
formula the author gives, in simplicity, good and truth
which were victorious in 1812 over the force that was anything but simple and full of evil and falsity. This is
the sense of 'War and Peace'.
In other words the author has given us a new, Russian
formula for *heroic life*, the formula according to which
Kutuzov acts and which Napoleon could in no way approach.
Of Kutuzov the author writes: '*This simple, modest* and
consequently *truly great figure* could not settle into the
false form which history has invented of that European

hero who pretended to control people.' One has also to
understand in this way all the Russians and all the other
characters introduced into 'War and Peace'. Their feelings, thoughts and desires, as far as they contain the
heroic, as far as they aspire to the heroic and an understanding of it, do not fit into those alien forms created
by Europe. The whole make-up of the Russian spirit is
simpler, more modest and presents that harmony and that
balance of forces which alone are consistent with true
greatness, and whose destruction we feel clearly in the
greatness of other nations. We are usually captivated,
and will long continue so to be, by the glitter and might
of those forms of life which are created by forces un-
controlled by a harmony stemming from mutual balance. A
purely Russian heroism, a purely Russian heroism seen in
all spheres of life, is what Tolstoy has given us, and
which is the main subject matter of 'War and Peace'.

If we look at our literature before 'War and Peace'
we shall see more clearly what a great service the artist
has done us and in what precisely lies this service. The
founder of our national literature, Pushkin, bore in his
great heart sympathy for all sorts and types of greatness, all forms of heroism,.which is why he also comprehended the Russian ideal and why he is the founder of
Russian literature. But in his wonderful poetry this
ideal appears only partially, it is only hinted at; unmistakably and clearly, but incomplete and undeveloped.

Gogol appeared but was not in control of the immense
task. A lament for the ideal burst forth, 'invisible
tears' poured out 'through the laughter seen by the world',
which bore witness to the author's not wishing to deny the
ideal but also to his inability to achieve its incarna-
tion. Gogol began to deny a life which so stubbornly refused to present him with its positive side. 'There is
nothing heroic in our lives; we are all either Khlestakovs
or Poprishchins' - this is the conclusion to which the
unhappy idealist came.

The only objective of all our literature after Gogol
became an attempt to discover a Russian heroism, to smooth
out that negative attitude to life of Gogol's, to understand Russian reality more correctly, in broader terms,
so as not to keep from us that ideal without which we
cannot live, as the body without the soul. A long and
hard labour was demanded to achieve this and all our
writers consciously or unconsciously took it up and attempted to complete it.

The first writer to complete the task was Tolstoy.
He was the first to overcome all the difficulties, to
suffer and conquer in his own soul the process of negation,

to free himself from it and begin to create forms containing within themselves the positive sides of life. He
was the first to show in unimagined beauty what was clearly
seen and understood only by the irreproachably harmonious
soul of Pushkin open to everything great. In 'War and
Peace' we have again discovered what is heroic in us and
now no one can take it away from us.

Let us try to define more particularly and accurately
what Tolstoy has done. Not all the problem has been resolved nor has all the breadth of the Russian soul been
exhausted, but that half of the task which at the present
time was most pressing and important has been completed in
'War and Peace'.

Tolstoy has not embodied completely the Russian ideal
but with inexpressible force and charm we hear in him
'the voice raised in our souls, speaking out for the
simple and the good against the false and the domineering'.
This voice was first heard in Pushkin and its sense was
first understood and witnessed by A. Grigoriev. *A voice
for the simple and the good and against the false and the
domineering,* this is the main sense of 'War and Peace'.
It is this essential, crucial element in our literature
which was discovered in it and traced with such subtlety
by Grigoriev. But the critic, so deeply understanding the
deepest strains of our poetry, scarcely foresaw or expected that this voice would burst forth after his death so
incomparably more loudly than he had ever heard it, or
that the mighty sound of this beautiful voice would ever
release for us the whole gamut of our literature and in
its incomparable purity and force unite with the marvellous sounds of Pushkin's poetry.

The particular thought of this voice is what we have to
define. If we trace all the characters and events in 'War
and Peace' we shall clearly see that the author's sympathies are a little one-sided but redeemed by the greater
penetration and depth of that side to which these sympathies are directed. There are in the world as it were two
types of heroism, the one active, anxious, fitful, the
other suffering, calm and patient. Grigoriev noticed
these two types in our literature and called them *domineering* and *submissive*. It is obvious with what great
sympathy Tolstoy treats suffering and submissive heroism
and it is equally obvious how little sympathy he feels
for active and domineering heroism. In Volumes V and VI
this difference in sympathy comes through even more
sharply than in the earlier ones. Into the category of
active and domineering heroism fall not only the French in
general and Napoleon in particular but many Russians too,
for example Rostopchin, Ermolov, Miloradovich, Dolokhov

and so on. Into the category of submissive heroism falls
in particular Kutuzov - the greatest example of this type
- Tushin, Timokhin, Dokhturov, Konovnitsyn etc., etc., the
large mass of our troops and our people in general. The
whole of 'War and Peace' has as its aim, as it were, to
show the superiority of a submissive over an active heroism which turns out everywhere to be not only defeated but
also ridiculous, not only powerless but also harmful. The
clearest and most vivid figure in which Tolstoy with
striking force characterized the type of person who thinks
he can be an active hero is Rostopchin. Before the grandeur of the events taking place people like Rostopchin seem
insignificant and pitiful not because they are weak in
themselves but because they attempted to interfere in a
course of events immeasurably beyond their powers. In
this exaggeration of their importance, in their clumsy and
crude self-seduction, the author points to the guilt of
not only individual characters but also whole nations, the
French for example. The author shows that a certainty of
one's own powers and a recognition in oneself of the ability to change and control events lead only to mistakes and
are unavoidably united with the play of the most base passions, conceit, vanity, envy, hate and so on.

Thus according to the sense of the novel, any field of
activity is removed from the domineering type. Furthermore, it is impossible, generally speaking, to deny that
decisive and brave people had no importance in the course
of the action, that the Russian people did not give birth
to those giving play to personal views and strengths. It
is completely just that with such a development of character they are marked for the greater part by the least
attractive characteristics; but there is no doubt, that in
these people there also appear the most beautiful aspects
of Russian spiritual strength.

Thus there is a side of the Russian character which has
not been fully caught or depicted by the author. One still
awaits the artist who can deal fully with this aspect, as,
for example, Pushkin did with Peter the Great in 'The
Bronze Horseman'.

[Quotation omitted.]

So while we still lack clear and pure forms of active
heroism, while this heroism has failed to find a poet to
express it, we must humbly bow before the poet who has
glorified and embodied for us submissive heroism. We can
only wonder about and darkly discern the characteristics
of that other greatness, also part of the Russian nature,
but that greatness which Tolstoy has depicted we can

already see clearly, fully incarnated.

In the essential point we cannot but agree with the poet, that is we fully recognize the superiority of submissive heroism over the active type. Tolstoy has depicted if not the strongest then at least the best sides of the Russian character, those sides to which the highest value is and should be given. If it is impossible to deny that Russia defeated Napoleon not through active but submissive heroism, so is it generally impossible to deny that simplicity, goodness and truth form the highest ideal of the Russian people to which the ideal of strong passions and exclusively powerful personalities must submit. If it is a question of force then it is resolved by which side gains the victory; but simplicity, goodness and truth are fine and beloved in themselves whether they win or not.

All the scenes of private life and private relationships introduced by Tolstoy have one and the same object - to show how that nation, whose highest ideal lies in simplicity, goodness and truth, suffers and exults, loves and dies, and leads its family and private life. The difference, so clearly stated, between Kutuzov and Napoleon exists in exactly the same form between Pierre and Captain Ramballe when they are talking over their amorous exploits, between Burenka and Princess Maria and so on. The same national spirit which showed at Borodino appears in the dying thoughts of Prince Andrey and in Pierre's spiritual processes, in Natasha's conversations with her mother and in the stamp of the re-formed families, in a word in all the spiritual movements of the private characters in 'War and Peace'.

Here and everywhere we see either the rule of the spirit of simplicity, goodness and truth or the struggle it has with the deviations of people of other persuasions and sooner or later its victory. For the first time we have seen the incomparable charm of the purely Russian ideal - humble, simple, endlessly tender and at the same time unshakeably stable and selfless. Tolstoy's huge canvas is a worthy depiction of the Russian people. It is a truly unique phenomenon - an epic written in the contemporary manner.

34.   DOSTOEVSKY ON 'WAR AND PEACE'

1869, 1870

Dostoevsky and Tolstoy never met but they followed each other's careers with interest.   These comments are taken from two of Dostoevsky's letters to N.N. Strakhov, of 26 March 1869 and 24 March 1870.

Have you noticed the following characteristic of Russian criticism?   Every important critic (e.g. Belinsky, Grigoriev) first presented himself to the public under the protection, as it were, of some outstanding writer; from then on he devoted himself completely to an interpretation of that writer and expressed his own ideas only in the form of a commentary upon that writer's works.   Thus Belinsky, when reviewing out literature, and even when he wrote articles on Pushkin, could only do so by leaning on Gogol, whom he had honoured in his youth.   Grigoriev relied on his views of Ostrovsky, and made his debut by championing him.   And for as long as I have known you you have had an immense and immediate sympathy for Lev Tolstoy.   When I read your article I felt sure that it was absolutely necessary, that you were obliged to begin with him and an analysis of his latest work ('War and Peace') before you could state your own ideas.   In the 'Voice', some writer says that you share Tolstoy's historical fatalism.   That silly phrase changes nothing; how on earth do people manage to find such amazing ideas and expressions!   What does 'historical fatalism' mean?   Why this eternal jargon, why do simple-minded men who cannot see further than the end of their noses so deepen and darken their words that no one can make out what they are getting at?   What you say in the passage about the battle of Borodino expresses the basic essence of Tolstoy's idea, and of your own thoughts on it.   I do not think you could have made yourself clearer.   The national idea of Russia stands out almost naked in that passage.   This is precisely what people have failed to understand and therefore have called it fatalism.

You state among other things that Tolstoy is equal to any of our greatest writers.   I just cannot agree with that passage in your letter.   It is something that must not be affirmed.   Pushkin and Lermontov were geniuses.   A writer who comes forward with 'The Negro of Peter the Great' and 'Belkin' brings with him a message of genius, a new message, which nobody before him has ever delivered anywhere. But when someone comes along with 'War and Peace', he comes *after* that new message which had been delivered by Pushkin; and this cannot be altered, however far Tolstoy may go in developing the message delivered before by another genius. I hold this to be very important.

35.   SHELGUNOV ON PIERRE BEZUKHOV, 'AFFAIR'

1870, no. 1

N.V. Shelgunov (1824-91) was a well-known journalist and critic. His review of 'War and Peace' is entitled The Philosophy of Stagnation.

There is a vast number of characters in the novel: men and women, grey-haired old men from the time of Catherine the Great and babies in their cradles, princes, counts, peasants, commanders-in-chief and clever diplomats, generals and common soldiers; three emperors even hold the stage; but all these characters are only introduced as further proof of the incontrovertible truth of the idea personified in Count Bezukhov and the Napoleonic campaigns. This is why, without going into details which would only lengthen the article, we shall direct the reader only to the novel's main idea.

Count Tolstoy's novel begins with a description of the emptiness of society morals with which he acquaints the reader in the salon of Anna Pavlovna Scherer, a lady-in-waiting and confidante of the Empress Maria Fyodorovna. The author also shows us his hero in this salon. Pierre Bezukhov is a fat and clumsy gentleman, of more than average height, broad-shouldered, with huge red hands, who does not know how to enter the salon or even less how to leave it, i.e. by saying something particularly pleasant as he goes. Besides this the hero is very absent-minded. For example when he gets up to leave, instead of his own hat he picks up a three-cornered one with a general's feathers in it and holds it looking like a sultan until the general asks for it back. But all his

absent-mindedness and ignorance on how to enter and leave
a room and speak in company - which he shows clearly in
his heated defence of Napoleon and his attack on the
Bourbons - is redeemed by his expression of kind-hearted-
ness, simplicity and modesty. Pierre, the illegitimate
son of Count Bezukhov, was sent abroad at the age of ten
with his tutor, a priest, and lived there until he was
nineteen. When he returned to Moscow the count dismissed
the tutor and told the young man to go to Petersburg, look
around and make his choice of a career and said that he
would agree to anything and gave him a letter to Prince
Vasiliy and some money. And so Pierre went to St Petersburg and did not know where to put his large, fat body. To
enlist? But that would mean fighting Napoleon and help
Austria and England against the greatest man in the world.
As he was unable to make up his mind about what path to
take he fell into the company of drunken scoundrels led by
Prince Kuragin. Just what sort of life this was the
reader may see from Dolokhov's escapade when he made a bet
when he was drunk that he could sit on the windowsill of a
second-floor room and drink a bottle of rum in one go.
Everyone was delighted at this and Pierre was so inspired
that he proposed doing the same thing and had already
climbed on to the windowsill before the others managed to
pull him back. Drinking bouts and dissipation, nocturnal
visits to certain shady ladies, games with a bear on to
whose back they once tied the caretaker of the building -
such are the heroic deeds of the hero through whose moral
enlightenment Count Tolstoy wishes to show the profundity
of the wisdom that should guide all humanity. There is
some strength in Pierre's large body, but where it is
hidden no one knows; he has nothing definite about him,
nothing fully developed. Giving himself over to his uncultured and unbridled nature Pierre does all sorts of
stupid things and just as he wanted to copy Dolokhov's
trick for no reason at all except from some simple mis-
direction of his energies, so he gets himself married to
the beautiful Hélène. Why did he feel the need to get
married? The fashionable Anna Pavlovna wanted to establish Hélène, and the good-natured Pierre went like a lamb
to the slaughter. Perhaps Pierre might have escaped the
net but it so happened that at a party at Anna Pavlovna's
Pierre finds himself so close to Hélène that even

his short-sighted eyes could discern the great charm of
her shoulders, neck and lips that he only had to bend
forward a little to touch them. He felt the warmth of
her body, smelt her perfume and heard the sound of her
corset as she moved. He did not see her marble beauty

which merged completely with her dress but he saw and
felt the utter delight of her body which was covered
only by what she wore.

Such is Count Tolstoy's wonderful description that we are
surprised that Pierre married her six months later and not
at the very minute he felt the warmth and delights of her
body.

Having indulged in this stupidity Pierre inevitably has
to go on to a whole series of new stupidities. He was
captivated only by a beautiful body and he had no other
more solid moral connections with Hélène. Therefore it is
not surprising that Hélène, who had married Pierre calcu-
latedly, and her body should then stretch out towards
other men more handsome than her husband; and then Pierre
gets jealous. Why? What on earth for? What did he have
in common with Hélène? Pierre knows nothing, understands
nothing. His broad, passionate nature, placed in a huge
body, can only become excited and agitated. He rages at
Dolokhov as he does at his wife's lover, finds fault in him
over nothing and calls him a rogue. A duel ensues, yet
another stupidity, a stupidity more gross than usual and
showing all the uncultivated breadth of Pierre's nature
because he has never in his life held a pistol before and
so is not only ignorant of how to load it but also how to
fire it. But Count Tolstoy thinks and tries to show that
there are forces beyond man's control which direct him
along one path and not another. Just before the duel
Pierre tries even to justify Dolokhov whom he had earlier
called a rogue.

Perhaps I would have done the same in his position,
thought Pierre, even probably; what is the point of
this duel, this murder? Either I shall kill him or
he'll shoot me in the head, the elbow or the knee.
It occurred to Pierre to leave, to run away and hide
somewhere.

In spite of these justifiable thoughts Pierre, on the
suggestion of his second who wishes to pacify the duel-
lists by saying that there was no insult intended on the
one side and should not he talk things over with Dolokhov,
replied: 'No, what is there to talk about; it doesn't
matter...' Thus that fate, which led him for no reason
to marry, and for no reason to fight a duel, so arranged
things that Pierre who does not even know how to fire a
pistol shoots that well-known duellist Dolokhov.

After the duel Pierre begins to wonder with his customary hindsight why he said to Hélène before their wedding,

'Je vous aime.'   I am guilty and must bear - what?   A
shameful name?   An unhappy life?   Everything is pre-
arranged; nothing depends on me.   Louis XVI was executed,
it occurred to Pierre, because he was dishonourable and a
criminal, and they were right from their point of view,
just as those who died in suffering for him and those who
canonized him.   Then Robespierre was executed because he
was a despot.   Who is guilty, who is innocent?   No one.
I am alive and well but tomorrow I might die, just as I
might have an hour ago.   Is it worth suffering when compared with eternity there is but a second to live?
Then Pierre decided that it would be better to divorce
his wife; he could no longer stay under the same roof as
her.   He leaves her a letter which explains that he intends to part from her for ever and will leave on the
morrow.   Then his wife comes in and tells him that she is
a fool and an ass as all the world knows and then when he
was drunk and forgetting what he was doing called out to
a duel a man of whom he was jealous without foundation.
Mmm ... mumbles Pierre at this.   'And how could you
believe he was my lover?   Because I like his company?
If you had been cleverer and more pleasant I should have
preferred yours.'   Pierre goes berserk, snatches a slab
of marble from the table, waves it at his wife and shouts:
'I'll kill you!'   If the reader recalls that Pierre has
pressed nails into the wall with his hands he will understand that a marble slab in the hands of such a Goliath
would present a certain danger.   'God alone knows what
Pierre would have done at that moment if Hélène had not
rushed from the room,' remarks the author.   It is clearly
incomprehensible why Count Tolstoy chose such a fat, wild
character as his hero.   He is a wild Mongol.   Why call
him a count?   Why give him a priest as a tutor?   Why send
him abroad for ten years?   Brute strength and emotional
outbursts are the basis of Pierre's character.   His un-
controlled strength in the body of a Goliath and his mind
of an ostrich can, of course, lead to no European result.
But this is precisely what Count Tolstoy needs; for otherwise his philosophy based on brute spontaneous strength
loses all grounds for its existence.   He needed precisely
the fatalism of the East and not the reason of the West.

[Description of Pierre's meeting the old freemason
omitted.]

The mysterious old man was one of the famous masons or
Martinists.   His influence was so strong that Pierre
joined the masons.   In masonry he discovered, as he
thought, that inner peace and satisfaction which he had

lacked till then. It seemed to Pierre that masonry was
the only expression of the best and eternal aspects of
humanity. Only the masons' holy brotherhood had any real
sense in life and everything else was but a dream.
Pierre gave himself over to this new influence whole-
heartedly. He organized lodges for feeding the poor and
for burials, he attracted new members, he worked for the
uniting of different lodges and for the acquisition of
documents. He gave his money for the building of masonic
temples and replenished as far as he could the alms collections at which most of the members were miserly and un-
punctual. Almost single-handed from his own resources he
supported a poorhouse built by the order in Petersburg.
In the course of the year, though, Pierre began to feel
that the masonic ground on which he was standing was more
and more slipping away from under him the more he tried to
stand firm. When he became a mason he experienced the
feeling of a man confidently stepping onto the smooth
surface of a bog. As he put his foot down he fell forward
and moving the other foot he fell in even more deeply. He
became disenchanted with his brothers and actually with
that self-perfectability towards which the masons apparently aspire. Among the members of the society he saw not
so much his brothers in the work of their mystic order
but rather some Prince B. and Count D., weak and insignificant people under whose masonic aprons and signs he saw
uniforms and the decorations which they had earned in
their lives. He understood the complete falsity and lie
of words which do not coincide with actions and became
depressed. Pierre began to seek a way out in prayer and
in spiritually edifying reading.

[Omitted: quotation concerning Pierre's flirtation with a
mystic religion.]

However Pierre did have some worldly moments too when
he again returned to his aimless, dissipated life but
these moments were of short duration. Pierre was living
in a kind of intoxication particularly intensified by the
general patriotic and military mood engendered by Napoleon's march on Moscow. Pierre's nerves were strained to
their limit. He felt the approach of some catastrophe
which would change his whole life and he sought in everything for signs of the approaching time. Our scribes had
concluded from the Apocalypse that Napoleon was the Antichrist and that his name was the number of the Beast 666.
It would appear that this was enough, but Pierre, half out
of his mind, was determined that come what may he would
find the number of the Beast in his own name. He wrote

his name in French and in Russian, changed or left out
some of the letters and finally arrived at the number he
was seeking, 666. This discovery agitated him. How and
in which connection he was joined with the great event
foretold in the Apocalypse he did not know; but not for
one moment did he doubt that connection.

The catastrophe actually arrived. Under the influence
of martial fervour Pierre, wearing different clothes now,
set out to view the battle of Borodino. He fell into the
company of soldiers and realized as if suddenly that these
strange people of whom he had been heretofore unaware were
indeed real people.

[Omitted: quotation concerning the simple, long-suffering
soldiers.]

This outburst of a sick, agitated man was far from solving the unsolvable which Pierre was seeking. Pierre did
not lead a healthy, active life nor did he have anything
real to do; he did not know what to do with his huge body
and at what to direct his Goliath-like strength. By
nature a man of passionate feeling, he needed to throw
some rocks around in order to cool the hot blood coursing
within him. But millions of contradictions, colliding in
this unshaped and unstable nature, forced him to seek a
point of reference which he had not yet found. A man of
simple democratic make-up, Pierre was born a count by
mistake, felt himself out of place in aristocratic salons
with their formality and conventional modes of behaviour
which he was incapable of learning. And so finding himself in the company of soldiers, having messed with them
and having heard simple soldiers talk, Pierre felt that
soldiers were his sort of people and in the simplicity of
their menial lives he saw where he should be. This is why
a man such as Karataev must have had an enormous influence
on Pierre.

Karataev had basically the same nature as Pierre. His
main pecularities were spontaneity and rapidity of speech.
He evidently never thought about what he had said or what
he would say and consequently in the flowing truthfulness
of his intonation there was a special irresistible conviction. He could do things not badly but not particularly
well either. He could bake, cook, sew, plane wood and
make boots; he would sing songs in a way different from
singers who knew people were listening to them but rather
like the birds, because these sounds just had to burst
from him; and the sounds were always gentle, tender,
almost feminine, rather doleful and while singing his face
was always serious. When he was taken prisoner he grew a

beard again and obviously threw off everything false, alien or martial and involuntarily returned to being the peasant he had been before. When he reminisced he did so primarily about his former and obviously beloved Christian peasant life. The sayings which filled his speech were not those generally coarse and vivid expressions used by the soldiers but those turns of speech of the ordinary Russian which seem so insignificant when heard out of context but which take on the appearance of profound wisdom when said in normal conversation. He often spoke in direct contradiction to what he said previously but on both occasions he seemed right. For Pierre, Karataev was some inscrutable, round and eternal personification of the spirit of simplicity and truth. His every word and action was a manifestation of some activity of which he was himself unaware but which was his life. But his life as he himself saw it had no meaning if looked at by itself; it only had any meaning as a part of the whole and this was something he constantly felt. His words and actions poure poured from him as evenly, inevitably and spontaneously as scent from a flower. He could not understand the value and meaning, though, of each word and action taken separately.

This idealization of spontaneous human feeling and of integrity of nature fully exposes the whole inconsistency of Count Tolstoy's philosophy. The author poses as the final result something at whose basis is the markedly uncultured brute force of a man whose development is no higher than that of a savage. Holding this point of view Count Tolstoy finds himself at the opposite pole from European civilization and the totality of knowledge which humanity has amassed over the centuries. 'There is no knowledge,' says Count Tolstoy. 'Surely facts plucked at random and results arrived at in isolation cannot form firm foundation on which to build the temple of human happiness? The truth of life is not to be found in books, in the studies of scholars, in the chemist's laboratory or in the heads of philosophers. It lives in the forests, the steppes, in trees and in the heart of Karataev.' But why does the light of truth reside in Karataev who grew like a mushroom in the woods or burdock in the field and not in the collective mental labours of the whole of humanity increasing its sum of knowledge from generation to generation? This light is understood only by Count Pierre Bezukhov and Count L.N. Tolstoy. Judge for yourselves. At one of the stopping-places Pierre as a prisoner has moved off from the others and sits by a lone wagon and gives himself over to his thoughts and the saving influence of Karataev and suddenly he bursts out laughing in his good-natured fat way so loudly that from all sides people look over at this strange and evidently private laughter.

[Quotation omitted.]

Karataev and the captivity, in which Pierre suffered much, renewed him. Not so much mentally but with his whole being he understood that man is created for happiness and that happiness lies within him in the satisfaction of his natural human desires and that unhappiness results not from any deficiency but from superfluity. When he was captured he realized that there is nothing terrible in life. He realized that as there is no place in the world where man can be happy and free so equally is there nowhere where he can be unhappy or not free. He realized that there is a line between suffering and freedom but that it is a narrow one, and the man who suffers when a single leaf turns in his rosebed is the same as the man who suffers now, sleeping on the bare cold earth, cold on one side and warm on the other; that when he used to pull on his narrow dancing shoes he suffered just as much as now walking barefoot and covered in sores. He realized that when he freely, as he thought, married his wife, he was no more free than now, locked up at night in a stable.

This submissive and appeasing philosophy along whose path Count Tolstoy walks is a philosophy without hope, of uninterrupted despair and declining strength. Karataev, of course, could not arrive at any other world outlook and as a saving grace, because good and suffering must receive their reward, if not on earth then elsewhere, had to seek the only way out of his hopeless position. But when Counts Tolstoy and Bezukhov come to the same conclusion it is quite a different matter. We agree that a child born to velvet and satin might feel as much suffering from a curled-up rose leaf as a child born on stony ground would feel from a flint which he finds under his side. But surely this is a question of powers of human endurance rather than human happiness. Count Tolstoy also erects a theory of individual human happiness and wishes to show how each of us can attain it. Count Pierre feels happy in a peasant's heavy coat with his legs covered in wounds and finds the soldiers' food tastier than all the viands of his lordly kitchen. Pierre is a fool and eccentric and we can well understand how he can arrive at any absurdity. But just imagine his philosophy becoming accepted universally, that every high-born baby will be convinced that a rose leaf under his side is just the same as a sharp flint sticking into a poor child whose poverty forces him to sleep on stony ground. Surely this is a philosophy of stagnation and murderous injustice, of oppression and exploitation. This philosophy of submissiveness passing from Karataev to Pierre shows only that Count Tolstoy felt his own impotence before the invincibility of the circumstances around him and thought of idealizing that very condition of individuals and whole societies which in thinking people calls forth different ideas and leads them to opposite conclusions. All of Russia is attempting to start off on a new road. The Emancipation of the Peasants, public trial and the Zemstvos suggest to us that our attempts must take us far beyond Mongolian traditions, yet Count Tolstoy gives Russia the advice that Rudin gave Natalya Alekseenva! This ascetic philosophy is presented by Count Tolstoy in an attractive form. He is lavish with his words of love but there is no real love or humanity in them. Count Tolstoy talks continually of that good inner feeling whose sense is given not by words but by man's whole being. Karataev's strength was not in words but in something else which Count Tolstoy does not presume to define but which appeared spontaneously and worked spontaneously. Having thus removed from himself the intellectual element and given himself over to spontaneous feeling in which he sees the source of all the world's wisdom, Count Tolstoy, under the influence of this feeling, falls into a contradiction. Putting love above all else in place of the practice of love, humanity and good, he preaches stagnation and the narrowest self-interest. The source of love brought the inward-looking Count Tolstoy to the advocacy of something which is evil, unhappiness and disaster - indifference and individualism.

All of Count Tolstoy's favourite characters are marked by the same depth of thought and so it is not surprising that starting from spontaneous feeling they finish in practical nonsense. For example when Natasha sees Pierre after his re-education by Karataev she remarks that Pierre has become somehow clean, smooth and fresh just as if he had had a bath, a moral bath. But Natasha has never appeared as a strong mental force and like all Count Tolstoy's heroes and heroines is marked by impulse, devotion and emptiness. There was a force roaming her innermost organism; she wanted a husband and the need for one was so great that when her wedding to Prince Andrey had to be postponed for a year she thought of eloping with Anatole simply to find herself a husband. Her mother remarked that Natasha always had strong maternal feelings. But what sort of feelings are they? Organic, spontaneous, Karataevian - and it becomes obvious through Count

Tolstoy's transparent idealization. Natasha became a
model mother; Pierre a model family man. Personal happiness shrank to the last limits of egoism in the pair and
the intellectual element took on the life of stagnant
water alien to everything that distinguishes a man from a
horse or a dog. A village at the back of beyond. Is this
really the object of all humanity's aspirations?

We understand why Pierre must have thought his family
life to be precisely the Promised Land towards which he
seemed to be striving. We certainly do! In his huge, fat
organism there was too much muscle and blood for them not
to show themselves in a burst of a certain strength seeking something. First of all he drinks and smokes, all but
fights bears, breaks marble tables, marries for unknown
reasons, fights a duel similarly, dresses in peasants'
clothes, rushes off to the field of Borodino and back to
Moscow and stays there also for unknown reasons when
everyone else is leaving, and only when he is a prisoner
of the French and Davout, that terrible, heartless Davout,
who threatens him with death, only as a prisoner, when
hunger, cold and physical suffering reduces some of his
size does he feel humility; for his strength has dimin-
ished. An elephant stronger than Pierre would have tired
in such escapades. It is clear why Pierre experiences
such happiness when he feels a young, beautiful woman
next to him, when he has acquired children and when
finally there is the satisfaction of those desires which
up till then have lain in the background. When one is
tired one always needs a rest.

If Count Tolstoy had given us in a simple form the
physiological and psychological processes which went on
in his hero we would have understood what he says. But
Count Tolstoy acts differently. He idealizes the weariness of a tired-out human organism. He idealizes the
absence of thought and points as a saving grace to the one
position which probably most of all prevents the social
development of humanity. Pierre starts with his marriage
to Hélène, a marriage without any sense. The same Pierre
ends with marriage to Natasha which is shown by Count Tolstoy as the consummation of family virtues. What can one
believe? Where lies happiness and where unhappiness?
Either Prince Andrey is right when he says that one should
marry when one has realized all one's social capabilities
or the spontaneous Karataev is right when he says one
ought to marry at eighteen. Count Tolstoy is silent and
we are glad for the Russian reading public who sees the
confusion of the author lost in his own ideas.

36.   TURGENEV ON 'WAR AND PEACE'

1868, 1869, 1870

See Introduction.

(a) From a letter to P.V. Annenkov, 14 February 1868.

I have read both Tolstoy's novel and your article on it...
the novel itself aroused in me the most intense interest;
there are whole dozens of pages which are quite marvellous - all the domestic and descriptive passages (the
hunt, the sleigh-ride at night, etc.), but the historical
addition, with which his readers are particularly delighted, is a puppet comedy and charlatanism. As Voroshilov
in 'Smoke' casts dust in people's eyes by quoting the last
pronouncements of science (not knowing either the first or
the second, which is something, for example, conscien-
tious Germans cannot conceive of) so Tolstoy amazes the
reader with the toe of Alexander's boot and Speransky's
laugh, forcing one to think that he knows *everything* because he has gone into even these details - but it is only
these details that he knows. A trick and no more, but the
public has fallen for it. And with regard to Tolstoy's
so-called psychology there is much that could be said;
there is no real development in any of the characters
(which by the way you noticed yourself) and there is the
same old way of transmitting the vacillations and vibra-
tions of one and the same feeling, situation and what he
so mercilessly puts into the mouths and consciousness of
all his heroes. I love, someone says, but actually I hate,
etc., etc. How sick and tired one is of these quasi-
subtle reflections, of these thought processes, of the
observation of his own feelings. Tolstoy is either unaware of any other psychology or he ignores it. And how
wearisome are those deliberate and insistent repetitions
of one and the same trait - the down on Princess Bolkonsky's upper lip, and so on. Despite all this, though,
there are things in this novel which no one in Europe save
Tolstoy could have written and which have aroused in me
the chill and fever of ecstasy.

(b) From a letter to A.A. Fet, 12 April 1868.

I have just finished the fourth volume of 'War and Peace'.
There are things in it that are unbearable, and things
that are wonderful; and the wonderful things, which
generally predominate, are so magnificently good that we
have never had anything better written by anybody and it
is doubtful if anything as good has ever been written.
The first and fourth volumes are weaker than the second
and third, especially the third, which is almost all a
chef d'oeuvre.

(c) From a letter to I.P. Borisov, 24 February 1869.

I am very pleased at the news that [another] volume of
'War and Peace' is coming out soon; with all his weaknesses and eccentricities, even with all his nonsense,
Tolstoy is a real giant among the rest of our literary
fraternity - and he produces on me the impression of an
elephant at the zoo: clumsy, even preposterous, but enormous - and how intelligent! May God grant he writes
another twenty volumes!

(d) From a letter to I.P. Borisov, 24 February 1870.

I still haven't received the fifth volume of 'War and
Peace'; but judging by the opinions that have reached me
our genius and crank has taken the bit between his teeth.
Is it possible that from hatred of philosophy and fine
phrases one can take into one's head philosophy and
phrases like this! What every peasant understands as
well as the benefits of bread - and I mean the benefits of
the human mind, of reason - is to be rooted out! There's
nonsense for you. And it has to be rubbish like that
which has got into the head of the most talented writer in
all European literature today. But I am overcome in advance by the delights which are sure to abound in this
fifth volume.

(e) From a letter to I.P. Borisov, 27 March 1870.

I have read the sixth volume of 'War and Peace'; of course
there are things of the first order: but without speaking
of the childish philosophy, I find it unpleasant to see
the reflection of a *system* even in the characters depicted
by Tolstoy. Why must all his beautiful women be not only
females but fools as well? And why does he try to convince the reader that if a woman is intelligent and cultured then she must be a phrasemaker and a liar? How did
he overlook all the *Decembrist* element in the twenties -
and why are all his decent people also nincompoops, with a
little of the holy fool? I am afraid that Slavophilism,
into the hands of which he seems to have fallen, has
ruined his splendid and poetical talent, by depriving him
of a free mind.

37.   SKABICHEVSKY ON TOLSTOY'S CHARACTERS

1872

From Count L.N. Tolstoy as Artist and Thinker, 'Fatherland
Notes', 1872, no. 8. A.M. Skabichevsky (1838-1910),
Populist writer and critic, saw in this review of 'War and
Peace' Tolstoy following the same sad path as Gogol - the
brilliant writer was becoming a mystic and preacher. His
dislike of what he thought was happening to Tolstoy was
even more marked in his review of 'Anna Karenina' (see
No. 58).

Evidently Tolstoy has no other objective in mind than the
presentation of a picture gallery of paintings of upper-
class life at the beginning of the century. In this respect the novel is not only irreproachable but may truthfully be called a phenomenon unknown of in Russian literature before and one of its most striking works. Indeed
you will find in our literature masses of novels, stories
and plays and even poems describing upper-class life but
you will not find such a complete, detailed and clear
depiction of this life as you will in 'War and Peace'.
You will find a whole series of real living types from the

world of the upper classes. In truth characters such as
the Bolkonskys, Kuragins and Rostovs, Pierre Bezukhov,
Dolokhov, Bilibin and so on are types no less realistic
than those in 'Dead Souls' and can serve as equally good
examples of their class as do Chichikov, Manilov, Nozdryov,
Plyushkin and so on who have already become by-words for
theirs. These types are examined in all the mainsprings
of their lives and the tiniest psychological movements.
They can be divided into four groups. First, those like
the Kuragins and Dolokhov who represent the final stages
of moral decadence causing them to have no fellow feelings
for people not only of lower standing but even for those
from their own level; they are like the Romans at the end
of the Empire, people with whom it is positively dangerous
to associate because if the need arises they are prepared
not only to take away your human dignity, remove your
honour and send you out into the world without a shirt to
your back but also to despatch you to the other world. In
this respect it must be pointed out that the most terrible
of these carnivorous animals are those who, like for
example Prince Kuragin, in all their monstrous actions
retain a certain amount of restraint, tact and shrewdness,
who are always in control of themselves and know how to
mask themselves in the various virtues. Dolokhov is no
less terrible with his awful impertinence, nerves of steel
and the fascination of the extraordinary forces that lie
within him. In the character of Dolokhov, Count Tolstoy
has finally dethroned and put in his rightful place that
demonic type of the thirties and forties who was beloved
of our writers and whom we even now cannot recall without
a sigh. Dolokhov is almost that same Pechorin, but
instead of amazement he arouses only loathing. Types like
Anatole Kuragin and his sister Hélène Bezukhov earn great
leniency for themselves in as much as their animal instincts have drowned to such a degree both reason and will
in them that for the most part they become sacrifices to
their own dissoluteness.

The second category is that of the careerists like
Boris Drubetskoy and Berg for ever earning promotion and
becoming rich. Always well dressed and well groomed,
moderate in their passions and habits, modest and respectful, they have the appearance of respectable people but
essentially they have no more humanity in them than those
in the first category. They do you no harm without
cause - and that's about all. But do not expect from them
good, help or concern; they are dry and cold towards
everything in which they can see no benefit for themselves. Their friendship and affection is determined by
various official aspects and no matter how deeply you are

attached to them you may rest assured that once they have
sucked you dry they will dispense with you without a second thought once you are no longer of any use to them.
Thus Boris dispensed with the friendship of Rostov who had
done him a great favour as soon as he was able to stand on
his own feet. In their official and other narrowly self-
seeking concerns they do not like to be seen in the company of people who are less important that they are or
even their equals but prefer to move in more important
circles where by cringing before people and doing them
services they can little by little worm their way into
people's confidence and then without being noticed rise
to the same level and crawl even higher.

To the third category belong the Rostovs. They are
people in whom you will find much humanity: they can love
and be friendly unselfishly, can rise to a noble impulse
on the spur of the moment, but they also have no objective
in their lives, no serious occupations and the least
understanding of people or life. They are as it were
grown-up children with the placid faith of children and
their views on life, blindly devoting themselves to the
present and ever thirsting for a wide-ranging happiness
and the good life. If life sometimes treats them to a
bitter moment or gives them a pat on the back or brings
them a new toy they will forget themselves for a moment,
then calm down a little and return to their usual contented and joyful lives; if circumstances suddenly crop up
which destroy the inviolability of their childlike conceptions they will rapidly chase away all doubt and think
it some sort of crime in themselves to admit to any independent thought. Thus when their estates are feeling the
effect of their too full lives they hurriedly write to
their son, who is in the army, imagining that he can
create miracles and somehow rescue them from their
troubles. Nikolay, who does not understand a thing about
running an estate or keeping accounts, attacks the bailiff, heaping abuse upon him, and throws him down the
stairs and the whole family calms down after such a scene
as if the whole estate will recover after this one act of
Nikolay's, and they begin again their cheerful festivities
and hunting parties... Thus the impressionable Natasha,
who considers it her duty to fall in love with every new
male acquaintance, suddenly takes it into her head to
elope with Anatole Kuragin just after she has become
engaged to Prince Andrey. After the scandal which ensues
she falls into despair and lies close to death but it only
needs Pierre Bezukhov to smile nicely at her and say a few
words of sympathy and she again begins to blossom as if
nothing has happened. Similarly Nikolay Rostov after the

Peace of Tilsit, whose injustice has been exposed by his
friend Denisov, and the terrible sight of the wounded in
the military hospitals is suddenly stricken by unexpected
doubts which threaten to disturb the ecstasy he experienced at the reviews and parades. He beats his fist
angrily on the table and shouts at a friend of his who has
similar doubts: 'It is our job to carry out our duty, to
fight and not to think, and that's all.' And all of his
doubts vanish.

To the fourth category belong those people who have
highly developed mental and moral aspirations coming from
their thinking and reading. They are continually asking
themselves what the purpose of their lives is and trying
to analyse and define the various phenomena surrounding
them and their attitudes to other people. Such people are
the Bolkonskys, father, daughter Maria, and son Andrey,
and Pierre Bezukhov. But because they continue to live
abnormal lives the objectives they set themselves do not
stem naturally from their lives or their natures but are
artificially invented in order to fill somehow the emptiness of their lives, and however beautiful their plans
appear in theory they are either not realized or have no
outcome or bring some unexpected misfortune to those who
are connected with them. In other words we have here yet
more Nekhlyudovism.

The old Bolkonsky, a retired general from the reign of
Catherine the Great living uninterruptedly in the country,
repeating again and again that there are only two sources
of human vice, idleness and superstition, in consequence
of which belief he spends his time in useless activity
working at his lathe, rebuilding parts of his estates and
solving problems of higher mathematics; he keeps the whole
household under the yoke of his firm despotism and imagines that the only real task left to him in life is the
education of his daughter Maria. This education consisted
in teaching her algebra and geometry until she was
twenty, mocking her lack of beauty and organizing her
life in ceaseless study. The young girl was so oppressed
by his despotism that when she entered his study she would
pray in advance that the meeting with him would turn out
happily. Under the influence of such terror the young
girl took refuge in a deep mysticism: she read books on
the subject, surrounded herself with wandering pilgrims
and cripples, dreamed of becoming a pilgrim herself and
imagined that her life's main task was self-sacrifice for
the sake of her father. Her depersonalization reached
such a degree that although suffering much from her father
she was horrified when her brother, Prince Andrey, was, in
her eyes, critical of her father. Furthermore, living

constantly in an abstract world of spiritual contemplation
interrupted by dry algebraic problems she had not the
slightest understanding of people or life in general in
which respect she was comically naive. For example, when
Prince Kuragin arrived to arrange a marriage between her
and his son she was immediately captivated by the young
man. He seemed good, brave, decisive, manly and generous.
Then she witnessed the scandalous scene between him and
the French governess, Mlle Bourienne; but this did not
disenchant her about him; in her innocence she believed
that Anatole and Mlle Bourienne had fallen in love, and
that she should not destroy their happiness for her object
in life was self-sacrifice, and so she refused his offer
of marriage on this basis. But even more comic is the
scene with her rebellious peasants during the French invasion. Excited by false rumours the peasants expected the
French to free them and not only wanted to stay in the
face of their advance but refused to let Maria leave
either, even though she had been left to manage things
alone after the death of her father. Princess Maria,
however, thought that the peasants were worried lest she
should leave them to the mercy of the French.

[Quotation omitted.]

   One feels a certain pity at the sight of a person
reduced to such idiocies for after all she is not unintel-
ligent and has certain admirable idealistic aspirations.
   As for her brother, Prince Andrey, at first glance he
appears as a man of great intelligence with a stable and
energetic character, strong and practical, but when you
look more closely at the various problems he meets in his
life you discover the same Nekhlyudovism which you know so
well. He married, Heaven knows why, an empty and flirtatious society girl and then gets bored with her and with
society life.

[Quotation omitted.]

   He later enlists in the army and here we see the striking dualism in such people: on the one hand you note in
him the belief that he is completely ignorant and worthless, but this does not prevent his dreaming that he will
do something that will save his fatherland and make him as
glorious as Napoleon. These ambitions have a particular
hold over him when he learns the French have crossed the
Tamborsky bridge and realizes the great danger this crossing presents to the Russian army.

[Quotation omitted.]

We meet here with one of those confrontations which are
a marked characteristic of Count Tolstoy's talent and so
sharply delineate the bankruptcy of his heroes. While
Prince Andrey is impatiently awaiting the moment when he
will seize the banner and save the entire Russian army
from certain defeat he meets on the eve of the battle of
Schöngraben the small, dirty and thin artillery officer,
Tushin, who is sitting barefoot having given his boots to
the sutler to dry out. There was absolutely nothing
heroic about him and indeed it had never occurred to him
to become the saviour of Russia. Modest and respectful
before his superiors he had the appearance of someone
special and utterly non-military, a little comic but
extremely attractive. Imagine Prince Andrey's surprise
when on the following day while he was pointlessly mooch-
ing about the battlefield this unprepossessing little
officer should show himself a real hero, and even more
striking was that this heroism should have been completely
unconscious.

[Quotation omitted.]

This meeting between Bolkonsky and Tushin is in my
opinion one of the brightest and might I say greatest
flashes of Count Tolstoy's genius.
After his failure to save Russia, and wounded into the
bargain, Prince Andrey retires from the army and soon
becomes depressed. To assuage his boredom he busies
himself with various liberal ideas which were current in
the society of the time; for example, he studies the
running of his estates and frees 300 of his serfs (he was
one of the first people in Russia to do this) and with
the others corvée was replaced by quit-rent. This was the
only good thing he did in his whole life. Do you think,
though, that he did it filled with a humane, warm Christian love for the unfortunate of this world which alone
could restrain his arrogance, soften his hard heart,
alleviate his vain melancholy and fill the emptiness of
his life? Evidently not. It is evident that the infinite
sky which he contemplated with such humility while lying
wounded on the field of Austerlitz instilled in him more
love for himself than for his fellows. We at least see
that after all his elevated thoughts he had become not a
whit more humane and could still make a cynical speech
like the one that follows.

[Omitted: quotation of Andrey's conversation with Pierre

on his completely selfish reasons for freeing his serfs.]

Just note to what an absence of any healthy logic a man can be brought by the inhumanity of a narrow prejudiced egoism. Andrey is incapable of understanding the simple truth that coarseness and cruelty can only be considered vices when they bring suffering to people and not just because they cause others a bad conscience. If Prince Andrey proposes that however much you flog the serfs and shave their heads that they will remain just the same and that the peasants are no worse off by being beaten, flogged or sent to Siberia then one wonders what he later found bad in the coarseness and cruelty of his own class? On what other basis do we not repent of our cruelty or become dehumanized when we chop a tree up into firewood or tear paper into pieces if not in the conviction that the tree or the paper will feel no moral or physical pain?

If in any case the best representative of his class appears before us in such a melancholy aspect then I wonder if there is any need to talk about Pierre Bezukhov, that pitiful toy in the hands of all those around him, whose whole life has been a series of unforeseen accidents throwing him like a doll first one way and then that, without the slightest show of opposition on his part. An abstract theoretician, attracted by the French Revolution and worshipping Napoleon, he is for ever seeking no matter what he is doing; suddenly he becomes immensely rich inheriting the title and estates of Count Bezukhov; he is drawn into the maelstrom of the social whirl, eats and drinks too much, marries Hélène Kuragin because he is attracted by the whiteness of her shoulders only to separate from her at her first show of infidelity and to challenge her first lover to a duel. Just as unexpected is his change from a Voltairean into a mason after meeting on the way to the station an old mason from the previous century; he writes a mystical diary, rides round his estates with the intention of improving the life of his peasants, sets up schools, hospitals and pharmacies and is satisfied with his activities, and especially with his triumphant meetings which the peasants organize for him on the orders of the foremen, and he does not notice how many fresh burdens the foremen have placed upon the peasants as a result of his virtuous rearrangements. Just before the war of 1812 he turns his name by some mystic nonsense into 'le Russe Besuhof' and decides that his fate has somehow been mysteriously joined with that of Napoleon and comes filled with joy at the thought that his love for Natasha, the Antichrist, Napoleon's invasion, the comet, the number 666, the Emperor Napoleon and le Russe Besuhof will all unite, mature, develop and remove him from the vicious, petty world of Moscow where he felt himself a prisoner and lead him to some great deed and then to great happiness. As a result of all this he flies off to active service without, however, enlisting and wanders aimlessly round the battlefield at Borodino, remains in Moscow as the French enter it and it then occurs to him to kill Napoleon; he dresses up in peasant clothes, buys a pistol and a knife, but instead of carrying out his fateful mission he has a very convivial talk over a bottle of claret with a French officer about love and is then arrested by the French on suspicion of being an incendiary and then rescues a child from a fire.

In a word we have in Pierre Bezukhov a Nekhlyudov of the beginning of the century in the full glory of his brilliance, with all his characteristics and idiosyncracies, all shown with such a naked truth, with which only Count Tolstoy is capable of investing his characters.

38.   COURRIÈRE: A FRENCH VIEW OF 'WAR AND PEACE'

1875

Courrière's book 'Histoire de la littérature contemporaine en Russie', published in Paris in 1875, contains probably the earliest French comment on 'War and Peace' (it was not translated into French until 1879). This extract is taken from chapter VI which is entitled The Historical Novel.

Count L. Tolstoy's novel 'War and Peace' is without doubt one of the best of all the masterpieces of Russian literature. When it appeared it was read with great enthusiasn and was a sensation. (I have counted some eighty-four critical articles on it in the Librarie de Méjof.) Its size is immense (it came out in five volumes) and contains innumerable characters. There are no less than three emperors and their ministers, marshals and generals, there are officers, soldiers, nobles and peasants. From the salons of St Petersburg the author transports us to the military camps, from Moscow to the country. Everything hangs together, the links are tight, there is no confusion; a mass of different pictures, ever changing, passes before our eyes; they are all equally beautiful, equally striking.

The novel can be divided into two quite distinct parts. 'Peace', although inferior in colouring and vividness to 'War', is none the less for that. It is a faithful picture of the Russian aristocracy at the beginning of this century - fickle, superficial, still influenced by the times of Catherine the Great, entirely French dominated and feeling ashamed to speak Russian, probably because the language was poorly known.... The hero of 'Peace' is Pierre Bezukhov. He is a product of a period of transition, typical of Russian society on the threshold of a new era. Pierre has no aim in life. Leaving Mme Scherer's, he goes off with his officer friends and ties a police official to the back of a bear and throws them into the River Moyka. He marries the young Hélène Kuragin under the influence of her charms without wondering why. Married to one of the leading beauties in the capital who is not slow in becoming a Ninon à la mode, he is not at all jealous and does not seem to notice that his wife is deceiving him. He is just a child who looks lost in an unknown, strange world. The mystical theories of the freemasons bring him a little peace but do not fully satisfy him. The author later shows us Pierre, lost and distracted, wandering casually through burning Moscow. Taken prisoner by the French he is converted to a true knowledge of life by a simple soldier, Karataev. Does one see an allegory here? Did the author wish to show that the salvation and the future of a young society at that time could only be found in abandoning the traditions of the past and in drawing near to the people?

The portrait of Natasha Rostov is far less successful. This young woman, despite the sympathetic traits which the author gives her, presents a shocking contrast. Engaged to Prince Andrey she cannot wait for his return. At times she screams to her mother: 'Give him to me! I want him!' Then losing all patience, she is almost carried off by Anatole Kuragin, for whom she develops a sudden passion. Finally, after Prince Andrey's death at Borodino, she marries Pierre Bezukhov and becomes a model wife and mother although tying her husband to her apron strings.

'War' in the beauty of its pictures, the grandeur and animation of its scenes and the vividness of its colouring is far superior to 'Peace'. The description of the battles of Schöngraben, Austerlitz and Borodino, the fire in Moscow and the retreat of the French army can rival anything we have produced in this genre. But why should the admiration one feels for all its beauties have to be ruined by the philosophic theories of the author? Count

Tolstoy sees in this gigantic struggle between two worlds,
in this huge movement of humanity, only the course and
amalgamation of accidental causes, independent of the
human will. Napoleon and Alexander, Kutuzov and Bagration, the French and the Russians are all nothing but
pawns set in motion by the hand of destiny on the vast
chess-board of the world. The author's fatalism is argu-
mentative and doctrinaire; it reduces to its own petty
level all the great events of this century. Not only does
he not show us the point where the action of the human
will ceases and the force of destiny begins but he confuses the issue by subordinating the former to the latter.

[Omitted: quotations and relation of Tolstoy's view of
free will.]

Of all those who played a leading role in this celebrated campaign only Kutuzov finds any mercy before the
pitiless theories of the author, probably because he unconsciously realized the impotence of the human will
before the laws of Fate.... On the eve of Austerlitz he
alone has a presentiment of the forthcoming defeat, and
we see him sleeping and snoring during the council of war
discussing the battle plans. During the retreat from
Moscow he divines the weakness of the French army; he
was of the opinion that it was best to let it founder of
itself without offering battle and make it a point of
honour that it should depart from Russia as quickly as
possible.

[Quotation omitted.]

   Napoleon not only passes like the others beneath the
Caudine Forks (we should be curious to know how the
author explains, in view of his fatalism, his famous
march from his camp at Boulogne to the Danube), but also
appears before us as a comic and ridiculous poseur, whose
only aim is to appear effective in the eyes of his
entourage. It is difficult to demand impartiality from
a novelist but in treating lightly the battles of Austerlitz and Borodino the author gives the activities of the
partisans the importance of real battles.

39.   RALSTON ON PIERRE BEZUKHOV, THE TYPICAL RUSSIAN

1879

From Count Leo Tolstoy's Novels, 'Nineteenth Century',
April 1879. W.R.S. Ralston (1828-89) was from 1853 to
1875 an assistant in the printed books department of the
British Museum. Interest in Russia was aroused at this
time in England and he taught himself Russian, and began
to write on Russian life and literature. He published
translations of the fabulist Krylov, Turgenev's 'Nest of
Gentlefolk', and two collections of Russian songs and
folk tales.

Pierre Bezukhov, the most interesting, though not at first
sight the most attractive, of the three heroes of 'War and
Peace', was in many respects a typical Russian. Good-
humoured, soft-hearted, well-meaning, emotional, indolent,
and all but destitute of moral backbone, he was everything
by turns, and nothing long, except in so far as that he
always remained true to the natural kindliness of his disposition. Among other weak points in the Russian character seems to be an incapacity to recognize the advantage
of telling the truth, the necessity of keeping a plighted
word. The tendency to colour or distort statements is
closely connected in many instances with the fervid imagination of a poetic temperament, or the desire to please of
an amiable disposition; the fracture of a promise is more
often due to a child-like forgetfulness than to any deliberate intention to play false.

40.   GUSTAVE FLAUBERT ON 'WAR AND PEACE'

1880

From a letter to Tolstoy from Turgenev, 24 January 1880.
A French translation in three volumes of 'War and Peace'
was published in Paris in 1879 and Turgenev did his best
to see that all the leading critics received a copy. He
admitted to Tolstoy that its spirit was alien to every-

everything the French looked for in a novel. However three hundred copies were sold in a few months.

I am copying out for you with diplomatic accuracy an extract from a letter to me from M. Flaubert - I had sent him the translation of 'War and Peace' (unfortunately a pretty anaemic one):

> I am grateful that you gave me the opportunity to read Tolstoy's novel. It is first rate. What an artist and what a psychologist! The first two volumes are sublime, but the third goes downhill dreadfully. He repeats himself. And he philosophizes. In a word here one sees the gentleman, the author, and the Russian, whereas hitherto one had seen only Nature and Humanity. It seems to me that there are some passages worthy of Shakespeare. I found myself crying out in admiration while reading, and that lasted a long time. Yes, it is powerful, very powerful!

> I think, *en somme*, you will be satisfied.

41. DE CYON ON TOLSTOY'S STYLE

1883

From E. de Cyon's article, Lev Tolstoy - a Russian Pessimist, 'Nouvelle Revue', 1 June 1883.

Count Tolstoy owes his pre-eminent position among contemporary Russian writers primarily to the incomparable subtlety and intensity of his psychological analysis; there is proof of this in everything he has written. In this respect there is nothing to distinguish between any of the works of this eminent novelist; the least of them shows the same supreme talent as the most vast. In 'The Cossacks', a simple sketch of military life in the Caucasus, in 'A Landowner's Morning', a rough draft for a story of village life, as well as in 'War and Peace', that huge epic with its innumerable characters and mass of events,

the author always allows us *inside* his heroes and initiates
us into every nuance of even the most fleeting of their
thoughts. Nothing which occurs within them is allowed to
pass unnoticed. Whether the idea results from previous
long thought processes or whether it bursts forth to leave
no trace of itself afterwards, it is always presented by
the author simply and clearly; he never even stops to consider the connection between the thoughts and the actions
which follow from them.

Like all realists Count Tolstoy presents his story in
minute detail; it is of little concern to him whether any
detail is pleasing or not, whether it is essential or not,
whether it adds to or detracts from the character to whom
it is attributed, even if it is one of those of whom he
seems to be especially fond.

When he paints moral life there is the same attention
to accuracy, the same absence of any bias. A guilty
thought can pass through the mind of the best of men just
as a good and generous one can arise in a scoundrel; our
author is careful not to neglect these contradictions
which lie at the root of human nature. Also it is impossible to read his works and not admire the absolute veracity of his analyses and pictures.

This exactitude is all the more striking in 'War and
Peace' as the work embraces the epic struggle between
Russia and Napoleon from Austerlitz to Berezina, repro-
duces all the political life from the beginning of the
century and places on the stage the principal heroes of
that troubled time: Napoleon, Alexander, Kutuzov, Rostopchin, Speransky, etc., are presented at the most critical
time in their lives. Thanks to an intuition which touches
on the marvellous, Tolstoy unveils those hidden springs
which move men. A few insignificant exterior details
suffice to paint them completely. Without stressing the
point or attempting to influence our judgment, he succeeds in stripping from several of them the masks in which
official history has clothed them, and in destroying our
most deeply rooted prejudices about them. He examines so
thoroughly the souls of his characters and the harmony of
their conscious and unconscious thoughts, and their
exterior actions are rendered so evident, that the less he
seeks to convince us the more we are struck by the justice
of his views.

There is only one modern writer who could possibly be
compared with Tolstoy in this respect - the author of 'The
Scarlet and the Black' and 'The Charterhouse at Parma'.
There is an analogy between them. Tolstoy made his début
while he was in the army and knows all the vicissitudes of
military life. Like Stendhal Tolstoy is both a sensitive

and a lucid writer; both of them were accustomed from
their earliest childhood to watch themselves thinking,
something which allows them to look into the hearts of
others with a wonderful perspicacity, and to create that
intense and sometimes frightening psychological life with
which they endow the creatures of their imagination.
Finally like Stendhal's, Tolstoy's style is sober, dry,
mathematical and free from all literary pretension. It is
clear that every word is chosen for the purpose it has to
serve, and that it is impossible to replace it with another without destroying the absolute precision of the
thought. Tolstoy often appears to take his contempt for
phrase-making to a complete disdain for syntax; his con-
structions, if looked at strictly logically, sometimes
appear incorrect and crude; but on the other hand he is
possessed of a range of vocabulary which few Russian
writers before him can approach. And thanks to his apposite use of contrast he can bring a quite unexpected meaning to the most ordinary expression.

The search for the correct word, however, is never taken
by Tolstoy to the excessive lengths indulged in by certain
French authors; it never becomes an exclusive preoccupation
to the detriment of all other artistic intentions. On the
contrary, nothing is further removed from Tolstoy's genius
than artificiality and falsity. Sincere in everything, he
loves only the simple and the natural. A characteristic
trait with Tolstoy is that the words which he employs most
happily and to which he gives a meaning different from
current usage are for the most part verbs. Stendhal always
seeks the most suitable adjective. Tolstoy, who relates
but never describes, gives verbs a greater importance.
Everything occurs through action; whether it is an external
event (a battle, a journey, or any ordinary occurrence) or
whether an internal one (a worrying thought, a hesitation
in the will, or a troubled emotion) makes no difference:
it is always action which he follows.

One cannot even say that the countryside, the towns, or
the battlefields whither Tolstoy leads his readers are
treated in a picturesque way. He never gives us pictures;
he shows us things not as they are in themselves but
through the impression they make upon his characters. It
seems as if he extends his psychological analysis to lifeless phenomena. The horrors of the battlefield, the mysterious charm of moonlight over the steppe, the tragic
sadness of Moscow abandoned before the invasion and a prey
to the incendiary - it is impossible to paint such scenes
with a more thrilling realism. And moreover, none of them
is ever described directly: Tolstoy confines himself to
relating their effects on Andrey Bolkonsky, Pierre

Bezukhov or Natasha Rostov.

These impressions are analysed with such a power of
truth that we participate ourselves in the horrors which
Andrey experiences during the massacres at Schöngraben
and Austerlitz; we submit with Natasha before the exhila-
rating delight of a ride across the steppe; and when
Pierre witnesses the destruction of Moscow and believes
himself called upon to take vengeance on the invader, we
are tempted to applaud his determination.

It is precisely in passages of this sort that Tolstoy
attains the peak of his art. Not content merely to reproduce all the details of the drama, external or personal,
he communicates to the reader the emotions in which the
drama takes place, he gives us the atmosphere surrounding
the characters and we understand the influences under which
they act because we are affected by them too.

If as a psychological analyst Tolstoy recalls Stendhal
more than anyone else, he is, however, superior to him in
the fertility of his imagination. Once one has recalled
the names of Julien Sorel, Morca and Mathilde de la Mole,
one has mentioned more or less all Stendhal's creations.
Let us also note that Stendhal deals almost exclusively
with exceptional people, grand, imposing designs, and
almost superhuman passions. Like some of Shakespeare's
heroes, his characters are at once both real and artificial: real because they possess, albeit idealized, inherent traits of human nature, but false in their expression of concrete reality. The number of types created by
Tolstoy is rather more considerable. In this respect he
can be compared only with Balzac. Only the 'Comédie
Humaine' offers a collection of characters as varied as
those we find in 'War and Peace'. This richness is all
the more remarkable in that the heroes, properly speaking,
of the novel as well as those who appear but briefly are
all painted with an equal finish, all stand out with an
equal clarity, and all are equally indelibly engraved
upon our imaginations, whether the author has devoted a
whole chapter to them or whether he merely depicts them
in a few lines.

42. UNSIGNED REVIEW, 'NATION' (NEW YORK)

22 January 1885

'Peace and War', as it now appears in the French translation, forms three volumes very closely printed. It is
called an historical novel, but hardly deserves that name.
It is not an historical novel; history is merely a thread
which binds together the heroes and heroines of a complex
human drama. It is not even a novel, as in a novel there
are always favorite heroes or heroines, surrounded with
accessory personages, and the novel is chiefly consecrated
to the delineation of a few central figures. Here we have
nothing of the sort. This single work might better be
compared to the series of novels by our great Balzac, in
which the same figures always reappear, sometimes more in
the light, but sometimes more in the shade. The personages
of Balzac, men and women, virtuous or criminal, weak or
heroic, form a sort of human medium, an atmosphere of passions, sometimes almost nebulous, and sometimes condensed
in brilliant constellations. Balzac himself gave to his
huge work, which fills so many volumes, the graphic name
of 'La Comédie Humaine'. The world in which all his
actors move, suffer, and die seems as real as the true
world. Such is the power of this writer that he gives
life, he creates; our memory preserves all his types as
easily as the men or women who have been thrown in our
path and in the vortex of our own destiny.
     This book of Tolstoi's might be called with justice
'The Russian Comedy' in the sense in which Balzac employed
the word. It gave me exactly the same impression: I felt
that I was thrown among new men and women, that I lived
with them, that I knew them, that none of them could be
indifferent to me, that I could never forget them. I
entered into their souls, and it seemed almost as if they
could enter into mine. Such a power in a writer is almost
a miracle. How many novels have I not read and after
reading them and admired their many qualities - the beauty
of the style, the invention, the dialogues, the dramatic
situations - have still felt that my knowledge of life had
not increased, that I had gained no new experience. It
was not so with 'Peace and War'.

[Summary of story omitted.]

     History, in this extraordinary work, merely plays the
part of a huge disturbing element; it acts on a host of

actors, high or low, as a foreign body would act if a
powerful hand threw it into the midst of our planetary
system. It does not change men, but it gives them new and
unforeseen opportunities. It changes the cold, heartless
profligate, the man of prey, who lives but for his material pleasures, into a brave man, and sometimes into a hero.
It brings out the dormant capacities and virtualities. It
reveals all sorts of secrets to man. It brings men constantly before a formidable unknown. It exasperates some;
it calms and soothes others. It gives to all the tender
relations of life a new intensity, by depriving them of
security. It is a powerful motor, but it is only a motor;
the masses which it puts into motion are already formed of
determined units, and each of these units is a human soul,
a world in itself, shrouded in mystery. Conceived in this
sense, Tolstoi's work has all the variety of human experience; it is less a novel than a succession of pictures, of
small scenes, in which we often see the same actors. The
book, in order to be well understood, must be read twice.
The first time, you have to make the acquaintance of a
number of people, and to become familiar with their bar-
barous Russian names. It is rather fatiguing at first,
especially as there is no *story*, in the English sense of
the word, as applied to a novel. You are constantly shifted from one place to another, from one set of people to
another set of people. By degrees, all becomes clear, the
action is fairly engaged, the drama - or rather, the
dramas, for there are several in one - develop themselves,
and you soon feel the keenest interest in all the actors.
I ran, so to speak, through the book the first time, in
order to form a conception of the aim of the author, and
then I read it a second time, *con amore*, interrupting
myself so as to prolong the pleasure, finding infinite joy
in some of its tableaux, in the descriptions of nature, in
the conversations, in the accessory details.

    It would be difficult to give a proper definition of
the talent of Tolstoi. First of all, he is an *homme du
monde*. He makes great people, emperors, generals, diplomats, fine ladies, princes, talk and act as they do act
and talk. He is a perfect gentleman, and as such he is
thoroughly humane. He takes as much interest in the most
humble of his actors as he does in the highest. He has
lived in courts: the Saint-Andrés, the Saint-Vladimirs
have no prestige for him - nor the gilded uniforms; he is
not deceived by appearances. His aim is so high, that
whatever he sees is, in one sense, unsatisfactory. He
looks for moral perfection, and there is nothing perfect.
He is always disappointed in the end. The final impression of his work is a sort of despair. The cherished

figures of his 'Russian Comedy' are all fatally condemned
to an untimely end, to continual mental and moral misery,
to undeserved misfortune. It seems as if suffering was
the mark of goodness, and as if a certain amount of virtue
was incompatible with happiness. Then, by a sort of physical and natural necessity, the element of evil is always
mixed up with the element of good. Natacha, one of the
heroines of the book, who is represented as so charming,
so good, so fascinating, has suddenly bad impulses. She
does things or wishes to do things almost horrible. The
women are all painted as somewhat irrational and unconscious; but it is not the privilege of their sex - the men
are irrational also, led by instinct much more than by
reason. Their courage, their honourable resolutions,
their heroic actions, do not seem to belong to them.
This fundamental idea of fatalism pervades the book. Fate
governs empires as well as men; it plays with a Napoleon
and an Alexander as it does with a private in the ranks;
it hangs over all the world like a dark cloud, rent at
times by lightning. We live in the night, like shadows;
we are lost on the shore of an eternal Styx; we do not
know whence we came or whither we go. Millions of men,
led by a senseless man, go from west to east, killing,
murdering, and burning, and it is called the invasion of
Russia. Two thousand years before, millions of other men
came from east to west, plundering, killing, and burning,
and it was called the invasion of the barbarians. What
becomes of the human will, of the proud 'I', in these
dreadful events? We see the folly and the vanity of self-
will in these great historical events; but it is just the
same in all times, and the will gets lost in peace as well
as in war, for there is no real peace, and the human wills
are constantly devouring each other. The mother is de-
voured by the child, the husband by the wife, the slave by
the master, the weak by the strong, the affectionate by
the heartless, the rational by the irrational. We are
made to enjoy a little, to suffer much, and, when the end
is approaching, we are all like one of Tolstoi's heroes
on the day of Borodino.

[Quotation of Andrey's fatal wounding omitted.]

I feel almost ashamed not to have been able to do
better justice to Prince Tolstoi. It will be something if
I can inspire a few with a desire to read his book, which
is by far the most remarkable work of imagination that has
been lately revealed to us.

43. NOTICE IN 'DIAL' (CHICAGO)

March 1886

From a review of a number of books by W.M. Payne. The comments on 'War and Peace' are occasioned by the publication of an American translation of the novel up to Tilsit, the period 1805-7.

'War and Peace' has been called a Russian 'Human Comedy'. It is not often that a single book presents so comprehensive a picture of an epoch in national history as this book presents of Russian society during the Napoleonic period. It begins in the year 1805, and the first part (which is all that is so far translated) reaches to the Peace of Tilsit in 1807. The second part carries on the national history, and the fortunes of the fictitious characters of the romance as well, through the period of French invasion and retreat. The writer's military experience enables him to treat with great vividness and precision the campaign of Austerlitz and the scenes preceding and following the French occupation of Moscow. At the same time his penetrative insight coupled with his keen observant faculties enable him to depict with rare sincerity the manifold aspects of Russian private life in the early years of the century. The writer of historical romance, and especially the one who narrates the course of battles, has the choice of two methods, both well approved. He can write from the viewpoint of the philosophic observer, who has studied the facts and reduced them to a system, or he can write from the standpoint of the participant, who descries but dimly the issues concerned in the struggle, and sees only what is going on in his immediate vicinity. These diverse methods are well illustrated by two famous descriptions of the battle of Waterloo - that of Victor Hugo in 'Les Misérables' and that of Stendhal in 'La Chartreuse de Parme'. Count Tolstoi's is the latter of these. He takes us to the field of Austerlitz, and we see the battle with the eyes of those contesting it. Of the struggle as a whole, we receive only the confused ideas of a few individuals who are engaged in it, but the loss of perspective is compensated for by the vividness of those scenes at which we thus play the part of actual spectators. After all, it is peace rather than war to which our attention is chiefly called.

In this rich and complex symphony of interwoven human
relations, the great national stir of resistance appears
as the bass, always present, but only at intervals giving
to the movement its dominant character. So various are
the types of character who appear, and so shifting are the
scenes, that we do not feel at home among them until we
are well along in the story. Having reached the point at
which they seem familiar, it would not be a bad idea to
begin over again. The work is certainly open to criticism
upon this point. It attempts to do more than any single
work ought to attempt, and a certain confusion is inevitable. Our state of mind is that of a visitor to a strange
country, who is introduced to all sorts of people and hurried from place to place with hardly time to look around
and get his bearings. After a while the surroundings
become intelligible, and he begins to understand the relations of these people to each other. But the novelist
ought to do more than reproduce this common experience.
He ought to smooth the way, and make the world of his
creation more intelligible than the everyday world in
which we actually live. All this, however, does not prevent the work of Count Tolstoi from being very remarkable,
and, what with the reader of jaded appetites is more to
the point, very stimulating in its fresh novelty.

44. UNSIGNED NOTICE, 'CRITIC' (NEW YORK)

31 July 1886

In 'War and Peace' Count Tolstoi has spread for us another
of those vast historical canvases which remind us of the
multitudinous pink-and-gold canvases of Paul Veronese,
with all their Babel of color and their Babylon of population. A circle as big as a dollar-disk is enough for
Meissonier or for Björnstjerne Björnson: each microscopic
detail is wrought in with exquisite delicacy and minute-
ness: each line within the illumined periphery is as fine
as a hair and as effective as a beauty-spot. But with Tolstoi or Thackeray it is different: they demand great moon-
like surfaces on which they play the wonderful fountains
of their imagery and experience; circumferences with
multiplying radii converging on a central incident; canvases crowded with figures, instinct with life and motion;
whole populations and cities - Londons, Moscows,

St Petersburgs - turned loose in their novels: all alive, all ebullient. The Meissonier-like effect - the exquisite fineness of portraiture - is lost; the Chinese whorl-within-whorl, as of some small but flaming Ezekiel-wheel, spreads out into great watery circles with hazy horizons, indistinctness, and a sense of the edges of things rubbed off.

So in 'War and Peace', an historical novel of the times of Napoleon the Great, with its axis of revolution in the years 1805-7. As usual with Tolstoi, the characters dwell on Olympian heights, like the Gods in Schiller's Tantalus ballad; they are all princes and princesses, counts and countesses, barons and baronesses. For Tolstoi, apparently, plain Misters and Mistresses do not exist; all these appear as Monsieurs and Madames and Mam'selles. Whether this is a fault of the author, or is an imitative reflex from French-loving Russian society, or is due to the translators, we cannot say; but its effect is that of a very odd affectation, and it is not at all agreeable. The book introduces us to the salon life of the times, and depicts with many realistic touches the terrors and tragedies of the Napoleonic campaigns. Young officers and officials with diamond orders abound; princesses sit beside samovars and dish out inexhaustible tea; young people make love in corners; the plot flits from St Petersburg to Moscow and from Moscow to the battlefields; there is a whirl of conversation, a buzz of gossip, a plague of small creatures nibbling at the plot and jerking this or that marionnette; behind all, mighty RUSSIA looming, full of vast cries, of unseen and unheard tragedies, of barbarians and serfdom, of inarticulate and as yet unuttered life, of intellectual potencies and physical suffering. One forgets all the shabby princes and princesses in this over-mastering impression: a something in the author greater than he has expressed; a something in the people that transcends any calculus of possibilities yet applied to it.

45.   UNSIGNED NOTICE, 'ATHENAEUM'

6 November 1886

In Count Leo Tolstoi's magnificent novel 'Voina i Mir'
many Russian critics hold that the literature, or at least
the prose fiction, of Russia reached the highest tide-
mark to which it has as yet attained. This is probably
a true judgment, and it is improbable that the achievement
will be surpassed, at all events in our own days, unless
Count Tolstoi shall beat his own record. Unfortunately
he has deserted the field of art in which he has reaped so
many laurels, and given himself up to religion and philan-
thropy. One of Tourguenief's last acts was to write a
letter from his death-bed to his great rival, beseeching
him not to abandon romantic literature. As yet no response has been made to this appeal. While speaking of
Tourguenief, we may mention that the author of 'Father and
Sons' was in the habit of declaring that he was inferior
in merit to the author of 'War and Peace'. But Tourguenief never seemed fully to realize his own immense, in
some respects unrivalled, merits as a novelist. As regards the two great writers generally, our own opinion does
not confirm that of Tourguenief. No single work of Tourguenief's is so grand, massive, colossal, as 'War and
Peace'. As an artist, however, Tourguenief stands, in
our opinion, higher than even Count Leo Tolstoi. But comparisons of this kind are not only odious, they are un-
justifiable, and we shall not pursue the theme. Nor do
we intend to give a summary of the plot of 'War and
Peace'. Something of that kind appeared in the 'Nineteenth Century' in April 1879. Nor do we pretend to have
perused the whole of the English translation, for we do
not care to disturb the profound impression made upon our
mind ten years ago by the careful study of the original.
That original was translated into French by a Russian lady
of rank. From the French version, which was literal and
faithful, the English translation has been made. Translations are apt to be so bad that it is a pleasure to be
able to say that such parts of the present work as we have
read do justice, even at third-hand as it were, to the
splendid work to which we wish to call special attention.
'War and Peace' is divided into three parts, each of which
forms a separate (and separately purchasable) volume. The
first gives a picture of Russia as it was just 'before
Tilsit'. In the second, the great panorama stretches on,
bringing before our eyes 'the Invasion', when the vast
army of Napoleon attempted to conquer the empire of the
Tsars. In the third, 'The French at Moscow', we witness
the 'battle of giants' at Borodino, the occupation of the
'white-stone Kremlin' by the almost exhausted invaders,
and then the terrible scenes which presented themselves
to the eye, first while the ancient capital of Russia was

burning, and afterwards when the tide of invasion ebbed backwards, involving in its course such an amount of misery as has but very seldom since the world began been inflicted upon suffering humanity. The canvas on which the picture is painted is so vast, the historical interest which attaches itself to many of the leading persons whose portraits are drawn is so great, the subject lends itself so well to the artistic expression of many of the strongest passions which stir the hearts of men, the skill of the artist who deals with the mighty theme is so remarkable, that it is impossible to regard the result without such an admiration as is seldom enforced by a work of art.

46. UNSIGNED REVIEW, 'SATURDAY REVIEW'

1 January 1887

From a review entitled Count Tolstoi's Novels occasioned by the publication of the English translations of 'War and Peace' and 'Anna Karenina', and the French versions of 'The Cossacks', 'Family Happiness', 'The Death of Ivan Ilich', and a collection of non-fictional writings under the title 'The Search for Happiness'.

Incomparably the greatest book, however, is 'War and Peace'. It has been called the Russian epic; and in the vastness of its scope as in the completeness of its performance it is not unworthy the name. It is the story of the great conflict between Koutouzoff and Russia and Napoleon and France; it begins some years before Austerlitz, and it ends when Borodino and Moscow are already ancient history. The canvas is immense; the crowd of figures and the world of incidents it is made to contain are almost bewildering. It is not a complete success. In many places the mystic has got the better of the artist: he is responsible for theories of the art of war which, advanced with the greatest confidence, are set aside and disproved by the simple recital of events; and he has made a study of Napoleon in which, for the first and only time in all his works, Count Tolstoi appears not as a judge but as an unjust and intemperate advocate. But when all is said in blame that can be said, so much remains to praise that one

scarce knows where to begin. Count Tolstoi's theory of
war is mystic and untenable, no doubt; but his pictures of
warfare are incomparable. None has felt and reproduced as
he has done what may be called the intimacy of battle -
the feelings of the individual soldier, the passion and
the excitement, the terror and the fury, which, taken col-
lectively, make up the influence which represents the
advance or retreat of an army in combat. But, also, in a
far greater degree, none has dealt so wonderfully with the
vaster incidents, the more tremendous issues. His Austerlitz is magnificent; his Borodino is (there is no other
word for it) simply epic; his studies of the Retreat are
almost worthy of what has gone before. For the first time
what has been called 'the peering modern touch' is here
applied to great events, and the result is that here is a
book unique in literature. Of the characters - Natasha,
Pierre, Marie, Dennissoff, the Rostoffs, Helen, Dolokhov,
Bagration, Bolkonsky and the others, above all Koutousoff
and Prince André - we have left ourselves no space to
speak. Of the two last, however, it may be said with
confidence that either is strong enough to make the book
live. Prince André we have already praised. Of Koutousoff it may be added that Count Tolsoi presents him as the
genius of Russia and the war, and that in terms that can
hardly be forgotten.

47. UNSIGNED REVIEW, 'SPECTATOR'

5 February 1887

Reprinted by permission.

It is not easy to give a name to such a work as Count
Tolstoi's 'War and Peace'. It is something more than a
novel, in that it deals largely with the history of actual
events; and, on the other hand, it is a work of far greater pretensions than the ordinary historical romance. In
it we are given a moving panorama of Russian life between
1805 and 1815, a panorama of the history of the most critical period that Russia has passed through, in the foreground of which the author has skilfully introduced the
fictitious personages who take part in the defeats, the

calamities, and the sufferings of the nation. So admirable is the painting, both of the background and foreground, so well blended is reality with fiction, that it
is hard to believe that the imaginary persons are any less
real than the historical ones, — that Prince Andrew Bolkonsky was not in real truth the aide-de-camp of Koutou-
sow, or that Anna Schérer's *salon* and its *habitués* were
never in actual existence. The *dramatis personae* are
innumerable, and yet there is not one that does not stand
out distinct from the rest, not one whose special character and individuality is not clearly portrayed. The
scene is constantly being shifted, passing from the Court
and *salons* of St. Petersburg to the quiet life of the
country-house, or the bivouac round the camp-fires; and
every scene is painted with equal truth and fidelity, so
that it would be hard to say in which the author feels
himself most at home. The *salon* of the Court official,
gay with beautiful women and splendid uniforms, with its
tainted air of incessant intrigue, its sham French court-
esy and hollow pretence: the lonely country estate where
the unhappy Maria Bolkonsky eats out her heart in vain,
unfulfilled longings: the open house kept by the improvi-
dent Count Rostow, who, if he only has roubles for today, lets the morrow provide for itself: the unnatural
calm of the camp on the eve of some great battle, the
indecision and futile councils of the leaders, the apathy
of the soldiers themselves, — all these varied scenes are
drawn with a fidelity that is almost merciless in its
severity. Long as the work necessarily is, one's interest
never flags, and although such epics are proverbially
wearisome in parts, with this author the task of following
him becomes a pleasure. That is almost the highest praise
that can be accorded to any book; but such a book as this
is rarely met with, and deserves the highest praise that
can be given.
    Were it necessary to label Count Tolstoi as an author,
we should have to call him a realist. But he is not realistic with the repulsive realism of the modern French
school, which seems to consist largely in dragging forward
and exposing to the light that shameful side of human
nature which it should rather be our interest and duty to
conceal. Setting aside what is unspeakably base, he is
content to aim at making his characters speak and act in
the way that men naturally speak and act, and to show us
by what thought and reasoning, by what causes in themselves or of circumstances, men are led so to act and
speak. There is no sprightly and unnatural dialogue, no
impossible plot to enchain one's interest; it is simply a
story of real life, the truth and reality of which prove

more attractive than all the wonders of fiction. It is in
depicting human nature that his chief strength lies, and
it is this power that should render his works invaluable
to foreigners, for no other author has succeeded in so
clearly expressing and explaining the character and spirit
of the Russian nation. It is needless to compare him here
with his two great compatriots, Turgenieff and Dostoieff-
sky, both now dead. They, too, were realists in the
fullest sense of the word, and in these Russia could boast
of possessing two of the most powerful writers of the day.
But this at least can be said in Tolstoi's favour, that he
takes a far more dispassionate view of Russian society,
that he writes with less class-feeling, and that his
descriptions are in consequence more just and of greater
value to a foreign reader. Of all European nations Russia
is the least known and understood by the others, and that
not so much on account of the vast extent of its territory
and the immense number of its inhabitants, as because the
real character of the people themselves is not European at
all. If the Turks can still be considered as a European
nation, we might say that the Russian national character
is far more akin to theirs than to any of the others.
Even in the highest classes, when one has got below that
artificial polish which intercourse with 'Occidentals' has
lent them, one finds evident traces of their Orientalism.
The hackneyed saying, *Grattez le Russe, et vous trouverez
le Tatare*, is as true to-day as when Napoleon first uttered it; but there are few people who know what kind of
man to expect in the Tartar that they find, and a study of
Count Tolstoi's works will do much to help them to this
knowledge. There is no exaggeration, nothing that may be
set down to malice. A pleasant, kindly tolerance pervades
his book, and so affects the reader that he too finds himself sympathising with the great powers for good that lie
below a rough exterior, and pitying rather than blaming
the ignorance that sometimes plunges the rude peasantry
into such brutal excesses. A childish simplicity, a
childish faith in any leader, a religious faith that lands
them in the grossest superstitions, — such are their leading characteristics. Easily led, easily impressed, they
are capable of an unassuming bravery in battle, of a stubborn endurance of suffering, and of a fanaticism which
stirs them equally to the most heroic self-sacrifice and
the most brutal cruelty. Yet outwardly they show little
but that careless *insouciance*, that want of calculation,
that eagerness to enjoy any pleasure that is within reach,
regardless of the consequences, that are so characteristic
of half-civilised people....

48. KAREEV ON TOLSTOY'S PHILOSOPHY OF HISTORY

1887

N.I. Kareev (1850-1934) was Professor of History at the
University of St Petersburg; he concentrated on modern
Western European history and the philosophy of history.
The following extract is taken from his Count L.N. Tolstoy's Philosophy of History in 'War and Peace', which was
first published in the 'Messenger of Europe', 1887, no. 7;
it appeared as a book the following year.

A general verdict on the philosophy of history in 'War and
Peace' may be formulated in the following manner. Count
Tolstoy takes the realistic tendency of his talent into
the realms of history and its philosophy and removes from
them both idealization and ideology; but where he talks
about the life of society as opposed to that of the individual, idealism, which he can well combine with realism,
deserts him. For him idealism is only concerned with
ethics, an idealism, as it were, of righteous living, and
is not at all a social idealism, one concerned with the
correct *forms* of social life apart from those which are
controlled by a personal ethic. This one-sidedness of his
whole outlook on life has its roots in a certain misconception of social life: he will declare that 'real' life
continues, quite independent of all conceivable social
change; he will affirm that only the criminal, ridden by
passion, knows where the real 'bien public' lies; he will
pour irony upon all the social activity which his characters engage in; he will develop the idea that only unconscious life has any sense; he will affirm that in the history of society everything happens of itself and that historical figures are but labels for events; he will discuss
historical laws which, according to his prescription, are
fulfilled only by people performing social activity, and
so on. At the same time as his realism leads him along
the correct path, this misconception of the real content
of history, its sociological aspect, makes him lose his
way and his philosophy of history appears as a mixture of
surprisingly true and strikingly false ideas, together
with a mass of inner contradictions which are explained
by the fact that their exposition has been little worked
out, by an insufficient consideration of the idea itself,
and by a complete disregard for any larger definition of

his concepts.

The basic idea in 'War and Peace' is the duality of
human life, both personal and historical, and the mutual
influence of the one upon the other; man acts in history
and history intrudes into his life. But this mutual
influence is understood by Count Tolstoy one-sidedly: the
individual acts in history, participates in events, in the
pragmatic side of history, and works at the changing of
socio-cultural forms, in which its sociological side consists, but Count Tolstoy sees and comprehends only the
first, the sum of consequential personal acts outside the
movement of social forms. Furthermore, the action of history upon the individual sometimes works in two ways,
namely: the direct influence of events upon the inner
world of the individual, and upon the the changing of the
social forms in which the individual must live; and here
Count Tolstoy recognizes only the first and illustrates it
clearly in the novel, while all conceivable changes he
declares as something having nothing to do with the personal life. Such a one-sided approach narrows Count Tolstoy's historical horizons and makes his philosophy
sceptical as soon as it comes into contact with social
activity and fatalistic as soon as it sees an individual
trying to do anything in the name of any social idea.
Personal initiative in social matters and an independent
attitude to their direction remains to him a mystery by
virtue of the unconscious 'swarm' activity of people, and
he wavers between looking at it all as something illusory
or as something in which one is forced to see a blind
force serving to bring into being the prescriptions of
historical laws. Count Tolstoy sees sense only in the
personal life and here he is the prophet of *moral rebirth,*
but the sense of historical life is closed to him; he sees
only external movement, only events, only the pragmatic
side of history, but the inner aspects of historical movement, the continual *changing of social forms,* not of
course indifferent to a good, full and free personal life,
a continual posing and a continual solving of social questions Count Tolstoy does not accept at all; he is like a
blind man who only feels the warmth of the sun on a hot
day but does not see the sun's rays or the sunlight. History, devoid of its real sense, could not receive from
Count Tolstoy any ideal sense in the understanding of that
purpose which it must realize in order to satisfy our sub-
jective demands from life, although it does give to personal life a purpose in an ethical ideal. A process without inner content, without purpose, the attainment of
which we could achieve for ourselves by participating in
that process, is a fatal advance of the insuperable power

of things, removing any possibility of judgment on it on
our part apart from a purely moral evaluation of the behaviour of those participating in the events, and the action
of some 'law' which turns living people into the parts of
some huge mechanism - that is what history is as Count
Tolstoy understands it. Here realism, remaining on the
summit of its setting in the poetry of 'War and Peace' and
in consequence of its combination with an ethical idealism, turns into the purest naturalism because Count Tolstoy sees in social ideals, in the form of 'freedom,
equality and culture', only simple 'attractions', although
they have the same meaning as his ethical ideal of 'simplicity, good and truth'. Naked realism, denying the
creation of any ideals, certainly moves over into naturalism, and the philosophy of history in 'War and Peace'
serves only to support this truth, along with the main
body of the novel where Count Tolstoy combines realism
with idealism.

It seems to me that Count Tolstoy's philosophy of history from this point of view can characterize all his
literary activity as that of a great realist who resolves,
however, all life's questions on the basis of a personal
ethic and is indifferent to social forms as forms, and
also posits that as it were social attitudes must be regu-
lated by a personal morality, the ethic of a personally
righteous life. Such a philosophy, however, cannot be
simultaneously a philosophy of *society* and of *history*.

49. WEDGWOOD COMPARES TOLSTOY AND THACKERAY

1887

From Count Leo Tolstoi by Julie Wedgwood, 'Contemporary
Review', 1887, no. LII. Reprinted by permission. The
review starts with some general comments on the fact that
literature has developed through three stages - that of
the ancient Greeks, which is equated with sculpture, that
of the Renaissance, which is equated with painting, and
the contemporary period which is that of the photographer.

Of this last division of literature we know no better
specimen than the great Russian writer to whose works we

invite the reader's attention today. He gives us the most
trivial and the most momentous circumstances of life with
scientific impartiality; no other novelist describes such
great things and such small things, as it would seem, with
equal interest. He shows us the destiny of nations, the
crash of armies; he forces us to gaze into that black
shadow which Hannibal, in his legendary dream, was warned
to leave unseen by avoiding any reverted glance; and he
takes us to the dressing-room where a young lady is hurry-
ing off to a ball, and tells us, although the fact has no
influence whatever on the story, that a tuck had to be run
in her dress at the last moment! The reader will be
grateful to us for sparing him further illustration of the
last half of our description. Something in the following
account of the effect of the first sight of Moscow has
recalled to us the raptures of Isaiah on the fall of
Sennacherib.

[Quotation omitted concerning Napoleon's entry into Moscow
which ends with the words: 'The city was deserted.']

These four words sum up not only Tolstoi's picture of the
path of a conqueror, but his view of life. They set forth
his judgment on all cruelty, all lust, all worldly endeavour. Whatever these are beside, they are, in the literal
and most emphatic sense of the word, *vanity*. They break
through the enclosure of law to find a vacuum.
   That deep-felt moral is only one of the reasons which
suggest a comparison between 'Peace and War' and an English
novel taking the same subject, and treating it with something of the same feeling — Thackeray's 'Vanity Fair'. In
both we see in the background the dust and smoke of the
great army, the thunder of cannon reaches our ears, the
figures of the *dramatis personae* vanish into that cloud,
and some reappear no more. The moral atmosphere of the
two writers, moreover, is somewhat similar. 'Which of us
has his desire, or having it is satisfied?' The last sentence in 'Vanity Fair' expresses something not unlike the
feeling in the words we have quoted. But what does the
reader remember of the elder novel? A great love, faithful through absence, through coldness, through disappointment, struggling on, through long years, to the satisfaction in which, after all, there lies hid a still greater
disappointment. What does he remember of 'Peace and War'?
A crowd of figures, a tangle of emotions, a hurried complex of incidents. Tolstoi gives a slice of experience.
He selects nothing but a certain area of vision, and
leaves its contents recorded in the proportion of their
actual dimensions. There is no concentration, no rapid

sweep of the brush, no broad shadow, everywhere only a
transcript of the bewildering variety of actual light and
shade.

Is it permissible, in view of the new fatalism of democracy, for the critic to condemn a method he acknowledges
to be characteristic of his day? When he translates his
own distaste for literary photography into a formula of
art, is he as ridiculous as Dr. Johnson criticising Shakespeare, Bentley emending Milton, or Voltaire improving upon
Sophocles? We find it very difficult to rise to the elevation of impartial modesty required for that concession,
and cannot express with any doubt our anticipation that
the reader will agree with us in finding many pages of
'Peace and War' insufferably tedious. They are at least
interesting only to that taste for the representation of
elaborate detail which finds satisfaction in mere accurate
description of things not in themselves interesting, such
a satisfaction as that which elderly people remember in
their first sight of the daguerreotype. But it must be
conceded that this is exactly the state of mind to which
the author addresses himself, and that he aims at a transcript of life which would be imperfect if it were never
desultory and seemingly purposeless. Experience, for the
most part, is undramatic. We often seem to be looking
back on a series of beginnings; an acquaintance full of
promise ends without ripening into friendship, or friendship fades into cold acquaintance without tragedy or
pathos, abandoned pursuits leave our path cumbered with
rubbish — everywhere we see the scaffolding side by side
with the ruin. Tolstoi's irrelevant detail, his painful
reproduction of what is fragmentary and disproportionate,
belongs to that search after truth which is the deepest
thing in him, and adds its influence to make his page reflect as it does the mood of our own time: its hurry, its
candour, its want of reticence, and then again its bewilderment, its questioning of all that its forerunners
assumed, and its new assertion of whatever is saved from
the wreck with the emphasis of individual conviction and
fresh experience.

But the characteristics which fit him to express the
life of the present seem to us somewhat to disqualify him
to describe the life of the past. His work is everywhere
redolent of the problems of the hour in which he writes,
and his picture of 'sixty years since' lacks the mellowness
of history. Thackeray's picture is not only characterized
by a method more suitable, we think, to historic treatment, but it much more nearly belongs to the period which
it undertakes to describe. It recalls a set of feelings
which are unknown to our generation. When the men of our

time assert what he assumed, it is a matter of individual
conviction formed in face of denial; his quiet reference
to a background of assumptions hallowed by the adherence
of a nation is now impossible. He belongs, in a peculiar,
but very real sense, to the world of Christian tradition.
He was a Christian as he was an Englishman. He accepted
his country's creed in the same spirit as he accepted its
laws. That this ceased to be possible about the same time
that photography became common, is, of course, a mere
chance. But it is not a chance that at the time of this
change literature altered its tone and lost its reserve.
As long as a country accepts some corporate expression of
faith in the unseen, the ultimate problems of life do not
invade the world of literature. We do not mean that there
ever was a time when these problems were not discussed.
But there was a time when they had to be discussed in face
of certain definite answers which formed objects of attack
to all opponents, and which might then be said to give a
framework to all thought. It was not only that anti-
theological writing was different as long as theology was
national, the influence of these theological assumptions
extended beyond the utmost verge of their logical scope,
they gave a training in reticence which influenced not
only all expression but all thought. Men see what they
look for, and when the ultimate questions of life are
problems awaiting solution, the whole of life is pervaded
by that spirit of research which finds everywhere the
petty and the trivial side by side with the colossal and
the momentous, and leaves no large impression undisturbed
by parenthesis and exception.

Yet here we must not be supposed to condemn when we
merely define. Perhaps when the subject is War, we do
better to contemplate the work of the photographer rather
than the painter. Open 'Vanity Fair', and read the summons to the field of Waterloo; note how the heartless
disloyal coxcomb at that trumpet call suddenly becomes a
man, and realizing for the few hours allotted to him of
his worthless life — so the brief mention with which he
is dismissed allows us to suppose — the description of
Wordsworth's Happy Warrior, 'turns his necessity to
glorious gain'. Or turn back from a great dramatic artist
to the great dramatic artist, read in 'Henry V' the night
before Agincourt. Shakespeare intensifies the lesson of
Thackeray. He shows us War as a source of the glow that
comes over a man when he feels himself to be the member
of a nation. 'We few, we happy few, we band of brothers!'
That is how war looks to the artist. But it is not thus
that it should be regarded by the statesman. Let him who
has power to involve his country in war learn from the

photographer what it is to be

> Forced to go in company with Pain,
> And Fear and Bloodshed, miserable train!

Let him, with Tolstoi, look upon war as a scene of horror and torture, of sudden terror, of selfish fear; and then again of bewildering confusion, of futile design, of wasted effort and planless sequence of event. Tolstoi, embodying, perchance, the actual recollections of his father, who served in the campaign he describes, and his own memories of the Crimean war, drags us to the surgeon's tent and turns his camera on the operating table, forces us to hear the shrieks of brave men, to see blood, torn and quivering flesh, to assist at the last convulsions of the dying. We feel the very opposite from all that noble emotion with which Shakespeare thrills us; we are made to sympathize with selfish cowardice, with an engrossing care for one's own skin. It is not that this is the true picture and the other the false one. Although Tolstoi is, and Shakespeare was not, a soldier, it is just as *true* that war makes a man feel himself to be the member of a nation as that it makes him feel pain. But the truth of the artist though it is also the truth of the historian, may be left to take care of itself; what he should remember who has to make history is the truth of the photographer.

50.   'A CURIOUS COMBINATION OF NOVEL AND HISTORY'

1888

From an unsigned article, Count Tolstoi's Life and Works, in the 'Westminster Review', 1888, vol. 103, no. 3; the article is one of the earliest attempts to explain the in some ways surprising acceptance of Tolstoy in England and America. For a summary of these and other reasons, see Introduction.

We now reach the work in which Tolstoi's genius has perhaps reached its highest elevation, though its flight is less sustained than in 'Anna Karenina' - the curious

combination of novel and history called 'War and Peace'.
It must be acknowledged that this book has the fault of
excessive length.   It recalls the Richardsonian epic
rather than the terse and nimble-footed tales which content the modest ambitions of the nineteenth-century
reader. The background of the group of stories that are
here combined is the Russia of the Napoleonic age. It is
difficult for a foreigner to imagine any phase of the
national life during that epoch which is left untouched.
The Court and the camp, town and country, nobles and
peasants - all are sketched in with the same broad and
sure outline. We pass at a leap from a *soirée* to a battlefield, from a mud hovel to a palace, from idyll to Saturn-
alia. As we summon our recollections of this prodigal
outpouring of a careless genius, a troop of characters as
lifelike as any in Scott or in Shakespeare defile before
our mental eye. The Rostov family, surely the most lovable
in modern fiction, appears and disappears, and returns anew
as the charming children whom we see when the curtain rises
attain youth and enter the great world, the boys to fight,
and one of them, alas, to die; the girls to spell the old
story of love given and taken, stolen and renounced, in
its changing tones of joy, sadness, and despair. We sal-
ute the old Count, expensive even in his economies; the
Countess, a very pattern of motherhood; the unsympathetic
sister Vera, whose marriage with Berg, the careful German,
the family frankly accepts as a relief; and Nicholas, the
hero in spite of himself, whose simple patriotism and
bravery are as admirable as his unconscious braggadocio is
absurd; the gentle Sonia, the daughter of the Countess's
protégée, and Nicholas's first love; Petia, the little
brother, who all but runs away to the war that takes his
life, and with it all the sunshine from his mother's; and
last, but most entrancing of all, the girl whose character
is Tolstoi's highest achievement, and, we venture to say,
one of the glories of literature, Natasha. To her we
shall return. Against this family another is set as a
foil, that of the old prince Bolkonsky, a fretful marti-
net, venomous in proportion to his affection. Bolkonsky's
son, Prince Andrew, and another typical Russian figure,
Count Peter Besoukhov, are with Nicholas the chief heroes
of the book. The study of Prince Andrew is one of those
psychological histories in which Tolstoi excels. Married
yₒng to a woman he loves, but who is incapable of understanding his deep and powerful nature, he leaves her to
join his regiment, returns to find himself alone with a
motherless infant, and for a time seeks consolation in war
and politics. Just as he thinks he has attained peace,
fate brings Natasha across his path, and in his love for

this young girl, at first repressed, then rising in an irresistible tide of mature passion; in the new vista of life and happiness which it discloses; in the realization of his hopes of winning her love, the subsequent separation for a year at his father's desire, and the life's tragedy to which it leads, Tolstoi finds endless opportunities of inculcating his favourite themes - the mastery of circumstance over will and desire, the weakness of man in the front of things, and the necessity of resignation.

A kindred moral is drawn from the history of Peter Besoukhov. After a youth, in which riot and aspiration are curiously blent, this ungainly inheritor of enormous wealth is dragooned into a marriage with a woman of fascinating personal attractions, but totally devoid of soul, and at heart as indifferent to him as he is to her. Such a union bears its natural fruits. Peter separates from his wife, and, like his friend Prince Andrew, seeks abroad and in society the happiness he cannot look for at home. Weary of excess, he finds a temporary moral stimulus in Freemasonry, and, when this likewise turns out to be vanity, casts himself in a frenzy of despair between the armies of Napoleon and the Czar. He sees as a spectator the battle of Borodino and the burning of Moscow, shares as a prisoner the terrible retreat of the Grand Army, and eventually returns home unscathed in body and purified in soul by the fiery ordeal through which he has passed. In the lesson of faith and courage which he learns from the simple peasant, who is one of the comrades of his privations, and whose death, just before the other prisoners are rescued, is one of the most pathetic incidents in the book, we again see the theory of 'simplification' at work. Its place in modern Russian thought and life has indeed been justly compared with that taken by the 'return to nature' in the French movements of the last century....

51. A. SOREL: TOLSTOY - HISTORIAN, 'REVUE BLEUE'

14 April 1888

Albert Sorel (1842-1906), French historian, is particularly known for his studies of the effects of the French Revolution on Europe at large. Joseph de Maistre (1753-1821), whom he refers to below, was Sardinian (Savoyard)

ambassador to Russia from 1803 to 1817; his 'Soirées de
Saint-Pétersbourg' was published in 1821.

In his novel 'War and Peace' Tolstoy covers the history of
Russia from 1804 to 1812. It is a colossal work of which
the true hero is the Russian people in the struggle against
Western ideas and Western armed force. 'The sum total of
modern Russia,' as M de Vogüé said, where everything is
portrayed - the Court, the Government, the provinces, the
people, the great of this world, the army, politics and
the Russian soul in all its gradations, in all its personal and social crises, in all its public and private
ordeals. An incomparable 'Comédie Humaine', conceived
from a single idea and cast in a single throw. It is
about this book that I wish to talk, while concentrating
on those historical sections which bear on French history.
    When Tolstoy considers the 1812 campaign, the dispro-
portion he sees between the vast scale of the events and
the contingent causes which most historians assign to them
offends him both as a thinker and a human being.

[Quotation omitted.]

    Tolstoy refuses to admit that this 'event as strange as
it is monstrous' issues from diplomatic incidents alone or
that an official dispatch from the Chancellery would have
sufficed to prevent it. He is consequently forced to analyse and discuss the great question of war, which is an
historical, human and political question; it is a question
which he is constantly asking himself. How is it started?
How is it resolved?
    I was struck by a similarity, which seems not at all
fortuitous, between his ideas and those of a man who was
the contemporary of those whose history he is relating, of
a man I can call French for the same reason that J.-J.
Rousseau is French - by the genius of his style - Joseph
de Maistre. He lived in Russia during the heroic part of
'War and Peace' and his correspondence is one of the most
valuable documents of the history of the time. He sets
his famous dialogues of the 'Soirées de Saint-Pétersbourg'
in 1809. It seems to me that Tolstoy was familiar with de
Maistre's correspondence and was influenced by the dialogues. I am thinking here especially of the words spoken
in the 'Soirées' by the Russian senator, that intimate
confidant of the author's most daring thoughts, that
interpreter of his most adventurous, and perhaps his
favourite, ideas, and in which he has set, by choice, the

future and the eternity of his spirit through which he
wishes continually to confound human reason before God
together with politics, war and knowledge. The basis of
Tolstoy's ideas on history is the same as that of Joseph
de Maistre's such that the philosophy of 'War and Peace'
is but local colour.

You will tell me that de Maistre is a theocrat while
Tolstoy is a nihilist; certainly, but both of them are
mystics and this is where they coincide, if not on politics or on the future of mankind, then at least in the
manner in which they consider the essence of things, the
mysteries of human destiny, the enigma of human life and
the ineffectiveness of human will; there is after all less
distance from a theocrat to a mystic and from a mystic to
a nihilist than from a butterfly to a larva, from a larva
to a chrysalis, and from a chrysalis to a butterfly.

For as long as I have thought, says the Russian senator
in the 'Soirées', I have thought about war; this awful
subject has monopolized my attention and I have still not
fathomed it. It is in connection with war that both Tolstoy and de Maistre treat causality in history; the same
curiosity with both of them or, in other words, the same
aspiration to discover the prime cause of things, the same
affirmation of this superior, absolute and inconceivable
cause which reveals its government only through its laws;
the same self-denial in finding it, de Maistre because he
loves the mystery in it, and Tolstoy because he thinks it
unfathomable. Tolstoy believed in showing at the same
time both superstition and impiety in making Fate inter-
vene in his story according to the demands of his theory;
in determining the designs of that Fate, in assessing its
effect, in making it act arbitrarily here and not there,
in reducing it especially to the role of a rhetoric divi-
nity, a literary *deus ex machina* and a pretext for antithesis. He would not expose himself to the reproach which
Buffon addressed to certain contemporary writers that they
granted to God only those ideas which they had about Him -
this always leads to appearing parsimonious.

'One believes in Fate *in toto*,' said Sainte-Beuve, one
believes in the rule of chance or its interference in
detail. Tolstoy dismisses providential causes as inaccessible and disdains as too facile fortuitous causes, luck,
or the 'spirit' of the times which historians call upon in
moments of difficulty to explain events which they do not
understand.... For Tolstoy chance is only the inexplic-
able. Consequently he never presents those false explanations beloved of novelists, the small unknown episode, the
glass of water which is spilt, which somehow determine the
fate of courts and empires; but certainly no genius

either, no personal free will, dominating, acting - in a word, no great men.

Tolstoy does not recognize them, and gives, in a parenthesis, a loaded reason which allows him to allege others. 'The Russian spirit hardly admits to great men.' I am in no position to disagree; however I believe that there are some intelligent men in Russia who have recognized great men; there are even those who have recognized great women - I speak, of course, only of politics - which is something which seems to me equally as difficult. But Tolstoy is not one of them; neither great men nor great women, in Russia or elsewhere, not even Peter the Great, have through the actions of their will been able to have a decisive influence on their times. The supposed great men, he says, are nothing but historical labels; they give their names to events without having even what labels have - at least some connection with the events themselves. He attacks with great vigour those men who claim to direct affairs - especially diplomats; he presents them as corks floating on the sea which the wind ruffles or calms. He has an inexhaustible supply of epigrams for fetishist historians who attribute to these bemedalled or crowned marionettes any influence whatsoever on history; he compares such historians with savages who imagine that the figurehead on the prow actually directs the boat.

Thus, no great men, especially in wars. It is here that Tolstoy develops his favourite paradox and that of the 'Soirées'. In the seventh 'Soirée' there is the following - the Russian senator is speaking: '....it is conviction which wins battles and conviction which loses them'.

Listen now to one of Tolstoy's heroes, one who, according to M de Vogüé, represents the author in his views on history, politics, war, and who represents him, what is more, with the most noble and sympathetic traits - Prince Andrey.

'The good generals I have known were foolish and careless. Bagration, for example, whom Napoleon by the way thought the best of all... A good captain does not need to be a genius or even possess any extraordinary qualities - quite the reverse.' His role is passive and fictive; he is never in the position - in which historians place him after the event - to judge; he is just a part of the event in which he is participating.

[Quotations from Tolstoy and de Maistre omitted.]

Victory, according to Tolstoy's Prince Andrey, is the result of 'innumerable and countless individual forces

which are never more active than during a battle'. The
moral self of the soldiers thrills under the influence of
a unique and solemn impulse; everything depends on that
'terrible moment of moral hesitation which decides the
outcome of battles'.

'Remember', says the senator in the 'Soirées', 'the
young soldier who describes in one of his letters that
solemn moment when, without knowing why, an army pushes
forward as if it were sliding down a slope.'

Furthermore both Tolstoy and de Maistre have a passion
for scientific comparisons and formulae. 'A body', says
de Maistre, 'which has a greater mass than another will
have more force even if the speed of movement is the same;
there is no difference if the proportion of mass to speed
is 3:2 or 2:3.' That is why one Horatius having more
force but less mass can kill three Curiatii who have more
mass but less force. And now Tolstoy: 'Force, the quantity of movement, is the product of the mass multiplied
by the speed... In war the force of the troops is also
the product of the mass multiplied by a factor of x. This
x is the spirit of the troops.'

Where does one seek this x which is the sole determin-
ant of the outcome of battles? Documents? Certainly not.
Documents are deceiving, they are based on false witness.
Everyone relates the story he is telling to himself, and
the more he is involved in the events the less he is exact
and reliable. He describes events not as they were but as
he would wish them to have been. According to Tolstoy one
must discount all isolated events; only everything taken
together will give a plausible explanation. Man is no
more the centre of humanity than the earth is the centre
of the world; one must consider history within a system
where everything is balanced, ordered and self-contained.
This universal gravitation of humanity Tolstoy defines as
the *concord of causes* and the *coincidence of wills*.

These are, however, abstract terms and Tolstoy is not
the man to be satisfied with them as such. He wants
something alive and he seeks it in the intimate movements
of the souls of the mass of the people, in the infinite
number of individuals who comprise that mass and who
secretly move it. It is a revolution in classical historiography and would have been a complete innovation if
Michelet had never lived.

Tolstoy applies this system to 1812. According to him
it was not Napoleon, or his genius, or his cold in the
head, or the snow, which created the events in Moscow and
which subsequently led to the French retreat. The real
cause is that the Russian people wanted to win far more
keenly than the French wished not to lose, and that under

these conditions Russia was saved because it was more in
the nature of things that it should be. That is why in
that campaign everything turned, both on the Russian side
and on the French, on the confusion of the strategists
and the self-styled geniuses who imagined they could control nature. Everything occurred in inverse proportion
to their plans.

At first sight this theory appears somewhat paradoxical; yet when one reflects upon it there are many historical events which are explained in this way and cannot be
explained otherwise. One such event which is still very
close to us and whose memory is as dear to us as 1812 is
to the Russians offers the best opportunity to develop
Tolstoy's theory - the retreat of the Prussians in 1792.
If ever a campaign was explained by general, non-specific
causes it is this one; if ever there was a battle won by
spirit it was Valmy - and it had the great advantage over
other similar military events in that it caused less
bloodshed.

52.   GEORGE MOORE ON 'WAR AND PEACE'

1903

'Lippincott's Magazine', 1903, no. LXII. Reprinted by
permission. These comments are taken from the third of
Moore's Avowals. George Moore (1852-1933), Irish writer
and critic, wrote much of his literary criticism in the
spirit of a defence of the 'Naturalist' school, and as
such differs from most Western European commentators on
Tolstoy who tended to use the latter as a stick with which
to beat the 'Naturalists'. If Moore's opinions are idiosyncratic, his facts are unreliable.

In my last article I spoke of Turgenieff as having come
out of the East telling tales. Now there is little of the
tale-teller in Tolstoy. Whereas Turgenieff's art came out
of the eternal East, Tolstoy's came out of the ephemeral
West. He took 'Vanity Fair' as his model, he adopted the
form of 'Vanity Fair', the division of a family into four
groups, and 'Anna Karenina' is a sort of 'Vanity Fair'
written with moral ideas substituted for social vanities.

With this rapid criticism I will pass on to the greater
book, 'War and Peace'. Here again we have the same form,
a family divided into different groups, and the life histories of each are told. In the fourth volume Tolstoy
draws the threads together, and he does this miraculously
well. The size of the book, the number of characters, and
the multiplicity of incidents have suggested to all critics the canvases of Tintoretto and Veronese, and Tolstoy's execution is as easy and as sure as theirs. But
the Venetians were tranquil pagans, content with the
kingdom of the earth, whereas Tolstoy is the reincarnation
of Luther as Luther was a reincarnation of Paul; and when
Tolstoy is not describing external things with a zeal and
patience equal to that of Van Eyck he is full of alarm at
the wickedness of the world, and it is difficult to give
any idea of the extent to which Tolstoy mixes up the
changing aspects of things that the eye perceives with the
unchanging affections that the heart ponders. As Wagner
seems to have attached the same importance to the flitting
horses in the flies as to the music in the orchestra, so
does Tolstoy seem to attach the same importance to the
number of freckles on the man's nose as he does to the
man's love of his children. In writing 'War and Peace'
he seems to have set out with no more subtle artistic
intention than a desire to describe the whole of life.
The first two volumes contain descriptions of hunting,
shooting, sledging, card parties, balls, duels! and I
laid aside the book to wonder. 'Flaubert,' I said to
myself, 'represented the external world in its many and
ever-changing aspects, for he wished us to see the external world flowing like water before our eyes as Brahma
sees it. But I can detect no such subtle intention in
this book.'
   I did not take up 'War and Peace' again for a year or
more, and the reason for my taking it up was that I had
read in a newspaper a mention of how Prince André lay on
a battlefield looking at the stars, and in seeking the
scene out I read the whole of the third volume, marvelling greatly at the ceaseless invention with which Tolstoy
takes Pierre from one regiment to another, from tent to
tent, showing us what is happening at every part of the
immense battle, explaining the different plans of the Russian generals. He explains Napoleon's plan for the battle
with an insight that makes us ask ourselves if he were not
as great a military tactician as Napoleon. But it was not
until Pierre is taken prisoner, until he is forced to
follow the French army from Moscow, and meets a philoso-
pher-peasant on the way who has a little pink puppy (the
puppy generally runs on three legs) that I began to

understand that everyone in the book set out to do something, but on-one did what he set out to do, not even
Napoleon, and I marvelled greatly how Tolstoy could have
described all the things he described in the first volumes without once indicating the idea that must have been
at the back of his mind all the time. In the fourth volume Natasha abandons her sensuous, frivolous girlhood and
becomes extraordinarily interested in her babies, even in
their disgusting little ailments; and we assist in the
sinking into old age of the generation we knew in the
first volume, and we watch the young people we knew in the
first volume sinking into middle age. While reading and
for some time after I thought I had never read anything
more poignant than the scenes in which Natasha's mother
talks only of things of twenty years ago. I marvelled
greatly at her son; it is only in the fourth volume that
Tolstoy allows us to know that he is a mere commonplace
man who married an ugly princess. Now he is interested in
farming, and the last time we see him he is standing on a
balcony watching the small rain that the thirsty oats are
drinking up greedily. Pierre too has grown older, and he
still goes up to St Petersburg to attend spiritual seances, but now he is only faintly interested in spiritual
things, and he knows that his life will know no further
change.

The end of the book is so great that we forgive the
description of the freckles on the left side of the
footman's nose, a footman who once brought in a samovar;
we forgive the coats that cannot be buttoned and the
waistcoats that overlap; we forgive even the description
of the Rostoffs moving their furniture from Moscow after
the battle; the scene in which Natasha and her mother
count the napkins and tablecloths and dusters ; the
description occupies several pages, and it would be difficult to say in what it differs from an auctioneer's
catalogue. We forgive and wonder that if we were to
reread the first and second volumes the knowledge of the
end would enable us to reread the hunting scenes, and the
sledging scenes, and the gambling scenes. We wonder but
we do not turn to the book again. Notwithstanding our
aesthetic curiosity, we shrink from the task of rereading
the first and second volumes; to reread them would be like
reliving some part of our lives over again. Now why did
Tolstoy describe so many things? He derived his literary
composition from the English novel, but the English novel
is free from realistic description. Did he get his realistic descriptions from the French novel? Are his novels
a stew of 'Vanity Fair' and 'Madame Bovary' with a little
remorse of conscience from Edgar Poe?

French realism proceeds from 'Madame Bovary'. 'Madame Bovary' was published in '57. 'War and Peace' was published in '60. And three years would not be sufficient for the composition of 'War and Peace'. Tolstoy must have begun it long before the publication of 'Madame Bovary'. But Flaubert's realistic description rests upon a philosophical basis. If you would understand 'Madame Bovary's' soul, the Normandy landscape must be described in its every detail. The novelist's business is like the entomologist's, not only the insect but the plant it lives upon must be described. Well, Tolstoy began as a materialist; the writings of Darwin and Spencer interested him as they interested Flaubert; maybe Tolstoy's realism was the spirit of the age, the result of the study of natural science. This may be a true explanation of Tolstoy's realism, but there is another explanation and a more interesting one, that Tolstoy's realism is the realism of a primitive people, comparable to the realism of the painters of the fifteenth century, the realism of children who stop at the wayside to tease a beetle, to investigate every bush. It pleases us to see something of the primitive painter in Tolstoy - in a word, to detect an element of 'folk' in his elaborate compositions.

53. MAUDE ON TOLSTOY'S REALISM

1908

Aylmer Maude (1858-1938), writer and translator, was the man who really made Tolstoy available to the English. He lived in Russia for over twenty years, knew Tolstoy well, and often visited him at his home at Yasnaya Polyana. He and his wife, Louise, translated most of Tolstoy's works into English and they are still among the best versions. The following extract is from his 'The Life of Tolstoy', published by Oxford University Press. Reprinted by permission.

Nothing can be simpler than most of the occurrences of 'War and Peace'. Everyday events of family life: conversations between brother and sister, or mother and daughter, separations and reunions, hunting, holiday festivities,

dances, card-playing, and so forth, are all as lovingly
shaped into artistic gems as is the battle of Borodino
itself. Whatever the purpose of the book may be, its
success depends not on that purpose but on what Tolstoy
did under its influence, that is to say it depends on a
highly artistic execution.

If Tolstoy succeeds in fixing our gaze on what occupied
his soul it is because he had full command of his instrument - which was art. Not many readers probably are concerned about the thoughts that directed and animated the
author, but all are impressed by his creation. Men of
all camps - those who like as well as those who dislike
his later works - unite in tribute to the extraordinary
mastery shown in this remarkable production. It is a
notable example of the irresistible and all-conquering
power of art.

But such art does not arise of itself, nor can it
exist apart from deep thought and deep feeling. What is
it that strikes everyone in 'War and Peace'? It is its
clearness of form and vividness of colour. It is as
though one saw what is described and heard the sounds that
are uttered. The author hardly speaks in his own person;
he brings forward the characters and then allows them to
speak, feel, and act; and they do it so that every movement is true and amazingly exact, in full accord with the
character of those portrayed. It is as if we had to do
with real people, and saw them more clearly than one can
in real life. We not only distinguish the form of expression and the feeling of each actor, but their manner,
their favourite gestures, and their way of walking. The
important Prince Vasily on one occasion, in unusual and
difficult circumstances, had to walk on tip-toe. The
author knows just how each of his characters walks.
'Prince Vasily,' we are told, 'could not walk well on tip-
toe, and his whole body jerked at each step.' With similar clearness and distinctness the author knows the movements, feelings, and thoughts of all those whom he depicts. When once they are before us he does not interfere with them, but lets each behave as is natural to him.

Similarly Tolstoy usually describes scenes or scenery
only as reflected in the mind of one of his characters.
He does not describe the oak that stood beside the road,
or the moonlight night when neither Natasha nor Prince
Andrew could sleep; but he describes the impressions the
oak and the night made on Prince Andrew. The battles and
historic events are usually described not by informing us
of the author's conception of them, but by the impression
they produce on the characters in the story. The battle
of Schöngraben is described chiefly by the impression it

made on Prince Andrew; Austerlitz by its impression on Nicholas Rostov; the Emperor's appearance in Moscow by the excitement it produced in Petya; and the effect of the prayer against invasion by the feelings of Natasha. Tolstoy nowhere appears behind the actors or draws events in the abstract; he shows them in the flesh and blood of those who supplied the material for the events.

In this respect the work is an artistic marvel. Tolstoy has seized not some separate traits but a whole living atmosphere, which varies around different individuals and different classes of society. He himself mentions the 'loving family atmosphere' of the Rostovs' house, but there are other instances: the atmosphere surrounding Speranski, or that surrounding the Rostov's 'uncle'; that of the big theatre in Moscow when Natasha went to the opera; of the military hospital Nicholas visited; of a crowded bridge when the French were preparing to fire on it, and so on. The characters who enter each of these atmospheres, or pass from one of them to another, inevitably experience their influence, and so do we with them.

In this way the highest objectivity is attained; we not only have before us the actions, figures, movements, and speech of the actors, but their whole inner life is shown us by equally clear and distinct traits - their souls and hearts are bared to our view. Reading 'War and Peace' we contemplate in the full meaning of that word, the object the artist has depicted. Tolstoy is an admirable realist who shows us alike the excellent and the contemptible traits in his characters. He does not spare us Natasha's infatuation for Anatole, or pretend that as the mother of a family she retained her youthful charm; and while he thus treats his most attractive characters he does full justice to the courage, firmness, and leadership of the rascally card-sharper Dolokhov. Again, no-one can doubt his sympathy for his country exposed to Napoleon's invasion, yet he never yields to the temptation to offer incense at the shrine of patriotic pride while depicting Russia's deliverance from a foreign yoke. How faithfully he deals with the shady aspects of Russian army life and its many defects!

The finest shades of spiritual life and its profoundest upheavals are alike depicted with clearness and fidelity. The feeling of holiday dullness in the Rostov's house at Otradnoe, and the feelings of the Russian army in the heat of the battle of Borodino; Natasha's youthful perturbations, and the excitement of the old Bolkonski when his memory was failing and he was on the verge of apoplexy; all are vivid, living, and exact, in Tolstoy's narration.

That is where the author's interest centres and

consequently his reader's interest also. However great
and important the events treated of - whether it be the
Kremlin crowded with people on the occasion of the Tsar's
visit, or the meeting of the two emperors, or a terrible
battle with guns roaring and thousands of men dying -
nothing deflects the author, or his readers with him, from
steady observation of the inner spirit of the individual
characters. It is as if he were concerned only with the
effect the occurrences produced on the soul of man - only
with what each soul felt and contributed to the event.

Tolstoy undertook to present the most heroic period of
Russian history, and he emerged triumphant from the contest with the difficulties of his theme.

We have before us a marvellous panorama of the Russia
that withstood Napoleon's invasion and dealt a death-blow
to his power. The picture is painted without exaggeration
and shows many of the shadows and ugly, pitiful features
belonging to the mental, moral, and political relations of
that day. But at the same time the strength that saved
Russia is indicated in a manner that by contrast with the
present makes the book painful reading for lovers of
Russia today.

The soul of man is depicted in 'War and Peace' with
unparalleled reality. It is not life in the abstract that
is shown, but creatures fully defined with all their limitations of place, time, and circumstance. For instance,
we see how individuals *grow*. Natasha running into the
drawing-room with her doll, in Book I, and Natasha enter-
ing the church, in Book IX, are really one and the same
person at two different ages, and not merely two different
ages attributed to a single person, such as one often
encounters in fiction. The author has also shown us the
intermediate stages of this development. In the same way
Nicholas Rostov develops; Pierre from being a young man
becomes a Moscow magnate; old Bolkonsky grows senile, and
so forth.

The spiritual peculiarities of Tolstoy's characters are
so clearly perceptible, so individual, that we can notice
the *family likeness* of those who are blood relations. Old
Bolkonski and Prince Andrew are evidently of similar
nature, though one is young and the other old. The Rostov
family, despite the great divergence of its members, presents features common to them all, and so remarkably reproduced that they merge into shades one feels but cannot
describe. For instance, we can feel that even the unsympathetic Vera may be a real Rostov, while the much more
attractive Sonya's mentality evidently springs from a different root.

The non-Russians present a very trying test, for had

Tolstoy been content to give a conventionally Russian view
of the nationalities presented, we, from our English point
of view, should at once note the artificiality of such a
presentation. But take, for instance, the French Mlle
Bourienne or Napoleon himself; the Austrian and German
generals Mack and Pfuel, or Adolph Berg, and (though we
today may feel more respect for German military capacity
than Tolstoy felt in the 'sixties) we readily recognize
the Frenchness of the Frenchman and the Germanity of the
Germans. As to the Russians in the book, not only is
every one of them thoroughly Russian but even the class
and condition to which each of them belongs is readily
distinguishable. For instance, Speranski, little as we
see of him, is from head to foot a 'seminarist', the product of a theological college.

And all that passes in their minds, each feeling, passion, or agitation, is distinct and true. Tolstoy never
makes the common mistake of representing a single state
of mind as always prevailing in the soul of any of his
heroes. Think for instance of Natasha, whose spirit is
so intense and full; in her soul everything is ardent;
her vanity, her love of her betrothed, her gaiety, her
thirst for life, her deep affection for her relations,
and so on. Or think of Prince Andrew when he stood over
the smoking shell. '"Can this be death?" thought Prince
Andrew, looking with a quite new, envious glance at the
grass, the wormwood, and the streamlet of smoke that
curled up from the revolving black ball. "I cannot, do
not wish, to die; I love life, love this grass, this
ground, this air"... He thought of this *and at the same
time remembered that men were looking at him.*' Or take
the feeling of animosity Prince Andrew nursed toward
Kuragin, with its strange contradictions, or the changes
of feeling in the Princess Marya: religious, amorous,
filially devoted, and so forth.

The dignity of man is hidden from us either by all
kinds of defects or by the fact that we esteem other
qualities too highly, and therefore measure men by their
cleverness, strength, beauty, and so forth. Tolstoy
teaches us to penetrate beneath their externality. What
can be simpler, more ordinary, and, so to say, meeker,
than the figures of Nicholas Rostov and the Princess
Marya. They have no brilliance, no ability, and do not
stand out from the most ordinary level of ordinary folk.
Yet these simple people, who go quietly along the simplest
of life's roads, are evidently admirable souls. The
irresistible sympathy with which the author has surrounded
these two, who seem so small but are really the peers of
any in spiritual beauty, is one of the masterly

achievements of 'War and Peace'. Nicholas Rostov is evidently a man of very limited ability, but, as the author
says, 'he had that common sense of mediocrity which showed
him what he ought to do'.

And really Nicholas does many stupid things and does
not show much understanding of people or circumstances,
but he always understands what ought to be done, and this
invaluable wisdom always preserves the purity of his
simple and ardent nature.

Is there any need to speak of the Princess Marya? Despite her weakness, this figure (which represented what
Tolstoy treasured as the image of the mother he had lost
before he was two years old) attains such purity and mild-
ness that at times she seems to wear the halo of a saint.

Then again Tolstoy is most masterly in the presentment
of what is hidden in the soul of man beneath the play of
passion, beneath his egotism, avarice, and animal desires.
Very pitiful, very senseless, are the passions which lead
Pierre and Natasha astray; but the reader sees that behind
it all these people have hearts of gold, and one never for
a moment doubts that when a demand comes for self-
sacrifice, or when there is a call for boundless sympathy
for what is good and admirable, these hearts will yield
warm and ready response. The spiritual beauty of these
two is remarkable. Pierre - a grown-up child with an
enormous body and terrible sensuality, impracticable and
unreasonable as a child - unites in himself a child-like
purity and tenderness of soul with a mind that is naive,
but for that very reason lofty, and a character to which
everything dishonourable is not merely foreign but even
incomprehensible. He has a child-like absence of fear and
unconsciousness of evil. Natasha is a girl gifted with
such fullness of spiritual life that, in Pierre's words,
she does not deign to be clever, that is, she has neither
the time nor the desire to convert this fullness of life
into abstract forms of thought. Her measureless pleni-
tude of life - which at times brings her into a state of
'intoxication' (to translate exactly the word employed in
the Russian original) - leads her into the terrible mistake of her senseless passion for Kuragin - a mistake
afterwards redeemed by severe suffering. Pierre and Natasha were people who by their very natures were bound to
commit many mistakes and encounter much disillusionment.
As if in contrast to them the author introduces the happy
couple Vera and Adolph Berg - people who commit no mistakes, encounter no disillusionment, and arrange their
life most comfortably. One cannot but be amazed at the
restraint with which Tolstoy, exhibiting all the paltri-
ness and pettiness of these souls, never once yields to

the temptation of treating them with ridicule or anger.
This is true realism and real truth! With similar truthfulness are the Kuragins, Hélène and Anatole, depicted;
these heartless creatures are exhibited unsparingly, but
with no desire to belabour them.

Amid all the diversity of people and events, we feel
the presence of some firm and indestructible principles on
which their lives rest. Family, social, and marital obligations are clearly discernible. The conceptions of good
and evil are clear and durable. Having shown us the artificial life of the higher spheres of society and of the
various staffs surrounding exalted personages, Tolstoy
sets in contrast two firm and real spheres of life -
family life and life in the active army. The two families,
the Rostovs and the Bolkonskis, present us with life directed by clear, indubitable principles, in the fulfilment
of which the members of these families set their duty and
honour, their dignity and satisfaction. Similarly army
life (which in one place Tolstoy compares to a swarm) presents us with a quite definite conception of duty and
human dignity; so that the simple-minded Nicholas on one
occasion even prefers to remain in the regiment rather
than return home, where he does not see clearly what his
conduct should be.

Tolstoy is peculiarly Russian and may at times be read
to find the differences of thought and feeling that separate Russians from ourselves; but what is more remarkable
is the way his penetration to the very souls of men convinces us that his Russians are of one nature with ourselves, and that the power that created us made 'of one
blood all nations of men', however we may vary superfi-
cially.

'War and Peace' presents us with a complete picture of
human life; a complete picture of the Russia of those
days; a complete historic picture of the struggle of
nations; and a complete picture of the things in which men
set their happiness and greatness, their sorrow and their
shame. It is a work so amazingly great that though many
have *felt* its greatness, few have *understood* how great it
is. Tolstoy is one who reveals the secrets of life and
death. The meaning of history, the strength of nations,
the mystery of death, the reality of love and family life
- such are the subjects he deals with. Are these matters
so easy that every casual reader may take up the book in
an idle hour expecting to fathom them? Is it strange that
'War and Peace' should prove both a touchstone testing the
quality of its critics and a stumbling-block to many who
undertake to judge it?

In judging such a work one should tread with caution,

but we think a Russian critic judged well when he said that the meaning of the book is best summed up in Tolstoy's own words:'There is no greatness without simplicity, goodness and truth'.

'Anna Karenina' 1875-7

54. CHUYKO ON TOLSTOY AND CONTEMPORARY SOCIETY

1875

V.V. Chuyko (1839-99) was a literary and art critic whose particular interest was England; he wrote on the Pre-Raphaelites and many English authors; his book on Shakespeare (1889) was the most far-ranging, interesting and well-written work on him to appear in Russia up to that time.

(a) From an article in 'Voice', 1875, no. 37, Count Tolstoy's Novel, signed X.Y.Z. He used the English letters.

This is but the beginning of the novel and all is not yet clear. The drama lies ahead, and drama there will be if the beginning is anything to go by. So far only the background has been sketched in and a few characters drawn. Kitty is certainly a re-working of the wonderful portrait of Natasha in 'War and Peace'; we can already see the same general characteristics, the same springs of spiritual life and the same sort of spiritual organism. Some of the other characters are already fully drawn and this is where Count Tolstoy's pre-eminence lies. I think that several of the characters in the new novel are better, are drawn in greater relief, than in his previous works; there is nothing incomplete in them, nothing left unsaid, nothing illogical; all of them are well constructed and integral; characteristic flows from characteristic naturally and

logically; they have none of the hazy outlines, none of
the posing and flabbiness of Pierre in 'War and Peace'.
In that novel Count Tolstoy was paradoxical to a marked
degree, but here there is no paradox; the author is the
same investigator of the varieties of humanity and not so
much the investigator of types as the analyst of various
psychological moments in a man's development. In this
respect he can probably be compared only with that other
great psychological writer, Henri Beyle (Stendhal): the
subject of their investigation is the same; equally they
both look into the smallest secrets of the soul; they are
both equally original, so original in fact that they
appear eccentric and paradoxical; they both equally dislike the smooth and beaten track in art; as well as talent
they both have a huge store of systematic knowledge and
consequently both are so dissimilar to the majority of
writers of fiction in our times who have been unable to
do away with customary forms and customary ideas. But if
the subject matter and the means are the same, the methods
employed by Beyle and Count Tolstoy are different. With
Stendhal theory and precise knowledge come before the creative process; with Count Tolstoy it is the opposite, and
whatever people may say Count Tolstoy is primarily not so
much a thinker as an artist, with him the creative process
itself takes pride of place, as it does with Mr Dostoevsky. But the creative process, kept within bounds, is
always accompanied by a severe mind which prevents it
descending into vague forms and unhealthy proclivities.
Stendhal's creative process is purely theoretical and
artificial; from one initial psychological fact he builds
the entire character and if this character seems alive it
is only thanks to the unusual logic with which Beyle develops what follows from this one general fact in all its
inevitability determined by the situation and by life.
With Count Tolstoy the main thing is life and people; he
loves this life and these people with all the passion and
impressionability of the artist; his creative process is
not a theoretical one but life itself as it is reflected
in his mind. But his mind never sleeps and consequently
one frequently meets suddenly a short, seemingly empty,
phrase which illuminates the character from a completely
new side and points to a psychological peculiarity which
could not be produced by a theoretical ideal alone. In
this Count Tolstoy is the undisputed master, and even
European critics can hardly suggest an artist who can
equal him in this respect. Take for example the portrait,
written evidently *au courant de la plume,* but which presents as something living the extremely pleasant Stepan
Arkadevich Oblonsky with his intellectual instability and

innate gentleness, although in this portrait there are no
heavy colours or quasi-profound touches.

[Quotation omitted.]

Note the manner in which this portrait is painted; it is
clear that the author has touched upon but a single trait
of his mental make-up which has no relation to the complicated apparatus of psychic motives which we call the personality; he speaks of a trait which is essentially quite
superficial, the more so since the attitude of a man to
this or that viewpoint cannot determine his moral physiognomy. Furthermore all this extract seems nothing more
than a witty comment on a very superficial quality, but
when you read it you begin very quickly to paint a picture
of Oblonsky in your mind's eye with his mental personality
and innate goodness, with his lack of drive and energy and
a certain mental shyness and pliability, with his indecision and the almost complete absence of a consciousness
of his own actions. Several times the author returns to
this theme and every time introduces a new trait which
suddenly illuminates the whole figure and presents it in
unusual relief. This is life itself in all its complexity
and all its natural simplicity... One last trait com-
pletes the portrait. Anna on her arrival persuades Dolly
to make peace with her husband.

[Quotation omitted.]

The actual kinship between Count Tolstoy and Beyle is
here visible; this kinship is to a certain degree so close
that from time to time when reading Beyle it seems that
one is reading Count Tolstoy and on the other hand several
pages in 'Anna Karenina' give an illusion of 'Le Rouge et
le noir' or 'La Chartreuse de Parme'. In any case Count
Tolstoy's novel promises to be very interesting.

(b) From 'Voice', 1875, no. 72, High Society and Count
Tolstoy's Attitude to it as Seen in the Section 'The Party
after the Ball'.

The February number of the 'Russian Messenger' contains
the continuation of Count Tolstoy's novel 'Anna Karenina'.
This continuation produces a less charming impression than
the beginning; it is, if one can so express it, paler,
although still interesting. The novel still revolves

around high society which in itself provides little of
interest for the artist. Levin leaves for the country in
despair after Kitty has refused his hand and his heart,
Anna departs for Petersburg and her husband; Vronsky who
is in love with her also sets out for the capital. Little
by little they draw nearer each other.

[Quotation and summary of the first two parts of the novel
omitted.]

All in all we have had more than one hundred and sixty
pages, and the novel's two main characters, Count Vronsky
and Anna Karenina, are still not fully developed and it is
still unknown what will become of them. Surely such a
leisurely development of the action and the characters is
a mistake and is harmful to the interest in the novel?
Furthermore the action takes place in high society circles
and the leading characters are from this society and neither these people nor this society can form the basis of
strong drama, even in the realm of personal relationships.
Count Tolstoy is a talented artist and, because of the
nature of his talent, a realist. He does not endow the
thoughts and feelings of these people with any independence because on account of their upbringing and social
position they could not possess it. He does not belong to
the number of those of our writers who endow the puppets
of their imagination with the title of Count or Prince and
fill them with unheard-of virtue and, copying the habit of
several French novelists, fill the boredom and emptiness
of their lives with a spurious drama.
  Count Tolsoy is a true realist in the broadest and most
exact sense of the word and consequently one does not meet
any sort of idealization in his works; he is the enemy of
everything affected, everything artificial, everything'
false and therefore the pictures he paints, while not
being simple photographs, present life in all its hard and
sometimes bitter truth; nor is there any hidden plan to
paint one phenomenon to the detriment of any other or to
present in an unfavourable light a fact which he himself
possibly does not like. This trait is especially clearly
seen in 'War and Peace' where Count Tolstoy set himself
the task of showing the utter inability of the upper
classes to help during the national disaster of 1812.
Count Tolstoy generally likes to remove from people and
phenomena everything done for effect or obviously theatrical and more often than not looks on life with an ironic
smile. Such irony shines through 'War and Peace' and a
similar pitiless and caustic irony is to be seen in 'Anna
Karenina' too, in relation to the same high society which

apparently comprises the novel's main subject matter.

[Quotation omitted concerning Anna's changing view of society life.]

Such is Count Tolstoy's view of high society and he knows
it not from hearsay or from dancing attendance upon it
like the majority of our upper-class writers. He has long
studied and observed it and has arrived at the negative
view of it which creeps over every page of 'War and Peace'
and which is so clearly and openly expressed in 'Anna
Karenina'.

(c) From 'Voice', 1875, no. 105, Literary Essays.

Something strange has been noticed both by society and
critics concerning Count Tolstoy's novel 'Anna Karenina'.
Before the appearance of the first chapters everyone
awaited the novel with the greatest impatience and eagerly
anticipated the same aesthetic and intellectual pleasure
which they had received from 'War and Peace'. Consequently a number of prejudices about the novel developed
from which the majority of the reading public have not yet
managed to free themselves. The first chapters were found
disappointing. It appeared that the idea behind the novel
was not as well thought out as that behind 'War and Peace'.
Instead of the history of a whole period of Russian society, 'Anna Karenina' presents the intimate story of several individuals almost without reference to the collective life of society; however at the beginning the reader
was struck by the masterly style, the subtly depicted
characters and the clear and interesting exposition of the
plot. The second series of chapters further disappointed
the reader; many saw that there were no particular types,
the external interest was somewhat weak and that although
the characters were consistent in themselves their psychological aspects were poorly delineated and were even
occasionally self-contradictory. Then the March number of
the 'Russian Messenger' completely depressed the reading
public. It turned out that from past custom and the pattern he had earlier established people were expecting precisely what Count Tolstoy had no intention of giving them
and that the belletristic side of the novel was decidedly
unsatisfactory and it was the general opinion that for the
author of 'War and Peace' the latest work was extremely
poor and did not possess even any general interest. It is

my opinion that just as the expectations for the novel
were unjustified so are the attacks upon it now that we
know what it is. I think that Count Tolstoy has been
found lacking in any aesthetic view about Russian society
but that the demands of this society will not in themselves stand up to even the most modest criticism. Our
babbling critics repeated the hesitations of public opinion and presented in their writings a series of contradictory and clumsy conclusions about the novel: some were
dissatisfied because 'Anna Karenina' was not 'War and
Peace', or because it did not display sufficient Slavophile tendencies; others that the author seemed to be too
pochvennik or Slavophile; or lastly those - the most persistent and at the same time most ridiculous - who considered that it was not worth the trouble to comment on the
novel and that besides obscenity and disgraceful goings-on
there was nothing in it, and then in all due seriousness
explained this as a sign of the decline and fall of society. But one also heard some rather more weighty criticisms.

The first of these concerned the fact that Count Tolstoy had narrowed down all the interest in contemporary
Russian society to that embodied in the so-called 'upper'
class. In the Russia of today are there really no more
interesting products of life than these which would give
the author of 'Childhood' and 'Boyhood' interesting and
original material for psychological comment? Is it really
worth studying this high society which has been exhausted
by our so-called upper-class authors and which Count Tolstoy himself does not regard at all favourably? An
upper-class dandy, be he even as well-behaved and intelligent a young man as Count Vronsky, is but a faded flower
of a former society and the circles in which he exists
have destroyed in him any original or individual characteristics and left only specific traces of a certain
nature.

The regiment occupied an important place in Vronsky's
life both because he loved his regiment but also and
more importantly because he was liked there. In the
regiment he was not only liked but also respected and
admired; he was admired because he was a man of great
wealth, extremely well educated and of immense talent
who had a clear road to any success to which his
vanity of ambition should lead him and who despised
all this and of all life's interests held closest to
his heart those of his regiment and his friends.
Vronsky was well aware of this view of him and over
and above the fact that he liked the life he felt

himself obliged to justify the opinions held about
him.

You will agree that this is rather meagre, especially
for a well-educated and talented young man. A good education should have certainly opened up for Vronsky wider
ideals and ambitions in life and his talents should have
opened up for him a wider field of activity. And to what,
by the way, have his talents led him? Besides his activities in the army and society he does have one other
interest - horses, for which he has an immense enthusiasm.
If we add to this his love for Anna Karenina then it would
seem that Vronsky is seized by two passions; but these two
passions do not get in each other's way although he looks
upon them both from the same point of view; in other
words for him love for a woman is in no way different in
kind from love for a horse. Such is Vronsky. His society friends are no better - nor, we might add, any worse.
Yashin, for example, is a gambler and hard drinker; far
from being a man who lives without principles, he is drawn
by Count Tolstoy as living by immoral ones. Yashin was
Vronsky's best friend in the regiment. Vronsky liked him
both for his unusual physical strength which was expressed
for the most part in the fact that he could drink like a
fish, go without sleep and show no ill effects and also
for his great moral strength which he displayed to his
superiors and his friends attracting both fear and respect, and also at cards when he would lay tens of thousands but always, in spite of the vast amounts of wine he
had drunk, carefully and deliberately, so that he was
looked upon as the leading player in the English Club.
Such is the psychological material which the author has
found in high society. It is unattractive and by no means
interesting; but Count Tolstoy did not intend to portray
contemporary heroes and if I were forced to comment on the
choice of milieu for the novel then I would say without
fear of erring greatly that he chose this one precisely
because it is not characteristic and does not present any
remarkable traits of its own. With no attempt at presenting the history of social ideas or of the morals of contemporary society and restricting himself to a specific
circle of psychological observations, the author evidently
chose such a milieu which in the realm of ideas contains
absolutely nothing and in that of morals has to such a
degree surrounded itself with certain rules and forms and
has to such a degree become petrified within them that it
gives the very best conditions for psychological observations. When he concerns himself with such a milieu the
writer is not obliged to anticipate, to evade, to explain

or even to comment upon the course of social ideas inasmuch as these ideas are reflected in that milieu - in high
society there are no ideas to be reflected; he is not
obliged to paint the morals of this milieu and consequently he can devote himself exclusively to the history of
psychic movements because in Yashin and even in Vronsky
there do exist such psychic processes. I think this is
the best excuse for Count Tolstoy, especially as he is not
at all drawn to that society and sometimes, albeit rarely
and in passing, as it were, paints it in such a way that
it could only bring a blush of shame to the face.

In the novel therefore the whole matter centres of psychological analysis. In this connection there is a further point of a more serious nature. Many people have
noticed inconsistency and illogicality in the actions of
Levin, who lives on his estates in the country. A man who
is clearly passionate and deeply sincere, Levin falls in
love with Kitty. He is completely absorbed in his love
and has arrived in Moscow with the determination (which
has cost him so much) to offer Kitty his hand and his
heart; he is agitated and ill at ease and the empty chat
of Oblonsky produces upon him a sharp and unpleasant dis-
sonance. When Kitty refuses him he recognizes that she is
attracted to Vronsky. In despair he immediately returns
to the country and although deeply depressed begins to
plan his future; despite his despair he listens with the
greatest interest to his steward who tells him that one of
his cows has just given birth and sets off with the passionate love of the estate owner and country dweller to
look over his land and forgets for a time his shattered
hopes and ruined life. It is said that there is something
lacking in Levin and that because of excessive originality
the author has made him a lifeless character. I think
that Levin is a remarkably alive person; there is not
only nothing lacking in him but on the contrary something
too much, namely that Great Russian lymph, a scrofulous
passion and an absence of impulse or irritability. This
trait marks both Levin's character and his actions. A
Russian who has suffered since his childhood from scrofula
and in whom both the drab natural surroundings and the
dark grey sky and the whole sum of social and historical
life have caused a huge amount of lymph just cannot act as
a vivacious Italian or an impressionable Frenchman. An
Italian would never settle for such an outcome of his
love; he would either put a bullet through his head like
Jacopo Ortis or take his revenge like Iago; a Frenchman
would probably soon forget the object of his passion but
then at the first opportunity perpetrate a multitude of
stupidities; but Levin as a lymphatic Russian could not

act in either fashion. Thanks to his lymph his spiritual
processes are much slower and as it were blunter. The
passion wanders darkly and sombrely through his soul, his
enthusiasms lack lustre and his habit of eternal mental
reflection (also the result of the influence of his social
milieu and his lymph) leads him not to any great spiritual
outburst but to a more or less dim analysis, to a fruitless mental vicious circle and not to the very process of
life but rather to a re-living of the reflection. Levin
is an extraordinarily well-described Russian in whom is
seen immensely clearly the whole complicated influence of
climate and social organism, a climate which oppresses the
nervous passion of a tender man living under a clear sky
and the warm sun, and a social organism which gives no
opportunity of developing the instincts of the community
and which in the absence of any live activity nips many
talents in the bud and allows only one characteristic to
develop: a fruitless theoretical philosophizing which lies
like a black spot upon the Russians.

Certainly 'Anna Karenina' presents no history of social
ideas but because of this it presents far more. It presents foreshortened and unusually clearly, profoundly and
with great talent, what the greatest European writers present to their readers: an ethnographic and spiritual history of Russian man, not as an individual or as an exception who has arisen because of this or that social phenomenon but as the representative of a certain nation or
race. O'Connell and a whole school of contemporary
European critics have shown that Shakespeare did essentially the same thing and his basic worth lies precisely
in this and is proof of his unusual genius. To achieve
the same objective Count Tolstoy did not, of course, need
to be such a genius, for science has considerably eased
his path, but nevertheless in Shakespeare's time it was
but an accidental result of his genius when then, as now,
everything was striving to solve the problem, and this is
why in 'Anna Karenina' Count Tolstoy shows himself to be
far more contemporary a writer than many of those who
depict contemporary heroes, make huge efforts to write a
history of social ideas, concern themselves with the pro-
pagation of unusual humaneness or unusual progressive
trends and forget that before ideas there exists life itself and in the present case Russian life, with its dull
skies, its dull ideas and its even duller spiritual processes.

The supporters of contemporary writing are dissatisfied
with Count Tolstoy for his apparent paradoxes in consequence of which Anna Karenina is some incomprehensible
moral monster. She is an intelligent and good woman, she

loves her son passionately, she is well disposed towards
her husband, and, moreover, once she has fallen in love
with Vronsky, she gives herself to him after some initial
hesitation without the slightest spiritual suffering,
without the slightest torment, and only after her so-
called fall as it were comes to herself and begins to
realize the consequences of her actions. On this basis
Count Tolstoy has been accused of a psychological paradox
and even of negligence towards the main character in his
novel. Of course the majority of contemporary Russian
novels are guilty of the same thing: they concentrate as
we all know on so-called psychological analysis; the
author will carefully and in detail describe all the processes of spiritual alarms, torments and pangs of conscience and will note all shades of feeling and every
doubt. This is all done in the most banal manner which
explains nothing yet at the same time fills dozens of
pages as, for example, in Mr Danilevsky's latest novel
'The Ninth Wave'. Naturally Count Tolstoy is not responsible for this banal ideal in modern writers and in 'Anna
Karenina' he shows that without turning to trite descriptions of spiritual processes one can nevertheless write a
great page from the history of the human soul.
    Discarding the dubious and essentially ridiculous de-
scriptions of pseudo-psycholoigcal processes he seizes the
spiritual life of man taken from the very facts of life;
he does not tell us that Anna Karenina is suffering from
this or that or that certain thoughts occurred to her - he
only tells us what Anna did, and this is quite sufficient
to explain her fully. And here we have one of Count Tolstoy's particular facets as a psychologist: he suggests
that man's spiritual processes are for the most part unconscious and that in the majority of cases we are controlled not so much by ideas as by words; the simple fact
is often of no great significance but when this fact is
given a code name in which is hidden a certain conventional concept the fact immediately is turned into consciousness and immediately is seen in all its striking nakedness. The author has noticed something similar in Anna.
The very fact of her love for Vronsky, although it had
radically affected the happiness of her husband and son,
destroyed her family and ruined Kitty's happiness appeared
to her as neither unfitting nor immoral; on the contrary
it all seemed natural, simple; she gave herself over to
the feeling unreasoningly, submitting herself to the im-
pulsiveness of her nature. But as soon as *her fall* has
been accomplished, when the rude fact appeared before her
eyes in all its clarity and logicality, she realized the
meaning of the fact for her life and the lives of those

near her; she gave the fact a name which explained to her
all its true meaning. This is unusually accurate: words
are as it were the receptacle of ideas where our impressions and convictions slowly and imperceptibly accumulate;
words are like mathematical formulae which for the most
part and in the normal run of things have little significance but which contain within themselves the sum total of
our experience and our convictions.

Precisely in the character of Anna Karenina Count Tolstoy has revealed a rare talent for subtle and vivid observation. The psychological law, so deftly caught by the
author, finds its application mainly in that sphere to
which Anna belongs by her birth, upbringing and habits.
In this milieu more than anywhere else people are governed
by words which encapsulate concepts and form an unchanging
moral code. Words themselves in this milieu are confined
in a certain legitimized framework and thus rules for all
the trivia of life are worked out. Anna's behaviour in
this milieu is up to a point not out of the ordinary and
is in itself in no way immoral or beyond the bounds of
propriety: consequently Anna submits to the emotions of a
new love with such ease and with the complete absence of
any inner struggle. It appears to her that with the
observance of certain external conventions her new feelings are as much of the accepted order of things as her
former behaviour towards her husband; it further appears
to her that in this milieu such a complication in her
feelings and passions would lead to no complications in
life because in essence there occurred there neither sincere liaisons nor deep passions but only a certain form
and caprice both vindicated by the code of behaviour of
this society. Unfortunately Anna Karenina is not fully a
society lady; her passion and enthusiasm for it are deeper
and when she finds herself face to face with the rough
fact of life, when all her past life and her peace of mind
are staked on this one fact there then wells up within her
that vulgar struggle of a bifurcated and ruined life which
is experienced by all mere mortals who do not belong to
the upper class and consequently do not have the slightest
idea of its moral code.

Finally one must understand that Count Tolstoy is an
artist who does not follow the beaten track but who
attempts to seek out new paths and new vantage points.
He is no routine copyist, taking ready-made paths and
taking on trust familiar conclusions. In the main he is
a lively observer bringing to his almost scientific researches the peculiarities of his nature and the turn of
his mind. Realist by nature and fatalist by general outlook, he looks at man's psychological mechanism from this

dual point of view. However great his errors might be,
however terrible his apparent paradoxes might seem, both
these errors and paradoxes are far more valuable and
important than the current and recognized truths and bana-
lities of the majority of our writers.

55. SOLOVYOV, REVIEW, 'ST PETERSBURG NEWS'

1875

Vsevolod Solovyov (1849–1903), brother of the influential
symbolist philosopher Vladimir, was an extremely popular
but not over-talented historical novelist. He was one of
the first critics to see 'Anna Karenina' as but a poor
sequel to 'War and Peace'. The first extract is from the
'St Petersburg News', 1875, no. 65, and the second from
no. 105.

The February number of the 'Russian Messenger' has appeared containing more of 'Anna Karenina'. We have the completion of the first part and the first ten chapters of
the second. Consequently the novel is now well under way
and the author has said enough for us to make certain
justifiable comments on his novel, which will remain true
when we look at the finished work. These new chapters are
indisputably wonderful, indeed they could not be otherwise; but the more one reads the more and more frequently
one is obliged to ask the question: Why in these marvellous scenes and all these wonderful and accurate pictures
of life is everything so familiar, so over-familiar that
one thinks one has read it all more than once before?
This question arises not because of that well-known sense
of a reality which one has lived through oneself and which
is looked at by someone else; this is in all truly artistic works. No, the further we go into Count Tolstoy's new
novel the more we see a certain familiar style, familiar
attributes and characteristics of the personages; finally
all the, so to say, feel of the novel has been long ago
sensed somewhere and remains in the mind. Where have we
read it? Have we really read it? We may answer these
questions with a Categorical 'yes'. We have read it all
before and we have read it in the works of the famous and

well-loved author, Count Lev Tolstoy.

'Anna Karenina', however the author might conclude it, will certainly turn out to be a remarkable and excellent novel and there is no doubt that there will be whole pages in it that will remain in the reader's memory for ever. Having read what has so far appeared we feel we must say that it was too early to embark on a new novel, for there is a lack of new material and the author has rather too often to rely on a previous rich source: 'War and Peace'. 'Anna Karenina' started off as a completely new and independent novel, but after the wonderful description of the ball, after chapter XV, the lack of fresh material has become apparent. Here and there pages from 'War and Peace' come to the surface; the figure of Levin becomes confused with that of Pierre Bezukhov; from behind Prince Shcherbatsky there appears, albeit rather more intelligent, Count Rostov; grandmother Natasha is embodied in her granddaughter Kitty. Perhaps Count Tolstoy consciously wanted to show this transmigration of souls, but as the novel is called 'Anna Karenina' and not 'Metempsychosis' we have as yet too little evidence for such a supposition....

Before us lies the wonderful passage describing the feelings, thoughts and ideas of Levin on his return from his unsuccessful meeting with Kitty.

Well, what is to be done?... I am quite guiltless. But I want to live now in a completely different way. Only it's impossible. Neither life, nor the past will permit it. So what can I do? Live as I used to? Only better, live in a much better way...

This, among other things, is what Levin says to himself. If you remember 'War and Peace' when you read this chapter you will be absolutely convinced that you see before you again Pierre Bezukhov, complete and unchanged, with all his thoughts, ideas and feelings, with all his decisions and conclusions, even with the self-same words that he uttered between 1805 and 1812. Only his circumstances, his external life, have changed; he is busy not with the freemasons or with Napoleon but with red skewbald cows and Tindall's book on heat.

Take the scene in the Shcherbatsky household during Kitty's illness, take the old prince, his attitude to his wife, his daughter and even to himself and you will see Count Rostov rising before you out of his grave. Look at Kitty closely throughout this period and note her

246 Tolstoy: The Critical Heritage

attitude to her father and her mother, her conversations
with Dolly, her movements, feelings and the trend of her
thought - and you will see Natasha.

Of course Levin or Shcherbatsky or Kitty will not
suffer from the fact that the souls of their ancestors
have been transferred to them for they remain vivid, very
accurately and artistically depicted creations and we
certainly do not wish to criticize them on this count. We
only wish to show their evident similarity to characters
whom we clearly remember from 'War and Peace'.

When we spoke of the first fifteen chapters of 'Anna
Karenina' we expressed the opinion that Count Tolstoy had
a command of a sense of measure and that it would be impossible to remove from and difficult to add anything to
these chapters. Now to our intense regret and great surprise we must reproach the honourable author for one particular page where this sense of measure has deserted him.
This page begins the novel's second part. Vronsky's
departure has so affected Kitty that she has fallen ill.
Her strength is failing and she is growing worse.

[Quotation of Kitty's examination by both a local doctor
and a specialist from the capital omitted.]

What is all this? Realism? Truth taken to its ultimate perfection? If it is then we can and must praise
Mr Nekrasov for the poetry of his 'their body lice burst
forth in song' and the many words of Mr Shchedrin which
we are too cowardly to repeat! Why is this passage necessary? What does it explain or elucidate? Why did the
author find it necessary to introduce into his wonderfully
written novel this unnecessary, cynical and even not particularly realistic passage? Yes, not particularly realistic because Kitty's suffering (as is seen later) was not
at all of the sort that either a famous or an unknown doctor could have demanded an examination which would stun
and shame the patient and then cause the doctor 'to stand
in the drawing-room carefully wiping his hands'. And
finally any examination by a doctor, whoever he might be,
cannot be terrible and immoral because every reasonably
intelligent and chaste woman or girl, precisely because of
her chastity, must not and cannot at a given moment look
on the doctor as a man and then speak, as Count Tolstoy
does, of 'the extremely handsome and not old man and the
young naked girl' - this is completely out of place. If
Kitty had been a corrupt and depraved person then it is
quite another matter; but the author depicts her as quite
the opposite. If we have lingered upon this awful passage
and have chosen to quote from it it is only because we are

forced to accuse Count Tolstoy of a serious blunder which
if it is repeated will be a serious matter, and to accuse
such a greatly talented author of anything is permissible
only with material evidence.

We left the heroine of the novel, Anna Karenina, last
time as a very shadowy figure and did not know what to
make of her. She has now turned out to be a woman of very
little interest, not particularly intelligent, without
either special goodness or special evil and without even
that primeval strength which in its clearest, most obvious
manifestations can be so involuntarily attractive that we
can forgive it much. We are still reluctant to pass a
final verdict on Anna; possibly as the drama develops she
will show some new side to her character which will then
justify the author in giving her the leading role in the
story; until then we can only repeat that she is not at
all interesting and that all the other women, who are but
secondary, are far more interesting.

[Quotation and description of the action omitted.]

Of course all Anna Kareninas will be very grateful to
the author for such beautiful passages, but we dare to be
dissatisfied with them. They would have been psychologically realistic if in place of Anna there had been some
little lovelorn girl or even woman but certainly not the
Anna whom we saw explaining things to her husband. It is
our opinion that Anna Karenina would hardly have 'stopped
and then fallen from the sofa', or 'found something
frightful and repulsive when she recalled what had been
paid for with the terrible price of shame' or would have
'felt herself overcome with shame' and so on. The author
must be reminded of the 'feeling of *joy*', of that feeling
which 'she did not want to *vulgarize* with words'. It is
the same author who has described for us the dreams which
she had every night. She dreamt that

> it seemed as if they were both her husband, that they
> were both showering her with caresses. Her husband
> cried as he kissed her hand and said: 'How pleasant it
> all is now', and Vronsky was there too and he was also
> her husband. And she was surprised by the fact that
> earlier it had seemed impossible and she explained to
> them, laughing, that it was all much simpler than
> before and that they were both happy and contented.

Now that's better and these dreams are pure delight!
The dreams which Anna Karenina has are real.

We did not expect that we should have to mention

passages from Count Tolstoy's novel except in great pleasure and with praise. We did not think that reading his
novel would give us anything but delight. But none the
less there is sufficient pleasure and 'Anna Karenina' remains at least so far a remarkable and highly talented
work.

When you read a new work by a talented and beloved author
and with every page you become more and more convinced
that there is no trace of that talent you begin to feel
sad; the sadness, however, is a little softened and starts
to fade away from the moment when you come to the conclusion that the author has written himself out. He has
written himself out and his work is over and lies in the
past. You know and remember him full of life and strength
and you look at the new, sorry work as something extraneous which has little to do with him. But there is a
strange feeling when there breathes from the page from
time to time the unexhausted power of the former talent
and you simultaneously feel that something odd has happened to that power, that it is for some reason devoid of
its former charm.

Such a strange feeling is left by the new chapters of
'Anna Karenina' which appeared in the March issue of the
'Russian Messenger'. You see the masterly brush of the
true artist and you notice here and there bright colours
and subtle shades. You pause on the details - and they
appear impeccable; but then you look at the sum total of
these details, at the picture as a whole and you unwillingly say that it is not worth the effort to write so
passionately or with such love.

Naturally every manifestation in life is worthy of
attention and reproduction; but if the writer devotes many
a chapter exclusively to human vulgarity and carefully,
with love, personifies this vulgarity, if he clearly does
not wish to create a single character with whom it would
be possible to stay and rest awhile then he is creating
something with which his attentive and unprejudiced readers will remain distinctly dissatisfied.

It is clear that only at the end of the novel will one
be able to judge the objectives which Count Tolstoy had in
mind in writing 'Anna Karenina'; possibly much will be
clarified that is at the moment unclear; possibly the
author will in the succeeding chapters take us away from
the melancholy company of Petersburg guards officers and
ladies with impeccable manners acquiring lovers; possibly
we shall find ourselves in another world, less fashionable
but more lively and interesting... We certainly hope so;
but the fact is that the author had better get a move on.

And so there is much that is still reparable and much
which cannot be judged until the end of the novel. There
is one thing, though, that is already irreparable and
which may be judged at the present time and this is Anna
herself. It is not a question of her character, her virtues or shortcomings but that she seems to bifurcate
before the readers' eyes and two Annas appear - one comes
directly out of the novel while the other from the
author's own attitude to her. Therefore when he writes
about her directly it seems that he is not speaking about
the woman he is describing.

What sort of a woman is Anna Karenina? Up to now she
has only appeared fleetingly as a mysterious and beautiful
shadow. But now she is filling out, materializing as habitués of seances might express it. Now we meet her
already having deceived her husband whom she hates and
awaiting her lover Vronsky. But instead of her lover her
husband arrives at her dacha. She sees again his familiar
moustache.

[Quotation omitted.]

This is the type, then, that Anna is beginning to shape
into. It is not a new type, it is extremely familiar and
in spite of all the art with which Count Tolstoy describes
it it remains extremely uninteresting.

Vronsky loves Anna in a way that 'this passion fills
his whole life', 'it is no joke, no light-hearted matter
but something, as on one card, his whole life could be
staked'. But his life is staked on a further card -
besides Anna he loves racing horses and loves his mare so
much that he forgets about Anna and her husband and that
Anna has just told him she is pregnant.

He loses on this second card - through his own clumsi-
ness he breaks his horse's back during the race. The description of this scene is marvellous.

[Quotation omitted.]

This episode of an extremely unhappy period of
Vronsky's life is impeccable from an artistic point of
view as is the whole description of the races. But is it
the reader's fault if in the final analysis all this unhappiness becomes unspeakably boring? That it is an accurate and artistic depiction of reality is quite true; but
the fact is that the reader expects descriptions of
another reality from a writer as talented as Count Tolstoy,
a reality for which there were high hopes at the beginning
of the novel. In those early chapters, in the Oblonsky

household, there was that truth that is close to the
readers, that truth which is worth examining and spending
time upon. In those chapters characters moved who demanded one's urgent attention, characters who more so at the
present time than ever before, cry out for the pen of a
talented author... For example Levin's brother and his
mistress, scarcely touched upon but demanding the right of
citizenship on a fully legitimate basis.

   It is time to return to such people, suffering both
from old diseases and those of our own time, it is time to
bring these complicated, intelligent people together with
people less complicated or intelligent, one of whom is
Oblonsky. When these people of different classes find
themselves together in whatever relations one to the other,
then from these relationships there will appear the actual
living truth of our time, that confused and murky truth,
the disentanglement and clarification of which would be a
rewarding task for such a highly talented author as we
consider Count Tolstoy to be.

56. TKACHOV ATTACKS TOLSTOY'S ARISTOCRATICISM

1875

P.N. Tkachov (1844-85), vitriolic publicist, revolutionary, and leader of the Russian 'Jacobins'; many of his
ideas were later taken up by Lenin. This essay, entitled
The Appearance of 'Anna Karenina' and written under the
pseudonym of P. Nikitin, appeared in the left-wing journal
'Affair', 1875, no. 5. His introductory summary of what
other critics (or pseudo-critics in his opinion) had said
is omitted.

If one looks at it closely, the basic idea behind 'War and
Peace' is worthy of attention. In Russian literature, and
I say this not without a certain trepidation because I
know that some will consider it the height of impertinence,
in Russian literature you will scarcely find another novel
that is imbued with a more dubious or a more corrupt morality than that put forward by the author in that 'epic
that will last for ever'. In the recent past Moscow critics have accused Mr Boborykin of putting forward immoral

ideas in his novels, but in this respect, as in many
others, Mr Boborykin is a mere beginner when compared with
Count Tolstoy. With Mr Boborykin it is not the content of
his novels which is immoral but surely, if I may so express it, their *façon*, their somewhat loquacious nature
distinguished by a generally Parisian *chic*; with Count
Tolstoy's novel the *façon* is excellent, he does not seek
after an exterior scabrousness in his works like the
author of 'The Solid Virtues' by replacing the scabrous
passages, as Mr Solovyov wrote, 'with rows of legitimized
and accepted full stops'. But because of this the internal morality of works such as 'War and Peace' and 'Anna
Karenina' becomes even more seductive. If our critics
were just a little more perceptive or a little bolder they
would see clearly that in the six volumes of that 'epic
which will last for ever' Count Tolstoy is attempting persistently to show that all so-called civic activity and
political aspirations adopted in the name of civilization
are all so much illusory nonsense; that their realization
and the form they take do not at all depend upon the efforts of separate individuals influencing the mass of the
others but upon accidental and purely spontaneous causes.
Starting from this viewpoint Count Tolstoy wishes to draw,
and indeed graphically does draw in 'War and Peace', the
following conclusion: the aim and meaning of life for
every individual must lie not in such activity or aspirations but in narrow egotistical self-satisfaction in
sexual relations and their consummation in family happiness in the crudest and almost cynical meaning of the
words. This is the basic idea which Count Tolstoy introduces with the most refined taste throughout his epic and
which is so attractive to those of our critics who wish to
compare it with 'Dead Souls'. Because of this idea Count
Tolstoy debunks the so-called great men in history and
presents them as fools; because of this idea he belittles
historical and fictional characters, moral relations and
feelings imbued with the highest aspirations and is prepared to permit no other ideals but sheepish obedience and
submission. Count Tolstoy makes it absolutely clear that
characters such as Napoleon and Speransky in no way express the movements of their times and that their roles are
even less than the individuals who formed the masses who
in turn formed the waves of these movements. Napoleon and
Speransky, according to Count Tolstoy, are but the spray
which is seen above the waves. The author of 'War and
Peace' paints Napoleon as no more and no less than an
impudent fop on the political stage lacking not only character and intelligence but military genius as well! In
contrast to the false Western greatness of Napoleon which

consists in an illusory energy and strength Count Tolstoy
presents in the shape of Kutuzov a real greatness consist-
ing entirely in an almost unconscious submission to circumstances, in a natural simplicity reaching all but
senile weakmindedness. The author regards Speransky with
an even greater contempt than he does Napoleon; he casts
this character over the general picture of Alexandrine
times specifically to show him as a conceited and petty
civil servant who thinks of himself as a serious reformer
but in reality is only a somewhat comic nonentity. The
hero of 'War and Peace', Andrey Bolkonsky, bearing in his
nature the instincts of protest, is passed by the author
through various impressions of the natural simplicity of
life and is enlightened finally by death, having comprehended the vanity of all aspirations to control any of the
manifestations of life. Another hero, Pierre Bezukhov,
who is the personification of the intelligent Russian
seeking the ways of goodness and truth, is led on these
paths by the philosophy of sheepish meekness which is
explained to him by the Russian soldier and wise man,
Platon Karataev, and finds peace from his searchings exclusively in family happiness. The novel's heroine,
Natasha, is one of those 'charming' female creations, so
subtly and poetically described which so delight our critics; this heroine in the flush of youth, full of absurd
romantic impulses and moving in the sphere of love, the
one suitable to her development, is of course turned by
the author at the end into, as he himself puts it, 'the
female of the species', the whole sense of which lies in
parturition, dirty nappies and being egotistically taken
by her husband. Alongside the heroes who erred and were
brought by the author on to the right road of old Russian
naturalness there are others in 'War and Peace' who are
true to the natural truth and simplicity of life by
nature, to whom any higher aspirations, any political or
civic activity, any impulse to protest against the surrounding reality seem completely stupid. These heroes,
who are distinguished by either meek submission or being
satisfied, so to say, simply by the instincts of plant
life, are extolled by the author precisely for such qualities. Such a man is Count Nikolay Rostov, the most wonderful and virtuous husband, the most noble family man,
the most marvellous master and landowner whose manifest
virtues are not spoiled even by his tendency to hit his
peasants across the face. His wife is the same; Princess
Maria, who is great because of her submission to her husband, her semi-nonsensical gentleness and primarily because of the fact that she never has astounded nor is she
ever likely to astound anyone with anything. And such

finally is the famous little soldier Platon Karataev - that sentimental insult to the national Russian character who has been taken by some of our critics as a marvellously and artistically-created truly national type.

Being certain in my own mind of the morality which Count Tolstoy brings into his 'undying epic' I am not at all surprised that in his latest novel the writer with his usual brilliance and the perfection of the novelist's art has distinguished himself by an unbelievable - one might almost say scandalous - lack of content: but an author with the philosophy of the creator of 'War and Peace' must logically come to writing 'Anna Karenina'. If of the important and remarkable historical events and the notable rise of the people during the first half of the reign of Alexander I Count Tolstoy had such a mystical opinion in which both those events and that social movement and the participants in it seem nothing but rubbish, then it is natural that the social movements of our time, by no means so remarkable, must remain quite unnoticed, insignificant and not worthy of the slightest attention. This is just what we have in 'Anna Karenina'. Because of his artistic and philosophical theories the author of the novel sees no interest at all in the general phenomena of life which go beyond the sexual, the personal or the family and feeds his creative talents only on the latter for they alone in his view are the be all and end all of human existence. He considers any so-called 'mood' of the times to be illusory nonsense; he has the same opinion of any action which tries to destroy those forces which are preventing the march of progress from so doing - in a word everything which forms life's inner content. Consequently for him and his work there is no such thing as a 'hero of the time', i.e. people who express in themselves either positive or negative aspects of their times. He neither wishes to have nor indeed does he have the slightest concern to reflect in his works these positive or negative aspirations nor to create characters to express them. Count Tolstoy's mystic outlook on life leads him to understand things as follows: the aim of life both for individuals and for whole societies consists not in intellectual, moral or civic development but exclusively in sexual and family relationships. Only these relationships are real, only they form the natural 'truth' of life: everything else is illusory or a superficial falsity serving as but a brake on human happiness and well-being.

An artist who possesses such a philosophy must of necessity direct his creative talents to the reconstruction of facts and characters from a milieu where sexual relations are the most exceptional and dominate all other aims

in life and one which is the most free from material and
idealistic concerns of another nature. Such a milieu is
one where satisfaction and ease are guaranteed, where
material well-being on the one hand and a sufficiently
superficial intellectual development on the other permit
the expression of sexual relationships in the fullest and
most apparently brilliant forms. In such a milieu sexual
relationships form almost the most important interest of
life and develop without hindrance in various combinations which could only be born of the lusts of an apparently highly cultivated human egotism. Artistic creation
which sees the apotheosis of life in lusts of this nature
must draw its material precisely from that milieu, for it
will find there a mine far richer and productive than in
any other.

Count Tolstoy has selected just such a milieu for his
latest novel. All the heroes of the novel, all these
Levins, Vronskys, Oblonskys, Annas, Dollies and Kitties
are characters who possess the material comforts, for
whom, as a consequence of the sort of upbringing they have
had together with a somewhat limited moral and intellectual development, the main 'duty for the day' lies in their
sexual relationships, interests and intrigues and in the
griefs and joys connected with these interests. All other
interests, all other aims in life touch all these people
in direct proportion to how they affect their sexual and
family relationships; only in this personal and private
sense does human existence have any meaning for them. It
is not that they do not understand any other meaning,
simply that they know of no other. A general sense of the
change and development of human life is unsuitable for
these well-off people: they live according to their own
interests, untouched by the current of life around them
and do not feel in their moral and intellectual cast of
mind any influence of the times, or if they do sense it
then they try to react to such influences as if to
trifles having no essential importance. Everything which
goes beyond the bounds of the sexual sphere is for them
something external and formal, having no intrinsic connection with their lives.

Take whichever of these amazing representatives of life
soured by the one-sided satisfaction of egotistic demands
and discern what they are like essentially, and except for
emptiness you will find nothing in them which would give
the critic any justification for seeing in the author a
realist like Gogol. Before you stands the country gentleman Levin, one of Count Tolstoy's favourite types, a man
of natural simplicity who knows 'the truth' about life.
He lives in the country and is fully taken up with the

cares of agriculture which are not, however, particularly
irksome and serve more as a diversion than as something
vital to his life. Certainly in those scenes from the
novel in which Levin's agricultural activity is depicted
we do not see that this activity has demanded any great
effort of will or any moral or intellectual energy. On
the contrary the author shows us scenes where Levin
appears, possibly despite Count Tolsoy, in a somewhat
humorous light in his desire for real peasant labour.
For Levin the running of his estates is not a specific
piece of work to which he must devote his whole existence,
it is not his 'business', but some pleasant way of passing
the time, it is unplanned and unsystematic and possesses
the charm of aesthetic sensations. Look, for example, at
the scene where Levin leaves his house one spring morning
with the aim of taking upon himself the burden of agricultural labour.

[Quotation omitted.]

    Thus, I repeat, for Levin, this natural-born landowner
who cures his anxieties with 'exemplary' ploughing and
sowing just as many of our aristocrats cure their ills
with taking the waters abroad, agricultural pursuits do
not mean any heavy and determined hard work. With his
aristocratic nature he is in general less inclined to hard
work than to fantasies about it, to an artistic, so to
say, conception of the benefits of agricultural labour.
The main objective around which all of his desires are
concentrated is marriage and the family.

[Quotation omitted.]

    Levin, what is more, is not free from several other
innocent diversions. As is often the case he devotes a
part of his seclusion in the country - naturally with the
aim of being useful to his fatherland - to the composition
of a profound book on agriculture in which he intends to
express his own opinions. One can see from the outset and
without fear of being mistaken one can say that even if
the book is finished it will be full of confusion, but it
is more likely that it will never be written and remain
but a vain hope. This conjecture is supported by the
following argument: in order to train oneself sensibly for
writing books it is essential that one should have a mind
capable of reading what others have written and this is
precisely what Levin lacks. On this matter the author is
interestingly sincere. Articles of a serious nature have
always caused unutterable tedium to Levin's apathetic,
vague brain.

He could not read them because when he did he was overcome by boredom. He was not at all interested in the
latest philosophical ideas and all these questions about
where man fits into the animal world, about reflexes,
biology and sociology all seemed to him plain boring.

That is the way it had to be if one takes account of the
superficial manner in which Levin reads any serious
article or book.

[Quotation omitted.]

This interesting example of Levin's attitude to mental
effort clearly shows the uncultivated nature of his mind
and at the same time makes an obvious comment on the
futility of his idea of family happiness which is, as we
well know, the main thing in his life. You will note his
conception of this happiness - it contains the basic element of boasting before his guests that his future wife
will make a fool of herself to such an extent that she
will go out to meet the herds of cattle and look after the
calves just like her own children! How is it possible not
to join with dear old Levin and cry: 'Excellent'!

If he carefully notes all these traits in Levin the
reader will gain a fairly clear idea of what the hero is
actually like although he personifies according to the
author of 'Anna Karenina' the naturally good and beautiful
country gentleman of our times. A self-satisfied and
limited egotism averse to mental labour and progress and
seeking his main aim in life in 'the lap of nature' -
such is the basis of this character which Count Tolstoy
describes with obvious sympathy for his delightful qualities.

Two other characters in the novel are even more unsympathetic than Levin: the brilliant Vronsky and the Moscow
landowner-cum-civil servant, Oblonsky. Their corrupt egotistical aspirations are not even softened by that meek
simplicity which makes it possible to regard Levin with a
certain leniency. The idle existence led by Vronsky and
Oblonsky has no justification at all and however much the
author tries to use 'artistic' methods and give them some
serious meaning they remain ultimately no more than idle
skivers.

Oblonsky, the 'working' aristocrat with the well-
groomed body, reacts with cynically genial politeness to
everyone and everything in high society, even to his own
debauchery which brings him sympathy from others precisely
because his decadent good-naturedness knows no bounds.
This good nature stretches even to conversing with his

servant about his relations with his wife who is annoyed
at his dissolute behaviour and to listening to that servant's friendly advice concerning the fact that the insulted wife will 'see reason', and further to feeling nothing
but happiness when a friend of his states that he, Oblonsky, can be bought for a twenty-copeck piece. For Levin
the most important thing in life is marriage, for Oblonsky
it is love which he understands, naturally, like all
people who are not concerned with moral questions, as
light-hearted affairs 'on the side'. The essence of the
vulgar nature and decadent ideas of this Moscow Don Juan
is fully expressed in the following words:

> I cannot live without love. There's nothing I can do
> about it, that's the way I'm made. And I don't do any-
> one any harm and bring myself so much pleasure.
> Woman is such a creature that the more you study her
> the more interesting she becomes.

Not for nothing is Oblonsky convinced that his amorous exploits do no harm to anyone and bring him nothing but
pleasure; he is such an egotist that even if he did do
harm he would never notice it and consequently he does not
suffer. Everything comes out well for him as it always
does for genial scoundrels - the most shameful type of
scoundrel there is. He has, unbeknown to his wife, seduced his children's French governess. His wife finds out,
is upset and then annoyed and wishes to leave her unfaith-
ful husband. Oblonsky is embarrassed by it all, but not
because he feels sorry for his family which is threatening
to break up, or his wife to whom he has delivered a cruel
moral insult, but only because it creates a tiresome dis-
turbance in his life, and he is a person used to living
off the fat of the land without a care in the world! He
does not suffer at all from thoughts that his attitude to
his wife has been reprehensible; it does not occur to him;
he is only disturbed by the fact that there might be a
scandal which will destroy the normal calm, pleasant
course of his life, a scandal caused by a quite insignificant event. When, thanks to the intercession of his
sister, the celebrated Anna Karenina, Oblonsky's wife expresses her readiness to forgive him, Oblonsky goes with a
light heart to her bedroom and leaves it quite satisfied
and glowing... Any idea of a crime before his wife and
family has slipped away like water off a duck's back and
he is even less likely to reprove himself.

[Quotation omitted.]

Happy-go-lucky types such as he are not anything new in
Russian literature. Previously they were usually presented
as something shameful and were looked upon disapprovingly,
but now artists draw them with scarcely concealed sympathy,
almost indeed as examples 'of people who retain amid all
the new social development the best traditions of a cultured society', as the critic of the 'Russian World' so
expressed it.

[Quotation omitted.]

Alongside this 'charming civilian' hero there figures
in Count Tolstoy's novel a no less charming hero from the
military: this is Count Vronsky whose deep and as they
used to say in novels in the good old days 'volcanic'
passion for Anna Karenina forms the novel's core. This
brilliant hero is seen in the novel only from the point
of view of his 'gallant behaviour' and he has done only
two things: he has inclined the wonderful wife of a
highly-placed Petersburg official towards illicit *amours*
and has broken the back of a pedigree English mare.

[Quotation omitted concerning Anna's conversation with
Vronsky about her suspicions that he is seeing another
woman.]

What a marvellous conversation, is it not? One does
not know whether to be surprised at the banality of the
explanations and the vulgarity of the heroes making them
or at the high art with which the author describes these
banal explanations. It has been a long time since our
great writers have described such amorous 'billy goats';
they have been the property of the rubbish written by our
belletrists of the salon. And now also it appears that
our greatly gifted writers are following the mediocrities
into the field of belletristic simplicity. And good luck
to them!
It is quite natural and not at all surprising that such
an experienced billy-goat 'with a sweet tooth' as Vronsky
should, after the annual labour of courting, achieve the
desired end, the as it were 'topping-out of the building'
of his affaires; it is quite natural and not at all surprising that such an empty woman as Anna Karenina should
have violated with Vronsky the rights of her highly-placed
but rather boring and wooden husband. But what is surprising and even unnatural is that the 'topping-out'
should be painted by the author as some tragic event in
the life of his hero who has up to now displayed only
naturally refined manners and gallant upper-class

behaviour. Vronsky's nature is evidently deep and capable
of a tragic passion. The 'topping-out of the building'
of his affaires is not the happy and pleasant business it
usually is for gentlemen such as he who are 'somewhat
carefree' in their relations with women and would on such
an occasion drink champagne with their friends - it is a
crime.

[Quotation omitted.]

   We suggest that weapon with which the first period of
Vronsky's love for Anna Karenina was killed - the kiss and
so on - is not all that terrible; but none the less the
reader will agree that the scene of the murder with this
weapon is presented in the novel as something tragic, and
Count Vronsky is unexpectedly raised in this episode on
to the pedestal of a tragic hero. And in the further
development of the story of his *amours* the author does
not attempt to remove him from it but on the contrary
makes him stand firmer and firmer. Vronsky's love for
Anna is no 'usual society passion, it is no game, no
joke, no mere pastime but a serious matter on which he had
staked his whole life as on a card'. This is what Vronsky
thinks and of course so does Count Tolstoy himself or else
he would not have bothered to write a vast epic about
amours.
   Such an unexpected discovery by Count Tolstoy of a
tragic element in the activities of upper-class Petersburg
cavaliers and ladies seems to me, I repeat, surprising and
unnatural. But the author goes even further in his illustrious analytical work: he discovers tragedy in Vronsky's
relations not only with Anna but with his mare Frou-Frou
too and makes these relations the object of as much detailed artistic analysis as he does those with Anna.
This might be astounding, but with his artistic views it
is a natural development for Count Tolstoy. If he wishes
to be even more consistent, if he wants his work to move
further along this new and original path then I permit
myself to suggest to the respected author a wonderful subject for his next novel, the main hero of which he could
make his favourite adolescent - Levin. Here briefly is my
outline for the story. Levin marries Kitty and lives with
her in seclusion in the country, scorning all political
and civic activity as fruitless and tedious concerns which
lead to progress and civilization which themselves put a
break upon the growth of happiness. In a short period of
time there appears in Levin's heart a more spontaneous and
consequently more powerful and legitimate feeling than
that of love for his wife: Levin experiences an

agricultural love for his cow, Pava. Kitty notices her
husband's new passion and seeing in it, because of her
feminine frivolity, a certain danger to family happiness
feels jealous and no longer wishes to look after Pava's
calves as if they were her own children. There follows a
series of peripeteia, both romantic and tragic, the sufferings of Kitty, the torments of Pava, the explanations
of Levin to Pava... Naturally in the depiction of all
these peripeteia, sufferings, torments and explanations
there must be the most artistic technique and the most
subtle psychological analysis of the feelings of humans
and cows which would stretch over scores of pages. The
novel might well end tragically with the suicide of Kitty
who cannot bear the triumph of her rival. After the
tragedy there will of course be a reconciliation in accordance with the accepted rules of literary composition:
having suffered sufficiently, Levin finds complete moral
satisfaction in his agricultural attachment to Pava and
grasps the fundamental idea that such an attachment is a
higher natural happiness on earth, higher even that family
happiness with a woman. As for Pava, well ... she is the
heroine. I had better stop; I might make a big mistake.
I have been imagining a future novel for Count Tolstoy
yet I might be anticipating the last part of the present
one. Who knows whether we might not yet see the artisi-
cally analytical depiction of the agricultural passion of
Levin for Pava? Who knows whether we might not yet see
Anna Karenina dying of jealousy for Vronsky's horse?

I trust the reader will forgive me for being carried
away by a joke; but joking apart, if we return to the
novel we shall indeed find that there already is the
tragic depiction of Vronsky's passion for his horse which
runs parallel to his passion for Anna. 'Vronsky', writes
Count Tolstoy, 'despite all his live for Anna, was passionately, albeit reservedly, fascinated by his mare
Frou-Frou' and these 'two passions did not interfere with
each other'. And not only did they not interfere with
each other, they were similar. Vronsky's love for women
and horses is painted with the same colouring. The author
tries to give them both the same tragic and serious character. Just compare Vronsky's passionate dealings with
the mare and with Anna and you will see the identical
nature of the two.

[Quotations omitted.]

Such is this epic of *amours* which Count Tolstoy has
created, where horses and people are treated in the same
tone, where heroes are gripped by fatal, tragic

attachments for society ladies and race-horses, and where
the attachments of people, cows and horses are all described with the same artistic analysis and detail.

57.   AVSEENKO, REVIEW, 'RUSSIAN WORLD'

1875, no. 69

Review signed A.O. and entitled Essays on Current Literature; it starts by stating that 'Anna Karenina' is the
only worthwhile novel of the year. V.G. Avseenko (1842-
1913) was a critic and anti-radical minor novelist.
Although he bemoaned Tolstoy's apparent lack of interest
in contemporary society, he nevertheless admired his
technique.

The lack of new ideas, new types and new elements is reflected at the moment even in works written by authors who
are above the average standard. This painting in dull
colours has also affected 'Anna Karenina'; one can sense
it through the freshness of the author's talent, through
the poetry of his ideas and through the elegance of his
pictures of his heroines. The basic idea behind the
novel is an attempt to disown those manifestations of
contemporary life which in their sum total Herzen called
'middle class'. Amid the general demand to mingle with
the impersonal masses and to live for their everyday practical interests, the author has sought out a corner of
contemporary society living as it were a separate life,
filled with the traditions of that epoch before the middle
class was knocking at everyone's door, a life which stands
aloof and is foreign to the interests and concerns of the
crowd and which seems to the majority of modern readers
something quite empty and vulgar. In fact, of course, it
is nothing of the kind. The author not only fills it with
content but also gives it a certain charm. But whence
this charm? How does the novelist create the magic with
which he surrounds the delightful figure of Kitty Shcherbatsky, the passionate personality of Anna Karenina, the
engaging nature of Konstantin Levin and the charmingly
frivolous character of Stiva Oblonsky? Alas, all the
magic, all the fascination, derives from the juxtaposition

of these characters with elements of contemporary life,
the life which is ruled by the middle classes. The secret
of the fascination which surrounds the novel's heroes and
heroines lies precisely in that it retains in itself and
its life characteristics of outmoded people of a bygone
age and that it is instinctively and organically opposed
to the middle class. Thus all the delight of life is
reduced to retaining its former charms and to sustaining
the vitality of tradition. Nowhere is the character and
sense of the outmoded epoch expressed with such evident
clarity as in the circumstances of the characters' lives.
We are present at *the moment when the flow of life has
ceased*. The best people have ceased pursuing new middle-
class ideals; all their concern is to preserve as well as
they can the old order which is being breached on all
sides by the middle class, i.e. a new form of life.

Earlier, when mankind had not yet worn out its creative
forces, its inner history consisted of the continual and
uninterrupted development and renewal of ideals. New
ideas flowed unceasingly into life bringing with them new
concepts of good, truth and beauty and everything which
was young, fresh and full of life strove after them.
Now a period of exhaustion and spiritual hunger has arrived. To cease accepting the new and to give it a strong
rebuff - this has become the task of a select minority of
the best people. A more complete or fateful exhaustion is
impossible to imagine.

Let us look more closely at the source of those charms
with which the author surrounds his favourite heroes, Konstantin Levin and Kitty Shcherbatsky. What is the nature
of that special magnetic attraction which Kitty has over
Levin? We recall the author's words from the first part
of the novel.

[Quotation omitted about Levin falling in love with the
Shcherbatsky family, a typical, traditional, landowning
milieu.]

Thus the whole basis for all the charm lies in the vitality of the old order, in the traditions of an hereditary
culture by which the old Moscow landowning families were
distinguished and which the newer social classes do not
possess. It is clear that the interests of today and the
elements of the new life, 'the new ideas', have only a
negative role among the charms of the old, and that they
play a very small part in them, if even that. Kitty herself is but a beautiful product of this old order with
its old-fashioned forms of education and social intercourse, and Levin was prepared to love her for the charm

which this milieu, the Shcherbatsky household, held for
him.

Let us look also at how Levin is made. His ideas and
feelings, his tastes and sympathies are divided between
two distinct social levels - the upper class and the
people. Levin feels quite at home both in the company of
the Shcherbatskys and the Oblonskys and on his own estates
among the people. All that huge intermediate level, i.e.
all the middle level, where new ideas and new currents of
life have full and free rein and where elements of Herzen's 'middle class' are developing at will, do not exist
for Levin and are indeed repugnant to him. And so here
too the novel's main motif is a distancing from the new
sources of life and its guiding tone and direction.

We note finally a strange fact: we have a great novel,
written by the hand of a great artist and containing a
multitude of contemporary characters - contemporary in the
sense that such people actually exist today - but at the
same time you will not only fail to see in this wonderful
novel the main trends of contemporary life, you will not
only fail to meet a single character who would be typical
of modern society (with the sole exception of Nikolay
Levin, who is a very minor character and who anyway destroys the general harmony of the story), but you will
feel that all these people and their lives are organically opposed to the bases of our present-day reality and
its main facet - the intelligent and moral middle class.
Is not this remarkable? Is it not a 'sign of the times'?

If Count Tolstoy were a tendentious pamphleteer, if he
were not first and foremost a sincere and great artist,
then the fact which we have pointed out would not be very
important. It would be just 'his opinion' and nothing
more. But Count Tolstoy, whatever convictions his turn of
mind might have led him to in social questions, is above
all a poet, i.e. a writer gifted with creative force. This
creative force should have led him to create new ideals,
if contemporary reality provided obvious material for him.
But the fact is that this new material does not exist.
Positive types, types coming more or less close to the
ideal, live according to concepts from the past. They
attract simply because they retain only the old yeast as
it were; they have not been touched by new varieties. It
is this, of course, which has led to the bitterness concerning 'Anna Karenina' expressed in certain literary ant-
hills. We read one article where this bitterness is particularly clearly expressed. In comparing the novels of
Mr Boborykin with those of Count Tolstoy the writer finds
the latter far more seductive and immoral than the former.
If our critics, he goes on, were a little more perceptive

or bolder, they would see perfectly clearly that in the six volumes of this great and 'everlasting' epic Count Tolstoy has tried persistently to show that so-called civic activities and so-called political aspirations adopted in the name of the principle of civilization are in essence an illusory nonsense. Developing this idea Count Tolstoy wished to draw, and actually clearly does draw, the following conclusion in 'War and Peace': that the object of life and its meaning for everyone must lie not in the above-mentioned activities or aspirations but in the self-indulgent pleasures of sexual relations and their consummation - in family life in its most crude and cynical sense. It is clear that the critic has mentioned 'War and Peace' only because the general idea behind the two novels is so similar; he then goes on to recommend to Count Tolstoy the following ending for 'Anna Karenina':

> Levin marries Kitty and lives with her deep in the country, despising any political or civic activity as fruitless and boring, engendered by civilization and progress. But in the passing of time there arises quite unexpectedly in Levin a more immediate and consequently stronger and more legitimate feeling than love for his wife: he is seized by an agricultural love for his cow, Pava.

There then follows something rather more disgraceful which we shall not repeat out of respect for the readers of the 'Russian World'. The critics of a certain camp have so far overreached the bounds of propriety that even the critic of the 'Voice' objected. However, what is the cause of this bitterness? Without doubt it arises from the complete disregard for the new elements in life which lies at the basis of Count Tolstoy's novel. These elements are so much a part of contemporary people *en masse* that they cannot but look with extreme displeasure on everyone who does not concur with their tastes and sympathies or who points at the middle-class cut of dress which they have just started to sport.

  To accuse the author of a negative attitude to contemporary reality, to accuse him of neglecting to show us the new ideals, that the milieu he has painted is attractive only because it retains elements of a bygone society, is of course not possible. If life had shown some new positive aspects he would doubtless have shown them in the novel. The author is not guilty - it is the organic exhaustion of creative powers which is felt in society itself. On the contrary the author has done all he could to find the most comfortable style of life under the new conditions. He thinks that it is possible to find utter seclusion, in the family, among the people; he does not wish to leave his readers without comfort or a way out. But the comfort and the way out are artificial in the extreme. Despite the remarkable freshness which fills the pages where Levin, far away in the country, is completely taken up with his agricultural interests, is drawing close to the people and spends days with them mowing, the reader senses in all this something strained and cannot believe it is possible to cut oneself off so completely. The author is holding something back from his hero at this stage - marriage and a family. But marriages turn out happily and unhappily and families can be friendly or full of discord. The solution is only apparent; the question actually remains open.

But we have already turned to broader themes and have spoken rather generally about the contents of the novel; it is time to look at it in detail. We shall limit ourselves to but a few comments.

As is well known Count Tolstoy is one of those authors who pay very little attention to the exterior plot or plan of their works. We would not for a moment suggest that either is as important as a novel's inner content; but there is no doubt that a poverty of imagination which leads to an excess of prolixity and lack of balance in the plan of the work is a disadvantageous method even in such remarkable works as 'Anna Karenina'. This fault has become even more apparent in the chapters that have just appeared. The drama, so powerfully and vividly enacted through Anna and Vronsky, is brought to a halt by the fact that both these characters disappear from the scene for a time. It is true that Levin's life in the country, the scenes of work in the fields, the mowing and so on all breathe with fresh healthy poetry; but one feels that they lack the dramatic element and slow down the development of the story. Levin himself is partially the cause of this, or rather his passive nature, lacking in any drive. Such people are very engaging but in the main their lives are without much interest because there are so few facts to relate in them. In general one can state that the novel's male characters are far inferior to the female ones. Both Vronsky and Levin cannot help appearing comparatively insignificant when put alongside Kitty or Anna. Levin has too little initiative and Vronsky's personality is too shallow. His nature is brilliant only externally and if Anna is attracted to him it is only because our society is devoid of remarkable people. It is also impossible not to think that the lack of comprehension which our critics have shown with regard to Anna is caused by the character

of Vronsky. In her choice of him they have seen evidence
of her own emptiness ... and immorality. We shall not
comment on the latter because we strongly doubt the morality of the theories on the basis of which our critics have
moralized about Anna. As for her emptiness and as our
newspapers put it her 'vulgarity' one must note that
'vulgarity' is an extremely relative concept. She is,
though, one of the most brilliant of all of Count Tolstoy's heroines. She belongs to that type of woman, as
the heroines of Pushkin, Lermontov and Turgenev, who live
exclusively by the heart. Such heroines are not to the
taste of contemporary society, but the author cares very
little about that.

58. SKABICHEVSKY ON TOLSTOY'S PROLIX TALENT

1875, 1876

(See also headnote to No. 37.) The first extract was published in the 'Stock Exchange News', 1875, no. 77, and
entitled Thoughts on Current Literature; the second
appeared in the same journal, 1876, no. 70. Both were
signed 'An Ordinary Reader'.

I had intended to limit myself simply to a short notice on
Count Tolstoy's new novel and say no more about it until
it was completed; then I would review it as a whole. But
I have been forced to change my plans. The section which
has just appeared is so full of special delights that I
just cannot refrain from speaking. What is more, everyone
is talking about them; everyone is so taken up with them
at the moment precisely because they are reading them;
later on they will probably not be so concerned about them
and will forget them. Furthermore it is possible that
such a large number of these delights will have accumula-
ted by the end of the novel that there will be too many of
them for a little article in a feuilleton and one will be
forced to mention only a few of them. For all these reasons I have changed by mind and shall chat to my readers
on each part separately.
    I shall begin with the fact that on reading the second
part, without forgetting, of course, the first, you start

to sense more and more the fragrance with which the novel is filled and which forms its so to speak philosophic content. And do you know what this fragrance is? (And one must admit it almost knocks one over.) It is that distinctive smell you get on going into a nursery - the idyllic aroma of babies' nappies. Please do not think I am saying this only to scoff or in any metaphorical sense. One must note in reading Count Tolstoy's novel that the author is only just beginning to warm to his theme, is only working up to that poetic spirit, when he tells us about how children are washed and nursed, how housekeepers order food and jingle keys, how husbands, dressed in dressing-gowns, shuffle around in carpet slippers and enter bedrooms where they sleep with their wives in double beds and chat to them before going to sleep.

[Quotation omitted concerning Anna's going to bed with Karenin without enthusiasm.]

It is remarkable that even in the last part of 'War and Peace' where the author presents to us with Homeric zest and in the most subtle strokes a complete idyll of the family life of his heroes, takes us through their bedrooms and nurseries and with a special relish forces us to breathe all the possible smells of these rooms hidden from outside and curious eyes, such idylls were somehow subsidiary and did not affect the general impression at all. You pay no attention to the author's attitude to them and assume that under the conditions of Russian life at the start of the present century the heroes and especially the heroines in 'War and Peace' perforce ended up in such idylls; the author, it seems to us, is standing aside, and you can even praise him for his perspicacity. Count Tolstoy's new novel, though, shows that his attitude to family idylls is not at all objective; quite the contrary; there is a subjectivity of the most savoury nature. It turns out that the whole novel is based on such idylls, that the author has spent his whole life looking at them in this way, drawing everything from them, leading everything to them, so that it appears as if whatever might happen in the world, it happens only so that with the tender emotion of a mother's love in their eyes wives may wash their little ones in the tub and husbands may come in at midnight, shuffling their slippers, and enter their wife's bedroom and say to them, smiling in a special way: 'Time for bed... Time for bed...'
On this the whole world rotates and everything else is vanity and decay.

'What?' the reader will say, frowning. 'Are you mocking
the family?' Calm down, dear reader; I am not mocking anything; I do not wish to shake anything. I am myself a
family man and am well aware of the delightful aroma of
babies' nappies; but it is not enough for me that poetry
should lie only there and force me to inhale continuously
these aromas and instil into me that there are no other
smells in life better than these. Let family interests
remain family interests; they must not prevent my having
any others or considering them any more or less important
than family ones; they must not prevent my demanding from
literature that it should correspond to these other interests of mine as well and to stand as it were on their
heights too. I have the right to demand this of Count
Tolstoy - the more so because once he used to satisfy
these other interests of the public. Recall all his previous works, including 'War and Peace'.

But what can be done about it? Such is obviously the
fate of all Russian writers, that whatever ideas they
might have introduced into their early works, and however
profound their analysis of life based upon those ideas
might have been, they are all forced to end up with the
same inevitable home-building-itis. We shall all catch
it. And when such first-rate writers as Count Tolstoy
reach the stage of delivering unto us such words of wisdom
about how a wife should behave towards her husband, how
she should go visiting and invite guests into her home and
how she must remember her vows, then we have the right, we
ordinary readers, as befits our advanced years, to call it
a day....

But what logic can you expect from our Russian writer,
albeit a first-rate one? What serious content can you
expect from his works when he proves himself so competent
at wasting his talent in describing scenes where a young
girl is examined by a doctor; and note well here that the
author is describing such scenes not from any artistic or
even simply entertaining objective, but tendentiously.
Can you think of the literature of any other country where
it is conceivable that an author would describe the medical examination of sick women with the aim of denouncing
such examinations for their impropriety? Such absurdities
could only occur to a Russian writer. The section concerns Kitty Shcherbatsky who is deserted by Vronsky and
falls ill. Naturally doctors are called in and one of
them is famous and he proposes the outrageously immoral
course of examining the patient.

[Quotation omitted concerning Kitty's shame at being examined by a good-looking and youngish doctor.]

There then follows the scene of the actual examination, during which the author does not omit such details as the doctor washing his hands afterwards, how the emaciated and blushing Kitty had a special sparkle in her eyes coming from the shame she felt, and how her eyes filled with tears when the doctor actually entered the room for a second time.

It is of course quite possible that Count Tolstoy introduces such attacks on medicine (which perpetrate such scandals as young and naked girls being touched by doctors) for no other reason than that which would be explained by his Slavophile tendencies. Do not forget that medical science, in whose name such shameful acts are carried out, was brought to Russia by the Germans. Russia had no doctors before the time of Peter the Great and consequently young ladies were not subjected to such examinations. It is true that virgins and women were taken out naked in freezing cold weather into the bazaars for the crowd to laugh at - but they were not well-born young ladies, were they, Count Tolstoy?

The section of the novel we are now reading ends with Vronsky finally achieving the ultimate victory over Anna, and after two lines of mysterious dots we read the following.

[Quotation omitted concerning Vronsky feeling that he has in some way murdered the first period of his love for Anna.]

Enough is enough, even though there is a whole page more of this. But the oddest thing of all, if you think about it, is that this melodramatic nonsense written in the spirit of French novels of a bygone age is lavished upon the banal love affair of a society fop and the wife of a Petersburg civil servant. And on top of that it is written by Count Tolstoy, the same Count Tolstoy who wrote 'War and Peace', and not some twelve-year-old schoolboy. It is the beginning of the end, a complete literary breakdown!

[The following extract begins with an attack on Avseenko's recently published review (see No. 57) where Skabichevsky ironically gives thanks that he is no critic but just an ordinary reader who can state freely what he thinks of the novel.]

Let Mr A. call me an ignoramus in aesthetic matters and may he be surprised and annoyed as much as he likes at my great impertinence at presuming to have a personal opinion,

but I am not at all inclined to rid myself of the following ideas: it seems to be that Count Tolstoy's novel ....
is very close to its conclusion. Anna has finally united
her fate with Vronsky's, even managing to become pregnant
by him, and in the end admits her guilt to her husband.
Konstantin Levin, after mournful meditations on unrequited
love and distracted by a whole series of hunts and idyllic
agricultural pursuits including mowing and threshing, sees
at last through the window of his carriage the little face
of his incomparable Kitty, who has succeeded in recovering
both from her disappointment concerning Vronsky and her
illness and has come to a neighbouring estate - straight
into the arms of her rejected suitor! It appears that
after this there will be but three or four pages, which
will be quite enough for the denouement of the plot and
the complete depiction of the fates of the heroes. This
is what the readers thought - that there would be just a
little more of the story and there would be an end to it.
But suddenly this expected ending has been dragged out for
some quite unforeseen reasons, the novel ceased appearing
in the 'Russian Messenger', the public became bewildered
and perplexed and there were various scandalous rumours
which all led in turn to different explanations and promises from the journal. Then in the first number this year
the continuation of 'Anna Karenina' finally appeared.
Unfortunately, however, it turned out that the novel was
not about to end, at least not yet; this caused of itself
no small scandal - the journal appears and is graced by a
little more of last year's novel. In all probability
there had been talks between the editors of the journal
and Count Tolstoy on the matter - that considering everything that had happened, could not the author perhaps
extend his novel for one more number, if not two or three,
or even four? After a multitude of requests the author
agreed, the more so since as a talented artist, an artist
whose talent is displayed pre-eminently in detailization
and subtle psychological analysis of the most insignificant areas of life, it would cost him nothing and he could
get it all off his hands. Consequently he began to drag
out the ending with all his might. In the January number
of the 'Russian Messenger' there were some one hundred and
fifty more pages of the novel. You might well expect the
plot to develop a little in these one hundred and fifty
pages; we repeat that Anna admits her liaison with Vronsky
to her husband, Levin lives near to his incomparable Kitty
and occupies himself with his agricultural pursuits and at
the end suddenly leaves for abroad. You need, dear reader,
a rather special art in order to write one hundred and
fifty pages of a novel and keep everything exactly where

it was when you started. But Count Tolstoy is an experienced and talented writer and knows how to overcome all
difficulties; he managed just that - his experience and
talent enable him to achieve it all with no trouble at all.
For example, this part starts with Anna's husband, Karenin,
thinking after her confession about what he ought to do
about his guilty wife; and he thinks, one must admit, like
a real bureaucrat - here one must acknowledge Count Tolstoy's great talent. To call his rival out? But Karenin
could not think of pistols pointed at him without horror,
and moreover had never in his life held a weapon in his
hands.

[Quotation omitted.]

Another solution for Karenin would be divorce; but a
divorce suit would lead to a scandalous hearing of the
case which would be a godsend to his enemies; there would
be slander and a decline in his elevated social position.
Furthermore with a divorce Anna would break off all relations with her husband and join her lover, and in Karenin's heart, despite his present apparent contemptuous
indifference to his wife, there was one feeling which he
still had for her - the desire that she should not be free
to join Vronsky, that her crime should not turn out to her
own advantage. The idea that the latter might come true
so irritated Karenin that no sooner had it occurred to him
than he felt a pain inside, sat up straight and changed
his seat in the carriage and for a long time afterwards
sat frowning, his thin legs wrapped in a woollen rug.
    Besides a formal divorce there was also the possibility
of a separation, but that presented the same prospect of
inconvenience and disgrace as a divorce and would also
only serve to throw Anna into the arms of Vronsky. 'No,
impossible,' he said. 'I cannot be happy, so neither shall
they.' Only one solution remained: to keep her with him,
to hide from the public eye what had taken place and to
take all appropriate measures to put an end to their relationship and most importantly to punish her. To sustain
him in his decision, once it had been taken, Karenin held
to one further fact: 'Only by taking this decision will I
act in accordance with the dictates of religion.'
    You and I, dear reader, in our simple-hearted sincerity,
once we read of this inhumane, Jesuit and bureaucratic
decision of Karenin's would have liked to hurry on to the
denouement of the novel and so it all would have ended
this January. Count Tolstoy, however, remembering that he
could not end the novel in January, acted differently. To
all of Karenin's complex cerebrations Count Tolstoy added,

for no apparent reason, a whole series of business matters; for example he describes in great detail a meeting of one of Karenin's state committees, everything Karenin says there, and his ultimate victory over his enemies concerning the problem of irrigation in Zaraysk Province.

For her part Anna, immediately after her confession, thinks for a long time about what to do and decides to go to Moscow. Then we have a detailed description of her packing. Then she receives a letter from her husband informing her of his decision, enclosing some money, and demanding that she leaves the dacha immediately and returns to their flat in town. Anna decides not to go to Moscow. All of this is described in the greatest detail. Later Anna goes to Princess Tverskoy's for a game of croquet, and once again we have the most detailed description imaginable of how our heroine passes her time there and of everyone else who was at the princess's.

As for Vronsky, well, we have a long, detailed description of how, after the steeplechase, he sits down to put his accounts in order and is extremely pleased with them when he has finished; then he goes off to his regiment where he meets an old friend of his, Serpukhovsky, and they have a long, long conversation about their careers; then finally there is his meeting with Anna during which our hero and heroine decide absolutely nothing and part in mutual incomprehension.

In all of this Count Tolstoy has, in my humble opinion, omitted many details which would have served him well in lengthening his novel even more. For example, it would be quite natural for Anna, after the usual muddy journey from the dacha, to take a bath before going to see Princess Tverskoy. The author has said nothing about this extremely interesting detail and it is a great pity. Besides the fact that it would have filled up ten superfluous pages he would have had a splendid opportunity to acquaint us with his heroine's marvellous figure and in so doing paint a picture which, considering his great skill in the genre, would have brought the whole Russian nation to ecstasy... At the same time as Anna is sitting in her bath thinking about her relations with her husband and her lover, Vronsky is not idle either. Having got filthy after his experiences in the steeplechase, he naturally would not let the day pass without deciding to take a bath too. Here again Count Tolstoy has missed a great opportunity, this time of describing the pleasures of a visit to a Russian bath-house. He could have filled another ten pages and would have dazzled us all not only with his artistic decpition of the scene and the subtle analysis of the most fleeting of sensations but also with his

patriotism. I cannot recall in any of Count Tolstoy's
works a description of our original Russian bath-houses of
which we can be eternally proud before all of Europe.
Luxuriating on the extremely hot bench and beating himself
with birch twigs, Vronsky (in order to tie things in with
the novel's general subject-matter) would ponder on the
heat generated by his passion and how best he ought to act
with Anna.

As for Konstantin Levin, both you, dear reader, and I
would have behaved in dealing with him very stupidly and
unthinkingly; on the very next page we would have arranged
an unexpected meeting between him and Kitty in the country
and then in another twenty pages or so we would have had
them legally married - and thus ruined the whole novel.
Count Tolstoy though as a brilliant virtuoso of the belletristic arts acts differently. In this section of the
novel Levin does nothing but worry about his lack of success on the farming front. Dolly Oblonsky, with whom
Kitty is staying, writes him a letter asking him to try
and find a ladies' saddle for Kitty and perhaps he would
deliver it himself. Levin, though, refuses to go himself
and sends the saddle, obviously frightened that if he went
himself the novel would come to a very sudden end. Instead he goes to see some landowner called Sviyazhsky;
and so we get a detailed description of this Sviyazhsky
and of the long conversation they have on agronomy with
several other landowners. Suddenly Konstantin Levin's
prodigal nihilist brother turns up; he is suffering from
the advanced stages of tuberculosis. The reader, disappointed in his hopes for a quick marriage between Kitty
and Levin, expects that at least he will get a touching
description of Nikolay's death. But no. All that is
described is the insincerity of the two brothers, one of
whom denies he has even a trace of tuberculosis and will
make a perfect recovery shortly, while the other plays
along with him and makes out that he believes him, while
being secretly convinced that his brother will soon snuff
it. Finally the brothers quarrel and Nikolay departs.
Konstantin goes abroad, weighed down by thoughts of death
brought on by the sight of his brother's condition.

When I read this long-drawn-out affair which caused me
fits of yawning and deadly boredom I had the brilliant
idea of suggesting to Count Tolstoy that he should never
finish his novel. Indeed why should he trouble his imagination thinking up subjects for future novels - subjects
which would arouse both the public and the critics to new
peaks of expectation and disappointment - when he could
quite easily, considering the breadth of his talent, continue 'Anna Karenina' for ever? In the further

development of the story Count Tolstoy could have the
Karenins travel abroad (an extremely detailed description
of their impressions of life abroad coloured by the torments of Anna's separation from Vronsky); there they would
meet the Levins and Anna would sweep that stoical agrono-
mist off his feet and take from Kitty her latest suitor;
Vronsky would finally be up to his ears in debt, there
would be a scandal, he would be exiled to Tashkent and
reduced to the ranks (what a wonderful opportunity for
Count Tolstoy to charm us anew with a number of scenes
from military life and with his essays on the ordinary
Russian soldier). Piling detail upon detail Count Tolstoy
could continue writing 'Anna Karenina' for years to come
and only stop when death finally caught up with him; and
year after year Mr A. in the 'Russian Messenger' will be
able to tell us of the universal and unanimous delight of
the public at the appearance of each and every new instal-
ment and the Ordinary Reader will go on crying and asking
when will it all end? Is not that, dear reader, a happy
thought?

59. MIKHAYLOVSKY ON TOLSTOY'S 'LEFT HAND'

1875

N.K. Mikhaylovsky, whom Tolstoy, with his usual charity to
critics, called a routine radical hack, was a literary
critic, sociologist and publicist but is more remembered
as one of the leading theorists of Russian Populism; his
ideas were put into practice by many members of the
Zemstva (local government organizations). His remarkable
essay, The Right Hand and the Left Hand of Count Tolstoy,
published in three parts in 'Fatherland Notes' in 1875, is
an attempt to counteract the prevalent opinion that Tolstoy was a brilliant writer but a poor thinker and stresses the idea that Tolstoy's 'right hand' (his talents as
a thinker) is in no way inferior to his 'left hand' (with
which he wrote his works of fiction). This extract is
from the second part.

However simple and clear are Count Tolstoy's ideas about
the significance for the people of those phenomena we have

come to call 'progressive' very few people indeed have
come to accept them. This is quite understandable. All
of us naturally hold dear the brighter sides of civilization. Civilization has awakened in us certain demands and
then satisfies these demands in a certain order and to a
certain degree. The pleasures of intellectual activity,
art, political activity and material well-being which
civilization has created are so great and tangible that
we quite naturally strive to attain them and then simply
enjoy them once we have attained them in this or that
degree. We are fully aware of the price we have paid in
getting them and consequently do not even ask ourselves
whether anyone else might be paying for them. If the
question should arise then we involuntarily brush it aside,
which is something extremely easy for us owing to the complexity and confusion of life's phenomena. For example, at
the present time there are widespread complaints about the
poverty of literary talent. The critics recall Pushkin,
Lermontov, Gogol, Griboedov and then a later group Lev
Tolstoy, Goncharov and Turgenev and bemoan the fact that
the source of pleasure in poetic works is as it were running out and is producing nothing new and is even threatening to dry up all together as soon as inexorable death
overtakes the representatives of the earlier brilliant
period of Russian literature. There are certainly talented authors around today and if we had not had even more
talented writers before we would possibly be quite content
with those we have. But in general the poets of the twenties, thirties and forties were much better than those who
have appeared in the last fifteen or twenty years. Of the
most recent writers who do not lack endurance and finish,
who possess subtlety of ideas and elegance of brush, all
of them have one defect - none of them gives us the pleasure which we have experienced in the past. We suggest
that the following explanation of this deplorable fact is
fully justified: the writers of the twenties to the forties were not particularly rich men but none the less landowners supported by their serfs. They had ample opportunity to develop their talents at their leisure, to receive
education more or less from the cradle, to study at foreign universities and to follow Gogol's advice of writing
a story and to let it 'lie around' for a year, then re-
write it, leave it for a year again and so on for eight
years. Under such a system no accidental spark of spiritual interest would be missed and would usually burst into
the flame of artistic talent, for poetry is possibly the
only reasonably unrestricted area for intellectual activity. Nowadays probably no fewer talents are born but
they are completely taken up with the merciless struggle

to survive, so that some of them never come to the surface, while others do not fully develop. Return to serfdom or wait until we have established and developed great
industrial capital and then Russian literature will again
blossom. I quite understand that this explanation is by
no means the whole story but it seems to me that it is
largely true.

[Passage omitted on arguments between various contemporary
critics, and on the fact that the intellectual pleasures
of the few are based upon the hard physical labour of the
many.]

Even Count Tolstoy cannot avoid this fact. In an article a critic has mentioned that Tolstoy is a rich landowner; from his novels it is clear that he knows high society very well and has close and various connections with
it; he is a very subtle artist and consequently speaks
warmly of art and must pay a high price for artistic pleasure. And this man who has the opportunity to enjoy all
the best gifts of civilization has had the thought that I
have expressed earlier. If such thoughts were to occur to
a man who was personally incapable or whose material circumstances made it impossible for him to taste the fruits
of civilization it would not be very surprising. And to
avoid the contradictions would be very easy for him. For
example a man who on account of his own fault or through
the force of circumstance is ignorant or lacking the need
for knowledge can very logically, without ever contradict-
ing himself, deny knowledge inasmuch as it is denied by
Count Tolstoy's point of view. But Count Tolstoy himself
is in a very different position. Let us take his literary
output. He is a brilliant writer who is immensely famous;
he is an artist, i.e. a creator who enjoys deeply the very
act of creation, he has published his own journal and has
appeared in others; yet he has come to the following conclusion about the printing of books.

[Quotation omitted of Tolstoy's views about publishing
being only of use to writers and those engaged in publishing and printing and of no use at all to the mass of the
people.]

I do not refrain from this quotation because I need an
exact statement of his views and also because I am sure
the views of his that I am expounding are unknown to the
majority of my readers. So marvellously well established
is his reputation as a poor thinker that the fourth volume
of his collected works, which contains his articles on

education, is hardly read by anyone in spite of the fact
that there are whole pages, even in a purely artistic
sense, which are quite superb, possibly as much as anything he has written. Furthermore it is precisely in this
volume that one may find the key to all the literary activity of our famous writer. Every writer can be, and is,
subjected to the most extreme and eloquent opinions about
him, first because his critics possess varying levels of
competence and, second because they are governed by differing points of view. Yet concerning Count Tolstoy there
is a third and truly wonderful reason: despite his great
fame he is still unknown. Let us look at him.

I ask the reader to enter mentally into the state of
mind of a writer who can state the above ideas about books
and publishing, a writer who is not creating to earn himself a living nor through any accidental circumstances,
but a writer like Count Tolstoy - a writer by calling, one
who is led into literature by an excess of creative force.
His position is truly tragic. Count Tolstoy quite
justifiably says that there is nothing reprehensible in
the desire to write a story and receive some money and
fame for it. Of course there is nothing reprehensible in
itself in this chasing after prizes, yet Count Tolstoy
knows that along this unreprehensible path great sums of
national wealth pass into the hands of those connected
with writing and publishing; that this is precisely how all
literature arises, all that 'exploitation which is of use
only to those who practise it and useless to the people at
large'. It is easy for a man who has never had a line
published in his life or who writes not from some inner
need to share with the readers the thoughts and ideas that
arise within him to say what Count Tolstoy says. On the
other hand there are many people who commit the grossest
of crimes and yet remain at peace with themselves simply
because the crimes they commit do not appear to them as
crimes. In a word when conscience and one's needs are in
harmony then one may live at peace. Count Tolstoy on the
other hand realizes that literature is exploitation of the
people and yet participates in it because like the Wandering Jew a mysterious voice does not cease saying: Go on!
Go on! Similarly, with Count Tolstoy there is a mysterious voice, the voice of his richly gifted talent, which
will not cease saying: Write, write! This collision between an uncontrollable need and an inexorable consciousness creates the drama whose peripeteia must be closely
studied by anyone who wishes to have a correct conception
of Count Tolstoy's literature. I do not intend to say a
lot about 'Anna Karenina', in the first place because it
is unfinished and in the second because one must either

say a lot about it or nothing at all. I shall only say
that in this novel the traces of the drama going on in the
author's soul are expressed incomparably more clearly than
in any other of his works. One wonders how such a man
exists, how he lives, how he avoids that bane of consciousness which intrudes at every minute into the pleasure of
satisfied need? Doubtless he must, albeit instinctively,
seek the means to end the inner spiritual drama and close
the curtain, but how can this be done? I think that if an
ordinary man should find himself in such a position then
he would either commit suicide or forget himself in unrestrained drunkenness. A man out of the ordinary will of
course find another solution, of which there are many;
Count Tolstoy has, it appears, tried them all. We also
see though a whole series of very natural variations in
the attempts themselves a series of deviations from his
basic task (of which possibly the author himself is not
fully aware). This task consists in, while continuing to
be a writer, to cease all 'clever exploitation' or at least
somehow to recompense the people for this exploitation.
For this there is a direct route - to become a writer
purely for the people, to contribute his mite by writing
literature which would 'catch on' with the people. But
even in the best of all possible worlds this is extremely
difficult in the technical sense. Count Tolstoy has tried
this way to some extent in a few stories which have
appeared in his 'ABC Book'. Here I should like to make
one observation. I have already pointed out that some of
Count Tolstoy's views on various 'manifestations of progress', albeit convincing and highly original, are often
simplistic and as it were straightforward in order fully
to respond to a complex and confusing reality. Both his
views on literature and on publishing suffer from this
over-simplification. It is true that our present-day
literature is not accepted, nor will it be accepted, by
the people. There are, of course, exceptions. I shall
not expand on them but just point to the example of Count
Tolstoy himself. He first published his 'Prisoner of the
Caucasus' in the journal 'Dawn', i.e. for 'society', and
later in his 'ABC Book', i.e. for the people. Possibly
'The Prisoner of the Caucasus', and one or two other
stories, were published in 'Dawn' only as examples of
stories for the people. There are other examples though.
Our critics, i.e. 'society', poured both praise and abuse
on the little soldier Platon Karataev in 'War and Peace' -
a novel not written for the people - and also Karataev's
very characteristic story of the innocent person sentenced
to exile also appeared in the 'ABC Book' under the title
'God Sees the Truth'. In any case Count Tolstoy's

activities as a writer for the people take up a comparatively small part of his work. To us, to 'society', he
gave 'Childhood and Boyhood' and 'War and Peace' but to
the people he gave nothing that is anywhere near as good.
This is primarily because he found another direct route to
serve the people - his pedagogical activities to which he
was led by another of his natural gifts, a pedagogical
bent. Count Tolstoy himself knows this .... but I think
he did not become a writer for the people simply because
he found in pedagogy another way of repaying the people
for his exploitation of them, something he did equally
with other writers. There is another reason. The range
of his intellectual interests is both too wide and too
narrow for him to become simply a writer for the people.
On the one hand he commands a store of images and ideas
that is unsuitable for the people on account of its
breadth and range, and on the other as a man from a certain section of society he holds too dear the petty and
narrow joys and anxieties of that class and is too occupied with them to abstain from their poetic expression.
The concerns of the aristocratic salons and the storms of
the ladies' boudoirs, despite their insignificance, are
known to Count Tolstoy and obviously interest him. These
interests, another element of the drama going on in his
soul, prevent him not only from being a writer for the
people but also from taking any other direct path to a
reconciliation of the need to write literature with the
consciousness of his own sin in so doing. Indeed, few are
those who are given the happiness of writing for the
people (I say happiness because it is better to make
millions of readers better off than just thousands or
hundreds) and possibly Count Tolstoy does not possess the
necessary strength and capacity for it. But once he is
sure the nation consists of two halves and that even the
innocent, 'blameless' pleasures of one half work to the
disadvantage of the other then this can prevent him devoting all his vast talents to this huge theme. It is difficult even to imagine what other themes could occupy a
writer bearing in his soul such a terrible drama as Count
Tolstoy carries in his; it is so profound and serious, it
so grips the roots of literary activity, that it would
seem it would smother all other interests like convolvulus
smothers all other plants. Surely it is not an insufficiently noble object of life to remind 'society' that its
joys and interests are not those of everyone, to explain
to 'society' the true sense of 'manifestations of progress', to awake in some more receptive natures a consciousness and feeling for justice? Surely there is room
in this broad field for literary creation? Count Tolstoy

has already achieved much in this direction. By contrasting the two halves of society in 'The Cossacks', in the
stories of Sebastopol, in many sections of 'War and Peace',
in 'A Landowner's Morning' and in others he has provided
much spiritual nourishment for social consciousness. This
also applies to his pedagogical writing and the very publishing of 'Yasnaya Polyana' which, being a product of
printing and consequently of 'clever exploitation', no
doubt brought some peace to Count Tolstoy's conscience.
There is no need here to mention the detailed study and
depiction of the joys and anxieties of aristocratic salons
and ladies' boudoirs. I hope the reader understands that
this theme satisfies in Count Tolstoy only the need to
create but that he recognizes he is digressing from the
path he considers the right one or at least recognizes
that he is following the wrong path. In truth he gets
satisfaction there and as a man from a certain section of
society to whom all humanity is not alien but who is particularly close to the thoughts, feelings and interests of
that class. But it is in this that the digression from
the path that Count Tolstoy considers the correct one consists and where precisely his *left hand* begins which
should be clearer to him than to anyone. What does it
actually mean to commit to print the subtle and most
detailed analysis of the changes in the love between Anna
Karenina and the aide-de-camp Vronsky or the story of
Natasha Bezukhov, née Rostov? Using the words of the
author himself the publication in many thousands of copies
of the analysis, for example, of the feelings of Count
Vronsky at the sight of the broken back of his favourite
horse is not in itself a 'reprehensible' act. He 'is
pleased to receive for it money and fame' and we,
'society' - not all of us of course, mainly upper-class
people and officers - are curious to see ourselves in a
wonderful artistic mirror. When we talk of the heroes of
Mr Turgenev's works hesitating between a young and inexperienced maiden on the one hand and a passionate impetu-
ous devil in a skirt on the other there can be no discussion about the spiritual state of the author; it is as
transparent as the lace on the passionate devil or the
light on the face of the young maiden because Mr Turgenev
is not embarrassed by considerations of the role of publishing and literature. But Count Tolstoy is. Consequently he should be extremely offended to listen to the
praise of people like the critics of the 'Russian Messenger', the Russian World' and the 'Citizen' who are convinced that, as one of them puts it, 'literature can feed
only on the interests of the educated class because they
alone are truly national interests, in a conscious form

coinciding with the interests of civilization'. Of course
it is only a suggestion of mine that Count Tolstoy should
be offended by such praise but the suggestion is none the
less valid. Another of these troglodyte critics declares
that the heroes of 'Anna Karenina' are 'people who retain
amid new social strata the best traditions of cultured
society'. These unhappy people do not know that in Count
Tolstoy's opinion 'among generations of workers (new
social strata) there lies more strength and a greater consciousness of truth and goodness than in those of barons,
bankers, professors and lords (cultured society)'. These
unhappy people do not suspect that for Count Tolstoy 'the
demands of the people for art are more legitimate than
those of a spoiled minority of the so-called educated
class', that for Count Tolstoy giants like Pushkin and
Beethoven are worth less than the song 'Vanka the Steward'
or the tune 'Along the Mother Volga'. These unhappy
people do not know that what they like in Count Tolstoy is
only his *left hand*, the sad digression, the *involuntary*
gift to 'cultured society' to which he belongs. They
would be as happy to turn him into a left-hander as he
would to have been born only with a right hand. I repeat
that I am only suggesting that Count Tolstoy should be
offended to listen to these praises from the troglodytes:
but the praise only refers to his left hand. But I am
always offended for Count Tolstoy when I see the not unsuccessful efforts of the troglodytes to disgrace him with
their moral proximity. Offended not because I should like
to stand next to Count Tolstoy, although that of course
has its attractions, but because by disgracing him with
their impure proximity they remove from society almost all
his right hand. Why is the reading public so decidedly
ignorant of Count Tolstoy's real opinions? Why have they
not touched the social consciousness? There are many
reasons but one of them is the moral proximity of troglodytes who, exaggerating some things and keeping silent
about others, servilely kiss his left hand. I have experienced this in myself. I came late to Count Tolstoy's
ideas because I had been put off them by the troglodytes
and was surprised to discover that he had absolutely nothing in common with them.

60.   NEKRASOV: TO THE AUTHOR OF 'ANNA KARENINA'

1876

    Tolstoy, with patient brilliance, you explain
    That a woman must not at all make free
    With aide-de-camp or Chamberlain
    If she a wife and mother be.

61.   ANONYMOUS NOTICE, 'RUSSIAN NEWS'

1876, no. 43

The notice is signed I-n. (Probably A.S. Suvorin.)

The long-awaited continuation of Count Tolstoy's novel
'Anna Karenina' appeared at last in the January number of
the 'Russian Messenger'. In reading it, one becomes
again convinced of the justice of the regret expressed by
the majority of critics that such a great talent is being
wasted on absolutely insignificant subject-matter such as
the depiction of empty lives, foolish concepts and petty
interests. Indeed, is it possible to interest oneself in
the life, thoughts, ambitions and spiritual suffering of,
for example, a character like the novel's hero, Vronsky,
whose intellectual and moral physiognomy is described as
follows?

[Quotation omitted concerning Vronsky's life being governed by a series of rules for every circumstance:
whether or not they were sensible did not matter, so long
as Vronsky's life was well-ordered and peaceful.]

    The brilliant qualities, however, of Count Tolstoy's
talent are well enough known to everyone. The most outstanding of these qualities and the one which contains
the very essence of his genius is that striking knowledge
of the process which governs the life of feelings and his
ability to draw down to the finest detail all their nuances - of age, sex, social position, education and so on.

Count Tolstoy's works form a kind of discourse on experimental psychology; take, for example, Karenin's thought processes when his wife tells him of her relations with Vronsky. With what a wonderful clarity the inner workings of the simultaneous confluence of various feelings and sensations are here depicted! The quantitative influence of each and every one of them leads Karenin to decide to keep her with him in his home and hide from the public gaze what had taken place and take all necessary measures to put an end to the relationship and most importantly, which he did not admit to himself, to punish her.

[Quotation omitted concerning Karenin's convincing himself that he was acting in accordance with the dictates of religion.]

What knowledge of the human heart! How wonderfully expressed the ability of a man to adapt the demands of religion and moral duty to his own egotistic interests and personal advantages! Furthermore man not only has the tendency and the ability to find in religion and moral dictates some justification for his own selfish inclinations, but in following them he is quite sincerely convinced that he is sacrificing his own interests to those of others.

[Quotation omitted.]

Look also at the scene of Anna's meeting with Vronsky when she announces to him that she has told her husband everything. What a subtle analysis of minute and quickly changing impressions and sensations! In half a dozen words, uttered by the characters with the smallest change of expression on their faces which the ordinary observer would not even notice, you immediately see the complex psychic processes which the characters themselves would like to conceal and which to describe would normally take many pages. To quote this passage or even to relate the contents of the novel or its best sections we consider quite unnecessary, for there must be very few people who are not reading 'Anna Karenina' for themselves.

62.   UNSIGNED NOTICE, 'CITIZEN'

1876, no. 11

It is generally agreed that the problems of serfdom referred to below were changed rather than solved by the
Emancipation of the Peasants in 1861.

Considering the remarkable poverty of our belles lettres,
the only work of literature which has been of interest of
late to our reading public has been Count L.N. Tolstoy's
'Anna Karenina'. The first two parts of this notable work
appeared last year .... and now, after a long interval, we
have its continuation. As a deeply knowledgeable expert
on the human heart and as someone who has studied the
state of our social life at all its levels, the author
paints for us a picture of that side of our life which has
attracted the attention of our greatest thinkers; but they
have only managed to lose themselves in their conclusions
about how to solve the problem. The story's main theme is
the family discord between Karenin and his wife Anna, who
has given herself with all the ardour of her passion to
Vronsky, one of the lions of the capital. The deceived
husband dispassionately considers his position and in
order to avoid any gossip retains his former relations to
his wife in public and demands from her the observance of
the customary decencies and imposes upon her the one condition that she does not receive Vronsky in their home.
This reasonable and modest enough demand is not fulfilled
by Anna and in the last chapter we see the unhappy woman
lying on her death bed after having given birth and begging her husband to forgive her and make his peace with
Vronsky.

[Quotation omitted concerning Karenin's realization of the
value of the Christian doctrine of forgiving one's
enemies.]

   Such a presentation of the question of family dissen-
sion, from which a huge number of people are forced to
suffer when they can see no solution other than a final
break, promises great interest in the novel's remaining
parts, about which we shall speak when we know their content. At the moment, however, we cannot pass in silence
over the remarkably typical personality of the landowner,

Levin; he is utterly devoted to the rational reorganization of his estates and sincerely loves the common people,
but despite all that he constantly fails in all his humane
and seriously considered undertakings.

In one of the chapters in Part III the author introduces a conversation between Levin and a friend of his who
has lived all his life in the country and who is an admirable farmer; the latter expresses his dissatisfaction with
the current state of agriculture and says that the only
way to farm successfully is still either to give half the
land to the peasants or to let them rent it, but that this
will, in his opinion, destroy the general wealth of the
state. Where under serfdom and good husbandry the land
brough in 9x, under a half-and-half system it will bring
in only 3x. Emancipating the peasants has ruined Russia,
he concludes. Levin does not find what he hears at all
ridiculous, indeed he understands it far better than he
does the opinions of other landowners. Much of what his
friend is to say later in showing why the emancipation had
ruined Russia also seems very true to Levin, if not irre-
futable. The landowner was evidently stating a personal
opinion and it was an unusual one; it was also not just
the result of a desire to occupy his mind with something;
it was an opinion that had grown out of the conditions of
his life and which he had developed in the seclusion of
his country estates and had examined in all its aspects.

In getting down to the business of reorganizing his
system of farming with the object of interesting his
labourers in the success of the enterprise, Levin consci-
entiously began to read everything that had been written
on the subject and he intended to go abroad to study how
things were done there. When he read the works of European experts he became convinced, however, that they had
nothing to tell him. He saw that Russia had fertile soil
and honest labourers and that in certain circumstances
these two factors could be most productive. He wished to
prove this - theoretically in his book, and in practice on
his estates.

Such is the personality of the landowner Levin and it
is drawn in the novel in great relief; one should also
note that this side of Count Tolstoy's new work might well
attract more general attention than the main intrigue between Anna and Vronsky.

63.   VEYNBERG LENDS TOLSTOY HIS SUPPORT

1876

The 'Bee', 1876, no. 1. P.I. Veynberg (1831-1908) was a
historian, novelist and leading man of letters. His support for Tolstoy is typical of those people, certainly in
a minority, who were prepared to forgive Tolstoy his apparent disdain for contemporary problems; artists of genius,
it was claimed, cannot be restricted in any way.

Count L. Tolstoy, whom one has no hesitation in calling an
artist of the first rank, has written a novel which is the
best literary prose work of the past year. The novel is
not yet finished and consequently it is impossible to pass
a final verdict upon it; nevertheless the majority of it
has already appeared and this enables us to see clearly
its merits and its faults. The reader cannot of course
expect us in this short, à *vol d'oiseau* review to discuss
all the belletristic works of the past year so we shall
limit ourselves only to some general comments.

'Anna Karenina' is worth, of course, considerably less
than the same author's 'War and Peace' which is a marvellous novel. The main faults of the latest novel consist
in the most extreme lack of colour and confusion of form
in the heroine, in the fragility and scantiness of the
foundations on which the so-called dramatic conflict of
the story is based, in the unfortunate interweaving of a
narrow tendentiousness, about which we have spoken earlier
as something epidemic in our literature, and in several
other, less important, slips and imperfections. These
faults are all but balanced out by the rare artistry of
certain of its details, which is the facility of only the
very best talents, that artistry which, expressed in high
style, provides a valuable contribution to the treasure
house of our literature, especially at a time when our
critics are striving to remove into the background the
aesthetic (in the full meaning of the word) qualities of
a given work. In this respect Count Tolstoy has done a
great service; for to turn away in all but contempt (as
certain of our critics have done) from this new novel
ostensibly because it is steeped in indifference towards
the burning questions of the day is extremely unjust: in
the first place because this last accusation is obviously
quite untrue (we are talking here about an attitude to

such questions, to a standpoint); and, second, because it
is impossible to impose upon an artist such demands or to
surround him with conditions that lie quite outside the
nature of his talent. 'Anna Karenina' will remain an important novel for those who are able, or who wish, to differentiate clearly between works of a truly artistic nature
and those which are but publicistic tracts.

64. DOSTOEVSKY, 'DIARY OF A WRITER'

1877

January.

....Our public is very fond of satire; however, I am convinced that this same public is incomparably more fond of
positive beauty and craves and thirsts for it. Count Lev
Tolstoy is without doubt the favourite writer of the Russian public of all shades of opinion.

February.

....My readers will perhaps have noticed that in publishing my 'Diary of a Writer' for over a year now I have
tried to say as little as possible about current works of
Russian literature and when I did allow myself a word or
two on the subject they were always eulogistic. In this
voluntary abstinence of mine however - what an untruth!
I am a writer and am writing my 'Diary of a Writer', and
I have perhaps been more interested than anyone this past
year in what literature has appeared, so why should I conceal my strongest impressions? 'You', I would say, 'are a
writer of fiction and what you might have to say about
fiction, with the exception of unconditional eulogy, would
be thought biassed; unless of course you dealt with the
dim and distant past.' This is the thought which has
stopped me.
  Nevertheless this time I shall risk ruining this consideration. Actually I shall say nothing about anything
in a purely literary sense unless I am forced to, unless
it is 'à propos'. And now there is something! The point
is that a month ago I cam across something that is so
serious and so characteristic of current literature that

I read it even with surprise, because it is a long time since I have read anything like it and on such a scale in the realm of fiction. In a writer and an artist of the highest quality, pre-eminently a writer of fiction, I read two or three pages of real 'topics of the day' - everything which is of the greatest importance in our present social and political life and as it were collected together. And what is most important the question which we are all asking at the moment is put and left unanswered with all the most characteristic nuances of the real-life situation. I am speaking of several pages in Count Lev Tolstoy's 'Anna Karenina', published in the January number of the 'Russian Messenger'.

About the whole novel I shall say only a word and then only by way of a most necessary preface. I started to read it, as we all did, a long time ago. At first I liked it a lot, but then, although I liked certain details from which I could not tear myself away, on the whole I began to like it less. It seemed to me that I had read it all before, namely in 'Childhood' by the same author, and in his 'War and Peace', where it was all even fresher. The same story of a family of Russian nobles although, of course, the plot was different. Characters such as Vronsky, for example (one of the novel's heroes), who can talk to each other only about horses, and who cannot even find anything to talk about but horses, are of course interesting as far as finding out what type of people they are, but they are very monotonous and all from the same class. It seemed to me, for example, that love for this 'stallion in uniform', as one of my friends called him, could be depicted only in ironical tones. But when the author began to introduce me to his inner world seriously and not ironically it all seemed rather tedious. But then all my prejudices were destroyed. I read the scene about the heroine's death (she later recovers), and I understood all the essential part of the author's intentions. In the very midst of that petty and insolent life there appeared a great and eternal living truth illuminating everything instantly. These petty, insignificant and lying people became suddenly genuine and truthful, worthy of being part of humanity, simply because of a natural law - the law of human death. All their outer shell vanished, leaving only truth. The last became the first and the first (Vronsky) became the last, lost all their halo and were humbled, but in their humiliation they became immeasurably better, worthier and more truthful than when they were the first and eminent. Hatred and lies began to speak in words of forgiveness and love. Instead of stupid, fashionable conceptions there was just love of other people. Everyone forgave and excused everyone else. Ideas of class and exclusiveness suddenly vanished and became inconceivable and these paper characters began to resemble real live people! None of them was guilty; they all accused themselves unconditionally and thereby immediately acquitted themselves. The reader felt that there is a living truth, a most real and inescapable truth in which they must believe, and that all our lives and all our troubles both the petty and shameful ones and equally those we often consider the greatest are all more often than not only the pettiest and most fantastic fuss over nothing which fades away and vanishes without trying to defend itself before that moment of living truth.

The most important thing in this indication was that the moment really existed although it rarely appears in all its blazing fulness and in some lives never. This moment was found by the poet and shown to us in all its terrible truth. The poet proved that this truth actually exists, not as faith or as an ideal but inescapably, inevitably and obviously. It seems that it was precisely this that the author wished to prove to us when he started his novel. The Russian reader needs to be reminded of this eternal truth only too well: many of us have begun to forget it. In this reminder the author did something good, to say nothing about the extraordinary artistic manner in which he did it.

The novel continues on its way; but then I was rather surprised to find in its sixth part a scene describing a real 'topic of the day' and more importantly it appeared not intentionally, or tendentiously, but arose from the artistic essence of the novel itself. Nevertheless, I repeat, it was unexpected and rather surprised me; I just did not expect such a 'topic of the day'. I somehow never thought that the author would decide to lead his heroes in their development to such 'pillars'. It is true that in these 'pillars' and the extremeness of the conclusions about them lies the whole sense of reality and without them the novel would have appeared even indefinite having little to do with either current or basic Russian interests: we would have had some little corner of life and a deliberate ignoring of the most important and alarming elements in that life. However, I seem to have become decidedly a critic which is no business of mine. I only wish to point to one scene. It is nothing more than two characters who show themselves precisely in that aspect in which they can appear most typical for us and thereby the type of person to which they both belong is shown by the author in its most interesting aspects and in its contemporary social classification.

They are both noblemen, hereditary peers and genuine
landowners; they are shown after the peasant reforms.
Both of them used to be serf-owners and the question
arises: what remains of these noblemen, in the sense of
belonging to the nobility, after those reforms? Inasmuch
as the type of these two landowners is extremely common
all over the country the question is partly answered by
the author. One of them, Stiva Oblonsky, is an egoist, a
refined epicurean, an inhabitant of Moscow and a member of
the English Club. These people are usually looked upon as
innocent, pleasant and witty, good fellows, who simply
enjoy life (agreeable egoists), living for its pleasures
and interfering with no one. These people often have
large families; they are kind to their wives and children
but give little thought to them. They are very fond of
women of easy virtue - the respectable sort, of course.
They have had little education but they love elegant
things, the arts and like talking about everything. When
the peasant reforms were introduced this sort of nobleman
immediately understood what they meant. He calculated and
understood that after all he still had something left and
consequently that there was no need to change anything -
après moi le déluge. He does not bother to worry about
the fate of his wife or children. He is saved from the
fate of the Jack of Hearts by the remnants of his fortune
and his connections; but if his fortune were ruined and it
became impossible to obtain a salary for doing nothing
then he would probably become a 'Jack' although he would
use all the efforts of his mind, which could be very sharp,
to ensure he became the most respectable and upper-class
one. In the old days, of course, when he had to pay a
debt at cards or his mistress he would just have sent some
of his serfs off into the army; but such recollections did
not disturb him at all and indeed he forgot all about them.
Although he is an aristocrat he never attached any significance to his noble birth and when serfdom was abolished
he just assumed it had vanished; for him the only sort of
people there were now were the lucky man, the civil servant with a certain rank and the rich man. When the railway owner and the banker became important he immediately
made their acquaintance and became friends with them.
This conversation begins with his being reproached by
Levin, a relation of his and a landowner (although of a
completely different type, and one who lives on his estates), for spending a lot of time with the railway owners
and attending their dinners and parties; in Levin's eyes
such men are ambiguous and harmful. Oblonsky caustically
refutes him. Since the time they had become related
rather caustic relations had developed between them.

Moreover in our day the rogue who refutes an honest man is
always in a stronger position because he has the appearance of dignity coming from common sense whereas the honest man, resembling an idealist, looks a fool. The conversation takes place during a hunting trip one summer's
night. The huntsmen are spending the night in a peasant's barn and sleeping on straw. Oblonsky is trying to
prove that contempt for the railway owners and their in-
triguing, chasing after quick profits, entreating for concessions and buying land for re-sale has no sense and that
they are people like everyone else who work hard and use
their brains - and the result is we get a railway.

[Quotation omitted where Oblonsky and Levin discuss the
disproportion in wealth between people and what can be
done about it.]

   Such is the conversation. And you must agree that it
is a 'topic of the day' and even one of the most urgent.
And how many typical, purely Russian characteristics!
In the first place these ideas had hardly been thought of
forty years or so ago even in Europe, and were there many
people even there who knew of Saint-Simon or Fourier, the
original 'idealistic' interpreters of these ideas? And
here! There could not have been more than fifty people
in the whole of Russia who knew about these ideas starting
up in western Europe. And suddenly these 'questions' are
being discussed by landowners out hunting and spending the
night in a peasant's barn, and they are being discussed
characteristically and competently so that at least the
negative side of the question is irrevocably signed and
sealed by them. It is true that these landowners from the
highest class, who converse in the English Club, read the
newspapers and follow the trials as reported in them and
from other sources; nevertheless the very fact that such
idealistic nonsense is considered as a most vital topic of
conversation by people who are no professors or specialists but simply society people, Levins and Oblonskys, is,
I repeat, one of the most typical peculiarities of the
present-day state of Russian minds. The second extremely
typical trait in this conversation noted by the author-
artist is the fact that the justice of these new ideas is
being judged by a man who would not care a brass farthing
for the happiness of a working man or a beggar and on the
contrary would fleece him if he had the chance. But with
a light heart and the cheerfulness of a punster he attests
at a stroke to the bankruptcy of the whole of mankind and
declares its present order the height of absurdity. 'I
am', he says, 'in full agreement with this.' Note that

these Stivas are always the first to agree with all this.
With one blow he has condemned the whole Christian order
of things, the personality and the family - and it costs
him nothing!   Note also that we do not know anything about
science and these gentlemen who realize quite shamelessly
that neither do they and only yesterday began talking about
it and in someone else's words are none the less deciding
problems of such a magnitude without the slightest hesitation.   But here is the third typical trait: this gentleman
openly declares: 'You must do one thing or the other;
either you recognize that the present order of society is
just and stand on your rights, or you admit that you are
enjoying unjust privileges, as I am, and enjoy them with
pleasure.'   In other words, having in essence passed sentence on all of Russia and having condemned along with his
family the future of his children, he openly declares that
it is none of his business.   'I admit I'm a scoundrel, but
I shall remain a scoundrel for my own pleasure.   *Après moi
le déluge*.'   He is still unconcerned because he still has
his fortune, but should he lose it, why should he not become a 'Jack'?   It is the most direct road.   This then is
the citizen, the family man and the Russian - what a typical Russian trait!   You will say that it is an exception.
What exception can it possibly be?   Just recall how much
cynicism you have seen over the past twenty years, how
easily we have changed our minds and our convictions, what
a lack we have of any firm belief in anything and how
quickly we take up the first person we meet only to sell
him on the morrow for what we can get.   No morality except
'*après moi le déluge*'.

65.   TOLSTOY ON 'ANNA KARENINA'

1876, 1878

(a) From a letter to N.N. Strakhov, 23 April 1876.

If I wanted to say in words everything that I had in mind
to express through the novel I should have to write the
very novel that I have written all over again.   And if
short-sighted critics think that I wanted to describe only
what I like, how Oblonsky has his dinner, and what Anna
Karenina's shoulders were like, then they are mistaken.

In everything, in almost everything, that I wrote I was
guided by the need to collect ideas, linked together, for
expressing myself, but each idea, expressed in words on
its own, loses its meaning, is terribly reduced, when it
is taken alone out of the linking in which it is found.
The linking itself is made not, I think, by ideas but by
something else, and to express the basis of this linking
directly in words is quite impossible; it can only be done
indirectly, by words describing images, actions and situations.

You know all of this better than I do, but I have been
interested in it lately. One of the most evident proofs
of this for me was Vronsky's suicide, which you liked.
This was never so clear to me before. That chapter about
Vronsky accepting his role after his meeting with the
husband had long been written. I began to correct it and
quite unexpectedly for me, but indubitably, Vronsky went
and shot himself, And now, much later, it appears that it
was organically necessary.

(b) From a letter to S.A. Rachinsky, 27 January 1878.

Your criticism of 'Anna Karenina' seems to me wrong. On
the contrary I am proud of its architecture - the arches
are so put together that you cannot see where the keystone
is. And this is what I most tried to bring about. The
structural links do not rest on the plot or on the relationships (friendships) of the characters, but on the
internal linking.

66.   STANKEVICH ON ANNA, VRONSKY AND KARENIN

1878

From Anna Karenina and Levin, 'Messenger of Europe', 1878,
nos 4 and 5. A.V. Stankevich (1821-1907) was one of the
first critics to divide 'Anna Karenina' into two all but
unconnected parts, the Anna/Vronsky/Karenin story and that
of Kitty and Levin. His review, occasioned by the novel's
publication in book form, epitomizes this not uncommon
viewpoint; its first part, an extract from which follows,

is concerned with the first of this division's parts, while
the second is a disparaging account of Levin's activities.

In 'Anna Karenina' the author presents the conflict between the family duties of a wife and mother and the demands of love, pleasure and happiness of the female heart
unsatisfied in the family and vainly seeking satisfaction
outside it - a conflict resulting in catastrophe - the
suicide of the woman who destroyed the sanctity of the
family. The author's chosen theme is full of dramatic
elements and highly suitable for a remarkable work of art.
This choice by a contemporary writer and more particularly
a Russian writer is fully explained by the multitude of
facets in contemporary Russian family life. In this respect the attacks on the author for his lack of originality
and the banality of his theme are quite unjustified. Love,
honour, the demands of the human personality and the conflicts and contradictions of the latter with the demands
and conditions of the world or with social or historical
conditions are ancient and continuing motifs of many new
and fresh combinations and forms created by artists.

[Passage omitted concerning the validity for writers in
treating an old theme.]

In Count Tolstoy's novel the subject of the story whose
hero is Konstantin Levin is possibly newer and fresher
than the theme of the Anna Karenina story, but as we hope
to show below the value of this does not fully mature and
serves the author as poor soil. Levin's happy marriage
and normal family life is intended by the author to contrast with the sad fate of the Karenin family and should
explain the whole novel; but the author has been seduced
by Levin's problematic personality which is something
extraneous to the novel's central theme, and the story of
the development of Levin's vagaries, lack of understanding
and intellectual meanderings is made the subject of a special story which has only a weak and external connection
with the story of Anna Karenina. Chapters from the one
novel cut into those from the other and the development
of each of them takes its turn without any integral connection with the other; this destroys the unity of the
work as a whole and the impression to be gained from it.
  The first novel opens with some unpleasant events in
the Oblonsky household. Stepan Oblonsky has become enamoured of his children's governess and has betrayed his
wife's trust. He feels embarrassed; he is sorry for his

wife, Dolly, for his children and for himself, and he is even a little sorry about failing to keep his misdemeanour from his wife. It is all so unpleasant and trivial! What is more it has led to certain complications in the even, quiet, pleasant and comfortable life which is as necessary to Oblonsky as water to a fish. He none the less has a vague feeling that all will pass and everything will sort itself out. He finds that the words 'sort itself out' are rather good; and indeed everything does. The tranquillity of Oblonsky's family and his pleasant life return to their usual course, even though some slight assistance was necessary from Oblonsky's sister, Anna Karenina, who has come to Moscow from St Petersburg to restore the union of the couple.

Oblonsky is described with unusual subtlety, completeness and consistency. He has a place among the best representatives of his type in Russian literature. Oblonsky may now be numbered by the reader as the latest in a long line of happy, good-hearted people whose object and calling in life is to live pleasantly and all of whose aspirations, ideas and opinions are determined by this calling. The worth of such people, their sociability, honesty and gentleness, just as their tastes, are determined by their aim in life. They are so indifferent to everything outside their basic objectives that they never find confusion or perplexity in life. They meet no difficulties or insoluble contradictions for they know that such things will all 'sort themselves out'. Their social, political and even religious needs, attitudes and opinions are all adjusted to and brought into harmony with their main objective - to live pleasantly.

The Oblonsky household is a model of those families which are based upon the patience and long-suffering of the wife. Oblonsky does not change essentially after making peace with his wife. Just as before, he does not interfere with her caring for the children or her running of the house, he caresses the children and gives them sweets, he arranges dinners for prima donnas and takes presents to ballet dancers, he gets into debt and intends to make up for it all, and continues to live pleasantly. There is no loving happiness between him and his wife, but they organize their lives well enough; Dolly even retains some humility before the father of her children and the family clearly lives in reasonable harmony.

[Quotation omitted.]

But what if it had not been Stepan but Dolly who had transgressed? What would have happened to the family

then? Would not the children have been deserted? Would
not the seeds of evil, doubt about their parents and mis-
trust have been sown in their hearts from an early age,
and would they not have borne fruit? Would the eternally
cheerful face of Stepan have retained its openness and
kindly smile? And what would have been Dolly's fate? All
the meaning of the family, all its potential and all its
morality depend, do they not, on the wife and mother, and
if she destroys the family will not the woman perish along
with the purpose of her life and any meaning she might
have as a person?

Such are the questions which form the content of 'Anna
Karenina' and explain the attention and interest of all
its readers.

[Omitted: relation of the story up to the time Anna and
Vronsky have become lovers.]

But what sort of a woman is this Anna? What is it that
forces us to participate in her fate and her fall? Are we
drawn by the fatal, inevitable conditions of the world
around her, the unsatisfied and insuperable demands of a
passionate woman's heart deprived of the treasures of love
and devotion? Or are there perhaps hidden in her soul
dark, evil and potent powers, energy of will and selfish
desires? This Anna - is she a fallen angel or a malevo-
lent devil? From what the author tells us about her we
can only see in her a beautiful butterfly, flying head-
long and falling into the flames which have attracted it.
Anna has been a wife and mother for eight years, she is
intelligent and she cannot be ignorant of evil, human
relationships, family and social duties and conditions or
of the consequences of disregarding them. This wife and
mother has strong ties with those close to her and definite objectives in her life. Her husband speaks to her
about them, reminds her of them, but in vain. From the
time she meets Vronsky we do not see in her any hesitation, any doubt. She never asks herself where the road on
which she has set out is leading. In this wife and mother
there are no signs of any inner struggle except for the
slight embarrassment she feels at the time of her first
acquaintance with Vronsky. How can this be explained
except in the shallowness of her character, which reminds
us of her brother Oblonsky? The key to the problem is
provided by Anna herself in her talks to Dolly about her
brother. 'I'm his sister; I know him and his capacity for
forgetting everything (she made a sign before her forehead); I know his capacity for enjoying everything but
also his ability to repent entirely.' The reader knows

the limits of both his enjoyment and his repentance. 'I
am not Stiva,' said Anna, 'I cannot have a moment's doubt
in myself.' Yet at the very moment she was saying this,
writes the author, she felt that what she was saying was
not true. In order to understand her attraction, fall,
repentance, actions, sufferings and even her death we must
not forget this levity, this butterfly nature, this innate
character of the Oblonskys, both brother and sister, however much the author might expound upon it during the
novel and however tragically he might depict the life and
death of Anna. The eight years they had lived together
had failed to create any strong moral union between Anna
and Karenin, although the latter, as far as may be seen
from the varied and in some ways contradictory characteristics which the author has given him, is a man not devoid
of all qualities and is even a man out of the ordinary.
He is intelligent, honourable and active, he has serious
aims and interests. The author portrays him as a bureaucrat, as a man divorced from real life and concerned only
with its reflection, but also as a man with intellectual
interests in politics, philosophy and even religion. Only
poetry and art are completely alien to him. This bureaucrat and man of reason appears in the family as a dry man,
a cold fish. His concern for his wife and his attitude to
her are accompanied by jokes as if they were not serious
or sincere and were beneath him. This at least is how
Anna understands him and how the author describes him at
the start of the novel. As far as her attitude to her
husband is concerned Anna often experiences a feeling of
pretence although she does not admit it, or so we are told
by the author. Only after meeting Vronsky and returning
to Petersburg does she clearly and consciously recognize
it. Later on in the novel we find that Karenin is a man
not only with a heart but someone capable of generosity
and great self-sacrifice and we are right to think that
his external coldness and dryness are only the cover for
strong and deep feelings, although Anna, having married a
man she does not love and who is twenty years older than
she, cannot be satisfied by such feelings. The author
himself gets lost in contradictions when he talks of the
relations between husband and wife. When Karenin notices
the impression made in society by the behaviour of Anna
and Vronsky he decides to speak to his wife about it, but
finds it extremely difficult.

[Quotation omitted.]

   No less contradictory are other parts of the characterization of Karenin. We already know from the author that

he is a bureaucrat and tries to keep himself at a distance
from real life but also that he hates his official life
and tries to be as direct as possible in his dealings with
real life. One cannot say that Karenin, depicted so laxly
and carelessly, stands before us clearly and firmly and
does not arouse in us the most justifiable doubts. And
for the author himself such a weak and disjointed portrait
surely has only the advantage that he can change at will
his original characteristics for others which have no connection whatsoever with those we see in him when we first
meet him. But whatever sort of man he might be and however
he might be described the only certain thing is that his
wife does not love him, does not respect him, and sees no
love for her on his part, or at least this is how she sees
it once Vronsky has captured her heart. It is not difficult for him to arouse passion in Anna. Vronsky is a
brilliant, elegant, very wealthy, intelligent and highly
educated man (he received his education in the Corps de
Cadets). All his fellow-officers consider that of all
life's interests he holds closest to his heart those of
the regiment and his friends. Besides his concerns with
the army and society Vronsky has one further passion - for
horses. Vronsky's interests and objectives in life -
regiment, friends, horses - are probably more comprehen-
sible to Anna than her husband's administrative affairs,
politics or science and in the imagination of this woman
of society give Vronsky a glitter her husband could never
acquire.

   But however important these qualities of Vronsky are
they could not by themselves conquer Anna's heart. The
most important things for her are his passionate love, his
pursuing her and his words that life and her are one and
the same thing for him. In him she finds everything that
is missing from eight years of family life - passion,
devotion, and the need to live only for her and through
her. Once attracted to Vronsky, Anna responds to all
attempts by her husband for some explanation with a wall
of happy incomprehension. The author lays the blame on
Karenin who feels that by goodness, tenderness and conviction he can save her, but he speaks to her in a tone not
at all like the one he wanted to use but in his usual
joking way. But did not Karenin say at the time of her
first explanation, 'I love you, but I am not important;
what matters here is our son and you yourself'? What can
a husband say to his wife and the mother of his child that
is more simple, forceful, touching and convincing? Did
these words have any meaning for Anna? Is Karenin to
blame for retiring into himself and finding himself capable only of bitter jokes? Karenin's outward attitude to

his wife remains as it was before except that it is a
little cooler. He grows cold towards his son as well. He
buries himself in his official duties in the attempt to
deaden his suffering and the thoughts which plague him.
He does not wish to admit, although he feels it, that his
life has been completely ruined.

Anna, however, having given herself completely to
Vronsky, cannot, nor does she want to, think about what
she has done or what will become of her: 'Later, later.'
Only her terrible dream of two husbands brings home to her
the horror of her situation. Anna is preparing to become
the mother of Vronsky's child.   'Shall I tell him? Will
he understand the full importance of the fact?' she thinks
as she is about to meet Vronsky at the dacha before the
steeplechase in which he is to participate. And she tells
him. He goes pale and bows his head; Anna senses he has
understood. Vronsky does indeed understand that a crisis
is looming, that her husband must be told, and that he
should join his fate to Anna's.

[Quotation omitted.]

Vronsky cannot understand, however, how Anna with her
strong and honest nature can bear a situation of deceit
and not wish to get out of it; he does not guess that the
main reason for it is the question of her son, about
leaving him, about how she could manage without him and
he without his mother. In Anna's words Karenin is such a
non-man, such an evil machine, that he would surely not
understand that it would be just and inevitable to hand
over his son to his wife's lover and substitute the latter
for his real father. A person in love is likely to be
mistaken in the object of his affections and so we should
not be surprised at the fact that Vronsky sees in Anna a
strong character, something which we have not seen before,
nor shall we see again.

Not knowing how to find a way out of her difficult
position, Anna tells Vronsky not to mention it again and
to leave everything to her. Vronsky rushes off to the
race. The lovers' conversation has no result. There then
follows the wonderfully vivid description of the race
which every reader remembers. The feelings and excitement
of the spectators and the riders and even all the sensations, instinctive enjoyment and thoughts of the horses
themselves are transposed with the greatest skill in the
fulness of artistic truth.

[Relation of the story omitted: the race, Vronsky's fall,
Anna's admission of being his mistress and Karenin's reaction.]

Leaving his wife after her confession, alone in his
carriage on the way back to Petersburg, Karenin is suddenly
and happily free both from any pity for his wife and the
doubts and torments of jealousy which he had recently suffered. He feels like a man who has just had a bad tooth
removed. He feels alive again and that he can think of
other things besides his wife; he feels irritated only by
her having spoiled his life for so long. Only one thing
concerns him now - the question of how best, most conveni-
ently and most properly, and consequently most justly, to
remove from himself the dirt in which his wife has covered
him in her fall and to continue along his road of active,
honourable and useful life. Here the author presents
Karenin with new characteristics of which we were previously unaware: as a man whose standard of justice is his
own convenience. Karenin recalls a number of deceived
husbands starting with Menelaus. Previously intelligent
and honourable, he now appears ridiculously stupid and
utterly selfish. In thinking of all the possible solutions
that would provide a way out from the position in which
Anna has placed the whole family, he finds that a duel, a
divorce or a separation would not release Anna from the
scorn and the condemnation of society; they would inten-
sify them; also a divorce or a separation would not present
his son with any clear distinction between his father and
his mother or save himself from insult and degradation in
the eyes of the world. The retaining of the outward *status
quo* appears to be the best of all the possible solutions
and would furthermore add to the sufferings of his faith-
less wife.

[Omitted: quotation and relation of the story up to Anna's
illness and reconciliation with Karenin.]

The novel could have ended here with Anna's death. A
pitiful Anna, in a late but complete repentance and in
death paying for her conscious and unconscious guilt, would
have retained her moral, albeit sad, beauty not only in
Vronsky's memory but also in Karenin's and the readers'.
But death appears as a cathartic sacrifice not when it is
presented as an external and accidental solution to the
contradictions of life but only as the inevitable result
of inner struggle and the outcome of the moral process
within a person's soul. For Anna's death to have had
such a meaning she would have had to have been a different
person and the whole story of her inner life would have
had to have been different from that which the author has
given us. Anna's death at this stage would have been accidental. If she had died it would have been from her fever

and not from the moral impossibility of going on living.
The author could not then have shown us in Anna either her
irreversible decision to follow the call of happiness and
the dictates of her own heart or her deep feelings of
moral guilt as a wife and mother. Her repentance as she
dies would be just a part of her ravings during the fever
and we would not know how real or profound it was. All we
would know is that she complained bitterly, cried out that
she was more angry than suffering, that she was more confused than repentant and that she had not been brought to
account for her life. She was waiting for her situation
somehow to change and the solution somehow came of itself.
Her attitude to her difficult position is essentially very
similar to the convictions and eternal hope of her brother
Oblonsky that everything 'will sort itself out'. Why
should she die anyway? She must live and wait. Furthermore Anna is without doubt a strong woman, at least physically. The doctors said that with her illness death was
99 per cent certain; but she does not die. She slowly recovers. Karenin forgives his wife and is sorry for her
suffering. He also forgives Vronsky and is sorry for him
too; and he loves his children, both his son by Anna and
Vronsky's daughter.

[Relation of the rest of the story omitted.]

    What is the point of Anna's suicide? Do we have the
inevitable outcome of unrecognized or unrequited love and
the profound sufferings of an insulted and self-sacrific-
ing heart or the despairing act of an unlimited self-
conceit, an ever-blind and hungry selfish passion, the
senseless action of a frenzied childish irritation and
mindless fear, or simply only the fatal consequences of
an intemperate use of opium on the weak organism of a
woman? Is Anna's death proof of the value and profound
but unsatisfied aspirations of the human soul, or proof
of childish impotence and senselessness, or is it but a
pathological manifestation of the physical body? The last
strikes the reader as the most likely when he considers
Anna's state in the hours leading up to her death and all
the confusion of her thoughts described by the author.
The reader recalls all the previous storms in her soul,
but all of them rose and fell in a normal pattern. Only
opium prescribes their ultimate limits. Without it Anna
would have come to her senses and calmed down as she had
often done before after similar upsets. Without it Anna
would have realized that when Vronsky replies to her
telegram he could not have replied to a letter he had not
received and that in promising to return in response to

her call in a few hours he is showing neither indifference
nor the desire to insult and torment her. She would have
thought he still loved her and that all that was required
on her part was trust in him. But has the author kept the
reader's attention in Anna's life and her fate simply to
show the fatal effect upon her of opium? There is much
confusion in the reader's mind over the last page of
Anna's life, before she takes her final decision. The
author shows this decision in Anna not as something which
is free and conscious but as a sick and dark whim. Going
to her death Anna asks herself why. Such a death preys on
our nerves and calls forth our pity like an accident but
it does not touch the depths of our souls with terror; we
feel no sympathy caused by a tragic outcome whose moral
sense we understand. We hear from Anna that no one knows
her and that she does not even know herself. Does not the
author place too much trust in her words and has he not
recognized in Anna a secret which one can discover in part
although not in its entirety? If Anna does not split into
two parts like Karenin the reader nevertheless cannot
easily grasp her unstable and changing nature. The author
himself sometimes grants Anna depth of character and
strength, more self-knowledge than is possible with her
childish levity and naive selfishness. In the scene where
Anna gives herself to Vronsky the author mistakenly makes
her feel her fall deeply. Her weakness and indecisiveness,
the mood of lies and deceit which overcome her and which
are expressed in her pretence before her husband when she
hides from him the true situation between her and Vronsky,
which she tells herself is something unusual for her and
which she later regrets, are shown by the author as the
result of her strong maternal instincts. He has forgotten
that he has told us that Anna assumed the role of a mother
living only for her son, a role which is partially sincere
but much exaggerated. The author places too much trust in
Anna's thoughts that what is easy for other women is a
torment for her. The loss of her position in society, a
loss she could never come to terms with, poisons her relations with Vronsky. At the beginning of the novel the
author does not hide from the reader Anna's own statement
that her position in society was dear to her and that however much she tried she would never be stronger than it;
but during her life with Vronsky the author sees as the
main and incurable wound to her heart that of being separated from her son and a woman unsatisfied by her love for
Vronsky. Intentionally or not the author has given Anna
only a one-sided illumination which picks out certain of
her traits of character in high relief but keeps others
in the shadows away from the reader's eyes. Without this

artificial illumination the reader would have seen that
in Anna there is more passion than warmth, that in her love
there is more selfishness than devotion, that in her passion there is more heat than depth, and that she can be
considered attractive in her childlike charm, playfulness
and grace but that she lacks all beauty, worth and strength
of character.

But if the author has not shown her clearly enough for
us to understand her completely he has nevertheless told
us many facts about her inner and external life from which
we may draw conclusions about Anna's character and personality. Anna is a woman of no great intelligence, she is a
suitable candidate for society life, but she is not capable of nor does she demand anything beyond these low
horizons. She is a woman not without a heart but it is
not a large one, she is not indifferent to her son but she
is not enough of a mother for her love for her son, or her
daughter, to be stronger than other demands she might have
as the desire for pleasure and personal happiness. Her
husband is a serious man but there is nothing serious
about her; she is bored and tired by his presence just as
a child is bored by being only with adults. The elegant
Vronsky is a worthy hero for such a heroine. In Anna
there is a complete absence of any moral sense; she never
makes any demands upon herself. In her life there are
neither strong attachments nor important objectives; there
is nothing to protect her from idle fantasies and ephemeral
pleasures. A grown-up child, she is weak and defenceless,
frivolous and irresponsible. With childish enthusiasm she
throws herself at delicacies in the shape of Vronsky and
then gets frightened at the thought that this delicacy will
be taken away from her, and at the slightest suspicion of
such a danger she gets agitated, cries and capriciously
demands that she be calmed down by caresses and a reassur-
ance that no one will take away her sweet. Just as she
threw herself upon the proferred delicacy without a second
thought so is she afraid that she will lose it in a dangerous but passing moment and once she is afraid this pitiable child throws herself in despair beneath a train and
ends her life. Anna was justified, Levin remarked. Up to
a point he is right. She was justified in living for the
moment, like a child. She is not only a child but even an
enfant terrible with her unexpected behaviour, escapades,
fears, ideas and decisions. Along with this justification
she was also not devoid of a certain childish cunning; we
recall her ability to withdraw into herself, to calm herself down, to reconcile herself, to put on a playful lack
of understanding to avoid unpleasant explanations and her
attempts to lavish attention upon Vronsky so that he should

want nothing new. To find happiness even in a difficult
union with the man she loves, a union which is recognized
neither by society nor by law, it is necessary to have a
strong personality and a moral basis within oneself.
There is not a trace of either in Anna. Such child-women
as Anna can be satisfied with a quiet and uneventful life
in some definite and secure surroundings, but not if their
heart's choice cannot be counted upon to go boldly ahead
with them even along a difficult road or to share with
them all life's difficulties. If Anna had become Vronsky's
wife then her secure position in society, especially the
concerns and enjoyments of society life which are so necessary to her and which she understands, could have softened
and diverted her constant feeling of fear of losing Vronsky, although actually her relations with him would not
have been any different. It is, of course, difficult to
see what marriage would have brought them. Anna could
have poisoned Vronsky's life just the same with her suspicions and persecution; she could have grown tired of him,
cooled towards him, if she did not receive the caresses
which were the only thing this grown-up child needed or
understood; she could have become attracted to another;
what had happened between her and Karenin could have happened to her and Vronsky. With her childlike naivety, her
impressionability and capacity for enjoyment anything is
possible, it all depends on chance. This is what leads
her to her death and what could have led her to future
confusion. If only this grown-up child could have loved,
desired and needed something other than delicacies and
caresses! This is what we cannot help feeling as we end
the novel. If only this wife and mother did not remain
for ever in her childhood, or if only children did not
become wives and mothers! If only for the majority of
women there were some serious aims in life, if they did
not see in life only a game and a pastime! If only they
could understand that in the self-denial and self-
sacrifice of a wife and mother there is more value and
more moral satisfaction than in the pursuit of their own
appetites and fantasies!
   'Anna Karenina' cannot be called a perfect work of art
because its basic idea and contents are not expressed in
the form best suited to them. None the less 'Anna Karenina' has an important place among the best works of Russian literature. In this field we no longer have the
strict criteria which we apply to other art forms and are
satisfied only by the relative worth and importance of
literature. We have here the usual superfluities and
longeurs; the explanations for the actions of the characters are not completely accurate or convincing; there is a

lack of a logical development in the events, a lack of
clarity and the effect of chance on normal events. We do
not have in the novel the usual completeness and finish
of a work of art, but there is variety and interest in
its contents; there is no complete revelation of the profundity of what is described but there are signs pointing
to many aspects of them. There is much to interest the
reader, but there is no complete satisfaction with the
answers to the questions raised by the novel.

67. V. MARKOV ON TOLSTOY'S ARTISTICALLY CONSERVATIVE
NOVEL

1878

From a review published in 'Week', 1878, no. 1.
V.S. Markov (1834-83) was a leading editor and journalist.

The theme of 'Anna Karenina' is concerned with personal
relationships and more particularly with those within the
family (excluding, that is, the final part which is a more
or less superfluous epilogue, although it does deal with a
few social questions) and the treatment of this theme is
entirely directed at supporting the foundations of a worn-
out but still current morality concerned with family life.
To identify this main idea and to justify it come what may
is the possibly unconscious but nevertheless tendentious
purpose of the novel. Count Tolstoy is often praised as a
'realist' because this gifted writer depicts very accurately and extremely truthfully many aspects of real life
and the spiritual side of things; such praise is well deserved; but this does not prevent him from having a very
marked tendentious and conservative streak which is very
similar to the attitude of the Old Believers and which is
seen clearly in all his works. There are many new ideas
in his books (especially in his articles on education) and
many perceptive and original comments of a democratic
spirit. One might well think: What a penetrating and
independent mind! But on looking more closely we notice
that these bold and true ideas are cast in that poetic
mould to which we were referring, in that subtle artistic
comprehension of certain sides of the life of ordinary

Russian people. This has enabled him to create several wonderful things but generally these illuminating rays do not destroy in him the cast of mind which was formed by his upbringing, social standing and the times when his talent was formed.

The basic tenet of his philosophy is sufficiently well shown in the following statement which catches the reader's eye in part VIII: 'Without a doubt a family should live just as our fathers and grandfathers lived, that is with the same upbringing, and children should be brought up in the same way.' Expressive, is it not?

The family relationships depicted in the novel take place in aristocratic circles. Why did Count Tolstoy choose this particular milieu? In one of his striking aphorisms he says that in his opinion 'among the working people there is both more strength and a greater consciousness of good and evil than among barons, bankers and professors'. Despite that, he none the less chose the highest social class as the setting for his novel, and there are many, if not barons, then counts and countesses, princes and princesses. One cannot actually state that this 'high society' appears in the novel in a very good light or that having read the novel we come to admire the sort of life led by the upper classes (and in this connection the hopes of certain conservative critics that they would have the honour to sense in the novel the fragrance and beauty of aristocratic drawing-rooms which had not yet betrayed the cult of the elegant, etc., were not realized. The fragrance is there but it is not strong; there is certainly a fragrance about Kitty (a very charming little doll) but one can scarcely say there is much fragrance about the heroine Anna).

What the conservative critics think about it is no concern of ours, but what is, is the fact that this world is drawn with unusual love and great accuracy, from which one must conclude that the author himself is prejudiced in its favour; he sings its praises to the skies and in all seriousness wants us to admire such scenes and characters, about which there is no need to speak here. Count Tolstoy finds it all entirely captivating and puts all his talents into motion in order to evoke in his readers laughter, tenderness and sympathy – the whole gamut of sensations, good and bad – concerning the adventures and exploits of his characters, all of which, surely, can only arouse a yawn or a mildly ironic smile. How is it that a writer who knows so much about the best sides of the life of the Russian people can lower himself to drawing such trifles and tawdry nonsense? The explanation is that Count Tolstoy in doing what he has is only obeying the

unchanging demands of his nature and his sympathies which
lie exclusively in these and similar interests and relationships. The idleness of the upper classes seems for
him to be something serious and he appears to make great
efforts to draw from it a strict morality; he is usurping
the role of the moralist; he draws frivolous, virtuous
people and destroyers, equally frivolous, of virtue - in a
word inner emptiness and utter insignificance; one feels
this on every page of the novel, although it is rich in
aesthetic beauties.

As a work of art, by the way, this epic of the upper
classes puts Turgenev's latest work, 'Virgin Soil', right
in the shade. But Count Tolstoy has not put Turgenev in
the shade; as a literary figure Turgenev is far superior
to the author of 'Anna Karenina' for the latter follows
only the chaotic ferment of his feelings and ideas while
Turgenev amidst all the confusing contradictions of human
life never rejects for a moment the light of reason and
continues living in sympathy with the highest aspirations
of humanity.

In 'Anna Karenina' there is a family morality which
would find approval from Zagoskin, a morality, we do not
deny, which flows naturally and inevitably from the given
facts and imparts to the story a definite edifying tone.
As everyone knows the novel concerns a beautiful, high-
society women, Anna Karenina, the wife of a high-ranking
Petersburg official, who enters into an *illicit* liaison
with a brilliant cavalry officer, Count Vronsky. Illicit
it certainly is, but what is there tragic or earth-
shattering about it? Count Tolstoy, however, finds both
horror and tragedy. One must also remember that Karenin,
the victim of his wife's infidelity, is a man in his declining years, more than twenty years older than his wife,
that she had not married him from love, that the marriage
had been arranged and that there are no tender feelings
between the couple, nor could there be. It is clear from
what the author tells us that the marriage had been a 'big
mistake'; the wife is a frivolous woman, knowing only how
to value the glitter of high society and devoting herself
to its customs and 'laws' and the husband, the worthy
official, is distinguished by a bureaucratic formalism and
buries himself in his civil service duties. Under such
conditions what could be more natural than discord between
them? It is quite natural that the young woman should
find herself a man more suitable to her tastes and inclinations, i.e. a man who attracts by an external elegance -
fetching manners and physical charms; she could have no
other hero, no other ideal. Such a hero is not long in
presenting himself in the shape of Count Vronsky, a man

endowed with an athlete's body and an expert on horses.
His passion for horses is so strong that it could be said
that his heart is divided between his love for his Arabian
mare Betsy and that for the splendid Anna. All this, we
repeat, is quite natural. Finally one must recognize that
the young woman - because she is frivolous and endowed
with a superficial culture - is bound to live the life of
the emotions and to seek the joys of the heart which she
cannot find in living with the man she married. Such is
the backcloth for this love story. If we are forced to
concern ourselves with such slight anecdotes, then what
morality can we find in it all? Is it not that in society,
high or low, marriages should not be arranged, that older
men should not marry young flibbertigibbets, and that many
society ladies, unaccustomed and disinclined to work, find
themselves dependent on their husbands materially and are
forced to seek in high society lovers in order to stop
themselves dying from boredom? It is difficult to come to
any other conclusion. But what does Count Tolstoy do? He
arms himself with the fulminations of the moralist and
decides to send the society lady who breaks her marriage
vows to the stake. To betray a husband, however repellent
and to live with whom is more awful and bitter than wormwood ... I shall not tell you what it can lead to! Anna
says she would rather kill herself than live with such a
husband; that is as maybe, but she still flaunts morality
and that is why an uncommon and melancholy death awaits
her. It is not necessary for the betrayed husband to take
his vengeance, however - the accursed morality, the moral
law, will do that. The novel is based upon this premise.
The author takes his text from the Bible: 'Vengeance is
mine; I shall repay.' He sets out to punish his criminal-
heroine. For greater effect he gives the couple a son,
who is the cause of great spiritual suffering to Anna
after her infidelity. She is separated from him and dies,
dies, to see him - all this will bring tears to the eyes
of all Count Tolstoy's sensitive lady readers. But because the whole novel is based on falsity and lies all
these pathetic scenes are essentially sentimental rubbish
even if they are described in an extremely touching manner
and the author squanders his not insignificant talent upon
them.

At the beginning Anna's liaison with Vronsky threatens
no danger. The husband is clearly deeply upset by his
wife's infidelity but demands only the observance of the
common decencies and, fearing a scandal, does not ask her
to leave his home. But then Anna becomes pregnant by
Vronsky. During the birth of this illegitimate child
there occurs in her, in her husband and in her lover a

complete moral transformation - all three are filled with grace, love and forgiveness. Karenin forgives Anna; Anna suddenly finds she loves her husband and goes into raptures over his nobility of soul when previously she had seen only hypocrisy; and Vronsky is deeply sorry for his action, i.e. seducing another man's wife, and almost shoots himself from pangs of conscience. Count Tolstoy has been widely praised as a psychologist who can look deeply into the human heart and unveil the essence of things. This reputation strikes us as somewhat exaggerated. It comes from the fact that he is always lavish with psychological motivations. We remember that sometime during the last ten years a critic praised Count Tolstoy for talking about a sparrow and saying that 'it made out it was pecking'; in this way he caught the whole psyche of the sparrow. In this connection, if you will, there is something even more interesting in his latest novel in the depiction of the wolfhound, Laska, which gives a wonderful example of animal psychology. The author tells us what the dog felt, thought and even how it used its powers of reasoning by the use of syllogisms. It must be admitted that Count Tolstoy displays here great powers of observation, but in this connection with people he is not always free from great psychological blunders and inaccuracies. For example, the psychological metamorphosis which takes place in the novel's main characters strikes us as rather dubious. It seems improbable that the heroine would suddenly experience tender feelings towards the husband she hated, and, what is more, during a childbirth resulting from a liaison with her 'admirer' and in his presence. It is possible that her husband could experience a real or apparent feeling of forgiveness if he were a colourless man whose moods swing from side to side under the influence of external factors. But Karenin? The truth of the matter is that the author needed this metamorphosis because he wants the husband to appear in a forgiving role so that the vengeance mentioned in the epigraph is left to higher authorities. This comedy of mutual reconciliation soon ceases, though, because of the impossibility of continuing it any longer. Anna leaves her husband and goes abroad with Vronsky. He soon begins to feel the onset of a slight tedium which presages grief for Anna just as clouds presage a storm and thus her retribution begins.

[Relation of the rest of the story omitted.]

This is the whole story with all its secrets, moral, social and philosophical. It is a squalid affair and all, we dare say, quite superfluous. Furthermore it is

absolutely misunderstood by the author. It has nothing at
all to do with the retribution which Count Tolstoy stresses
in his epigraph. It is not Anna who is guilty and it is
not necessary to punish her, or even her husband, who relatively speaking is more guilty than she for he was freer in
his choice of a wife than Anna had been in hers of a husband. The answer lies in the general style of the life depicted, a life which must result in such false relationships, and in the fact that Anna, who is possessed of no
moral resources, could do nothing to turn her life into
something better, to direct it along a different path, and
that none of her friends, least of all Vronsky, could give
her any moral support - they are all variations of the same
type of personality which Anna herself exemplifies.

68.   SHEVITCH ON TOLSTOY'S IDEAL OF FAMILY LIFE

1879

From a review of Turgenev's 'The Diary of a Sportsman',
'Smoke' and 'Virgin Soil', and Tolstoy's 'Childhood and
Youth', 'War and Peace' and 'Anna Karenina' entitled
Russian Novels and Novelists of the Day, by S.E. Shevitch,
'North American Review', 1879, no. CXXVIII.

An illustration of Tolstoy's ideal of family life, which he
but slightly touches in 'War and Peace', we find in his
last novel, finished a year ago, 'Anna Karenina'. As a
true and artistic picture of 'high life' this novel is a
masterpiece without an equal, perhaps, in any literature.
In one frame the author has combined two love-stories -
the one pure and quiet, the other passionate and criminal.
The latter, the love between the heroine, Anna, and the
brilliant aide-de-camp, Prince Vronsky, is conducted by
Tolstoy step by step to its tragical end with a pitiless
logic, and a profound knowledge of all the subtle instincts
of the human heart, of all the innumerable prejudices and
peculiarities of Russian aristocratic life. The scene of
the heroine's suicide, which she commits by throwing herself under the wheels of a railway-train, is in its tragical grandeur one of the most remarkable dramatic effects in
modern literature. Beside these two rebel hearts, who seek

their own way to love and happiness in open defiance of
the decrees of society, the author has placed another pair
- the plain, unsophisticated country gentleman Levin and
the young girl who ultimately becomes his wife. Their
romance, disturbed for a moment by the interference of
the disorderly element in the person of Vronsky, flows on
quietly and peacefully. The young Mrs Levin becomes an
utterly prosaic and even somewhat slovenly *materfamilias*;
her husband remains what he always had been, a quiet country gentleman, ignoring entirely all manner of social
'problems' or political 'questions', raising his corn and
potatoes with the persistency, if not with the civic
courage, of a Cincinnatus. And at the close of the book
we seem to hear the author exclaiming: 'Go and do likewise!'

Such is the moral and social creed of this great poet
of the Russian aristocracy. The reader will not be slow
in detecting all its shallowness. An author who says to
the class he represents: 'You are estranged from the rest
of the people - you are by nature lazy and indolent, that
is true, but no matter; be still more indolent, retire
once for all from public life, bury yourselves in your
families, on your estates, and you shall be saved!' -
such an author is unconsciously writing a bitterer satire
on that class than any of its most implacable enemies
could have done.

Thus the two greatest novelists (1) of modern Russia,
both born and bred in that class of Russian society which
has until now held undisputed the sceptre of intellectual
and political power - both, the one with a set purpose,
the other unconsciously, pass a death warrant against the
present social organization of their country. In their
works, as in a mirror, the actual condition of Russian
society is reflected with a merciless accuracy. They are
not only the poets, they are the physiologists, the historians, of their people, and, by the powerful influence
they exert on the public mind, they may yet prove to be,
in defiance of the proverb, 'prophets in their own land'

Note

1 The other is Turgenev. (Ed.)

69.   GROMEKA ON KARENIN

1883-4

In his book 'On L.N. Tolstoy's latest work: "Anna Karenina"', 1885, M.S. Gromeka (1852-83) judges Tolstoy from a
traditional nineteenth-century moralistic standpoint.
He states that many critics have failed to understand Tolstoy because they criticize him from nationalistic bases;
Tolstoy must be judged on his own terms; his poeticism
looks at individuals rather than societies; the latter is
composed of the former; consequently 'Anna Karenina' is
the social novel. Gromeka's critique was first published
in 'Russian Thought', 1883, nos 2, 4, 11, and 1884, no.
11, appearing as a book the following year. The fifth
edition, 1894, contained two additional chapters which
attempted to explain Tolstoy's conversion to Christianity
and linked it to certain ideas in 'Anna Karenina'. Tolstoy did not like Gromeka's comments. His main criticism
was that Gromeka had thrown light on things best left un-
illuminated - at least by critics. This extract is from
chapter 4.

It is probable that the character of Karenin and the importance of his personality is the most difficult problem
for the critic in the whole of Count Tolstoy's novel.
First of all the reader's sympathy is so clearly on the
side of Anna that the form of the husband she hates takes
on of itself an unsympathetic appearance and it is difficult for him not only to be fair but also to comprehend
the profound secrets of the human heart, which the author
has revealed through his character and which makes Karenin
far more artistically valuable than even Anna herself. It
is not only the reader's sympathy but also his interest
that is directed exclusively at Anna and only transfers in
passing to the colourless and apparently insignificant
figure of her husband. Furthermore the reader is also a
human being and as such he bears within himself the same
tendency to have a cold, despising and negative attitude
to the external degradation and disgrace which Count Tolstoy has drawn so profoundly and pitilessly accurately in
the people around Karenin - and he is also inclined to
condemn Karenin for his unhappiness. Finally the wide
range of the author's talent hampers the reader's understanding of his creation: however strange this might

appear it is nevertheless true. Count Tolstoy has pene-
trated too deeply into Karenin's inner world and the
heterogeneous traits of his character are presented so
clearly and individually that it is impossible at first
sight to grasp their deep interrelation. The reader is
also hampered by the chronology of the story in which
Karenin takes part. When at first you see the obverse
of the coin and then the verso slips briefly before your
eyes you see neither its qualities nor the connection of
one side with the other. There is some mysterious connection between love and knowledge and that which we do
not love we often do not wish to know and consequently
we never do know.

However difficult it is to imagine that there could be
any common ground at all between the young, beautiful,
passionate, sincere and vivacious Anna and the cold, lifeless, unprepossessing and formal Karenin there is none the
less no doubt that between them there is a greater parallel than could be given simply by the external ties of
marriage or their life together. They both neglect something in their lives and because of the inevitable punishment they both perish. For a long time neither of them
know themselves and in their ignorance they both commit
errors which later cause their downfall. They both realize their mistake when actual death for one and moral
death for the other have become inevitable. Both of them
break the same law of human nature without noticing it in
their short-sightedness and self-confidence and draw down
upon themselves those negative forces with which this law
punishes people for their every digression. Both of them,
although from different causes, despise feeling and love
which are alone the real source of life and find no place
for them in their hearts and are in turn rejected by them.

Karenin is a man of ambition, of abstract thought, a
man of naked will and cold reason who scorns on principle
emotion, of which he feels so little anyway. He is emo-
tionally cold, but the fact of being orphaned at an early
age, his lack of friends, his exclusively bureaucratic
existence and his devotion to ambition have all made him
colder still. From his conception of abstract duty he
has so subdued all manifestations of feeling in himself
that even an accidental and involuntary expression of it
is considered by him to be an unworthy weakness.

Possibly his upbringing and his profession, possibly
his innate phlegmatic temperament have both played their
part in the formation of such a man - we do not know. But
in the novel he appears at once as the typical model of
the St Petersburg bureaucrat of pure blood, as a man for
whom there is a time and place for everything, and despite

his honesty, nobility, education, inquisitiveness and
serious attitude to the affairs of state a man who has no
room for living thoughts or living feelings and whose
capacity for the latter is utterly atrophied. He is a
man of strong will and great intelligence but completely
lacking in feeling, like his thin, big-boned body with its
sinews and large hands but without muscle or blood, like
his large eyes with their steady but weary and lifeless
expression. He lives in the paper world he has constructed around himself and in losing his tiny store of feeling
he gradually loses the ability to understand feelings when
they appear in others and consequently withdraws from real
life.

Up to that time he has not admitted to the main moving
force of real life - feeling; and when he unexpectedly
stumbles against its demands he is taken unawares and
loses his balance for ever. And now, wishing to warn
Anna, he finds, however, that questions about her feelings
are not within his competence; they touch her conscience
but do not enter the realm of their general family interests for they belong to that of religion, and then he
feels relieved at the realization that he has found a
point of reference for the circumstances he has to face.
He does find in himself at that moment a strong flood of
feeling which alone could support and save Anna; he only
constructs an abstract theory of logical arguments which
cannot have any real effect on Anna's behaviour. When he
is developing his line of argument and says to Anna: 'I
am your husband and I love you', Anna feels that he is
incapable of love and that he does not know what love is,
and this becomes the strongest refutation of all his artificial arguments.

The closer Anna draws to Vronsky, the more Karenin
understands that only goodness and tenderness, that is the
showing and influence of *feeling*, can save her; but any
attempt on his part to do this is doomed to failure from
the outset because he cannot find any feeling in himself
nor the knowledge of how to express it.

Anna gives herself to Vronsky and Karenin instinctively
feels that he has a wife no longer. But he does not want
consciously to admit it because it is too terrible a
thought.

[Quotation omitted.]

Precisely because he feels crushed by the event, when
he is asked about his wife there is in the expression on
his face something stern and proud. When he goes to see
his wife at the dacha and hears her insincere and empty

tone of voice he does not attribute to that tone any particular meaning. 'He only listened to her words and gave
them only the basic meaning that they had.' When he hears
from the weeping Anna about her unfaithfulness he is
silent for a long time and his face bears the solemn expression of a corpse, and only as they approach the house
does he say to Anna that she must observe the outward
conditions of propriety until he decides on the measures
to take which will preserve his honour. If Karenin had
been capable of the slightest feeling or had loved Anna
with a real, living love and not simply the habit of extended cohabitation he would have killed her or Vronsky
or done something else - separate from his wife, call
Vronsky out for a duel - but certainly not what he actually does do. He only discusses things and these discussions are remarkable for their lack of feeling and their
egotism. For everyone in Karenin's position there is no
way out, no happy way out at least. But one man might
feel despair over his broken marriage, or jealousy, and
would take care to rid himself of the tormenting feeling
and thus find a way out; while with another, as Karenin,
it is his outward *amour propre* which suffers and he is
only concerned with keeping what he has and not losing
face in public. Consequently Karenin cannot accept
either of the radical solutions to his problem. He
rejects a duel because he fears being killed or injured -
and he is quite capable of thinking about his own health
in this situation - and he also refuses to consider a
divorce or separation and all its accompanying scandal
which would inevitably shake his important position in
society and the government. He puts the outward respect
of his position above his own inner worth. He insists on
the retention of the outward *status quo* with the one condition that Anna stops seeing her lover, in which his
single living - cruel but still living - desire is satisfied, the desire to take revenge upon his wife, the desire
that she, who has taken away from her husband his peace of
mind and his honour, should suffer herself and not benefit
from the fruits of her crime. In Karenin's attitude there
is nothing religious; but in the thought that by not freeing his wife he is acting in a religious way, as if giving
her the chance to repent, is extremely pleasant for him,
and this insincere and concocted sanction gives him peace
and satisfaction.

He was pleased to think that even in such a crucial
matter no one would be able to say of him that he had
not acted according to the rules of that religion whose
banner he always held high amid general apathy and indifference.

He looks up an article in an official publication and is
taken by a certain sentence. He writes his wife a letter
in fluent French in which he does not say a word about his
real and extremely petty motives, but there are fine words
about the impossibility of undoing a knot tied by a higher
power, about repentance and about money. And he sends the
letter off, pleased with his style, decisiveness and the
use of his beautiful and apposite epistolary accomplish-
ments. He then starts to think of affairs of state.

But as soon as he actually sees Anna his artificial
superiority and assumed indifference disappear like smoke
in the wind and the realization that he is crushed over-
whelms him again.

The conditions imposed by Karenin and silently accepted
by Anna and Vronsky are, of course, too artificial and
soon all three realize it and each of them, for different
reasons, attempts to break them. The hand on the clock,
which during the meeting in the garden had not yet reached
the hour, now does so and the clock begins to strike.
Anna forgets all about society and gives herself body and
soul to Vronsky. Vronsky forgets about his ambitions and
consumed by his infatuation for Anna joins his fate to
hers more and more securely. Karenin, vainly attempting
to bury himself in official duties, feels ever more deeply
his unhappiness and loses his capacity to be satisfied
with his affected grandeur. All three suffer and instinctively await the first external impulse which will break
their unnatural union. This impulse is found in the accidental meeting of Vronsky and Karenin at the latter's home
which Vronsky is visiting to see Anna who is ill and unhappy after they have been parted for a week. Anna has
not seen Vronsky for a week, is missing him and is jealous
of that life he leads which is completely unconnected with
her and which she cannot understand.

[Quotation omitted.]

The passion in Vronsky's feelings for Anna begins to
cool but his moral union with her is intensified. They
both feel the need for a full union. Karenin, thinking
that he should be angry with Anna for breaking one of his
conditions - of receiving her lover in his house - is
actually pleased at the event as it gives him the opportunity to finish with her, and he uses it as the excuse
for a separation. In the repulsively accurate scene
when Karenin tells Anna of his decision, both of them
feel profoundly their mutual degradation. The cup of
degradation overflows and there is nothing for them but
to part. But when it seems that the final step has been

taken the situation unexpectedly changes completely.
Karenin has already handed over the affair to a solicitor
and has gone to Moscow, intending never to return to his
wife, when everything is overturned. Anna lies at death's
door with puerperal fever, and is calling for her husband
and begging forgiveness.

The scene between Vronsky, Karenin and Anna when she is
lying in bed in delirium is possibly the finest in the
whole novel. But it is so unexpected and the idea behind
it so profound and intense that it has aroused confusion
among the critics. No one can be indifferent towards this
scene; everyone instinctively feels that here is something
much out of the ordinary and experiences the strong sensation of sublimity and spiritual emotion. But it is precisely because we so unexpectedly see here the very best,
the most valuable movements of the human heart, so rare in
their sublimity, and they move us all so much that they
consequently cannot satisfy the abstract demands of everyone's reason. And this is quite understandable.

All of us, whether we are religious people or not, talk
a lot about Christianity and about the value of the human
being, yet in the depths of our souls we are all material-
ists. The animal side of our natures is still too strong
and although we use idealistic terminology like money
pressed into the service of our daily requirements, in the
depths of our souls we cannot give our ideals a definite
meaning and we do not believe in their final victory over
the negative side of human nature. And so when we come
across this quite unique example in our experience of the
triumph of good over evil we are struck by it but stand
uncomprehending and unbelieving, feeling a little ill at
ease. We are ill at ease because of its inconsistency
with what we are accustomed to see every day and all
around us.

So is it here. Up to this point we have followed step
by step with involuntary sympathy the appearance and
growth in Anna of love for Vronsky and a simultaneous
hatred for her husband. And suddenly we see Anna's eyes
looking at her husband with such a plaintive and rapturous
tenderness of which we did not know she was capable; suddenly we see her taking her husband's balding head in her
arms and with defiant pride raising her eyes which glitter
with expression. Although we are touched and moved we
still say it is impossible. We are used to seeing Karenin
as a callous, hard, heartless man; we consequently feel
antipathy, disgust and repugnance towards him. And suddenly we see him full of the joyful feeling of love, with
forgiveness for his enemies, and we see him sobbing from
this new higher happiness of the soul which he had not

experienced before. We unexpectedly but quite clearly
hear Karenin's quiet voice, full of feeling, telling Vronsky that the happiness of forgiving has shown him his duty
and that although his name has been dragged through the
mud and he has been made the laughing stock of society he
will not desert Anna and will not reproach his enemy. We
are touched by Karenin's tears; the expression in his
eyes, which before had been so stubbornly cold and dull,
and are now so bright from a deep and complete peace of
mind, creates a deep and serious response in us. We are
deeply touched, yet this so contradicts our accustomed
feeling that we cannot immediately believe, cannot immediately comprehend. It appears that the author has forcibly
given his characters feelings which are quite unsuitable
to them and inconsistent with their characters as we know
them.

Actually all of this is the most profound truth, a
truth without which it would not be worth man's while
staying in the world. If he cannot, albeit late in the
day, albeit just for a moment, elevate himself to the
heights of real goodness from where he may look with firm
and complete faith, his daily slavery to the instincts of
his sensual nature and to that pitiful compromise which we
call worldly morality would make life too unbearably insignificant. And if Karenin or Anna or anyone else is
incapable of remaining on that eminence for ever, it none
the less exists, and its presence even for the minutest
period of time, and even if in just one person, gives us
all absolute criteria and an absolute aim.

If the story of Anna is followed attentively up to this
crucial crisis it will appear that her instinctive feeling
that her husband is in the right - that special right
which depends neither on his faults nor on his qualities,
neither on his character nor even on his attitude to Anna,
the right that consists in the fact that he is a human
being, of what type it does not matter, but who has placed
in her care *without hope of return* both his honour and his
peace of mind, that right which Anna cannot understand yet
accepts - will never desert her.

It had already been expressed long ago in that vague
feeling of guilt which Anna felt and the responsibility
for which she had transferred to Vronsky but which had
issued from herself. It manifests itself in that lively
ability to lie and that assumed naturalness in which she
instinctively clothes herself in order successfully to
deceive her husband. The recognition of the fact that her
husband, as a husband, was in the right is said loud
enough for us to hear during her meeting at the dacha with
Vronsky before the race when she recalls her husband 'with

all the details of his figure, his way of speaking, and
reproaching him for everything she could find wrong about
him, not even forgiving him for that terrible fault *of
which she was guilty before him*'. But the voice of this
recognition speaks loudest of all in Anna when she feels
annoyed at her husband's patience and admits to herself
and even to Vronsky that if her husband were to kill her
or them both then she would bear it without opposition
and would forgive him everything. 'Oh,' said Anna, 'had I
been in his place I should have killed and torn that wife
of mine to pieces long ago - that's the way I'm made.'
And precisely for the fact that her husband has not killed
her and has not exercised that right which he had, according to Anna, but had on the contrary addressed her as 'ma
chère Anna' - for this she hates him all the more. She
hates him all the more because she feels guilty before
him, because he did not behave towards her according to
that right which she thinks he had, that he is in the
right before her in another, better, way which she could
not take away from him. While she was in good health her
passion for Vronsky ruled everything she did and prevented
her obeying the indistinct voice of that instinctive conscience. But when she is dying and her body lies weak her
soul softens at the sight of death and that voice, formerly indefinite, comes out of its depths and speaks with
such force and beauty that she transfers these qualities
to her husband whom she formerly so hated, and in those
moments she loves him with a deep and pure love which can
only occur in an ideal impulse as death approaches. And
the light from this pure impulse fills Karenin's formerly
dry and long embittered heart and he kneels before her and
sobs like a child feeling the unexpected softening of his
heart and 'the very same thing which had been the cause of
his sufferings now became the source of his inner joy -
what had appeared insoluble when he condemned, reproached
and hated became simple and easy when he forgave and
loved'.
  The feeling which raises Anna and Karenin to such
heights must sink Vronsky to the bottom. The condition of
a man suddenly removed from his false pedestal, having the
last piece of ground removed from beneath his feet, suffering intensely and near to mental derangement and suicide, is shown by Count Tolstoy in inimitable fashion.
  But to remain for ever on such a moral peak is not possible for human beings. Even if he wishes so to do with
all his heart other things will interfere and forcibly
remove him. Anna is the first to leave. As soon as the
softening in her character brought about by the proximity
of death has passed, all her former feelings return and

she again begins to want Vronsky, again begins to be burdened by her husband, to fear and hate him. Why do all
these things return to her? Is it because she is naturally less of a spiritual person than anyone else? Is it
because once this charming creature has returned again to
the living it becomes impossible to remove her again from
it?

But Karenin is equally incapable of remaining for long
on the peak of exclusively spiritual feeling. He passes
hours and days standing over a helpless and strange baby,
and the feeling of sympathy and love for this desolate and
weak little girl as he looks at her sleeping face at first
fills his heart with a world he did not know before. He
does not know that that cruel force has gathered outside
and has long been standing at the ready to destroy his
new-found happiness against his will, without pity, with
spite and laughter. Betsy and the whole of high society
regard his position differently. They have no interest
in the soul, in forgiveness or spiritual happiness; they
feel an unrestrained joy at this new entertainment for
their idle attention, at the sight of what appears to
them the ultimate *ridicule* - a minister of state caressing
in his arms a child which he knows his wife has had by her
lover. And they burst into the sanctuary of a husband who
forgives such insults, commit outrages upon him and destroy him. As they said to Vronsky earlier so now they
say to the deceived husband: You are ours and you must not
aspire to love, to forgive and to ascend to spiritual
heights unknown to us.

But such is the life-giving force of real feeling in
this unhappy man that even the decadent spirit of those
around him does not immediately emerge victorious. It
struggles for a long time and Karenin is prepared in the
fulness of his love to accept all the shame and degradation of a divorce simply to give Anna her freedom. Anna
understands this and values it, however repellent to her
this magnanimous man has become, but she turns down a
divorce point-blank. She does not stay with her husband,
however. The noble Betsy brings her and Vronsky together
and in the ecstasy of their reunion, made even more so by
the horror of their position, they forget everything else
and leave for the place where they think this passionate
oblivion will last for ever.

70.   STRAKHOV, REVIEW, 'RUSSIA'

1883

(See also headnote to No. 33.)   The following passage is taken from Strakhov's View of Current Literature, 'Russia', 1883, no. 1; basically it is a comparison between Turgenev's 'Virgin Soil', Dostoevsky's 'Brothers Karamazov' and Tolstoy's 'Anna Karenina'; all three deal with suicide and despair and are typical of the mood of contemporary educated society, but at least, thinks Strakhov, a solution is offered by the last two, and it lies in religion.

'Anna Karenina' is a work not without its faults but it also possesses some great artistic qualities. First of all its subject matter is so simple and ordinary that many people long thought that it had no interest mainly because they did not think the novel was contemporary or instructive. The novel falls into two parts or onto two levels which are poorly connected on the external plane but which none the less have a strong inner unity. In the foreground we have urban life in the capital and we are told how Anna Karenina falls in love with Vronsky, gives herself to him and leaves her husband; but having lived with Vronsky for a time suffers so much because of her passion that she throws herself under a train. There is also the story of the landowner Levin; we are told how he declares his love, proposes, fasts, marries and has a son. The author's great originality consists in the fact that these ordinary events are given striking meaning and interest by the clarity and depth with which they are described. The novel's main idea, although not shown everywhere with the same skill, comes through extremely clearly; the reader cannot escape an inexpressibly oppressive impression, despite the absence of any melancholy characters and events and the mass of completely idyllic pictures. It is not only Anna who comes to suicide for no clear *external* cause or suffering, but also Levin; Levin, who is successful in everything, who leads such a normal life, feels at the end inclined towards suicide and saves himself from it only through some religious concepts which are suddenly aroused in him when a peasant says that one must remember God and live for the good of one's soul. This is a moralizing novel the introduction to which is provided by 'What do men live by?'.

Anna Karenina lives for her passion. Before it happened she was empty at heart; the life in the capital and at Court in which there is no spiritual nourishment and where all interests are artificial and illusory is depicted with a striking subtlety and clarity. Anna and Vronsky are among the best people in this circle because their natural feelings take precedence over all artificial distractions which form the joys and griefs of their circle. They are completely given over to their love and for Anna it remains to the end the only thing she lives for and which finally kills her. 'Anna Karenina' is one of those rare works where the passion of love is really shown. Despite the fact that love and voluptuousness form the invariable theme of novels and stories, authors are usually satisfied with bringing onto the stage a young couple and describing various meetings and conversations, leaving to the reader's imagination all the emotions and excitement which these meetings and conversations occasion. In 'Anna Karenina' on the other hand the very spiritual process of their passion is accurately described - this is something so new that many critics and readers could not even understand it and expressed their bewilderment in print. Passion is aroused at the first glance with no preparatory conversations about mutual tastes and ideas. In the novels of yore this was to be expected but we have somehow forgotten these old stories. Then the passion grows and the author relates its every phase as clearly and comprehensively as he does the couple's first glance. Then a certain emotion opens out more and more: Anna begins to feel jealous - 'He who is in love will involuntarily become jealous', as Pushkin says in 'Ruslan and Lyudmilla'. The essence of this jealousy and the inner struggle between Anna and Vronsky is related so convincingly and in so much detail that it is terrible to see the inevitable consequence of its development. The unfortunate Anna who has staked everything on her passion must inevitably burn in its flames. When she feels that the only blessing in her life has betrayed her she summons death. She cannot wait for the final cooling or for Vronsky's unfaithfulness; she dies not from insults or unhappiness but from her own love. It is a moving and bitter story and if the author had not been so pitiless to his heroes, if he could have betrayed his incorruptible veracity, then he would have forced us to weep bitter tears over the unfortunate woman who perishes from an irrevocable devotion to her emotion. But the author has taken things further. In subtle but utterly clear details he has shown us the *impurity* of her passion which cannot be subdued by any higher ethic or controlled by any subordination.

Furthermore, within both Anna and her husband during moments of shock or illness there occur conscious rays of spirituality (remember only Anna when she is ill after childbirth or Karenin when he bids Vronsky farewell), rays which are quickly extinguished in the mire of feelings and thoughts which are hostile to them. Only Vronsky remains completely *carnal* from beginning to end.

Thus we are shown with terrifying truth this world full of blindness and darkness. As a contrast to it there is the world of Levin, a world obviously brighter. Levin is a sincere and simple man with many faults but who has a pure heart. Karenin and Vronsky are typical of the bureaucrat and the officer while Levin is typical of the landowner. In fact there are three Levins. The eldest, by a different father, is Koznyshev; he is a Slavophile; the second, Nikolay, is a Nihilist; the third, Konstantin, the hero of the novel, is seen simply, as it were, as a Russian without any set ideas. This contrast is very instructive; it shows us examples of the main intellectual trends in society, a picture of our intellectual ferment. The best representative of this ferment and who has all the sympathy of the author is Konstantin Levin, eternally reflecting upon general questions and not finding any convincing solutions. Of course this tendency for philosophizing is a purely Russian phenomenon and all contemporary literature bears witness without exception that never was such philosophizing so common as it is today.

The novel, though, depicts Levin's life more than his philosophizing, even the full flower of his life, and the author wants particularly to show us how Levin's thoughts are occasioned by the events of his life and the unexpressed feelings of his heart. Evidently he has a completely successful life; Levin is self-sufficient, he is young, strong, he enjoys hunting and is devoted to his study of agriculture, he marries the girl he loves and becomes the happy father of a family. The pictures of all these pleasures and joys belong to the best and truly remarkable pages in the novel. One wonders whence his mournful thoughts come and especially those of suicide. If we look closely we feel the emptiness of his life and we begin to understand Levin's spiritual hunger. The author brings Levin into contact with various people and events and with his amazing clarity shows on every page how Levin could feel at ease with none of them. He is terribly alone, alone on account of his sensitivity, his uprightness and sincerity, his refusal to make any compromises and rejection of everything false. Consequently the best of all the characters in the novel is the least capable of coming to terms with the life around him. He rejects it and this rejection is all the stronger because it happens without catalyst and involuntarily; Levin denounces nothing, attacks nothing - he simply puts distance between himself and what he finds distasteful. At the end of the novel the author describes the enthusiasm in society during the war between the Turks and the Serbs; Levin has no part in this and buries himself among the ordinary people who remain unmoved by it although it affects every corner of their lives. At one time this episode caused some stir and even the journal which was printing 'Anna Karenina' refused to publish this section. But the novel contains some even more cheerless pages. Despite the extreme restraint of Tolstoy's methods, never has Russian life been described in so melancholy a light. Only the life of the peasants, which is right in the background and only rarely appears clearly, ever glows with the calm, clear light of life and it is only into this world that Levin wishes to merge. He feels, though, that he cannot.

What is there left for Levin to do? What is there left for any man to do who has become so cruelly alienated from the life around him? All that remains is himself, his own personal life. But such a life is always the plaything of fate. When his brother Nikolay lies fatally ill, when his wife is in the torments of childbirth, when thunder rattles the tree beneath which his little son is asleep and in thousands of other less important events, even at the height of his joys and successes, Levin constantly feels that he is in the hands of chance and that the very thread of his life will snap as easily as a cobweb. Thence his despair. If *my* life is the only purpose in being alive and that purpose is so insignificant, so fragile, so obviously unattainable that it can inspire only despair then it can only weigh down upon a man and not inspire him. This is where to look for the origin of Levin's turning to religion.

This is the clear meaning of 'Anna Karenina'. The problem is boldly grasped, the eternal problem of human life, and not simply of contemporary man or contemporary interests.... The whole novel is a picture of the general spiritual chaos which reigns in all social levels except the very lowest.

71.   DUPUY ON 'ANNA KARENINA'

1885

Although less analytical in his approach than de Vogüé
(see No. 87), E. Dupuy (1849-1918) was part and parcel of
the wide interest in Russian literature in France in the
second half of the 1880s. His book, which deals with
Gogol, Turgenev and Tolstoy and is entitled 'Les Grands
Maîtres de la littérature russe au dix-neuvième siècle',
1885, was only the second full-length treatment of Russian
literature to be published in France.

As in 'War and Peace', so in 'Anna Karenina'; Count Tolstoy will be seen just as his own confessions have permitted us to see him. As in 'War and Peace', all his
characters have a little of him in them, and both Vronsky
and Konstantin Levin in turn represent him in some particular aspect just as clearly as Nikolay Rostov, Prince
Andrey, or Pierre. For example, in the conversation where
Count Vronsky proposes to reorganize his estates and takes
as the foundation stone for the new arrangements an
agreement between the peasants and their former landlord,
Count Tolstoy is propounding a theory which he had long
held but which he has since developed further; for he has
arrived, as we shall soon see, at Communism.
     Similarly we shall recognize the ideas of 'What I
Believe' in Levin's resistance to patriotic bravura or, to
use his own words, the unreflecting enthusiasm which
arouses the youth of Russia and pushes one of the novel's
characters, Vronsky, to enlist voluntarily to defend the
cause of the Serbs. In protesting by his abstention and
even in his speech against the Slav committees and conscription, Levin is already applying the doctrine which
Count Tolstoy will later formulate in the maxim: 'Do not
engage in war', and on which he will comment:

     Jesus has shown me that the fifth temptation which
     deprives me of my well-being is the differentiation we
     make between our own countrymen and foreigners. I can-
     not but believe in that; consequently if in a moment of
     forgetfulness I experience a feeling of hostility to-
     wards someone of a different nationality then I cannot
     help recognizing, when I think calmly about it, that
     this feeling is false; I can no longer justify to

myself, as I could earlier, that my own people are
superior to others or that they are less ignorant,
cruel or barbaric; I cannot refrain at the first
opportunity of being more affable towards a foreigner
than to a fellow-countryman.

If Vronsky behaves differently from Levin, it is not because Tolstoy wishes to contrast the actions of the one
with the opinions of the other. In effect Vronsky enlists not through conviction but through despair; he
leaves in the attempt to forget, amid the excitement or,
as Pascal wrote, the 'divertissements' of a soldier's
life, the effects of the inner drama which had disturbed
his being to the core and which by a fatal, albeit unexpected, conclusion has just bespattered him with blood.

'Anna Karenina' is the story of an adulterous affair
which ends in suicide. Is this suicide in the author's
view a moral judgment? If it is then it would be quite
barbaric, a sort of divine judgment such as an author in
the Middle Ages might have imagined; but Tolstoy seems to
have wished to refute in advance such a vulgar interpretation of his tale. In the novel there are other illicit
love affairs and the completely immoral liaison between
Princess Betsy and her lover is carried on with impunity.
On the other hand the passion which unites Anna and Vronsky is something sincere, profound, almost austere, despite the irregularity of their actions. The love between
the couple is illicit but it is also deep; besides, the
more sympathy with which the author depicts them the more
forcibly he is able to draw the moral he desires from
their inner torment. All the ideas behind and the interest in the novel lie in this. What anguish this union, so
desired, brings to the guilty woman! What deep sorrows,
what vulgar discomforts, what profound humiliations and
what prosaic tedium arise from their false situation and
which render it in the end so hateful and so painful that
it must be escaped, in a moment of despair, by an act of
madness!

Yet never did conditions so well unite to facilitate
this union outside the law. Vronsky's rank is too elevated for him to worry about public opinion; he makes a sort
of point of honour in defying it and he installs his mistress in his luxurious home as if she were his legal wife;
without much apparent difficulty he gains the respect of
his family and friends for this liaison. For her part
Anna loves Vronsky absolutely and the consciousness of the
sacrifices she has made, instead of cooling her ardour, in
fact excite her. She only asks in exchange from her lover
to be loved by him; she has made it a point of honour on

her part to refuse the advantages of the divorce which her husband Alexey at first offers in that he would declare himself the guilty party. She refuses from a double feeling of delicacy; she does not wish to add this gratuitous insult to the guilt she feels before this unsympathetic but honest man, and above all she does not want a suspicion of calculation to cast its shadow over the feelings she has avowed to the count.

A divorce, furthermore, would overcome many of the equivocal feelings which create misunderstanding and many of the subtleties of conduct which lead only to argument. Vronsky desires the divorce with all the strength of his generous pride; Anna avoids it with all the jealous anxiety of a naturally noble woman wishing to preserve the last remnants of her dignity which the shock of passion has thrown down and shattered like an expensive vase. This antagonism creates a source of secret bitterness between the two lovers. There are other latent troubles. From her marriage Anna has a son from whom she is separated but whom she adores, a son the slightest remembrance of whom causes her body to thrill in the same way as it did before motherhood. As a result of her love for Vronsky she has a daughter. By a strange paradox she does not love the daughter she has by the man she loves; she thinks of her daughter as somehow occupying a place usurped, of demanding from her all her maternal care, in being deprived of which, it appears to her, her son is suffering so much. If as a mother she has her fits of jealousy, unfounded but touching, as a woman she has other fears whose absurdity does not prevent them from being extremely distressing. She passes her time and eats her heart out in divining her lover's attitude to her. She knows that he has renounced for her the most brilliant of futures; she fears she cannot fill his pointless existence; she takes every attempt of his to return to some activity or to any distraction as proof that he is becoming weary of her, as evidence that he is bored, or as some sign of regret.

Vronsky, who has given himself to her completely without wanting anything in return, begins to suffer from this distrust; the more it shows itself the more he resorts to deception and feelings of spite. Here the nobility of character which attaches him to his mistress and which has made it easy for him to brave all for her turns against the unfortunate woman and forces him to resist the efforts she makes to possess him the more completely. One can imagine where this incessant struggle will end. With every day the angles become more acute, the feelings less secure, and the actions more annoying; these two beings

who set out from the bright and carefree heights of love
have descended, without being aware of it, to the sombre
and suffocating regions of hate. This result of the inevitable decay of passion is rendered not less cruel but
more evident by a completely external circumstance. The
divorce which Karenin had once offered is now refused when
his wife, weary from so much suffering, at last decides to
ask for it. It is here that the future author of 'What I
Believe' appears with his precise theory of the immorality
of divorce. The group of mystics, to which the deserted
husband had been led by his need for consolation of a
religious nature, declares through the mouth of Countess
Lidia Ivanovna that Karenin should not accede to his wife's
wishes and grant her her freedom, because if he did he
would himself fall into a state of mortal sin.

From the day when they are told of this refusal Anna
and Vronsky speed, in spite of themselves, towards a
separation. In fearing it, Anna hastens it. Vronsky is
irritated by her ever-increasing restlessness and faced
with what appears to him as plain ingratitude, he affects
an indifference which he does not feel; arguments, once
rare, become more frequent and turn into quarrels; this
daily conflict ends in an explosion followed by a rupture.

Vronsky leaves her. He goes to his mother, the natural
enemy of his mistress. Left alone Anna feels torn apart
in every fibre of her body; he must return to her; she
will fall at his feet; she will humiliate herself like a
naughty child. She writes to him to return, but she has
not the strength to wait for him; she hurries to meet him
and stopping at an intermediate station she informs him by
telegram that she is coming. The train arrives; only a
valet of the count appears, bearing a note. Vronsky drily
announces he is returning and Anna interprets the tone of
the letter as further proof of the death of a love which
in her alone has deepened with time and possession. She
tells herself that she has no more reason to live and a
series of fatal circumstances unite at this critical
moment to throw her to her death. She wishes to escape
the inquisitive looks of the people at the station who
had been struck by her strange behaviour and she descends
to the lines. She recalls the terrible accident when a
railway worker had been crushed before her eyes in Moscow
on the very day of her first meeting with Vronsky; a sort
of reflex action occurs in her brain; a goods train approaches; she walks in front of it.

[Quotation of Anna's death omitted.]

Certainly when one reads this brutal denouement and

recalls the epigraph to the novel: 'Vengeance is mine, saith the Lord' one is tempted to interpret Christ's words in their Judaic sense. This would be, however, a gross error. It is quite certain that this sudden and tragic end is meant, in the novelist's eyes, to be Anna's deliverance; it is out of pity for her that he has granted her the favour of death. Death alone is capable of terminating the torment of this soul, and the torment had started with the sin. Here is the true punishment for an illicit love; all illusion which exalted the senses as long as they resided in 'love's shadow', as one of Shakespeare's characters expressed it, disappears as soon as one is sated of love itself.

[Quotation of Anna's dream of two husbands omitted.]

This is the real moral sanction. What penetrating psychology! What an admirable commentary and what a powerful interpretation of the *surgit amari aliquid*! And it is not only her punishment as a wife that Tolstoy has described but also that of her as a mother, when separation, so long postponed by the husband himself, becomes indispensable to the two lovers who have returned from the jaws of death, returned more morbidly and more deeply in love with each other than before.

At the beginning of the separation Anna became accustomed to thinking that it was her duty to renounce everything which had beforehand made her happy and to leave with her husband as compensation, such as it was, all the elements of their past happiness which she has exchanged for that of a different kind. 'I renounce everything I love, everything I most value in the world - my son and my reputation.' She manages for a certain time to push into the background and to deceive her maternal instincts and to substitute for her love for her son a continuous and tender care for her daughter by Vronsky. But suddenly Vronsky is obliged to return from abroad where the two lovers have been living together; he arrives with Anna in St Petersburg; the mother finds herself again near the house where her son is living; she wishes to enter, to see him again; she asks permission, but it is coldly refused; she decides that she must go to her husband's home, whatever the cost, and visit her son; she bribes the servants.

[Quotation of Anna's secret visit to her son omitted.]

It is in these scenes, in these moral analyses, that one must look for the sense of and the idea behind 'Anna

Karenina'. There is also a continuous lesson concerning
the intentions, which it would be easy to verify with
'What I Believe' to hand, of the husband, the statesman
Karenin. He is punished for having sacrificed everything
to ambition, even the love and care for the woman he had
taken for his wife. He does not fight a duel with Vronsky because he lacks the courage, but above all because
his religion has made it a duty for him not to kill a
fellow human being. He hates his errant wife up to the
point of wishing even for her death and he thinks himself
deceived when he finds her alive after the childbirth
which she had feared so much; but he gives in during her
delirium and at the words of repentance which she utters
at that moment she believes to be her last; he forgives
her. From the day when he tastes the divine sweetness of
mercy he is another man; he finds the meaning of life;
from then on he will apply Christ's doctrine.

> 'I offer my other cheek to him who smites me; I give my
> last vestment to him who robs me; I ask from God only
> that He allows me to keep the joy of forgiving.'
> Karenin stood up, his voice choking, sobbing. Vronsky
> stood up too and with bowed head looked up at Karenin
> without saying a word. 'He was incapable of under-
> standing feelings of this nature, but he none the less
> realized that they were somehow superior, and irrecon-
> cilable with a vulgar conception of life.

72. BARINE ON 'ANNA KARENINA' AS AUTOBIOGRAPHY

1885

From an article entitled Count Leo Tolstoy: concerning
'Anna Karenina' by Arvède Barine, 'Revue Bleue', 5 December 1885.

Tolstoy wrote 'Anna Karenina' when he was in the prime of
life and at the height of his creative powers. None the
less the second half of the novel seems uncertain and confused, which was something which surprised his friends
when the book appeared in Russia. Turgenev found the
second half tedious and thought it a great pity. The

novel was completed during the approach and clearly under
the influence of that great moral crisis after which Tolstoy thought he had found spiritual peace but which was for
him nothing but the onset of madness. His preoccupation
with the problems to the solution of which he felt his life
devoted became too strong and too pressing for him to iso-
late himself from them in favour of fictional characters.
Under the pretext of telling us of the adventures of Levin
and Anna Karenina he was actually unburdening himself of
his own ideas, his doubts and worries. The second volume
thus became a kind of platform where his characters discuss those great questions which exercise the mind of an
educated and upper-class subject of the Russian emperor.
Consequently what takes place in the story shows that the
spiritual history of one of the heroes is composed, in all
important respects, of the author's personal reminiscences.
When one reads 'Anna Karenina' and bears this in mind the
story takes on a completely different aspect. It is not
only the fictional characters who speak; it is also the
great and unhappy Tolstoy who places his ravaged soul
naked before us.

73. BULGAKOV ON 'ANNA KARENINA' AND TOLSTOY'S VIEW OF
MARRIAGE

1886

F.I. Bulgakov (1852-1908) was a leading editor, art critic
and journalist and served for a short period as one of the
censors dealing with translations into Russian of foreign
literature. These comments are taken from his 'Count L.N.
Tolstoy and Criticism of his Works both Russian and
Foreign' of 1886.

It is said that 'Anna Karenina' was begun quite accident-
ally. The story is that one of Tolstoy's relations was
staying at Yasnaya Polyana and she was reading the fifth
volume of the works of Pushkin. The count somehow picked
the book up and opened it; he quickly read the first line
('The guests were arriving at the dacha...') and involuntarily carried on reading. Then someone came into the
drawing-room. 'Delightful,' said Tolstoy, 'that's how one

ought to start a story. Pushkin gets down to things
straight away. Another author would have described the
guests, the rooms, but he enters right into the action...'
     When he had finished reading aloud the whole section,
Tolstoy went to his study and immediately wrote: 'Everything was in disorder in the Oblonsky household.' The
sentence which actually begins 'Anna Karenina' was added
later but the general story the novel tells had already
been thought out. It is said that it is based on an
actual event; the author had seen the mutilated body of a
woman who had thrown herself under a train.
     However that may be, there is at least no doubt that
'Anna Karenina' describes more than anything the state of
mind of the author himself. It is Tolstoy, with his
search for the meaning and truth of life, who is drawn in
the figure of Konstantin Levin. At first Levin, just like
Pierre Bezukhov, leads an utterly selfish life - he is
idle, tiresome and artificial. Then, after his marriage,
there begins a new period of joyfully productive family
life. Once he has tasted these joys, however, Levin soon
comes to the view that they too are just as ephemeral,
incidental and unstable as everything else connected with
the personal life. He is filled with despair and torment
until he comprehends the truth of the words of his servant
Fyodor that one must 'live for one's soul' and 'remember
God'.
     Such a conception of the meaning of life was already
apparent in the author's own spiritual development, in
that fundamental change in him which is fully explained
in his latest works. Having lost all faith in the wisdom
of the people of his own class, he began to seek answers
to the questions which tormented him about the secret of
life in the teachings of Christ and in the fact that 'the
life of people uncorrupted by wealth is ruled by these
teachings'. Only then did it become clear to him that
man is not a haphazard conglomeration of elements, that
life is not evil, and that in life there is a deep meaning
which is understood by the vast majority of humanity who
are not called upon 'to pass their lives in idle amusement
living off the labour of others, but to create life'.
     Before this conversion Tolstoy saw all the life around
him as cheerless and gloomy in its emptiness and falsity
and as a real evil from which one should hasten away. In
just this way the life of the intellectual circles in
Russia is depicted in 'Anna Karenina' and the unstable and
precarious moral bases of this life are personified. In
this respect the story of Anna's love for Vronsky is particularly edifying.
     It would be difficult to find more interesting heroes.

Anna is beautiful, vivacious, happy, good, energetic and
captivating; Vronsky possesses the nobility of soul and
the good breeding of the highest society; he is able to
brave the opinions of the world. For her part Anna loves
Vronsky with a passion which knows no bounds. Their only
obstacle is Karenin. But he is unable to arouse much
sympathy. His main concern lies in observing the normal
conventions. All the circumstances in which Vronsky becomes attached to Anna are such that it would apparently
never occur to anyone that anything but happiness would
come from their liaison. Everything is seemingly in their
favour.

  But then the morality lying behind the unhappy ending
begins to act more and more irresistibly. No sooner has
Anna given herself completely to Vronsky than her life
begins to fill with torment. In the first place she has to
carry on a battle with herself in order to betray her husband; second, which she finds more distressing, is the
fact that she realizes Karenin will endure it. After the
steeplechase when Vronsky falls from his horse Anna has
not the strength to control herself and despite all her
husband's attempts somehow to conceal her relations with
Vronsky in a fitting matter she firmly says to him: 'No,
you are not mistaken, you are not mistaken. I was horrified and I could not conceal it. I listen to you but I
think of him. I love him. I am his mistress and I cannot
bear it. I am frightened; I hate you... Do with me what
you will.'
  Such a confession could only complicate the situation
for Anna and Vronsky. Karenin announces that he will continue to pretend he knows nothing so long as society
remains ignorant and no shame is attached to his name.
He requests Anna not to receive Vronsky in their home.
Then Anna lies at death's door during childbirth. Vronsky
tries vainly to shoot himself in despair; Anna recovers
and she and Vronsky leave for Italy, exhausted by the falsity of their position. There, of course, they are free.
But they are accustomed to the carefree life of high society and their solitude becomes clearly burdensome and
forces them to return to Petersburg. Once there they are
forced to bid farewell to their peace of mind. Various
insults which Anna has to suffer drive them once again
from the capital and they settle on one of Vronsky's
estates.
  No sacrifice on Anna's part can cool her ardour. On
the contrary her passion flares even more brightly. She
is proud she has refused the convenience offered by a divorce in which her husband was prepared to declare himself
the guilty party. She does not want a divorce for two

reasons. In the first place in the event of a divorce new
insults would be added to everything in which she felt
herself guilty before Karenin. Second, and more importantly, Anna does not want to give the slightest occasion
to any shadow of suspicion of calculation falling over
her feelings for Vronsky. For his part Vronsky strives
for a divorce with all the strength of his pride. This
difference of opinion is one of the sources of misunderstanding between them.

Furthermore, when they are living apart from society
all the falsity of a situation which follows from a passion unbridled by any moral boundaries is hidden from
them. Feeling that her only happiness in the world lies
in her love for Vronsky, Anna takes the temperature of
this love every day. She becomes jealous. Because she
lacks any activity these ordeals add to her already bitter
suffering. She knows that Vronsky has forsaken a brilliant career for her and she cannot stop feeling anxious
about whether she can fill his life. His every attempt
to engage in any business matter or to amuse himself elsewhere she takes as a sign of boredom, regret about their
liaison, or disappointment. Vronsky, who is utterly devoted to her, is hurt by these suspicions and in order not
to succumb completely to this jealous tyranny he attempts
to contradict them from time to time.

Thus the situation develops to the point that while
not ceasing to love one another they become mutually hostile. Every day unpleasant incidents occur, bitter complaints, heated explanations. From the light and carefree peaks of love they both descend into the suffocating
shadows of animosity. The situation is further complicated by Karenin's refusal at this stage to grant Anna a
divorce when she overcomes her pride and asks for one herself.

Once the refusal has been received Anna's and Vronsky's
love, albeit unnoticed by themselves, moves towards its
final collapse. Fearing such a finale, Anna hastens its
approach.

Vronsky for his part cannot bear these ever-
increasing anxieties. He leaves for his mother's with
distressing thoughts about Anna. Anna writes to him, but
not having the strength to wait for his reply sets off to
see him and then sends him a telegram from a station. A
train approaches, but Vronsky does not appear. A servant
of his gives her a message from Vronsky in which he replies coolly that he is coming back. She interprets the
tone of his words as further proof of the death of their
love. Life no longer holds any attraction for her. A
whole succession of accidents all combine at this decisive

moment and Anna hurls herself beneath a train.

Anna, who gave herself over completely to an uncontrollable passion, suffers more than simply the torments of an unhappy woman. Tolstoy, with supreme mastery, depicts her torments as a mother too. From her marriage to Karenin she has a son. She is separated from him. From her union with Vronsky there is a daughter. By some strange anomaly she does not love this daughter. She thinks the daughter has taken her away from her son, has usurped his place, and demanded all the maternal affection her son lacks. As a mother Anna is torn by jealousy. When separation from her husband becomes inevitable Anna, it is true, decides at first that she must give up everything which had formerly brought her happiness and as a sort of consolation to her husband leaves him her son. She manages to subdue for a time her maternal instincts and to replace the tenderness she feels for her son by affection for her daughter. But once she has returned to Petersburg from abroad the mother awakes in her again with renewed force and this increases her unhappiness even more.

The denouement of the novel (and its epigraph 'Vengeance is mine, I shall repay') has led certain critics to regard her suicide as a kind of punishment sent from above for her unfaithfulness to her husband. Such an explanation does not at all recommend itself to the rather more perceptive critic. It would seem that Tolstoy has specifically removed the possibility of such an interpretation. There are other cases of adultery in the novel. Princess Betsy and her lovers escape punishment for their dissolute behaviour. Stiva Oblonsky also occupies himself in such matters. What is more, all these people even flourish and are quite without a care. The point is that the illicit passion which unites Anna and Vronsky is sincere, profound and one might even say pure in its sincerity and selflessness - as far that is as a love may be called pure which knows no moral boundaries.

And how the poor woman suffers from her illicit union! What profound grief! So many unpleasantnesses, so many insults, and so much unbearable unhappiness result from the false position she is in, and this position finally becomes so tormenting that out of pity for her rather than from any malice one is forced to wish that she might be released from her suffering. In deciding to kill herself while in the depths of despair which cloud her reason she is punishing not herself but Vronsky, 'repaying him' for the fact that his coldness towards her has removed the meaning from her life, a meaning which had consisted in her passionate love.

The love of Kitty and Levin is the complete antithesis

of that of Anna and Vronsky. It is interesting that here
too Tolstoy's ideas about the arbitrary nature of chance
which can change men's lives stands out in all its force.
The love of Anna and Vronsky which began under such pro-
pitious circumstances has a deeply unhappy outcome. By
contrast the relationship between Kitty and Levin begins
unsuccessfully but ends in complete happiness.

Levin falls in love with Kitty and his attempt to marry
her has no success initially for at the time Vronsky is
courting her. When Vronsky ceases to frequent the Shcherbatsky household (much to Kitty's mother's regret as she
is apparently pleased at the prospect of such a wealthy
son-in-law) Kitty is left alone. She is tormented by
shame because of her refusal to Levin to whom she is
favourably disposed. Levin for his part finds it difficult to forget all thoughts of marriage.

[Quotation omitted.]

He buries himself in his country estates and devotes
himself to various attempts to improve their management
in the name of the general good. He tells himself that
he will not give Kitty a thought, while Kitty swears that
she will not degrade herself by feeling sorry over the
loss of such a good man.

None the less they both find it possible to convince
themselves that they love eath other and can be happy
together. Tolstoy describes with love how this marriage
comes about, the ecstasy this eternally philosophizing
Levin experiences at the thought that Kitty is to be his
wife and of all the bright joys their marriage will bring
to his life. In the depiction of this fully legitimate
love there is nothing deliberate or preconceived. The
family happiness of Kitty and Levin is described with the
same impartiality that was used to depict the illicit love
of Anna for Vronsky. Their happiness is no pure Arcadian
idyll. Tolstoy does not hide the misunderstandings and
arguments which arise when two people of differing characters live together.

[Quotation omitted.]

Nor does he refrain from describing all the smallest
details but this does not prevent his drawing a remarkably
attractive picture of a very happy family, the most important event in whose life is the birth of a child. But
despite all the happiness, all the charm and all the joys
of family life, Levin can find no satisfaction in his
existence. In his depiction of Levin's state of mind

Tolstoy is surveying the contemporary life of the Russian
intelligentsia in the seventies from all its various aspects, in all its complexities and with all the worries,
ideas and malice of the day. Nothing succeeds in deceiving
the sincere and upright Levin. Our public figures, so concerned with the general good, seem to Levin only sterile
philosophizers who have embraced the general good not
from their hearts but from their minds. Our Populists
look upon the ordinary people as something different from
everyone else, even their antithesis. Political and economic ideas which promise general wealth in place of poverty and the unison and identity of interests in place of
enmity appear easily realizable only on paper.

Levin feels himself completely alien to the aspirations
of his own circle. Everything around him seems to be
built upon sand, brittle, unstable and ephemeral. Everywhere there are irreconcilable contrasts and parties
attacking one another. Everywhere there is artificiality,
falsity and moral disorder. There is nothing to side with
and nothing to rely upon which would enable one to consider one's life useful either to oneself or to others.
Levin is consequently dubious about any social activity
and considers all work for society to be unnecessary. To
love humanity at large and to despise its parts is granted
only to philosophers who are content with their own theories and systems. But Levin belongs specifically to that
type of person who has no ready-made theories, who lives
by the heart and obeys only the promptings of the spirit.
The current problems which concern the Russian intelligentsia neither concern him nor inspire him to action.
All of them are somehow inessential, artificial and exaggerated for the idle amusement of the crowd. American
friends replace heterodoxies. The interests of society
are transferred from the famine in Samara to exhibitions.
Then the Slavophile question becomes the fashionable pastime. For Levin the current concerns, when hundreds of
people were rushing off to Serbia, and where Vronsky went
himself to forget his grief, mean only that 'in a nation
of eighty millions you will find not hundreds but tens of
thousands of people who find they have no place in society
and are quite recklessly prepared to join Pugachov's gang
or leave for Serbia...'. And this same disillusion was
experienced by the author himself in the mid-seventies.

[Quotation omitted.]

Tolstoy, just as Levin, was deeply struck by a feeling
of horror at the mystery, proximity and inevitability of
death as it overcame his brother. His whole world

appeared to him then but 'a small mould which had grown on
a tiny planet'. All thoughts and actions seemed but
grains of sand. Under the weight of such thoughts he
tried to do anything which would prevent thoughts of
death. But then he began to feel horror not so much of
death but of life and the fact that he had not the slightest idea whence it came, why and what it was for.

[Quotation omitted.]

And the happy family man, the healthy and strong Levin,
just like Tolstoy himself, came several times so close to
suicide that he had to hide rope away lest he hanged himself with it and was afraid to go out with a gun in case
he shot himself.
    In general the whole story of the spiritual hunger
experienced by Levin is quite similar, in places almost
identical, with that which Tolstoy describes in his confessions which he wrote in 1879. Both Levin and the
author of 'Anna Karenina' after much tormented searching
found the answers to their questions about the meaning of
life in a belief in God and Good which are man's only purpose in the world. Armed with this faith Levin dreamed of
achieving that which was possible to everyone, to the millions of different people, wise men and fools, children
and old men, everyone - peasants, beggars, Kitty, tsars -
to understand without a doubt the one important thing and
to embrace the life of the soul for which alone it is
worth living and which alone is of any value.

[Omitted: Tolstoy's story of his vision of death.]

    Tolstoy and Levin were both illuminated by the light of
faith and found in it the source of spiritual peace and
the real meaning of life. The sphinx of life which had
for so long sat across the author's path was despatched
and lost all its power. Tolstoy had tried to unravel its
treacherous questions and the result of his solution is
apparent in his latest works.

74. UNSIGNED NOTICE, 'CRITIC' (NEW YORK)

10 April 1886

The world has lately waked up to the knowledge that Russia
is not only the land of nihilism but that it is also the
land of great novelists. Everybody knows and loves
Tourgueneff; but Tourgueneff is no more the only Russian
novelist than one swallow makes a summer. Hitherto people
have identified the literary aspiration of the great Muscovite race with the one figure of this celebrated exile:
Tourgueneff was Russia, and in him alone Russia lived and
moved and had its being. So, for generations, Voltaire
was France, Goethe was Germany, England was Shakspeare.
Suddenly new names are whispered; new heads emerge from
the dim Muscovite horizons; as from the background of one
of Correggio's ceilings a far-withdrawn perspective has
suddenly become peopled with nebulous forms which take
shape and life and grace, and grow in beauty and distinctness till the ceiling becomes an overshadowing canvas
crowded with intelligence and motion. Thus Russia has
suddenly become alive. Ossianic dimness - the difficulties of a most difficult language - have faded gradually
away, and in their stead have come clearness, definiteness
of view, and knowledge: Russia reveals itself as no less a
wonderland than the Arabia of the Khalifs did to the cru-
saders.
    Count L. Tolstoi is the last of these literary revela-
tions: a man of whom nobody had heard except through the
medium of a garbled French translation; a man of whom
nobody knew that he had written anything except perhaps
spellers and readers. Now, it seems he has been the
writer of copious and prolix romances - 'Infancy',
'Adolescence', 'Youth', 'The Cossacks', 'The Two Hussars',
'War and Peace', and many others - not to speak of pedagogical works and war sketches. A Russian nobleman of
high rank, a philanthropist, a student of political science, he began in 1875 to publish 'Anna Karenina' in the
columns of the 'Russki Sovyestnik' ('Russian Contemporary').(1) The publication awakened intense interest - the
kind of interest awakened by the publication of George
Eliot's novels in 'Blackwood's'; and though it dragged on
for months and even years, and was even interrupted for
many months by a break between its parts, interest in its
hundreds of pages never flagged; and it now appears, in an
excellent and idiomatic English version, by Mr N.H. Dole,
who has translated at first hand from the Russian, and

whose work consequently has the ring of the true metal.
     We have spoken of George Eliot. Count Tolstoi is a
sort of 'double' of the English novelist. 'Anna Karenina'
is a strange and pathetic work, characterized by all the
breadth and complexity, the insight and the profound analysis of 'Middlemarch'. George Eliot's humour is not
there, but her great power of generalization, her life-
likeness, her knack of looking into people's hearts and
dragging thence all their reluctant secrets, are there,
and there in fulness. Anna Karenina herself is a lovely
creation - lovely but miserable as Gwendolen. The Russian
life and society around her - the balls, the gaieties of
Moscow and Petersburg, the peasant life, the Russian songs
and folk-lore, the passion and corruptions, the frivoli-
ties and splendors - all this is depicted with the hand of
an artist and a master, and at such length that at the end
of it one knows Russian official, aristocratic, social and
peasant life in the nineteenth century as well as it is
possible to know them from one book. Brilliant, unhappy
Anna, fascinating Vronsky, interesting Levin and his desperate loves, Dolly, Kitty, Stepan, and the rest of this
complicated and wonderfully described company; love,
guilty passion, fidelity, unfaithfulness - Read for yourself, gentle reader; we will not spoil a noble story by
revamping it in these few lines.

Note

1 Actually 'Russkiy vestnik' ('Russian Messenger'). (Ed.)

75. UNSIGNED REVIEW, 'LITERARY WORLD' (BOSTON)

17 April 1886

Count Tolstoi's 'Anna Karenina' is a long, intricate, and
crowded novel of Russian life. It is really two novels,
we might almost say three novels, in one. It sets out
with an unhappy domestic experience, in which Prince
Stepan Oblonsky is detected by his wife Darya, in a liaison with the French governess of their children, the husband barely escaping an irretrievable rupture with her
whom he has wronged. But this is only an introduction -
a dish of soup before meat. From this beginning the story

branches in two lines: one following the innocent but
tearful experiences of Konstantin Levin and Kitty
Shcherbatskaia, together with the fortunes of Levin as a
large landed proprietor in connection with agrarian problems of a socialistic kind; the other the guilty love of
Count Aleksei Vronsky for Anna Karenina, the wife of
Aleksei Karenin, their defiant and illicit union, and the
tragic fate which concludes their history. This variety
of interests and motives, the multiplicity of characters,
and a confusion as to names which the translator might
have saved his readers by a stern independence of Russian
nomenclature, make the opening chapters perplexing and
toilsome; until the stream of the story gets fairly under
way and falls clearly into its several channels. Then
it becomes interesting, at times absorbing, and will
retain the attention of those who have leisure, throughout
the entire 769 capacious pages, to the end.

The two leading themes act as if one were set as a foil
to the other; Vronsky's and Anna's lawless passion and its
fruits over against Levin's agrarian experiments on his
country estate of Pokrovsky. The great mass of materials
employed gives cumbersomeness and complexity to the product, moulded though it be by a powerful and steady hand.
The reader does not ever feel that the guide is losing his
way, but rather that he is being led through a mountainous
and rugged country, with an immense range of ground to
cover, and ground of a difficult character. The story
oscillates, swings, sways from side to side like an express train at forty miles an hour over the twistings and
climbings of the Baltimore and Ohio Railway; one chapter,
for example, ends in a most dramatic passage between Anna
and her wronged husband, the next begins in the hay loft
at Pokrovsky.

As a socialistic novel 'Anna Karenina' is wholesome,
and for a novel on the transgression of the Seventh Com-
mandment it is inoffensive. Yet on its latter side, on
these relations of the sexes, on the facts of parentage
and motherhood, the book speaks with a plainness of meaning, sometimes with a plainness of words, which is at
least new. We do not know that we have ever before read
a novel in which the details of an *accouchement,* for
example, were made to do service for one chapter. A very
effective chapter of its kind, but...!

With the moral intent of the book no fault can be
found. The sinfulness of sin, the wretchedness of sin,
the bitter fruits of sin, are all in the sad story of
Vronsky and Anna. The stern virtuousness of Aleksei
Karenin when he suspects the error of his wife, and as
suspicion settles into discovery; the first severity of

his anger, his later compassion, his final magnanimity;
these are some lines only in a noble and majestic figure,
a lay figure, in whose person and purpose the author would
incarnate the Sermon on the Mount. If there are few
scenes in fiction, which for pure vividness of portraiture
equal the snowy journey by night from Moscow to St Petersburg, upon which Vronsky, dominated by his passion, follows Anna, so are there few which for dramatic intensity
and tender pitifulness equal that in which Karenin and
Vronsky meet by Anna's bedside, as she lies hovering between life and death over the birth of a daughter, of whom
her husband is not the father.

The book has many striking portraits among its subordinate characters; and there are graphic descriptions of
Russian scenery and incident - the farmyard at Pokrovsky;
the brilliant wedding of Levin and Kitty, at which Levin
is late for a ludicrous reason; the exciting races at
which Vronsky has his fall; the salon receptions in which
nobles and statesmen figure; the officers' mess in the
barracks; the sojourn in Italy; and the two tragedies of
the railway station. Impressions the book certainly makes,
makes and leaves; and impressions on the moral sensibilities as well as on the imagination.

The great lesson of Anna Karenina's melancholy history
is that for a woman to marry a man twenty years her senior
when she does not love him, is to place her under conditions of terrible temptation when afterwards she comes to
be thrown with a man whom she can love, and who is not
unselfish enough to save her from herself when she has put
herself in his power; and that, surrendering to that temptation, the wages of her sin is - death.

It must have taken some resolution to translate this
book, and some courage to publish it; and the reading of
it some persons will find a work which requires persever-
ance and application. But it is large and strong; we
remember nothing with which exactly to compare it since
Elizabeth de Ville's 'Johannes Olaf' of 1873.

76. W.M. PAYNE, NOTICE, 'DIAL' (CHICAGO)

May 1886

....'Anna Karenina' (1875-7) was first published in a
Russian review. It is the most mature and probably the

greatest of the products of its author's imagination.
Unlike 'War and Peace' it is purely domestic in its subject matter, but there is no lack of variety in its scenes
and characters. It is indeed a world in itself, so comprehensive is its grasp, and so intimately does it bring
us into relations with the manifold aspects of country and
city life in Russia. Were this work the sole available
document, it would be possible to construct from its pages
a great deal of Russian contemporary civilization. It is
of course realistic to the last degree. But its realism
is not confined to minute descriptions of material objects,
and is no less made use of in the treatment of emotion.
There are few works of art in which the art is so well
concealed; few works of fiction which give so strong a
sense of reality as this. We seem to look upon life
itself and forget the medium of the novelist's imagination
through which we really view it. And right here we are
brought to compare the methods of Tolstoi with those of
his better known and unquestionably greater countryman,
Tourguenieff. In the marvellous novels of Tourguenieff
we have this same feeling of immediate contact with the
facts of material existence and of emotional life, and the
effect is produced with much less machinery than Tolstoi
is compelled to use. The work of Tourguenieff surpasses
the work of Tolstoi, in revealing that final sublimation
of thought and imagination which give to it an artistic
value beyond that of almost any other imaginative prose.
Tolstoi lacks this power of concentration and this un-
erring judgment in the choice of word or phrase. He
cannot sum up a situation in a single pregnant sentence,
but he can present it with great force in a chapter. Now
that this story of 'Anna Karenina' has been brought to the
cognizance of the western world, it is not likely to be
soon forgotten. It will be remembered for its minute and
unstrained descriptions, for its deep tragedy, unfolded
act after act as by the hand of fate, and for its under-
current of gentle religious feeling, never falling to the
offensive level of dogmatism, yet giving a marked character to the book, and revealing unmistakably the spiritual
lineaments of the Russian apostle of quietism.

77.   UNSIGNED REVIEW, 'NATION' (NEW YORK)

6 May 1886

From a review entitled Tolstoi and Turgeneff. The American translation of 'Anna Karenina' by Nathan Haskell Dole
had just appeared.

How Count Tolstoi writes we are not informed, but anyone
who reads him in the original soon becomes breathless at
the earnestness and rapidity with which chapter after
chapter seems to have been dashed off and never afterwards revised - an earnestness so concentrated and glowing
that the reader seems to feel at once the heartbeats of
the characters as they are introduced, and, above them
all, the passionate throb of the author's own heart, with
an almost personal sense of his very presence. This dash
results in an apparent indifference to some of the com-
monest rules of writing and of novel manufacture, in
which far inferior performers excel. It is not uncommon
for him to repeat himself on the same page, to begin
several consecutive sentences with the same name in the
most awkward manner, to contradict his own statements.
Thus Varenka in 'Anna Karenina' is made to wear a yellow
dress and a white one in the same breath (both are omitted in the translation), and Vronsky's wealth in Italy is
not accounted for after the description of his embarrassed
circumstances in St Petersburg. But this habitual disregard for nice points does not detract from the effect,
and it serves to accentuate still more strongly the contrast between Tolstoi's ardent temperament and Turgeneff's
phlegmatic nature. The latter would never have permitted
such technically imperfect work to leave his hands, but,
with all his art, he appears cold beside his brother
writer. It may be argued, and with some justice, that the
removal of these blemishes by a translator is an improve-
ment; but it interferes with the proper psychological
study of the author, whose personality is as interesting
as any of his characters, in the same degree that the
mistakes foisted upon Turgeneff by the same means prevent
a proper appreciation of him.
   The methods of the two writers are as different as
their styles. Turgeneff viewed all Russian subjects and
people from a double standpoint - that of an impartial
foreigner who regarded Russians as new and curious animals

to be studied, and that of a native who understands
thoroughly the manners and customs of his country. An
epigrammatic and critical treatment is the natural result
of this. Tolstoi's method is the exact reverse. He never
consciously treats his characters as Russians, nor does he
criticize them. He simply becomes, for the time being, an
integral part of the mind and the very essence of the
character whom he is depicting. Nevertheless no-one can
deny that his characters are as genuinely Russian as any
of Turgeneff's creations. But they are something more -
they are universal types. The situations in 'Smoke' and
'Anna Karenina' are sufficiently similar to render a comparison interesting. Vronsky deserts Kitty for Anna, as
Litvinoff deserts Tania for Irene. After showing us the
fashionable Russians at Baden-Baden, with their airy
French, superlatively fresh clothes, and elaborate grace
of manner, picnicking in the morning and mesmerizing their
crab in the utter inanity of their evening, Turgeneff
exhibits another set behaving like lunatics at Gubareff's
rooms, and confides the task of summing up Russia as a
whole to Potugin. Like Pigasoff in 'Rudin', Potugin does
little but utter pithy criticisms, which, though highly
amusing, are as unpalatable to the victims as are certain
Anglo-American sketches to people in this country. After
giving the impression that high-class Russians are frivolous, narrow-minded, and overburdened with foreign affec-
tations, and that Russia is utterly devoid of originality,
the story proceeds. But there is very little analysis of
character, or of the motives and feelings which inspire
any course of conduct. The people and events are simply
photographed under a brilliant light, and the reader is
left to supply the rest, as he is in the dramas which go
on about him in real life. Irene is frail, shallow,
heartless - eminently Russian if we are to believe the
author. No-one will ever pause to inquire Anna Karenina's
nationality; she will be accepted unquestioningly, in her
weakness and remorse, as a world type by anyone who has
once followed the vivid history of her mental processes.
      Varvara in 'A Nobleman's Nest' is another example of
the same eminently national delineation. Tania hardly
appears on the scene, any more than Natalia in 'Rudin',
and much less than Lisa in 'A Nobleman's Nest'. All three
lose their lovers through the interference of a married
woman. That they are all strong characters is evident
enough; but Turgeneff is very reserved in his portraits
of young girls, and the reader never feels that he has
been very thoroughly introduced to them. They are simply
the ideal young girl of romance. Irene at first forms an
exception. But Tolstoi's young girls are among the most

wonderful of his creations. Had Kitty been dropped after
the description of her feelings at Vronsky's desertion, as
Turgeneff's girls are, she would still have lived in the
hearts and memories of all readers. As Levin's wife she
reigns equally as the typical young married woman.
Natasha in 'War and Peace' is an example, quite as perfectly drawn, of another type - the fickle, forward, capricious girl, who eventually settles down with the last
and most unexpected of her many admirers, and develops
into the most domestic of matrons, without a care for her
appearance or an idea beyond her much-governed husband and
children. That Levin is an autobiographical sketch is
generally accepted, and there are portions of Pierre
Besukhof's story which seem to come under the same head.
Yet he is not a whit more true to nature than any other
character in the author's two great novels. Lavretzky in
'A Nobleman's Nest' is somewhat similar to Alexey Karenin,
but the contrast is as marked in this case as in the
others. Like Litvinoff he forms the subject of a psychological study within the narrow limits to which Turgeneff
limited himself, or was restricted by his lack of sympathy.
One curious result of the latter's attempts at analysis is
that the people to whom he devotes the most of his attention in that line turn out the weakest characters, and
eventually fade out of the story in a nerveless way, which
speedily banishes them also from the reader's mind, leaving behind, in vivid colours, only the portraits of the
brave young girls who suffer unanalysed in silence. 'All
is smoke,' says Litvinoff. 'Words, words, that is all,'
echoes Rudin; if Lavretzky does not utter the sentiment,
he feels it. The married women are too shallow to dis-
sect. The young girls do not yield their secret hearts to
his touch.

In short, Turgeneff's art is always transparent, and
never more so than when he is contrasted with Tolstoi,
whose utter absence of that quality (consciously and deliberately, at least) results in something as much above any
deliberate artistic product as a rose or a tree is beyond
the utmost effort of a painter or a flower maker. But
although Tolstoi appeals more directly to the heart than
Turgeneff, the latter never appears so well as when read
directly after one of the former's great works. They complement each other in a marked manner and to a singular
degree, and, united, they reveal Russian life in a way
that is fairly startling in its vividness.

[Omitted: adverse criticism of the poor quality of the
translation - from the French.]

It makes the heart bleed to see the havoc that is made
with beautiful things.   Turgeneff and Tolstoi deserve
better treatment than they have received; and though they
are great enough to rise superior to misrepresentation,
only those who can make their acquaintance in their own
magnificent language will ever be able fully to appreciate
them.

78.   UNSIGNED NOTICE, 'ECLECTIC MAGAZINE' (NEW YORK)

July 1886

'Anna Karenina' is the story, told by a genius of extraordinary insight, of a great social tragedy, the elements
of which are universal, though the background is thoroughly Russian.   It is the greatest of all social tragedies, the fall of a pure and high-minded woman, who is
introduced to us as a model of her sex, a good wife and
devoted mother, before the power of an illicit passion.
The theme in some way or other enters largely into most
modern fiction.   Count Tolstoi treats the topic with a
lofty dignity and splendid purpose which, even for those
repelled from the theme, redeems it.   The heroine, her
husband, and her lover seem from the first to be the victims of some terrible fate, like the personages in an old
Greek tragedy.   They are borne on to their end in spite
of all their struggles.   The misery of the guilty woman,
happy as she is in her unlawful love, which finally over-
throws the whole balance of her originally strong and fine
nature, and causes her to commit suicide, is painted with
a terrible brush.   Retribution for broken social obligations dogs her slowly but surely, till the fateful close,
when she throws herself under the wheels of a railway
train.   The sombre elements of the story are relieved by
some most charming and idyllic scenes, and the contrast
between a noble and upright marriage life, full of all joy
and sweetness, is very vividly contrasted with the woeful
picture of Anna Karenina.   This great novel could not be
adequately treated in less than a special essay, it is so
full of suggestiveness.   It is not a book, perhaps, for a
very young person to read, but those who have already
eaten of the tree of knowledge of good and evil could
scarcely find a book more compact with interest and in-
struction.

79.   HOWELLS, REVIEW, 'HARPER'S MAGAZINE'

1886, vol. LXXII

W.D. Howells (1837-1920), American novelist, editor,
critic and poet, first read Tolstoy in the 1880s and soon
became an avowed 'Tolstoyan'. Tolstoy, he wrote, 'has not
influenced me in esthetics alone, but in ethics too, so
that I can never again see life in the way I saw it before
I knew him'. What particularly attracted him in Tolstoy
was his moral force, something Howells considered more
important than any rules of art. The articles written by
Howells, especially in the 'North American Review' and
'Harper's Magazine', did much to pave the way for Tolstoy's
popularity in America. These comments are taken from his
Editor's Study, the title of his regular column.

It is this conscience, present in all that Tolstoi has
written, which has now changed from a dramatic to a hort-
atory expression. The same good heart and right mind are
under all and in all. Their warmth and their light are
not greater in 'My Religion' than in 'Anna Karenine', that
saddest story of guilty love, in which nothing can save
the sinful woman from herself - not her husband's forgiveness, her friends' compassion, her lover's constancy, or
the long intervals of quiet in which she seems safe and
happy in her sin. It is she who destroys herself, persistently, step by step, in spite of all help and forbear-
ance; and yet we are never allowed to forget how good and
generous she was when we first met her, how good and generous she is, fitfully and more and more rarely, to the
end. Her lover works out a sort of redemption through his
patience and devotion; he grows wiser, gentler, worthier,
through it; but even his good destroys her. As you read
on you say not 'This is like life', but 'This is life'.
It has not only the complexion, the very hue, of life, but
its movement, its advances, its strange pauses, its seem-
ing reversions to former conditions, and its perpetual
change; its apparent isolations, its essential solidarity.
A multitude of figures pass before us recognizably real,
never caricatured or grotesqued or in any way unduly
accepted but simple and actual in their evil or their
good. There is lovely family life, the tenderness of
father and daughter, the rapture of young wife and husband, the innocence of girlhood, the beauty of fidelity;

there is the unrest and folly of fashion, the misery of
wealth, and the wretchedness of wasted and mistaken life,
the hollowness of ambition, the cheerful emptiness of some
hearts, the dull emptiness of others. It is a world, and
you live in it while you read, and long afterward; but at
no step have you been betrayed, not because your guide has
warned or exorted you, but because he has been true and
has shown you all things as they are.

80.   UNSIGNED NOTICE, 'ATHENAEUM'

26 February 1887

Reprinted by permission.

We owe an apology to two very remarkable works for having
kept them for some time waiting. We will try to make
amends by strongly recommending every one to read them.
The one is Count Leo Tolstoi's 'Anna Karenina'; the other
is Dostoyefsky's 'Injury and Insult'. From each of them a
great deal may be learnt with respect to the manners and
customs, the thoughts and feelings, of that great Russian
people whose onward march is now disquieting many nations,
and of whose inner life so little is known outside the
frontiers of its own land. Each of them also tells a most
interesting tale and is full of such minute and subtle
studies of character as are but rarely to be met with in
romantic fiction.
    Count Leo Tolstoi's 'Anna Karenina' is not so grand a
work as his 'Peace and War'.... but as a picture of Russian upper-class life it deserves cordial admiration.
The canvas on which Count Tolstoi has painted is not so
vast as in 'Peace and War'; the figures which he has
delineated are not, as in that great work, those of historic heroes; the impression made upon the mind of the
spectator is not likely this time to be so deep or so
lasting as it was in the case of 'Peace and War'. But no
one can study 'Anna Karenina' without recognizing in its
admirable pictures of Russian society, and in its portraits of charming women, the handiwork of a great master.
    We do not propose to give a summary of the story. The
plot is simple; the charm of the book arises from the

skill with which the various characters are portrayed, the
power which the author displays in dealing with pathetic
or humorous incidents, and the grace and fitness of the
language in which the tale is told. The life of the heroine, after whom the book is named, is full of shadow and
she meets with a terrible death. She realizes the fact
towards the end of her career that when a woman has
stooped to folly and finds that a man can betray, the best
thing she can do is to die. Similarly sad stories have
been told over and over again by novelists, but there are
few instances on record of such a story being so well told
as in the case of the trusting, loving, ill-fated wife of
the cold and puzzling Aleksei Karenin. His character is
depicted with a skill which reminds the reader of Balzac,
Thackeray and George Eliot by turns; and that of Vronsky,
the unscrupulous and light-hearted man of the world who
ruins the happiness of Karenin's wife, deserves similar
praise. But the most delightful parts of the work are
those which are devoted to the charming Kitty Shcherbat-
skaya, who flirts with, refuses, but ultimately marries
Levin, a young landed proprietor, in whose character
Count Leo Tolstoi has evidently depicted his own. Not
one of the three great novelists we have mentioned could
have made manifest to our eyes so charming, winsome, and
pleasingly capricious a young girl as the Kitty of this
tale. The Russians have a saying that 'A maiden's heart
is a dark forest', but through that forest the author has
threaded his way with a dexterity which, as Mrs Oliphant
once said of Anthony Trollope on a similar occasion, is
almost 'uncanny'....

81. TYLER, REVIEW, 'NEW ENGLANDER AND YALE REVIEW'

March 1887

From an article entitled Tolstoi's Novels by M.F. Tyler.

'Anna Karenina' is a book of more regular form. It has a
beginning, an artistic progress of interest in a single,
definite chain of actions and events, it has a distinct
denouement, it has its controlling sub-plot. In a word,
it is more like the Western novels, it is more dramatic.

It is the story of a wife's unfaithfulness, and of its
consequences to herself and to those dependent upon her
for their happiness or their training. Anna Karenina, a
delicate, highly organized creature, who is unsympathetic-
ally mated - evidently by a *mariage de convenance* - is
seized with a passion for a young prince, a man in every
way worthy and fit for her, except that he is not her husband. The book is the story of how this relation, that
was an offence to both God and man, worked out the destruction of the two lives through their consciences,
leading in the woman's case to suicide, and in that of the
man to a military death not far removed from it. It is
not the picture of a common passion. The error of these
two souls is ennobled by the qualities that make love the
power that it is. They are devoted and faithful to one
another. If the woman has given up her reputation and her
home for her lover, he sacrifices as cheerfully for her
the position to which he is by birth entitled, and the
consideration of his friends and family. There is nothing
sordid or degrading in their attachment save its sin.
But that it is sin, and that it must work out its proper
fruit, are written with the iron pen of holy truth in
every chapter and line. The abstract hero of the book is
Duty, as opposed to unrestrained passion. But this is not
all of it. The secondary thread of the story is a charming idyll of honest love, not romantic, but true and real,
leading as it ought to the life of the family and the
home. The character of Levine, the speculator on the
things of life, the uneasy doubter, this hoper for the
better times for all men, this natural optimist, the
lover of love, whom the sober facts of life make a pessimist, probably speaks for the author as much as any of his
characters. The writer evidently loves him, sympathizes
with him, and wishes that life could be easier for him.
Side by side with the story of the destruction of two
lives runs this tale of the love, the wooing, the marriage, and the domestic life of Levine, the phases of his
development, his optimism, his struggle with the obscure
problems that life presents to him, his resulting pessi-
mism, and his ultimate believing fatalism. Levine is the
typical young modern Russian. It is the production of
such characters in their novels that has led a French
critic to say of the Russian writers that it seems as if
the wind that wanders aimlessly over their mountainous
steppes had imparted to the souls of these men something
of its own to and fro. But it is in the research of the
motives of such a heart, in portraying the play of the
experiences of life on such a soul, in tracing to its last
source every emotion and every act, that Tolstoi is at his
best.

82.   MATTHEW ARNOLD ON 'ANNA KARENINA'

1887

From Count Leo Tolstoi, 'Fortnightly Review', December
1887.   Matthew Arnold (1822-88), poet, writer and critic,
did for English readers what de Vogüé did for the French
(see No. 87) in that he more or less introduced them to
Tolstoy.   Arnold and Tolstoy possibly met briefly in
London in March 1861 when Tolstoy was in England to take
a look at the English educational system; as Arnold was a
prominent school inspector for most of his working life it
was not unnatural that Tolstoy should have tried to meet
him.
    Arnold's views of Tolstoy are coloured by the fact that
he read him in French.   When Tolstoy read this article he
found Arnold's comments 'well-founded and just'.

Count Leo Tolstoi is about sixty years old, and tells us
that he shall write novels no more.   He is now occupied
with religion and with the Christian life.   His writings
concerning these great matters are not allowed, I believe,
to obtain publication in Russia, but instalments of them
in French and English reach us from time to time.   I find
them very interesting, but I find his novel of 'Anna
Karénine' more interesting still.   I believe that many
readers prefer to 'Anna Karénine' Count Tolstoi's other
great novel, 'La Guerre et la Paix'.   But in the novel one
prefers, I think, to have the novelist dealing with the
life which he knows from having lived it, rather than with
the life which he knows from books or hearsay.   If one has
to choose a representative work of Thackeray, it is
'Vanity Fair' which one would take rather than 'The Vir-
ginians'.   In like manner I take 'Anna Karénine' as the
novel best representing Count Tolstoi.   I use the French
translation; in general, as I long ago said, work of this
kind is better done in France than in England, and 'Anna
Karénine' is perhaps also a novel which goes better into
French than into English, just as Frederika Bremer's
'Home' goes into English better than into French.   After I
have done with 'Anna Karénine' I must say something of
Count Tolstoi's religious writings.   Of these too I use
the French translation, so far as it is available.   The
English translation, however, which came into my hands
late, seems to be in general clear and good.   Let me say

in passing that it has neither the same arrangement, nor the same titles, nor altogether the same contents, with the French translation.

There are many characters in 'Anna Karénine' — too many if we look in it for a work of art in which the action shall be vigorously one, and to that one action everything shall converge. There are even two main actions extending throughout the book, and we keep passing from one of them to the other - from the affairs of Anna and Wronsky to the affairs of Kitty and Levine. People appear in connection with these two main actions whose appearance and proceedings do not in the least contribute to develop them; incidents are multiplied which we expect are to lead to something important, but which do not. What, for instance, does the episode of Kitty's friend Warinka and Levine's brother Serge Ivanitch, their inclination for one another and its failure to come to anything, contribute to the development of either the character or the fortunes of Kitty and Levine? What does the incident of Levine's long delay in getting to church to be married, a delay which as we read of it seems to have significance, really import? It turns out to import absolutely nothing, and to be introduced solely to give the author the pleasure of telling us that all Levine's shirts had been packed up.

But the truth is we are not to take 'Anna Karénine' as a work of art; we are to take it as a piece of life. A piece of life it is. The author has not invented and combined it, he has seen it; it has all happened before his inward eye, and it was in this wise that it happened. Levine's shirts were packed up, and he was late for his wedding in consequence; Warinka and Serge Ivanitch met at Levine's country-house and went out walking together; Serge was very near proposing, but did not. The author saw it all happening so — saw it, and therefore relates it; and what his novel in this way loses in art it gains in reality.

For this is the result which, by his extraordinary fineness of perception, and by his sincere fidelity to it, the author achieves; he works in us a sense of the absolute reality of his personages and their doings. Anna's shoulders, and masses of hair, and half-shut eyes; Alexis Karénine's updrawn eyebrows, and tired smile, and cracking finger-joints; Stiva's eyes suffused with facile moisture — these are as real to us as any of those outward peculiarities which in our own circle of acquaintance we are noticing daily, while the inner man of our own circle of acquaintance, happily or unhappily, lies a great deal less clearly revealed to us than that of Count Tolstoi's creations.

I must speak of only a few of these creations, the
chief personages and no more. The book opens with 'Stiva,'
and who that has once made Stiva's acquaintance will ever
forget him? We are living, in Count Tolstoi's novel,
among the great people of Moscow and St Petersburg, the
nobles and the high functionaries, the governing class of
Russia. Stépane Arcadiévitch — 'Stiva' — is Prince
Oblonsky, and descended from Rurik, although to think of
him as anything except 'Stiva' is difficult. His *air
souriant*, his good looks, his satisfaction; his 'ray',
which made the Tartar waiter at the club joyful in contem-
plating it; his pleasure in oysters and champagne, his
pleasure in making people happy and in rendering services;
his need of money, his attachment to the French governess,
his distress at his wife's distress, his affection for
her and the children; his emotion and suffused eyes, while
he quite dismisses the care of providing funds for household expenses and education; and the French attachment,
contritely given up to-day only to be succeeded by some
other attachment to-morrow — no never, certainly, shall
we come to forget Stiva. Anna, the heroine, is Stiva's
sister. His wife Dolly (these English diminutives are
common among Count Tolstoi's ladies) is daughter of the
Prince and Princess Cherbatzky, grandees who show us
Russian high life by its most respectable side; the Prince,
in particular, is excellent — simple, sensible, right-
feeling; a man of dignity and honour. His daughters,
Dolly and Kitty, are charming. Dolly, Stiva's wife, is
sorely tried by her husband, full of anxieties for the
children, with no money to spend on them or herself,
poorly dressed, worn and aged before her time. She has
moments of despairing doubt whether the gay people may not
be after all in the right, whether virtue and principle
answer; whether happiness does not dwell with adventuresses and profligates, brilliant and perfectly dressed
adventuresses and profligates, in a land flowing with
roubles and champagnes. But in a quarter of an hour she
comes right again and is herself — a nature straight,
honest, faithful, loving, sound to the core; such she is
and such she remains; she can be no other. Her sister
Kitty is at bottom of the same temper but she has her
experience to get, while Dolly, when the book begins, has
already acquired hers. Kitty is adored by Levine, in whom
we are told that many traits are to be found of the character and history of Count Tolstoi himself. Levine
belongs to the world of great people by his birth and
property, but he is not at all a man of the world. He
has been a reader and thinker, he has a conscience, he
has public spirit and would ameliorate the condition of

the people, he lives on his estate in the country, and
occupies himself zealously with local business, schools,
and agriculture. But he is shy, apt to suspect and to
take offence, somewhat impracticable, out of his element
in the gay world of Moscow. Kitty likes him, but her
fancy has been taken by a brilliant guardsman, Count
Wronsky, who has paid her attentions. Wronsky is described to us by Stiva; he is 'one of the finest specimens
of the *jeunesse dorée* of St Petersburg; immensely rich,
handsome, aide-de-camp to the emperor, great interest at
his back, and a good fellow notwithstanding; more than a
good fellow, intelligent besides and well read — a man who
has a splendid career before him.' Let us complete the
picture by adding that Wronsky is a powerful man, over
thirty, bald at the top of his head, with irreproachable
manners, cool and calm, but a little haughty. A hero, one
murmurs to oneself, too much of the Guy Livingstone type,
though without the bravado and exaggeration. And such is,
justly enough perhaps, the first impression, an impression
which continues all through the first volume; but Wronsky,
as we shall see, improves towards the end.
    Kitty discourages Levine, who retires in misery and
confusion. But Wronsky is attracted by Anna Karénine, and
ceases his attentions to Kitty. The impression made on
her heart by Wronsky was not deep; but she is so keenly
mortified with herself, so ashamed, and so upset, that she
falls ill, and is sent with her family to winter abroad.
There she regains health and mental composure, and discovers at the same time that her liking for Levine was
deeper than she knew, that it was a genuine feeling, a
strong and lasting one. On her return they meet, their
hearts come together, they are married; and in spite of
Levine's waywardness, irritability, and unsettlement of
mind, of which I shall have more to say presently, they
are profoundly happy. Well, and who could help being
happy with Kitty? So I find myself adding impatiently.
Count Tolstoi's heroines are really so living and charming
that one takes them, fiction though they are, too
seriously.
    But the interest of the book centres in Anna Karénine.
She is Stiva's sister, married to a high official at St
Petersburg, Alexis Karénine. She has been married to him
nine years, and has one child, a boy named Serge. The
marriage had not brought happiness to her, she had found
in it no satisfaction to her heart and soul, she had a
sense of want and isolation; but she is devoted to her
boy, occupied, calm. The charm of her personality is felt
even before she appears, from the moment when we hear of
her being sent for as the good angel to reconcile Dolly

with Stiva. Then she arrives at the Moscow station from
St Petersburg, and we see the gray eyes with their long
eyelashes, the graceful carriage, the gentle and caressing
smile on the fresh lips, the vivacity restrained but waiting to break through, the fulness of life, the softness
and strength joined, the harmony, the bloom, the charm.
She goes to Dolly, and achieves, with infinite tact and
tenderness, the task of reconciliation. At a ball a few
days later, we add to our first impression of Anna's
beauty, dark hair, a quantity of little curls over her
temples and at the back of her neck, sculptural shoulders,
firm throat, and beautiful arms. She is in a plain dress
of black velvet with a pearl necklace, a bunch of forget-
me-nots in the front of her dress, another in her hair.
This is Anna Karénine.

She had travelled from St Petersburg with Wronsky's
mother; had seen him at the Moscow station, where he came
to meet his mother, had been struck with his looks and
manner, and touched by his behaviour in an accident which
happened while they were in the station to a poor workman
crushed by a train. At the ball she meets him again; she
is fascinated by him and he by her. She had been told of
Kitty's fancy, and had gone to the ball meaning to help
Kitty; but Kitty is forgotten, or at any rate neglected;
the spell which draws Wronsky and Anna is irresistible.
Kitty finds herself opposite to them in a quadrille
together:-

> She seemed to remark in Anna the symptoms of an over-
> excitement which she herself knew from experience -
> that of success. Anna appeared to her as if intoxi-
> cated with it. Kitty knew to what to attribute that
> brilliant and animated look, that happy and triumphant
> smile, those half-parted lips, those movements full of
> grace and harmony.

Anna returns to St Petersburg, and Wronsky returns
there at the same time; they meet on the journey, they
keep meeting in society, and Anna begins to find her husband, who before had not been sympathetic, intolerable.
Alexis Karénine is much older than herself, a bureaucrat,
a formalist, a poor creature; he has conscience, there is
a root of goodness in him, but on the surface and until
deeply stirred he is tiresome, pedantic, vain, exasperat-
ing. The change in Anna is not in the slightest degree
comprehended by him; he sees nothing which an intelligent
man might in such a case see, and does nothing which an
intelligent man would do. Anna abandons herself to her
passion for Wronsky.

I remember M.Nisard saying to me many years ago at the
École Normale in Paris, that he respected the English
because they are *une nation qui sait se gêner* — people who
can put constraint on themselves and go through what is
disagreeable. Perhaps in the Slav nature this valuable
faculty is somewhat wanting; a very strong impulse is too
much regarded as irresistible, too little as what can be
resisted and ought to be resisted, however difficult and
disagreeable the resistance may be. In our high society
with its pleasure and dissipation, laxer notions may to
some extent prevail; but in general an English mind will
be startled by Anna's suffering herself to be so overwhelmed and irretrievably carried away by her passion, by
her almost at once regarding it, apparently, as something
which it was hopeless to fight against. And this I say
irrespectively of the worth of her lover. Wronsky's gifts
and graces hardly qualify him, one might think, to be the
object of so instantaneous and mighty a passion on the
part of a woman like Anna. But that is not the question.
Let us allow that these passions are incalculable; let us
allow that one of the male sex scarcely does justice,
perhaps, to the powerful and handsome guardsman and his
attractions. But if Wronsky had been even such a lover as
Alcibiades or the Master of Ravenswood, still that Anna,
being what she is and her circumstances being what they
are, should show not a hope, hardly a thought, of con-
quering her passion, of escaping from its fatal power, is
to our notions strange and a little bewildering.

I state the objection; let me add that it is the triumph of Anna's charm that it remains paramount for us
nevertheless; that throughout her course, with its failures, errors, and miseries, still the impression of her
large, fresh, rich, generous, delightful nature, never
leaves us — keeps our sympathy, keeps even, I had almost
said, our respect.

To return to the story. Soon enough poor Anna begins
to experience the truth of what the Wise Man told us long
ago, that 'the way of transgressors is hard.' Her agitation at a steeplechase where Wronsky is in danger attracts
her husband's notice and provokes his remonstrance. He is
bitter and contemptuous. In a transport of passion Anna
declares to him that she is his wife no longer; that she
loves Wronsky, belongs to Wronsky. Hard at first, formal,
cruel, thinking only of himself, Karénine, who, as I have
said, has a conscience, is touched by grace at the moment
when Anna's troubles reach their height. He returns to
her to find her with a child just born to her and Wronsky,
the lover in the house and Anna apparently dying. Karénine has words of kindness and forgiveness only. The noble

and victorious effort transfigures him, and all that her
husband gains in the eyes of Anna, her lover Wronsky
loses. Wronsky comes to Anna's bedside, and standing
there by Karénine, buries his face in his hands.

[Quotation omitted.]

    She seems dying, and Wronsky rushes out and shoots him-
self. And so, in a common novel, the story would end.
Anna would die, Wronsky would commit suicide, Karénine
would survive in possession of our admiration and sympathy. But the story does not always end so in life:
neither does it end so in Count Tolstoi's novel. Anna
recovers from her fever, Wronsky from his wound. Anna's
passion for Wronsky reawakens, her estrangement from
Karénine returns. Nor does Karénine remain at the height
at which in the forgiveness scene we saw him. He is formal, pedantic, irritating. Alas! even if he were not all
these, perhaps even his *pince-nez,* and his rising eyebrows, and his cracking finger-joints, would have been
provocation enough. Anna and Wronsky depart together.
They stay for a time in Italy, then return to Russia. But
her position is false, her disquietude incessant, and
happiness is impossible for her. She takes opium every
night, only to find that 'not poppy nor mandragora shall
ever medicine her to that sweet sleep which she owed yesterday.' Jealousy and irritability grow upon her; she
tortures Wronsky, she tortures herself. Under these
trials Wronsky, it must be said, comes out well, and
rises in our esteem. His love for Anna endures; he behaves, as our English phrase is, 'like a gentleman'; his
patience is in general exemplary. But then Anna, let us
remember, is to the last, through all the fret and
misery, still Anna; always with something which charms;
nay, with something, even, something in her nature, which
consoles and does good. Her life, however, was becoming
impossible under its existing conditions. A trifling
misunderstanding brought the inevitable end. After a
quarrel with Anna, Wronsky had gone one morning into the
country to see his mother; Anna summons him by telegraph
to return at once, and receives an answer from him that he
cannot return before ten at night. She follows him to his
mother's place in the country, and at the station hears
what leads her to believe that he is not coming back.
Maddened with jealousy and misery, she descends the platform and throws herself under the wheels of a goods train
passing through the station. It is over — the graceful
head is untouched, but all the rest is a crushed, form-
less heap. Poor Anna!

We have been in a world which misconducts itself nearly
as much as the world of a French novel all palpitating
with 'modernity.' But there are two things in which the
Russian novel — Count Tolstoi's novel at any rate — is
very advantageously distinguished from the type of novel
now so much in request in France. In the first place,
there is no fine sentiment, at once tiresome and false.
We are not told to believe, for example, that Anna is
wonderfully exalted and ennobled by her passion for
Wronsky. The English reader is thus saved from many a
groan of impatience. The other thing is yet more important. Our Russian novelist deals abundantly with criminal
passion and with adultery, but he does not seem to feel
himself owing any service to the goddess Lubricity, or
bound to put in touches at this goddess's dictation. Much
in 'Anna Karénine' is painful, much is unpleasant, but
nothing is of a nature to trouble the senses, or to please
those who wish their senses troubled. This taint is
wholly absent. In the French novels where it is so abundantly present its baneful effects do not end with itself.
Burns long ago remarked with deep truth that it *petrifies
feeling*. Let us revert for a moment to the powerful novel
of which I spoke at the outset, 'Madame Bovary'. Undoubtedly the taint in question is present in 'Madame Bovary',
although to a much less degree than in more recent French
novels, which will be in every one's mind. But 'Madame
Bovary', with this taint, is a work of *petrified feeling;*
over it hangs an atmosphere of bitterness, irony, impotence; not a personage in the book to rejoice or console
us; the springs of freshness and feeling are not there to
create such personages. Emma Bovary follows a course in
some respects like that of Anna, but where, in Emma
Bovary, is Anna's charm? The treasures of compassion,
tenderness, insight, which alone, amid such guilt and
misery, can enable charm to subsist and to emerge, are
wanting to Flaubert. He is cruel, with the cruelty of
petrified feeling, to his poor heroine; he pursues her
without pity or pause, as with malignity; he is harder
upon her himself than any reader even, I think, will be
inclined to be.
    But where the springs of feeling have carried Count
Tolstoi, since he created Anna ten or twelve years ago,
we have now to see.
    We must return to Constantine Dmitrich Levine. Levine,
as I have already said, thinks. Between the age of twenty
and that of thirty-five he had lost, he tells us, the
Christian belief in which he had been brought up, a loss
of which examples nowadays abound certainly everywhere,
but which in Russia, as in France, is among all young men

of the upper and cultivated classes more a matter of
course, perhaps, more universal, more avowed, than it is
with us. Levine had adopted the scientific notions current
all round him; talked of cells, organisms, the indestruct-
ibility of matter, the conservation of force, and was of
opinion, with his comrades of the university, that religion no longer existed. But he was of a serious nature,
and the question what his life meant, whence it came,
whither it tended, presented themselves to him in moments
of crisis and affliction with irresistible importunity,
and getting no answer, haunted him, tortured him, made him
think of suicide.

Two things, meanwhile, he noticed. One was, that he
and his university friends had been mistaken in supposing
that Christian belief no longer existed; they had lost it,
but they were not all the world. Levine observed that the
persons to whom he was most attached, his own wife Kitty
amongst the number, retained it and drew comfort from it;
that the women generally, and almost the whole of the
Russian common people, retained it and drew comfort from
it. The other was, that his scientific friends, though
not troubled like himself by questionings about the meaning of human life, were untroubled by such questionings,
not because they had got an answer to them, but because,
entertaining themselves intellectually with the consideration of the cell theory, and evolution, and the indestruct-
ibility of matter, and the conservation of force, and the
like, they were satisfied with this entertainment, and
did not perplex themselves with investigating the meaning
and object of their own life at all.

But Levine noticed further that he himself did not
actually proceed to commit suicide; on the contrary, he
lived on his lands as his father had done before him,
busied himself with all the duties of his station, married
Kitty, was delighted when a son was born to him. Nevertheless he was indubitably not happy at bottom, restless
and disquieted, his disquietude sometimes amounting to
agony.

Now on one of his bad days he was in the field with his
peasants, and one of them happened to say to him, in
answer to a question from Levine why one farmer should in
a certain case act more humanely than another: 'Men are
not all alike; one man lives for his belly, like Mitio-
vuck, another for his soul, for God, like old Plato.' —
'What do you call,' cried Levine, 'living for his soul,
for God?' The peasant answered: 'It's quite simple —
living by the rule of God, of the truth. All men are not
the same, that's certain. You yourself, for instance,
Constantine Dmitrich, you wouldn't do wrong by a poor man.'

Levine gave no answer, but turned away with the phrase, *living by the rule of God, of the truth,* sounding in his ears.

Then he reflected that he had been born of parents professing this rule, as their parents again had professed it before them; that he had sucked it in with his mother's milk; that some sense of it, some strength and nourishment from it, had been ever with him although he knew it not; that if he had tried to do the duties of his station it was by help of the secret support ministered by this rule; that if in his moments of despairing restlessness and agony, when he was driven to think of suicide, he had yet not committed suicide, it was because this rule had silently enabled him to do his duty in some degree, and had given him some hold upon life and happiness in consequence.

The words came to him as a clue of which he could never again lose sight, and which with full consciousness and strenuous endeavour he must henceforth follow. He sees his nephews and nieces throwing their milk at one another and scolded by Dolly for it. He says to himself that these children are wasting their subsistence because they have not to earn it for themselves and do not know its value, and he exclaims inwardly: 'I, a Christian, brought up in the faith, my life filled with the benefits of Christianity, living on these benefits without being conscious of it, I, like these children, I have been trying to destroy what makes and builds up my life.' But now the feeling has been borne in upon him, clear and precious, that what he has to do is to *be good*; he has 'cried to *Him*.' What will come of it?

> I shall probably continue to get out of temper with my coachman, to go into useless arguments, to air my ideas unseasonably; I shall always feel a barrier between the sanctuary of my soul and the soul of other people, even that of my wife; I shall always be holding her responsible for my annoyances and feeling sorry for it directly afterwards. I shall continue to pray without being able to explain to myself why I pray; but my inner life has won its liberty; it will no longer be at the mercy of events, and every minute of my existence will have a meaning sure and profound which it will be in my power to impress on every single one of my actions, that of *being good*.

With these words the novel of 'Anna Karénine' ends. But in Levine's religious experiences Count Tolstoi was relating his own....

83. W.J. DAWSON: THE SINCERE ART OF 'ANNA KARENINA',
'CRITIC' (NEW YORK)

9 May 1896

It is, like all Tolstoi's earlier novels, a book conceived
and executed upon a vast scale. There is not a page in it
that does not witness to the minute and unflagging patience of his observation of life. It reminds one in this
respect of the great cathedrals of the middle ages in
which the humblest piece of carving or sculpture, which is
thrust furthest out of sight, and which the artist must
have known would rarely or never be observed, is executed
with as much nicety of finish as those parts of the work
which were meant to challenge criticism. Its chief interest centres, of course, in Anna herself, and her temptation, fall and shame. But side by side with her story
there run other stories, full of pure, idyllic love, of
sweetness, sanity and natural affection, so that while Anna
always remains the supreme object of interest, and her
tragedy is that which the mind is never permitted to forget, yet the reader is made to realise that she is but one
figure upon a crowded stage. Now, this is not merely fine
art, but it is true realism. It is relatively easy to
create a one-part drama and excite intense interest by
making the one figure in the drama a woman struggling in
the throes of a disloyal love. Such a drama appeals to
the widespread sensationalism which cares for nothing but
strong lights and shades, and has no sense of moral equi-
poise and artistic perspective. But to fill the stage
with a crowd of figures, each individual and defined, and
yet hold the eye by one supreme figure, who appeals in the
strongest way to our pity and indignation, is a great
achievement, and this is what Tolstoi has achieved. But
he has done much more than this. His daring is great, for
he has withheld nothing in the story of Anna's shame. Yet
from first to last his appeal is made entirely to the
moral sense of the reader, nor is there anything more
piteous in literature than Anna's own cry, in the very
climax alike of her love and her shame: 'It is horrible'.
Think of how the ordinary French novelist would deal with
such a theme, and then you will appreciate the method of
Tolstoi. One cannot but feel that there is a sort of
divine simplicity about the man; an innermost purity of
mind and spirit which controls the situation, and awes
while it amazes us. And this divine simplicity is the
result of perfect sincerity as applied to art.

84. UNSIGNED REVIEW, 'BLACKWOOD'S EDINBURGH MAGAZINE'

November 1901

From a review by Charles Whibley (1859-1930), English
writer and critic; he contributed 'Musings with Method'
to the 'Edinburgh Magazine' for many years. Reprinted
by permission.

It is a commonplace that the most of men have a dual
nature, but no one ever lived two lives so distantly
separate as those which have made Count Tolstoi famous.
On the one hand he is an artist, on the other he is a
fanatic. The present generation knows him best as a
preacher of impossible dogmas, as a pietist who deems
renunciation the first and last duty of man, and who looks
with a kind of guilty regret upon the brilliant works of
earlier years. It is unlikely that his gospel will ever
be more than the sport of cranks and interviewers. The
excellence of manual labour, a favourite article of his
faith, is disputed by no one, while his communism has been
tried and has failed too often to be of interest or importance. But the very simplicity of his fanaticism would be
engaging, if it had not been made common by the newspapers; for Count Tolstoi is that rarest of creatures — a
fanatic who has lived. If he believes today that a
primitive life is best for us all, he has arrived at that
belief by proving to his own satisfaction that most other
lives are unsatisfying. He is a noble, he has great
estates, he has served in a distinguished regiment; yet
he now sees no beauty save in the life of the peasants
who till the soil, who sow the grain, and who reap the
harvest. But his fanaticism will pass and be forgotten
with other systems of the same kind; his masterpieces of
fiction will guard their niche in the temple of fame for
all time.
     To attach him to this school or that would be an imper-
tinence, since, indeed, he seems to have fashioned his own
method. For such mechanical contrivances as the novelists
call plot or construction you will look in vain in his
pages. He is not a professed psychologist, though he
pierces deeper than most into human character. He makes
no claim to realism, though he is always closer to the
truth than the rhapsodical M. Zola. But he exhibits the
characters of his personages as much in deed as in thought;

he does not analyse their motives as does Turgenev;
he prefers that their qualities, either good or evil,
should be displayed in action. For this reason he packs
his canvas full of figures. He attains his effects by a
mass of details introduced into a vast space. Some of
them, at a first reading, may seem superfluous; but there
are few which do not add a new touch to the portrait, or
show a character in a new light before his friends or
foes. And it is this method which creates the impression
of realism. In reading such works as 'Anna Karenin' or
'Peace and War' you seem to be confronted not by fiction
but by life. There are no jerky 'curtains' to disturb
the illusion; the chapters do not end upon a note of
interrogation, designed to force the interest on to
another page. The plot develops itself as does life,
simply, inevitably, and without accent; and in accord with
this simplicity the characters are rarely either above or
below the stature of men. That is to say, he deals neither with giants nor pigmies. His characters are not grotesquely sombre, like Dostoievsky's; nor grotesquely
humorous, like the characters of Dickens. They are,
indeed, merely the men and women that he has encountered
in his career — nobles and peasants, statesmen, sportsmen,
and soldiers. And here we may note the result of an
aristocratic prejudice: for him the great middle class
does not exist. Even the lawyer in 'Anna Karenin' is not
treated quite seriously; when he is not enunciating foolish platitudes in a pompous style, he is catching moths
to save his rep curtains.

But with this limitation Tolstoi knows the world of
Russia intimately, and he pictures it with a philosophic
calm and impartiality which should belong to the perfect
realist. But his books have no construction, the critic
may object. Nor has Life; and though you might leave out
half of 'Peace and War,' or 'Anna Karenin,' without destroying its meaning, there is still more in Life, at
whose significance we cannot guess. Again objects the
critic, the artist should select no more than is useful to
his purpose. But Tolstoi only differs from other novelists in that he selects with a more generous hand. He is
no symbolist attempting to represent the world in a blade
of grass; rather he sets Life impartially before you, and
leaves you to draw your own conclusions.

But there is one limit even to Tolstoi's impartiality.
Though he holds the scales of justice with an even hand,
though he looks with hatred upon none of his personages,
though even Karenin in his eyes (and in ours) is redeemed
from contempt, he is still partial where he himself is
concerned. In other words, he cannot keep himself out of

365 Tolstoy: The Critical Heritage

his books, and in some subtle fashion lets you know when
fiction turns to autobiography. There is little doubt
that in the vacillant, magnanimous, simple-hearted Levin
he is drawing his own character, not with any slavish
accuracy in fact, but with a perfect fidelity to thought.
The actions of Levin may not have been Tolstoi's; the
opinions of the two men (one is sure) are always identical.
So, too, we detect the author in the valiant Peter, a hero
in the heroic 'Peace and War.' But while these resemblan-
ces are intuitive, as it were, the student may judge how
much Tolstoi borrowed from his own experience, if he will
study his 'Memoirs,' and compare their incidents with the
incidents of his two great romances. To give an impression of his gallery would be impossible, but surely no
artist every boasted so noble an array of portraits.
Prince Andry is the noblest gentleman known to fiction,
and though only the greatest hand can draw a gentleman, it
is not only by this supreme test that Tolstoi excels: he
has depicted gamblers and men about town with a clairvoy-
ant sympathy which can come of experience alone. His Cossacks are living heroes; and Turgenev, with all his sympathy with young Russia, never saw so deep into the peasant's mind as Tolstoi. He has unfolded war with all its
accessories of splendour, courage, and passion in a grandiose panorama. In 'Ivan Iliitch' he has softened by his
art the common, hopeless horror of death; and he has done
all this with so deep a knowledge of human nature, with so
fine a sympathy with human weakness, that he can rank only
with the great ones of the earth. Such is Tolstoi the
artist, and as for Tolstoi the fanatic, we may leave him
to other fanatics who, not having his genius, are proud to
ape his folly. But all the fanaticism in the world cannot
recall or abolish a published masterpiece, and not even
the indecent folly of the 'Kreutzer Sonata' can dim the
brilliancy of 'Peace and War.'

85. KROPOTKIN: 'SUPERHUMAN JUSTICE' OR 'SOCIETY'?

1905

Prince P.A. Kropotkin (1842-1921) was an eminent geogra-
pher in his younger day, and later a revolutionary. He
left Russia after escaping from prison in the Peter and
Paul Fortress in St Petersburg in 1876, and he lived in

England from 1886 until 1917 when he returned to Russia
after the February revolution. He is best known as the
leading theorist of Communist Anarchism; he opposed all
state power and private property and proposed a federation
of mutual-aid communities. Besides a number of theoretical works, he wrote a fascinating autobiography, 'Memoirs
of a Revolutionist' (1899-1906); his 'Russian Literature:
Ideals and Realities', from which the following extract is
taken, was written in English and published in London in
1905.

Of all Tolstoy's novels, 'Anna Karenina' is the one which
has been the most widely read in all languages. As a
work of art it is a masterpiece. From the very first
appearance of the heroine you feel that this woman must
bring with her a drama; from the very outset her tragical
end is as inevitable as it is in a drama of Shakespeare.
In that sense the novel is true to life throughout. It is
a corner of real life that we have before us. As a rule,
Tolstoy is not at his best in picturing women - with the
exception of very young girls - and I do not think that
Anna Karenina herself is as deep, as psychologically complete, and as living a creation as she might have been;
but the more ordinary woman, Dolly, is simply teeming with
life. As to the various scenes of the novel - the ball
scenes, the races of the officers, the inner family life
of Dolly, the country scenes on Levin's estate, the death
of his brother, and so on - all these are depicted in such
a way that for its artistic qualities 'Anna Karenina'
stands foremost even amongst the many beautiful things
Tolstoy has written. And yet, notwithstanding all that,
the novel produced in Russia a decidedly unfavourable impression, which brought to Tolstoy congratulations from
the reactionary camp and a very cool reception from the
advanced portion of society. The fact is that the question of marriage and of an eventual separation between
husband and wife had been most earnestly debated in Russia
by the best men and women, both in literature and in life.
It is self-evident that such indifferent levity towards
marriage as is continually unveiled before the courts in
'Society' divorce cases was absolutely and unconditionally
condemned; and that any form of deceit, such as makes the
subject of countless French novels and dramas, was ruled
out of question in any honest discussion of the matter.
But after the above levity and deceit had been severely
branded, the rights of a new love, serious and deep,
appearing after years of happy married life, had only been

the more seriously analysed. Tchernyshevsky's novel 'What is to be Done?' can be taken as the best expression of the opinions upon marriage which had become current amongst the better portion of the younger generation. Once you are married, it was said, do not take lightly to love affairs, or so-called flirtation. Every fit of passion does not deserve the name of a new love; and what is sometimes described as love is in a very great number of cases nothing but temporary desire. Even if it were real love, before a real and deep love has grown up, there is in most cases a period when one has time to reflect upon the consequences that would follow if the beginnings of his or her new sympathy should attain the depth of such a love. But with all that, there are cases when a new love does come, and there are cases when such an event must happen almost fatally, when, for instance, a girl has been married almost against her will, under the continued insistence of her lover, or when the two have married without properly understanding each other, or when one of the two has continued to progress in his or her development towards a higher ideal, while the other, after having worn for some time the mask of idealism, falls into the Philistine happiness of warmed slippers. In such cases separation not only becomes inevitable, but it often is to the interest of both. It would be much better for both to live through the sufferings which a separation would involve (honest natures are by such sufferings made better) than to spoil the entire subsequent existence of the one - in most cases of both - and to face moreover the fatal results that living together under such circumstances would necessarily mean for the children. This was, at least, the conclusion to which both Russian literature and the best all round portion of our society had come.

And now came Tolstoy with 'Anna Karenina', which bears the biblical epigraph: 'Vengeance is mine, and I will repay it', and in which the biblical revenge falls upon the unfortunate Karenina, who puts an end by suicide to her sufferings after her separation from her husband. Russian critics evidently could not accept Tolstoy's views. The case of Karenina was one of those where there could be no question of 'vengeance'. She was married as a young girl to an old and unattractive man. At that time she did not know exactly what she was doing, and nobody explained it to her. She had never known love, and learned it for the first time when she saw Vronskiy. Deceit, for her, was absolutely out of the question; and to keep up a merely conventional marriage would have been a sacrifice which would not have made her husband and child any happier. Separation and a new life with Vronskiy,

who seriously loved her, was the only possible outcome.
At any rate, if the story of Anna Karenina has to end in
tragedy, it was not in the least in consequence of an act
of supreme justice. As always, the honest artistic genius
of Tolstoy had itself indicated another cause - the real
one. It was the inconsistency of Vronskiy and Karenina.
After having separated from her husband and defied 'public
opinion' - that is, the opinion of women who, as Tolstoy
shows it himself, were not honest enough to be allowed any
voice in the matter - neither she nor Vronskiy had the
courage of breaking entirely with that society, the futility of which Tolstoy knows and describes so exquisitely.
Instead of that, when Anna returned with Vronskiy to St
Petersburg, her own and Vronskiy's chief preoccupation
was - how Betsey and other such women would receive her,
if she made her appearance among them. And it was the
opinion of the Betsies - surely not Superhuman Justice -
which brought Karenina to suicide.

86.   BARING ON 'ANNA KARENINA'

1910

Maurice Baring (1874-1945), novelist, essayist, poet and
playwright, worked as a journalist in Russia for a number
of years up to 1912 and wrote extensively on Russian
affairs. The following extract is taken from chapter IV,
Tolstoy and Tourgeniev, of his 'Landmarks in Russian
Literature', first published in 1910. Reprinted by permission.

Manners change but man, faced by the problem of life, is
the same throughout all ages; and, whether consciously or
unconsciously, Tolstoy proves this in writing 'Anna Karenina'. Here again, on a large canvas, we see unrolled
before us the contemporary life of the upper classes, in
Russia, in St Petersburg, and in the country, with the
same sharpness of vision, which seizes every outward
detail, and reveals every recess of the heart and mind.
Nearly all characters in all fiction seem bookish beside
those of Tolstoy. His men and women are so real and so
true that, even if his psychological analysis of them may

sometimes err and go wrong from its oversubtlety and its
desire to explain too much, the characters themselves seem
to correct this automatically, as though they were independent of their creator. He creates a character and
gives it life. He may theorize on a character, just as he
might theorize on a person in real life; and he may theorize wrong, simply because sometimes no theorizing is
necessary, and the very fact of a theory being set down in
words may give a false impression; but, as soon as the
character speaks and acts, it speaks and acts in the
manner which is true to itself, and corrects the false
impression of the theory, just as though it were an independent person over whom the author had no control.

Nearly every critic, at least nearly every English
critic, (Matthew Arnold is a notable exception), in dealing with 'Anna Karenina', has found fault with the author
for the character of Vronsky. Anna Karenina, they say,
could never have fallen in love with such an ordinary
commonplace man. Vronsky, one critic has said (in a brilliant article), is only a glorified 'Steerforth'. The
answer to this is that if you go to St Petersburg or to
London, or to any other town you like to mention, you will
find that the men with whom the Anna Kareninas of this
world fall in love are precisely the Vronskys, and no-one
else, for the simple reason that Vronsky is a man. He is
not a hero, and he is not a villain; he is not what people
call 'interesting', but a man, as masculine as Anna is
feminine, with many good qualities and many limitations,
but above all things alive. Nearly every novelist, with
the exception of Fielding, ends, in spite of himself, by
placing his hero either above or beneath the standard of
real life. There are many Vronskys today in St Petersburg, and for the matter of that, *mutatis mutandis*, in
London. But no novelist except Tolstoy has ever had the
power to put this simple thing, an ordinary man, into a
book. Put one of Meredith's heroes next to Vronsky, and
Meredith's hero will appear like a figure dressed up for a
fancy-dress ball. Put one of Bourget's heroes next to
him, with all of his psychological documents attached to
him, and, in spite of all the analysis in the world, side
by side with Tolstoy's human being he will seem but a
plaster cast. Yet all the time in 'Anna Karenina' we
feel, as in 'War and Peace', that the author is still
unsatisfied and hungry, searching for something he has not
yet found; and once again, this time in still sharper outline and more living colours, he paints an ideal of simplicity which is taking us towards Ivan Durak in the
character of Levin. Into this character, too, we feel
that Tolstoy has put a great deal of himself; and that

Levin, if he is not Tolstoy himself, is what Tolstoy would like to be. But the loneliness and the void that are round Tolstoy's mind are not yet filled; and in that loneliness and in that void we are sharply conscious of the brooding presence of despair, and the power of darkness.

After 'Anna Karenina' 1886-1910

87. DE VOGÜÉ ON TOLSTOY'S NIHILISM

1886

E.M. de Vogüé (1848-1910) was secretary at the French
Embassy in St Petersburg from 1876 to 1882 and it was
during this period that his interest in Russian literature was aroused. His six articles on various Russian
authors appeared in the 'Revue des deux mondes' in 1883-6
and were published as a book, 'Le Roman russe', in 1886;
it appeared in Russian the following year. De Vogüé is
as important a figure in introducing Tolstoy to his
fellow-countrymen as Matthew Arnold is in England (see
No. 82) or W.D. Howells in the USA (see No. 79).
   The extracts which follow are taken from the book,
chapter VI: Tolstoy: Nihilism and Mysticism.

We have seen the birth of the *roman de moeurs* in Russia
with Turgenev; we have seen him move from the very first,
as if through a natural inclination of the Russian national spirit, towards the psychological observation of
general types; perhaps it would be more just to say
towards their contemplation as this better describes the
serenity which, in this great artist, tempered his interest in the morals of his time. Dostoevsky has shown a
genius of a completely opposite nature, uncultivated and
subtle, full of compassion, tortured by tragic visions and
with an unhealthy preoccupation with unusual characters.
The former will always carry on a flirtation with liberal
doctrines while the latter is an intransigent Slavophile.

Tolstoy has other surprises for us. Younger than his
predecessors by a dozen years he was scarcely affected by
1848. Free from any attachment to any 'school', indifferent to political parties which he disdains, this lonely
and thoughtful gentleman acknowledges no master or grouping; he is a spontaneous phenomenon. His first great
novel was written at the same time as 'Fathers and Sons'
but between him and Turgenev there is a great difference.
One holds to the traditions of the past and of a European
teacher; he retains the instruments of precision as a
writer, which he obtained from us. The other has broken
with the past and dependence on foreigners. He is the new
Russia, thrown into the shadows in the search for her own
path, scornful of our advice on matters of taste and
often incomprehensible to us. Do not demand of her that
she should set bounds on herself, which she is quite incapable of doing, or concentrate her activities on one
thing in particular, or subordinate her conception of life
to a doctrine; she wants a literature which reflects the
moral chaos from which she is suffering. Tolstoy has come
to provide it. Before all others and more than all others
he is both the interpreter and propagandist of that state
of the Russian soul which is called Nihilism.... Critics
have called Turgenev the father of Nihilism because he
gave the disease that name and described a few cases; this
is like saying that cholera was introduced by the first
doctor who diagnosed it rather than by the first person
who suffered from it. Turgenev diagnosed the disease and
studied it objectively but Tolstoy had suffered from it
from the day he was born without at first having a clear
idea what was the matter with him: his afflicted soul
cries out on every page of his books with the anguish
which weighs on the souls of so many of his countrymen.
If the most interesting books are those which faithfully
represent the lives of a part of humanity at a given time
in history then our century has produced nothing more
interesting than the works of Tolstoy....
By a strange and frequent contradiction this troubled,
restless spirit who floats about in the mists of Nihilism
is gifted with a lucidity and penetration without equal
for studying life's phenomena scientifically. His gaze is
sharp, immediate and analytic on everything on earth to do
with both the inner and exterior life of man; first the
tangible realities, then the play of the passions, the
most mobile and fleeting of actions and the slightest
feelings of disquiet in the conscience. One might say he
has the spirit of an English chemist in the soul of a
Buddhist or Hindu which alone can explain this strange
combination and which can explain Russia. Tolstoy walks

through human society with a simplicity and naturalness
which seems forbidden to writers in France; he looks, he
listens and he paints the image and fixes the echo of
what he has heard. It is permanent and has a truthfulness
which we are forced to applaud. Not content with assemb-
ling the different characteristics of social life he then
breaks them down into their constituent parts with an in-
definable subtlety; always obsessed with knowing how and
why an action is performed, he pursues the initial thought
behind the visible action and does not let go until he has
stripped it naked and pulled it from the heart with all
its secret roots revealed.

Unfortunately his curiosity does not stop there; these
phenomena which offer him such firm ground when he studies
them in isolation lead to his wanting to know the general
laws which govern and harmonize them, and to find their
inaccessible causes. And then his clear gaze is clouded,
the intrepid explorer loses his footing and falls into the
abyss of philosophical contradictions; within him and all
around him he senses nothing but the void and the night;
to fill this void and to illuminate this night he makes
his characters propose the feeble explanations of meta-
physics; then suddenly, irritated by their juvenile ramb-
lings, they are made to expose their own explanations for
what they are.

As Tolstoy advances in his work and in his life, continuously plunged in universal doubt, he continues to
treat with cold irony those children of his imagination
who make an effort to believe and apply an established
system; but beneath this apparent coldness one can determine the beating of a heart hungering after the eternal.
Finally, tired of doubting, tired of searching, convinced
that all the workings of the reason end only in shameful
failure and fascinated by the mysticism which has been
haunting his troubled soul for some time, the Nihilist
throws himself suddenly at the feet of God - which God
we shall soon see....

88. OSCAR WILDE COMPARES TURGENEV, TOLSTOY AND
DOSTOEVSKY

1887

Oscar Wilde (1854-1900), the Irish-born poet, novelist

and dramatist. His series of critical writings forms as it were the middle section of his literary life, between the time when, as a disciple of Walter Pater, he was the leader of an aesthetic movement advocating 'art for art's sake' and the later period of his most famous works. The review with which this extract begins, entitled A Batch of Novels, appeared in the 'Pall Mall Gazette', 2 May 1887 and was concerned among other works with the then just published English translation of Dostoevsky's 'The Humiliated and Insulted' (1861) which was called then 'Injury and Insult'.

Of the three great Russian novelists of our time Tourgenieff is by far the finest artist. He has that spirit of exquisite selection, that delicate choice of details, which is the essence of style; his work is entirely free from any personal intention; and by taking existence at its most fiery-coloured moments he can distil into a few pages of perfect prose the moods and passions of many lives.

Count Tolstoi's method is much larger, and his field of vision more extended. He reminds us sometimes of Paul Veronese, and, like that great painter, can crowd, without over-crowding, the giant canvas on which he works. We may not at first gain from his works that artistic unity of impression which is Tourgenieff's chief charm, but once that we have mastered the details the whole seems to have the grandeur and the simplicity of an epic.

Dostoieffski differs widely from both his rivals. He is not so fine an artist as Tourgenieff, for he deals more with the facts than with effects of life; nor has he Tolstoi's largeness of vision and epic dignity; but he has qualities that are distinctly and absolutely his own, such as a fierce intensity of passion and concentration of impulse, a power of dealing with the deepest mysteries of psychology and the most hidden springs of life, and a realism that is pitiless in its fidelity, and terrible because it is true.

89.   EDMUND GOSSE ON TOLSTOY

1890

Sir Edmund Gosse (1849-1928) was a critic, minor writer
and leading man of letters. His essay Count Lyof Tolstoi,
part of which follows, was first published in 1890 and
reprinted in his 'Critical Kit-Kats' of 1896. Reprinted
by permission.

Tolstoi was thirty-two when he published his first great
novel,'War and Peace', in 1860. Very soon after its
appearance, he took himself out of society, and began his
retirement at Yasnaya Polyana. For fifteen years the
world heard comparatively little of him, and then he
crowned the edifice of his reputation with the successive
volumes of 'Anna Karenine' (1875-77). It is by these two
epics of prose fiction, these massive productions, that
he is mainly known. By degrees the fame of these amazing
books passed beyond the ring of the Russian language, and
now most educated persons in the West of Europe have read
them. They dwarf all other novels by comparison. The
immense area of place and time which they occupy is un-
exampled, and the first thing which strikes us on laying
them down is their comprehensive character.
    The work of no other novelist is so populous as that of
Tolstoi. His books seem to include the entire existence
of generations. In 'War and Peace' we live with the characters through nearly a quarter of a century. They are
young when we are introduced to them; we accompany them
through a hundred vicissitudes of disease and health, ill
fortune and good, to death or to old age. There is no
other novelist, whose name I can recall, who gives anything like this sense of presenting all that moves beneath
the cope of heaven. Even Stendhal is dwarfed by Tolstoi,
on his own ground; and the Russian novelist joins to this
anthill of the soldier and the courtier, those other
worlds of Richardson, of Balzac, of Thackeray. Through
each of Tolstoi's two macrocosms, thronged with highly
vitalised personages, walks one man more tenderly described and vividly presented than any of the others, the
figure in whom the passions of the author himself are en-
shrined, Pierre Bezouchof in the one case, Levine in the
other. This sort of hero, to whose glorification, however, the author makes no heroic concessions, serves to

376 Tolstoy: The Critical Heritage

give a certain solidity and continuity to the massive narration.

These two books are so widely known, that in so slight a sketch as this, their constitution may be taken as appreciated. Their magnificent fulness of life in movement, their sumptuous passages of description, their poignancy in pathos and rapidity in action, their unwavering devotion to veracity of impression, without squalor or emphasis — these qualities have given intellectual enjoyment of the highest kind to thousands of English readers. They are panoramas rather than pictures, yet finished so finely and balanced so harmoniously that we forget the immense scale upon which they are presented, in our unflagging delight in the variety and vivacity of the scene. No novelist is less the slave of a peculiarity in one of his characters than Tolstoi. He loves to take an undeveloped being, such as André in 'War and Peace', or Kitty Cherbatzky in 'Anna Karenine', and to blow upon it with all the winds of heaven, patiently noting its revulsions and advances, its inconsistencies and transitions, until the whole metamorphosis of its moral nature is complete. There is no greater proof of the extraordinary genius of Count Tolstoi than this, that through the vast evolution of his plots, his characters, though ever developing and changing, always retain their distinct individuality. The hard metal of reflected life runs ductile through the hands of this giant of the imagination.

90. LEONTIEV ON TOLSTOY'S QUALITIES

1890

From 'Analysis, Style and Atmosphere: On the Novels of Count L.N. Tolstoy', published as a book in 1911, but first appearing in the 'Citizen', 1890, nos 157-8, and the 'Russian Messenger', 1890, nos 6-8. K.N. Leontiev (1831-91) was a conservative and anti-democratic thinker and arguably the most brilliant literary critic of his day. He was concerned with the aesthetic nature of literature and not at all with what 'message' authors might or might not have. His book on Tolstoy has been regarded as a landmark in nineteenth-century Russian criticism.

One of our most eminent scholars and writers when discussing the merits some years ago of 'Anna Karenina' mentioned, among other things, that: 'He who studies "Anna
Karenina" studies life itself.' I think that the expert
was right, and that this novel is in its way a notable
achievement both in its extraordinary truthfulness and the
depth of its poetry, neither of which has been equalled in
nineteenth-century literature. In some ways it is better
than 'War and Peace'.

To study these two great works of Russian literature is
extremely interesting and instructive. It is also a pleasure.... [They] not only can but they must be compared
with each other. When one compares them and examines them
in detail, preferring first one and then the other, one
must finally admit that the sum of their merits is the
same.

In 'War and Peace' the task is more elevated and the
choice more gratifying; but for the very reason that in
'Anna Karenina' the author was left more to his own
devices and was not helped from outside by the grandeur of
the historical events and so had to choose for himself
from the motley events flashing across the contemporary
scene and to 'fasten onto' what he had chosen some 'lasting idea' makes one wish to give preference to the author
of 'Anna Karenina' over the creator of the national epic.

In 'War and Peace' there is, of course, more tragedy,
there are more striking scenes. Moreover the very nature
of the tragedy is better. In the epic, people are fighting for their native land (on both sides, even, for the
French were waging wars of aggression for the predominance of France and the benefit of their native land).
In the contemporary novel the war of the Russian 'volunteers' fighting for Serbia appears in the distance and is
condemned out of hand by the author. There are two sui-
cides (one successful, the other not) and Levin thinks
about it; it is incomparably more sombre and even more
vulgar; but this is not Count Tolstoy's fault, it is that
of contemporary life. It was given to him from outside as
were the fire of Moscow and the battle of Borodino in 'War
and Peace'. It is difficult to write a great, truthful
and interesting novel about contemporary Russian life
without including in it at least some thoughts of suicide
inasmuch as it has unfortunately become so common in our
lives.

In any case the great service of 'War and Peace' is
that the tragedy in it is sober and healthy and not distorted as in so many of our other writers. It is not, as
it is with Dostoevsky, the tragedy of doss-houses, bro-
thels or the Preobrazhensky Hospital. The tragedy of 'War

and Peace' is useful: it disposes one towards military
heroism for one's country; Dostoevsky's tragedy can probably only stimulate certain psychopaths living in furnished rooms. And even in 'Anna Karenina' both the sui-
cides, both Vronsky's and Anna's, are covered in such an
abundance of health, strength, physical beauty, sparkle,
peace and enjoyment that they cannot deeply offend the
heart or taste of the normal reader.

In both novels the incredible subtlety of Tolstoy's
mind could not kill his feelings for the healthy or, shall
we say, his 'flair'. The historical or more precisely the
directly political service done by the author is immense.
Did many of us ever think about 1812 before he so wonderfully and unforgettably reminded us of it? Very few! And
in spite of the fact that the count so 'tendentiously' and
theophilanthropically condemns war, now himself, now
through the lips of the good but ever absent-minded Pierre,
he is none the less such a truthful artist that it is very
easy for the reader not to listen either to him or to
Pierre and to continue to regard war as one of the highest
and most ideal of the manifestations of life on earth despite all the private misfortunes it occasions. (These
misfortunes are constantly - let us note in passing -
accompanied for many people by special joys which peace
does not bring!) And in our times when the craze for
'general utilitarian bliss' is far from cured this is a
great political service....

When Turgenev, according to P. Boborykin, said so
justly and nobly that his talent could not be compared to
Tolstoy's great gifts and that 'Levushka Tolstoy is an
elephant' I think that he must have been thinking at the
time of 'War and Peace' in particular. It is indeed an
elephant. Or, if you like, something more monstrous, an
excavated Sivatherium in the flesh - a Sivatherium whose
huge skulls are kept in Indian temples to the god Siva.
The trunk, the immense body, the tusks, and besides the
tusks there are also horns, all of which go against every
zoological law.

For it is also possible to compare 'War and Peace' to
an Indian idol: three heads or four faces and six arms!
The enormous proportions, the precious material and the
eyes made of rubies and diamonds not only below the brow
but on it as well. And the sustaining of the general
plan; and the inexhaustible details which become even a
little ponderous; the three heroes of almost equal importance (in the eyes of both the author and the readers) and
the four heroines (Bezukhov, Bolkonsky, Rostov, Natasha,
Maria, Sonya and Hélène). The psychological analysis in
the majority of cases is striking precisely because the

most different of people are subjected to it: Napoleon,
ill at Borodino; the peasant girl at the council at Fili;
Natasha and Kutuzov; Pierre and Prince Andrey; Princess
Maria and the modest Captain Tushin; Nikolay - both the
Rostov brothers, and let us note in passing the great
difference between these two brothers - Nikolay and Petya
- in their first encounters with danger: Nikolay who later
turns out to be a brave and reliable officer is timid and
afraid in his first battle but the sixteen-year-old Petya
is quite the opposite. I noticed this difference when I
first read the novel and wondered was it only because the
author did not wish to repeat himself or was there in the
two characters a physiological difference? I found that
there was. Petya has more imagination and enthusiasm
while Nikolay is more obtuse and conditioned; if the
young man is not an utter coward by nature it is because
his strong imagination, militarily inclined, can so take
control of him that he just does not think of personal
risk, his heroic fantasy drowns his natural feelings of
fear; Nikolay has a poor sense of imagination which could
not replace his habits; he had to 'receive his baptism of
fire'. One could make many such observations.

Which of our writers has described minor and bloody
battles so well, so excitingly, so horrifically and so
Homerically and at the same time in such a modern way?
Gogol in his 'Taras Bulba'? Yes, but only Homerically
and not contemporarily; we cannot live in the souls of
these distant and crude people as we can in those of the
civilian, Pierre, or the energetic idealist, Andrey, or
the ordinary but good Russian officer, Nikolay Rostov.

And who, on the other hand, in our time has described
so beautifully, so subtly and as it were so fragrantly
scenes from high society? For example the ball for the
tsar where the rejuvenated widower Bolkonsky, dressed in
his white uniform, dances with Natasha who is almost mad
with success and where 'at every third step in the waltz
Hélène's velvet dress seems to flash and swirl out'.

And in whom else would we find this? Only in Markevich's 'Quarter of a Century' and 'Turning Point'. But
even here the path was laid by Tolstoy (*without a single
negative nuance*).

In both the description of this ball in Petersburg and
later in that of the ball in Moscow in 'Anna Karenina'
(the one where Anna unexpectedly takes Vronsky away from
Kitty) and in the scenes of the courtiers' horse-race (in
the second novel too) we see only the poetry of truth and
can find no shadow of negation, ridicule or malevolence
as we always do in Turgenev when he crosses the threshold
of a real drawing-room; he never even dared enter a grand

ballroom with complete freedom and impartiality as Tolstoy
and Markevich did. Or, as a third example of the unusual
breadth and wealth of content of 'War and Peace' let us
take the author's attitude to religious feeling. Of the
main characters in the novel there are only three,
strictly speaking, truly religious Orthodox people from
the upper classes: the old Kutuzov, Nikolay Rostov from
time to time and Princess Maria constantly. I shall leave
Nikolay Rostov and His Excellency to one side for the
moment and compare in this respect Princess Maria with
Liza Kalitina in Turgenev's 'A House of Gentlefolk'. Liza
is, of course, the most charming and noble of Turgenev's
heroines; her pure, saintly image will remain for ever an
adornment of our literature; but none the less in this
connection, too, we must give Tolstoy preference in the
matter of creativity and once again give Turgenev moral
honour for the impartiality of his 'Tolstoy is an elephant'. (It is well known that an elephant can lift a
large log with his trunk and cast it aside as well as
carefully lift a butterfly from a flower.)

Of Liza Kalitina we know that she believes in and
fears God; she says to Lavretsky: 'We shall all die.' We
know the stories told by her nanny about martyrs in whose
blood flowers bloomed; we remember with tenderness little
Liza's 'Were they wallflowers?' when she asked about the
holy blood and the wonderful flowers. We feel exactly
what the noble Lavretsky felt when she has become a nun
and passes from one choir to another with bowed head. We
are grateful to Turgenev that he did not start analysing
this event but merely said that there are occasions in
life when one need not expand; one should 'only point
them out and pass by'. I have not forgotten those words
and am now writing them from memory but when I think of
them I am even now, twenty-eight years later, moved to
tears. But (again this 'no' and again in Tolstoy's
favour; but what is there to be done?) we see everything
about Liza only from the outside, we see her as Lavretsky
saw her because Turgenev analyses almost always only one
of his main characters, and that one who is closest to
him spiritually; but for Tolstoy there are no limits to
his analysis, not in a person's temperament, or in age or
sex or even in *zoological* differences for he can in a moment show us the feelings of a bull or a dog or a horse.
One perhaps notices only that national qualities resist
him more than anything for he analyses the French in 'War
and Peace' far more weakly than the Russians. We see
nothing human in Napoleon, for example, only pride,
cruelty and vanity. Was it really like that?

We see Liza through Lavretsky's eyes but Princess

Maria's religious nature we see from closer at hand because along with the author we more than once penetrate
the very depths of her soul and see not only the purity of
her Orthodox principles but we are also present at the
inner struggles of her thoughts and feelings. The young
Kuragin comes to Bald Hills to seek her hand; and her
sister-in-law, Princess Liza, and her companion, Mlle
Bourienne, make her wear her best clothes, but they do
not manage to make the princess more beautiful; on the
contrary she looks even less attractive.

[Quotation omitted.]

    Count Tolstoy can depict with equal success not only
the various kinds of passionate feelings but also the
workings of the mind in people of different faiths. Let
us recall for comparison with the princess's genuine train
of Orthodox thought only those poetic and vague dreams of
some philanthropic pantheism with which her gifted and
unhappy brother dies.
    And that is not all. What contrasts! The fire of
Moscow and the children's games, the charming make-believe
of the children of the good Rostov family; those married
couples, so different from each other, yet all of them
interesting; the frosts on the fields and the balls in
the palaces; the emperors, and the peasants in their best
shoes; the hunts in the country; the drinking of the
soldiers; and the gossip in the army. Chastity and sensuality are shown with equal truth. That stout and senile
warrior, Kutuzov, now praying, now being cunning, now
crying and on the eve of the battle of Borodino calmly
reading a French novel and joking with the priest's wife!
By doing hardly a thing, he achieves everything - it is
amazing!
    And another of the author's originalities: having
halted both the course of the action and the workings of
his own external observations, sometimes for a long
period, he will suddenly throw open wide as it were the
doors of the human soul before the reader and place in
front of his eyes (sometimes almost forcibly) a kind of
psychological microscope of his own and plunge the reader
into a world of fantasy at one time wide awake, at another
drowsily or in a dream, at another in the heat of battle
or on the bed of someone dying a slow and gently reconcil-
ing death.
    Even this philosophy of fatalism is introduced into the
story in whole large pieces contrary to all accepted practice; and finally that obvious philanthropic tendency
which reveals its sense more and more clearly as the end

of this strange, absolutely unique but great epic is
approached.

Possibly one might not sympathize with this tendency;
it is necessary even to be able strictly to differentiate
it from true Christianity but one cannot help marvelling
at the author's originality and daring in not fearing the
usual reproaches concerning irrelevant philosophizing.

91.   HAVELOCK ELLIS ON TOLSTOY'S CONDITIONS FOR HUMAN
HAPPINESS, 'THE NEW SPIRIT'

1890

Havelock Ellis (1859-1939), psychologist, essayist and
critic, was best known for his, in their time, scandalous
writings on sexual psychology. His book, 'The New
Spirit', is an attempt to trace the development of the
scientific spirit of truth and inquiry, the general soci-
alization of life, and the spread of democracy, and looks
to art, especially literature, for their expression; he
deals with the social aspects of Diderot, Heine, Whitman,
Ibsen and Tolstoy in whom he sees 'the manifestation of
another great modern force', i.e. the growth in power and
influence of Russia, and 'no keenness or clearness in the
interpretation of life, though such a marvellous power
of presentation; yet a massive elemental force, groping
slowly and incoherently towards the light, so interesting
to us because we seem to be conscious of the heart of a
whole nation, the great nation of the future, towards
which all eyes are turned'. The following extract concludes his chapter on Tolstoy. Reprinted by permission.

Tolstoi sums up his own doctrine under a very few heads:
Resist not evil - Judge not - Be not angry - Love one
woman. His creed is entirely covered by these four
points. 'My Religion' is chiefly occupied by the exposition of what they mean, and in his hands they mean much.
They mean nothing less than the abolition of the State and
the country. He is as uncompromising as Ibsen in dealing
with the State. 'It is a humbug, this State,' he remarked
to Mr Stead. 'What you call a Government is mere phantasmagoria. What is a State? Men I know; peasants and

villages, these I see; but governments, nations, states, what are these but fine names invented to conceal the plundering of honest men by dishonest officials?' Law, tribunals, prisons, become impossible with the disappearance of the State; and with the disappearance of the country, and of 'that gross imposture called patriotism', there can be no more war.

In place of these great and venerable pillars of civilization, what? The first condition of happiness, he tells us, is that the link between man and nature shall not be broken, that he may enjoy the sky above him, and the pure air and the life of the fields. This involves the nationalization of the land, or rather, to avoid centralizing tendencies, its communalization. 'I quite agree with George,' he remarked, 'that the landlords may be fairly expropriated without compensation, as a matter of principle. But as a question of expediency, I think compensation might facilitate the necessary change. It will come, I suppose, as the emancipation of the slaves came. The idea will spread. A sense of the shamefulness of private ownership will grow. Someone will write an "Uncle Tom's Cabin" about it; there will be agitation, and then it will come, and many who own land will do as did those who owned serfs, voluntarily give it to their tenants. But for the rest, a loan might be arranged, so as to prevent the work being stopped by the cry of confiscation. Of course I do not hold with George about the taxation of the land. If you could get angels from Heaven to administer the taxes from the land, you might do justice and prevent mischief. I am against all taxation.' The second condition of happiness is labour, the intellectual labour that one loves because one has chosen it freely, and the physical labour that is sweet because it produces the muscular joy of work, a good appetite, and tranquil sleep. The third condition of happiness is love. Every healthy man and woman should have sexual relationships; and Tolstoi makes no distinction between those that are called by the name of marriage and those that are not so called; in either case, however, he would demand that they shall be permanent. The fourth condition is unrestrained fellowship with men and women generally, without distinction of class. The fifth is health, though this seems largely the result of obedience to the others. These are the five points of Tolstoi's charter. They seem simple enough, but he is careful to point out that most of them are closed to the rich. The rich man is hedged in by conventions, and cannot live a simple and natural life. A peasant can associate on equal terms with millions of his fellows; the circle of equal association becomes narrower and narrower

the higher the social rank, until we come to kings and
emperors who have scarcely one person with whom they may
live on equal terms. 'Is not the whole system like a
great prison, where each inmate is restricted to association with a few fellow-convicts?' The rich may, indeed,
work, but even then their work usually consists in official and administrative duties, or the observance of
arduous social conventions which are odious to them: 'I
say odious, for I never yet met with a person of this
class who was contented with his work, or took as much
satisfaction in it as the man who shovels the snow from
his doorstep'. From this standpoint Tolstoi has never
since greatly varied.

92. LÖWENFELD ON WHY TOLSTOY WAS MISUNDERSTOOD BY HIS
CONTEMPORARIES

1892

Raphael Löwenfeld (1854-1910) was lecturer in Slavonic
languages at Breslau University and visited the Tolstoys
at Yasnaya Polyana in 1891. On his return to Germany he
began to publish a German translation of Tolstoy's
works; it started to appear in Berlin in 1891. His
extensive book on Tolstoy, 'Graf Tolstoi, Sein Leben,
seine Werke, seine Weltanschauung', was published in 1892
and translated into Russian by S. Shklyaryov in 1895 and
reprinted the following year. The extract which follows
is taken from the book's final chapter.

It is obvious that once Tolstoy had attracted the attention of Russian society there would not be long to wait
before an appreciation of his great importance as a
writer was made. It is true that Tolstoy's contemporaries, prejudiced by tendentious ideas, were hardly capable of evaluating the quality of the harmony between the
artistic form and the unusually rich content which is the
mark of all of his works. The remarkable artistry shown
by Tolstoy in the depiction of people from all classes and
levels of society, peasants and nobles, soldiers and civilians, officers and privates, Europeans and Asiatics, and
the amazing powers of his psychological analysis from

which no movement of the human heart could escape, were
all quite capable of being understood by his Russian
readers. The only innovation in Tolstoy's works for these
readers was his attitude to love, which is something which
plays a less central role in his works than in those of
other writers, and his unparalleled sincerity which sometimes reached naivety but which stemmed from a unique
spiritual purity. Under the influence of this sincerity
Tolstoy had no fear of depicting all the unattractive
nakedness of much of what was generally regarded as
sacred; under the influence of that very special spiritual
nature he strips the mask from the disguised emptiness of
society life, not without a certain cruelty exposes all
the secrets of the marriage market (see chapter XXII of
'The Cossacks') and ridicules certain sections of society
whose representatives make use of general trust and
shroud themselves in mystery and attempt to usurp the
position of those acting according to religious rites, as
for example doctors (see the end of chapter II of 'Polikushka').

Whatever might have been the attitude of this or that
reader to him, Tolstoy showed in a long series of works
that he was not only a productive but also a many-sided
writer.

He began his career with a sort of autobiographical
novel, the story of a man's intellectual and spiritual
development. By means of the description of the slightest
changes in the form of the thoughts and emotions of his
hero, Tolstoy drew a picture of the change from a small
boy into an adolescent, from an adolescent into a young
man, and from a young man into a fully mature person. The
influence of the milieu surrounding Irtenev in the first
years of his life, the effect on him of his school-
fellows, his friends and close relations are all noted by
the reader and at the root of the conclusions to which he
comes is the interrelation of inherent characteristics and
upbringing in the widest sense of the word. Thus the
artistic task of the novel is the depiction of aspirations
to self-perfection and the artistic methods employed to
this end are based on psychological analysis.

Psychological analysis has long been a favourite artistic device among Russian authors; it is for this reason
that such a method has not been surpassed in other literatures. Tolstoy brought, however, to his first work an
unusual skill in the dissecting of spiritual conditions, a
skill which can only be compared to Dostoevsky's. Consequently the whole idea of the novel was something completely new for the Russian reader. Tolstoy's first work
is remarkable for the fact that he was attempting

something positive and was erecting definite ideals which
was something markedly different from other works of
Russian literature of the time, the majority of which were
full of a pessimistic and satirical spirit. In this connection, though, the ideals put forward by Tolstoy in
'Childhood, Boyhood and Youth' are not at all unattainable
and are indeed realizable for more than just a chosen few.
Whosoever's attitude to himself is one of continuous and
pitiless honesty can reach the heights on which Nikolay
Irtenev places his aspirations to self-perfection, because
between the feelings of such a man and the ignoble ones of
a society which has utterly lost all *naturalness* there is
nothing in common.

In his early works Tolstoy often draws the contradiction between artificiality, the apparently unavoidable
companion of civilization, and simplicity, which exists
only where education has had no influence. In each of the
works mentioned above Tolstoy has pointed to a different
side of the problem.

In 'A Landowner's Morning' Tolstoy has described the
irreconcilable contradictions in Russian society and
country life. In those tales where the action takes place
in the capital or other large towns Tolstoy draws with
cruel accuracy characters who have had the benefits of
further education and they are absolutely good-for-nothing.
In those stories, as for example those in the Caucasus or
Sebastopol where an ordinary man is forced to live alongside an educated man from society, the simple man always
and clearly has the overwhelming superiority. All the
emotions of the man from society are insincere and immoral. Even his idea of love is far removed from the
natural feeling of love and it becomes an end in itself
and not, as it is in nature, the means.

In order to throw off the fetters in which culture has
chained us we must bring up the younger generation in such
a way that they are free from all our prejudices. We have
no right to propound to our children truths, the validity
of which we ourselves doubt. On the contrary we must listen to the voice of the instincts of the child and further
the full development of everything which Nature has given
him. This is the link between Tolstoy's fiction and his
articles on education. In all his works Tolstoy is
attempting to express a morality which is neither complete in itself nor ready-made; it is one which is continually renewing itself. It is this characteristic which is
the main difference between Tolstoy and his fellow-
countrymen and contemporaries. This difference went unnoticed at first by his critics, although they all, as it
were unconsciously, pointed it out. Tolstoy's

contemporaries selected for themselves a particular point
of view and forced into its service their more or less
considerable skills as writers. With all the force of his
spiritual beliefs Tolstoy sought a philosophy which would
resolve all the strange paradoxes which exist everywhere
where the cultured world comes into contact with the
natural one. In his searches Tolstoy came more and more
to favour the natural and the spontaneous. He contrasts
pride with self-denial, the struggle for material posses-
sions with love for all humanity, and hatred between
nations with everlasting peace.

93. SHESTOV ON TOLSTOY'S LACK OF COMPASSION

1900

L.I. Shestov (1866-1938), real name Shvartsman, was an
anti-rational and anti-moral philosophical thinker. Most
of his writings are directed towards proving the principle
summed up in the closing lines of his 'Good in the Teaching of Tolstoy and Nietzsche' of 1900 (from which the
following extract is taken) where he states: 'Good - we
know it from the experience of Nietzsche - is not God.
"Woe to those who live and know no love better than pity."
We must seek for that which is *above* pity, *above* Good. We
must seek for God.' Shestov is consequently more in tune
with Dostoevsky in whose works he sees a 'philosophy of
tragedy'; he has little time for Tolstoy the moralist,
indeed many of his most destructive arguments start from a
critique of Tolstoy's ideas.

'What is Art?' is but the last word of a long sermon which
was begun many years ago. I use the word sermon because
all of Tolstoy's works of the last few years, even the
fictional ones, have but one object: to make the philosophy of life which was worked out in them compulsory for
everyone. Such an attempt is clearly seen even in 'Anna
Karenina'. The epigraph is taken from the Gospels:
'Vengeance is mine, and I shall repay.' We are accustomed to interpreting this in the sense that the final
judgment on man is and must be pronounced not by man himself, and that the success or failure of his life on earth

is no proof of his innocence or guilt. But in 'Anna
Karenina' one senses a completely different understanding
of the gospel text. Here Tolstoy not only depicts human
life but also sits in judgment over people. And he judges
them not as a dispassionate and calm judge should, showing
neither anger nor pity, but as a man deeply and passionately interested in the outcome of the case under examination. Every line of this remarkable work is directed
against an unseen but defined enemy or in the defence of
a similarly unseen but also completely defined ally. And
the more powerful the enemy, the sharper and more refined
are the weapons Tolstoy uses to defeat it and the more
skilful, complicated and imperceptible are the methods by
means of which the author undermines it. Stepan Arkadevich Oblonsky is easily dealt with - by ironic comments
and the comic difficulties in which he always finds himself. With Karenin it is a little more serious but even
on him, comparatively speaking, one does not need to
spend much effort. But it is another matter with Vronsky
and Koznyshev. These are stronger people; if they cannot
create something new on their own initiative they know how
to develop sufficient strength to support both the things
and the people they consider their own. They are supported by a certain construction, they are pillars whose sta-
bility guarantees the solidity of the whole building.
Tolstoy rains down on them, too, with all the force of
his huge talent. Not only everything they do but their
whole life is reduced to nothing. They struggle, they
work, they rest but it all turns out to be nothing more
than running round in small circles. They serve some
senseless idol whose name is Vanity. Listen how Tolstoy
characterizes Vronsky's moral convictions:

> Vronsky's life was made particularly happy by his hav-
> ing a set of rules which determined for him without a
> doubt what he should and should not do... These rules
> determine without a doubt that he needed to pay a
> cardsharper but did not need to pay his tailor, that
> one should not lie to one's peasants but one could to
> women, that one must deceive no one but one could a
> husband, that one could not forgive insults but could
> insult others.

You will see that in the author's opinion the sources of
Vronsky's moral convictions are but simple, social prejudices. With Koznyshev it is the same or almost the
same. His enthusiasms are but imitations of fashion, the
workings of his soul are the superficial activity of his
mind and the less meaning they have, the stronger and more

consistently are they expressed. The sum total of his
life is a book which nobody needs, witty drawing-room
conversation, and useless participation in various private
and social institutions. Vronsky and Koznyshev are all
that Tolstoy could find among the representatives of
Russian intellectual society of recent times whom he has
called to judgment. Besides them there are some even more
fleetingly outlined figures but all of these people have
no meaning and are incapable of saying anything definite
to the readers.

But the last and most important defendant, on whose
behalf evidently the gospel text at the head of the book
was introduced, is Anna. Vengeance awaits her and Tolstoy
will repay it. She has sinned and must be punished. In
all of Russian and possibly even foreign literature no
artist has so pitilessly and calmly led his hero to the
awful fate which awaits him as has Tolstoy Anna. And not
only pitilessly and calmly but joyously and triumphantly.
For Tolstoy the shameful and tormented end of Anna is a
pleasing sight. Once he has killed her he leads Levin to
a faith in God and ends his novel. If Anna could have
survived her shame, if she could have retained a sense of
her rights as a human being and had died not overwhelmed
or destroyed but righteous and proud then from Tolstoy
that fulcrum, thanks to which he could retain his spiritual composure, would have been removed. Before him was
the alternative - Anna or himself, her downfall or his
salvation. He sacrificed Anna who had gone with Vronsky
while her husband was alive. Tolstoy well knows what
sort of husband Karenin was for Anna; no one but he could
describe the horror of the position of a gifted, clever,
sensitive and vital woman, chained by the ties of marriage
to a walking automaton. But these ties he must consider
obligatory, sacred, because in the existence of obligations in general he sees proof of some higher harmony.
And in the defence of these obligations he rises with all
the strength of his artistic genius. Anna, because she
has broken the rules, must perish in an agonizing death.

All the characters in 'Anna Karenina' are divided into
two categories. The first keep to the rules and along
with Levin find grace and salvation; the others follow
their own desires, break the rules and in proportion to
the boldness and decisiveness of their actions suffer a
more or less cruel punishment. From those to whom much
is given, much is exacted. Because Anna is the most
gifted, the ultimate shame awaits her. The others suffer
less. One is forced to think that if Tolstoy in 'Anna
Karenina' had taken all his heroes to the end of their
life then all would have been repaid in proportion to how

and by how much they had broken the rules.

However, in 'Anna Karenina' the sum of the rules which Tolstoy considers obligatory is none the less relatively small. At the time he was writing this novel he gives 'good' only a relative power over human life. Moreover, serving 'good' as the exclusive and conscious aim of life is still denied by him. Just as in 'War and Peace' so in 'Anna Karenina' Tolstoy not only does not believe in the possibility of exchanging life for 'good', but considers such an exchange unnatural, false and a sham leading in the final analysis only to reaction in even the best of men. In 'War and Peace' he gives a severe sentence to Sonya, that virtuous and loving girl, who is so deeply devoted to the Rostov family. In the Epilogue where the young families of Nikolay Rostov and Pierre Bezukhov come on to the scene the life of the people who have grown up under our eyes - Pierre, Natasha, Nikolay and Princess Maria - is depicted as sensible and full. They have all found their place and their work and quietly continue what their fathers had started. Their existence is necessary and understandable. Only Sonya, that shy, alien figure, sits despondently at the samovar, half nanny, half dependent. Behind her back the friends of her youth, Natasha and Princess Maria (who is so moved by ideas of virtue but then takes Nikolay away from Sonya), discuss her life and introduce a text from the Gospels in which her pitiable condition is completely deserved. This is their conversation:

> 'You know', said Natasha, 'how you have read a lot of the Gospels: there's a place there which is directly about Sonya.'
> 'Where?' asked Princess Maria in surprise.
> '"To him that hath shall be given and from him that hath not shall be taken away," do you remember? She "hath not". I don't know why; perhaps it's because she hasn't any egotism, I just don't know. But from her will always be taken away and always has been. I'm sometimes awfully sorry for her; earlier I did so want Nikolay to marry her, but I always somehow foresaw that it was not to be. She is a *barren flower* (Tolstoy's italics), like on a strawberry bush.'

One scarcely needs to say that the 'barren flower' and the explanation 'she has no egotism' and that 'everything has been taken away' from her, is not only the opinion of Natasha but also of Princess Maria, who although interpreting the Gospels differently, none the less 'looking at Sonya' agreed with Natasha; it is clear to everybody that

this opinion of the two happy women, albeit not having
suffered the test of virtue, is also the opinion of the
author of 'War and Peace' himself. Sonya *is* a barren
flower; she *is* guilty of the absence of egotism, in spite
of being all devotion, all self-sacrifice. These qualities in Tolstoy's eyes are not qualities, they are not
worth living for; he who does have them only approximates
to, but is not, a man. Natasha, who married Pierre
several months after the death of Prince Andrey, and
Princess Maria, whose 'situation had an influence on
Nikolay's choice', both of them who were able at the
decisive moment to take happiness from life are right.
Sonya is not; she is a barren flower. One has to live
as Natasha and Princess Maria. One may and even has to
try 'to be good', to read sacred books and be moved by the
stories of pilgrims and beggars. This, though, is only
the poetry of existence and not life. A healthy instinct
must prompt man towards the true path. He who is seduced
by the teachings of duty and virtue and looks through life
and does not assert his rights in time is a 'barren
flower'. Such is the conclusion drawn by Tolstoy from the
experiences he had during the time of writing 'War and
Peace'. In this work where the author expresses the sum
total of forty years of his life, virtue *an sich*, the pure
service of duty, submission to fate and the inability to
stand up for oneself are with what man is directly
charged. Over Sonya, as later over Anna Karenina, the
sentence is read - over the former because she did not
break the rules and over the latter because she did.

But even in 'Anna Karenina' Tolstoy's antipathy to
people who devote themselves to *serving* 'good' appears in
all its strength. How pathetically Varenka is depicted
with her poor, unhealthy and uncomplaining life with
Madame Stahl! And with what repugnance Kitty recalls her
attempts at serving good and her meeting with Varenka
abroad. She prefers her husband to be an unbeliever -
'she who considers that lack of faith will destroy him in
the future life' - rather than he should be as she was
when she was abroad. Finally the novel's main hero, the
alter ego of the author (even his surname comes from Tolstoy's Christian name: Lev - Levin) clearly states that
the conscious serving of good is an unnecessary lie. As
Tolstoy says:

> earlier (it began almost in his childhood and grew into
> full manhood) when he (Levin) tried to do something
> which would have been *good* for everyone, for mankind,
> for Russia, for the whole of his village, he noticed
> that thinking about it was very pleasant but that

actually doing it was invariably absurd and led nowhere; but now after his marriage when he began more
and more to limit himself to living for himself and
although he no longer experienced any joy at the
thought of what he was doing he felt certain that he
needed to do it and saw that it went much better than
before and grew all the time. Now, against his will,
he cut deeper and deeper into the earth like a plough
which could not be removed without leaving a furrow.

Thanks to the fact that he had cut himself off from his
past and refused to think about serving good, the whole of
Russia, all his village, etc., he always knew in all the
circumstances of life what he had to do and how to go
about it, what was necessary and what was not. Family
life must be lived as it was by his fathers and grandfathers, one must organize the land as well as one can and
to this end hire workers as cheaply as possible. One must
worry about the affairs of one's brother and those of all
the peasants who come to one for advice but the worker
who goes home during working hours because his father has
died must not be forgiven. Levin is tormented by the
thought that he does not know why he is alive or how to
live, but none the less he is laying his own special
defined road in life and in the end is convinced that
although previously he was not seeking good but his own
happiness nevertheless, or more accurately actually because of it, his life 'was not only not senseless as it
had been before *but had without doubt the sense of good*'.
From where, then, does this 'sense of good' come? Why
has 'good' arrived to bless Levin but not the other
characters in the novel? Why does Anna perish and
deserve to, why is Vronsky ruined, why does Koznyshev drag
out an illusionary existence, while Levin, who enjoys all
the blessings of life, still acquires the right to a profound spiritual world - the prerogative of a very small
and exclusive group of people? Why has fate favoured
Levin so unjustly and dealt so cruelly with Anna? For
another writer, a naturalist for example, such questions
do not exist. For him the unfairness of fate is the basic
principle of human life, so evidently flowing from the
laws of natural development that he does not have to be
surprised at it. But such a writer does not quote from
the Gospels nor does he speak of retribution. With Tolstoy, on the contrary, the novel 'Anna Karenina' is occasioned by such questions. He does not describe life but
interrogates it, demands answers from it. This is why
all his works, both large and small, both 'War and Peace'
and 'The Death of Ivan Ilich', and his publicist articles,

have a completely finished character. Tolstoy always
appears before the public with answers given in a specific
form, which completely satisfy the most demanding and
strict, in this sense, person. And this, of course, is no
accident, nor could it possibly be one. In this lies the
basic characteristic of Tolstoy's works. All that immense interior labour which was needed to create 'War and
Peace' or 'Anna Karenina' was occasioned by the most
urgent demand to understand himself and life about him, to
beat off the doubts which pursued him, and to find for
himself, albeit only temporarily, firm ground. These
demands are too serious and constant for him to hide
behind the simple description of aspects of reality which
continually come before his eyes or the relation of recollections from his past. Something else is needed. He
needed to discover a strength greater than any man has,
which would support and defend this right. Personal
tastes, sympathies, partialities, enjoyments, passions,
all those elements into which realist authors usually
break down human life, guarantee nothing and are incapable
of reassuring Tolstoy. He seeks a strong, all-powerful
ally. All Tolstoy's great genius is directed towards
finding such an ally and winning him over. And in this
Tolstoy is pitiless. There is nothing he will not destroy if it stands in the way of achieving his goal. And
there is no limit to his spiritual exertions when dealing
with this most sacred interest of his. To lie, to pretend, to concoct false facts is beyond Tolstoy, nor would
he wish to. He writes not for others, but for himself.
This is why he not only does not invest his Levin with any
quality other than those he possesses but honestly and
sincerely depicts all his faults and his ridiculous side.
'Such is Levin', Tolstoy tells us, 'both excessively
jealous and an egotist, a fugitive from society's affairs
and a clumsy, unsociable lone-wolf, but nevertheless good
goes with him, his life has a definite sense of good.' He
not only arranged his life according to his demands and
desires but also accurately defined where to go and what
to do for good to be on his side. And 'good' is exactly
that might which makes Levin a giant in comparison with
other people because there is nothing mightier than good.
And at the moment of 'Anna Karenina''s appearance you
could convince Tolstoy of anything except that good is not
for Levin. Not only is it *for* Levin it is *against* everyone who does not think, feel and live like Levin; it is
against Koznyshev, Vronsky and Anna and will have its vengeance upon them, it will punish them however temporarily
they may celebrate their victory over Levin. Like a
plough Levin digs into the earth. That strength which

Tolstoy needed is found in him too. All the Varenkas,
Sonyas and other virtuous creations do not serve a real
good because they do not live as Levin lives, and Tolstoy
lumps them together with Vronsky and Anna. No tragedy or
cruel strokes of fate are prepared for them but their
hateful existence is worse than any unhappiness. Tolstoy
feels sorry for none of his sacrifices. You will never
hear from him any gentle note of compassion as you so
often hear in the works of Dickens, Turgenev and even in
experimental writers like Zola and Bourget who never miss
a chance of underlining their human feelings. It might
appear strange to Tolstoy but many readers accuse him of
being cold, of being without feeling, of callousness. To
push Anna Karenina under a train and not to utter a single
sigh! To follow the agony of Ivan Ilich and not to shed a
single tear! This seems so impossible to understand and
upsetting to many readers that they are ready even to deny
Tolstoy's artistic genius. It seems to them that to call
Tolstoy a genius means to insult a morality which places
before all its demands the ability to feel sympathy for
the unhappiness of one's fellows. They consider it their
most important duty to place Tolstoy in the ranks of the
second rate who just cannot compare with Dickens or Turgenev, suggesting that in this way they are defending
their sacred right to compassion. In their opinion a
writer who cannot show sufficient sympathy for the sufferings of his fellows cannot be called a great artist.
And they, these readers, are in their way absolutely
correct. They wish to be sympathetic because sympathy is
all that they can give of themselves to people stricken by
fate. In feeling sorrow for the unhappy, in shedding
tears over those that are lost, they assuage the eternal
prickings of their conscience. 'One cannot put somebody
who has fallen down back on their feet so we'll cry over
them and all will be well,' they say. For whom will all
be well? They do not answer this question, they do not
even ask it, they dare not ask it. And it is understandable that Tolstoy who shows no human feelings frightens
them and they rush away to 'A King Lear of the Steppes',
to stories by Dickens and even to Lourdes, because there
the horror aroused by pictures of unhappiness is resolved
by noble feelings of sympathy transferred by the authors
to the reader. Even Zola, the Zola whom Tolstoy so disliked in all his works, calms us by his ability to sympathize with the grief of his heroes.

In Tolstoy there is not a trace of such soft-hearted-
ness.

94. CHEKHOV ON TOLSTOY

1888-1900

A.P. Chekhov, 1860-1904, usually regarded as Russia's greatest dramatist, but also a short-story writer of the first rank, first met Tolstoy in 1895, and the two men, so different in age and temperament, became friends. Chekhov was a great admirer of Tolstoy's fiction, although not of his philosophical and religious beliefs; Tolstoy, however, in spite of his liking for Chekhov the man, disliked his plays, primarily for the fact that, as he saw it, they had no action, and even Shakespeare, whom he could not bear, he considered better in this respect.

(a) From a letter to A.S. Suvorin, 27 October 1888.

....You are right to require from the artist a conscious attitude, but you mix up two ideas: *the solution of the problem* and *a correct presentation of the problem*. Only the latter is obligatory for the artist. In 'Anna Karenina' and 'Onegin' not a single problem is resolved, but they satisfy you completely only because all their problems are correctly presented....

(b) From a letter to A.N. Pleshcheev, 15 February 1890.

....Don't you really like 'The Kreutzer Sonata'? I won't say it is a work of genius, or one that will last for ever, I am no judge of these matters, but in my opinion, among everything being written here and abroad, you will hardly find anything as powerful in seriousness of conception and beauty of execution. Without mentioning its artistic merits, which in places are outstanding, one must thank the story if only for the one thing that it is extremely thought-provoking. As I read it I could hardly stop myself crying out: 'That's true!' or 'That's wrong!' Of course it does have some very annoying defects. Besides those you enumerated, there is one further point which one will not readily forgive its author, namely the brashness with which Tolstoy pontificates on

things he does not know and out of stubbornness does not
want to understand. Thus his pronouncements on syphilis,
foundling hospitals, women's repugnance for copulation and
so on are not only debatable but also show him to be a
complete ignoramus who has never taken the trouble during
the course of his long life to read a couple of books
written by specialists. Still these defects fly off like
feathers in the wind; considering the merits of the story
you simply do not notice them, or, if you do, it is only
annoying that the story did not avoid the fate of all
works of man, all of which are imperfect and possess
faults....

(c)   From a letter to A.S. Suvorin, 25 October 1891.

....I wake up every night and read 'War and Peace'. One
reads with such curiosity and naive astonishment as though
one had never read anything before. It is wonderfully
good. But I don't care for the passages where Napoleon
appears. Wherever Napoleon comes on the scene, you get a
straining after effect and all sorts of devices to prove
he was stupider than he was in reality. Everything that
Pierre, Prince Andrey or even the utterly insignificant
Nikolay Rostov say or do is good, clever, natural and
touching; everything that Napoleon thinks and does is unnatural, stupid, inflated and lacking in meaning....

(d)   From a letter to M.O. Menshikov, 28 January 1900.

To finish with Tolstoy, I shall say something about
'Resurrection', which I did not read in fits and starts
but all at one go. It is a remarkable work of art. The
most uninteresting section is that concerned with Nekhlyudov's relations with Katyusha; the most interesting things
are the princes, generals, old ladies, peasants, prisoners
and overseers. As I read the scene at the home of the
general, who is the commandant of the Peter and Paul Fortress and a spiritualist, my heart almost stopped it was so
good! And Mme Korchagin in her armchair, and the peasant,
Feodosya's husband! This peasant calls his old lady
'adroit'. So it is with Tolstoy; he has an adroit pen.
The story has no end; what there is can hardly be called
one. To write on and on and then to settle everything on

the basis of the Gospels is extremely theological. It is
as arbitrary to use such a solution as it is to divide
criminals into five classes. Why five and not ten? Why
use a text from the Gospels and not from the Koran? First
you ought to make people believe in the Gospels to show
them that they are the truth and then you can resolve
everything with a gospel text....

(e) From a letter to A.S. Suvorin, 12 February 1900.

....'Resurrection' is a remarkable novel. I liked it a
lot, only you must read it at one go, at a single sitting.
The ending has no interest and is false - false in technique.

95. GARNETT: TOLSTOY'S PLACE IN EUROPEAN LITERATURE

1901

Edward Garnett (1868-1937), critic, biographer and essayist, did much to publicize Tolstoy both in England and
America. It was his wife, Constance, who through her
translations of Turgenev, Dostoevsky and Tolstoy made the
Russian novel available to a wider public in the West.
This article first appeared in the 'Bookman' (London),
1901, no. XIX, and was reprinted together with articles
by G.K. Chesterton (see No. 98) and G.H. Perris in a book
'Leo Tolstoy', two years later. Reprinted by permission.

Tolstoy's significance as the great writer of modern
Russia can scarcely be augmented in Russian eyes by his
exceeding significance to Europe as symbolising the spiritual unrest of the modern world. Yet so inevitably must
the main stream of each age's tendency and the main movement of the world's thought be discovered for us by the
great writers, whenever they appear, that Russia can no
more keep Tolstoy's significance to herself than could
Germany keep Goethe's to herself. True it is that
Tolstoy, as great novelist, has been absorbed in the

peculiar world of half-feudal, modern Russia, a world
strange to Western Europe, but the spirit of analysis with
which the creator of 'Anna Karenina' and 'War and Peace'
has confronted the modern world is more truly representative of our Age's outlook than is the spirit of any other
of his great contemporaries.

Between the days of 'Wilhelm Meister' and of 'Resurrection' what an extraordinary volume of the rushing tide
of modern life has swept by! A century of that 'liberation of modern Europe from the old routine' has passed
since Goethe stood forth for 'the awakening of the modern
spirit.' A century of emancipation, of Science, of unbelief, of incessant shock, change and Progress all over
the face of Europe, and even as Goethe a hundred years ago
typified the triumph of the new intelligence of Europe
over the shackles of its old institutions, routine, and
dogma (as Matthew Arnold affirms), so Tolstoy to-day
stands for the triumph of the European *soul* against civilisation's routine and dogma. The peculiar modernness of
Tolstoy's attitude, however, as we shall presently show,
is that he is inspired largely by the modern scientific
spirit in his searching analysis of modern life. Apparently at war with Science and Progress, his extraordinary
fascination for the mind of Europe lies in the fact that
he of all great contemporary writers has come nearest to
demonstrating, to *realising* what the life of the modern
man *is*. He of all the analysts of the civilised man's
thoughts, emotions, and actions has least idealised, least
beautified, and least distorted the complex daily life of
the European world. With a marked moral bias, driven onward in his search for truth by his passionate religious
temperament, Tolstoy, in his pictures of life, has constructed a truer *whole*, a human world less bounded by the
artist's individual limitations, more mysteriously living
in its vast flux and flow than is the world of any writer
of the century. 'War and Peace' and 'Anna Karenina',
those great worlds where the physical environment, mental
outlook, emotional aspiration, and moral code of the whole
community of Russia are reproduced by his art, as some
mighty cunning phantasmagoria of changing life, are superior in the sense of containing a whole nation's life, to
the worlds of Goethe, Byron, Scott, Victor Hugo, Balzac,
Dickens, Thackeray, Maupassant, or any latter day creator
we can name. And not only so, but Tolstoy's analysis of
life throws more light on the main currents of thought in
our Age, raises deeper problems, and explores more untouched territories of the mind than does any corresponding analysis by his European contemporaries.

It is by Tolstoy's passionate seeking of the life of

the soul that the great Russian writer towers above the
men of our day, and it is because his hunger for spiritual
truth has led him to probe contemporary life, to examine
all modern formulas and appearances, to penetrate into the
secret thought and emotion of men of all grades in our
complex society, that his work is charged with the essence
of nearly all that modernity thinks and feels, believes
and suffers, hopes and fears as it evolves in more and
more complex forms of our terribly complex civilisation.
The soul of humanity is, however, always the appeal of men
from the life that environs, moulds, and burdens them, to
instincts that go beyond and transcend their present life.
Tolstoy is the *appeal* of the modern world, the cry of the
modern conscience against the blinded fate of its own
progress. To the eye of science everything is possible in
human life, the sacrifice of the innocent for the sake of
the progress of the guilty, the crushing and deforming of
the weak, so that the strong may triumph over them, the
evolution of new serf classes at the dictates of a ruling
class. All this the nineteenth century has seen accomplished, and not seen alone in Russia. It is Tolstoy's
distinction to have combined in his life-work more than
any other great artist two main conflicting points of
view. He has fused by his art the science that defines
the way Humanity is forced forward blindly and irrespon-
sibly from century to century by the mere pressure of
events, he has fused with this science of our modern
world the soul's protest against the earthly fate of man
which leads the generations into taking the ceaseless
roads of evil which every age unwinds.
     Let us cite Tolstoy's treatment of War as an instance
of how this great artist symbolises the Age for us and so
marks the advance in self-consciousness of the modern
mind, and as a nearer approximation to a realisation of
what life is. We have only got to compare Tolstoy's
'Sebastopol' (1856) with any other document on war by
other European writers to perceive that Tolstoy alone
among artists has *realised* war, his fellows have *idealised*
it. To quote a passage from a former article let us say
that '"Sebastopol" gives us war under *all* aspects — war
as a squalid, honourable, daily affair of mud and glory,
of vanity, disease, hard work, stupidity, patriotism, and
inhuman agony. Tolstoy gets the complex effects of "Sebastopol" by keenly analysing the effect of the sights and
sounds, dangers and pleasures, of war on the brains of a
variety of typical men, and by placing a special valuation
of his own on these men's actions, thoughts, and emotions,
on their courage, altruism, and show of indifference in
the face of death. He lifts up, in fact, the veil of

appearances conventionally drawn by society over the
actualities of the glorious trade of killing men, and he
does this chiefly by analysing keenly the insensitiveness
and indifference of the average mind, which says of the
worst of war's realities, "I felt so and so, and did so
and so: but as to what those other thousands may have
felt in their agony, that I did not enter into at all."
"Sebastopol," therefore, though an exceedingly short and
exceedingly simple narrative, is a psychological document
on modern war of extraordinary value, for it simply rele-
gates to the lumber-room, as unlife-like and hopelessly
limited, all those theatrical glorifications of war which
men of letters, romantic poets, and grave historians alike
have been busily piling up on humanity's shelves from
generation to generation. And more: we feel that in
"Sebastopol" we have at last the sceptical modern spirit,
absorbed in actual life, demonstrating what war is, and
expressing at length the confused sensations of countless
men, who have heretofore never found a genius who can make
humanity realise what it knows half-consciously and consciously evades. We cannot help, therefore, recognising
this man Tolstoy as the most advanced product of our
civilisation, and likening him to a great surgeon, who,
not deceived by the world's presentation of its own life,
penetrates into the essential joy and suffering, health
and disease of multitudes of men; a surgeon who, face to
face with the strangest of Nature's laws in the constitution of human society, puzzled by all the illusions,
fatuities, and conventions of the human mind, resolutely
sets himself to lay bare the roots of all its passions,
appetites, and incentives in the struggle for life, so
that at least human reason may advance farther along the
path of self-knowledge in advancing towards a general
sociological study of man.'

Tolstoy's place in nineteenth-century literature is,
therefore, in our view, no less fixed and certain than is
Voltaire's place in the eighteenth century. Both of these
writers focus for us in a marvellously complete manner the
respective methods of analysing life by which the ration-
alism of the seventeenth and eighteenth centuries, and the
science and humanitarianism of the nineteenth century have
moulded for us the modern world. All the movements, all
the problems, all the speculation, all the agitations of
the world of to-day in contrast with the immense material-
istic civilisation that science has hastily built up for
us in three or four generations, all the *spirit* of modern
life is condensed in the pages of Tolstoy's writings,
because, as we have said, he typifies the soul of the
modern man gazing, now undaunted, and now in alarm, at the

formidable array of the newly-tabulated *cause and effect* of humanity's progress, at the appalling cheapness and waste of human life in Nature's hands. Tolstoy thus stands for *the modern soul's alarm in contact with science*. And just as science's *work* after its first destruction of the past ages' formalism, supersition, and dogma is directed more and more to the examination and amelioration of human life, so Tolstoy's work has been throughout inspired by a passionate love of humanity, and by his ceaseless struggle against conventional religion, dogmatic science, and society's mechanical influence on the minds of its members. To make man more *conscious* of his acts, to show society its real motives and what it *is* feeling, and not cry out in admiration at what it pretends to feel — this has been the great novelist's aim in his delineation of Russia's life. Ever seeking the one truth — to arrive at men's thoughts and sensations under the daily pressure of life — never flinching from his exploration of the dark world of man's animalism and incessant self-deception, Tolstoy's *realism* in art is symbolical of our absorption in the world of fact, in the modern study of natural law, a study ultimately without loss of spirituality, nay, resulting in immense gain to the spiritual life. The *realism* of the great Russian's novels is, therefore, more in line with the modern tendency and outlook than is the general tendency of other schools of Continental literature. And Tolstoy must be finally looked on, not merely as *the conscience of the Russian world* revolting against the too heavy burden which the Russian people have now to bear in Holy Russia's onward march towards the building-up of her great Asiatic Empire, but also as the soul of the modern world seeking to replace in its love of humanity the life of those old religions which science is destroying day by day. In this sense Tolstoy will stand in European literature as the conscience of the modern world.

96.   MEREZHKOVSKY ON TOLSTOY, THE 'SEER OF THE FLESH'

1901

From 'L. Tolstoy and Dostoevsky: Life, Works and Religion', 1901, part II, chapter I.   D.S. Merezhkovsky (1865-1941) was a leading figure in Russian Symbolism, a

novelist and critic. His literary criticism marks a break
from the sociological approach and a return to a concentration on the aesthetic qualities of literature. His
book on Tolstoy and Dostoevsky, which was translated into
English in 1902, with its thesis that Tolstoy is the 'seer
of the flesh', describing man from the outside, and Dostoevsky the 'seer of the spirit', ignoring man's externals
and dealing more or less exclusively with his inner world,
however debatable was probably the most influential of all
Russian comments on the two writers and also coloured much
criticism in English for a number of years. The emphasis
throughout is Merezhkovsky's.

Princess Bolkonsky, the wife of Prince Andrey, as we discover from the first pages of 'War and Peace', was
'pretty, with a slight dark down on her *upper lip,* which
was short to the teeth, opened extremely sweetly and even
more sweetly lengthened at times and met the lower lip'.
For twenty chapters this lip keeps appearing. Some months
have passed since the opening of the story: 'The little
princess, who was pregnant, had grown stout in the meantime, but her eyes and the *short downy lip* and its smile
curled up just as gaily and sweetly'. And two pages
later: 'The princess talked without stopping; her *short
upper lip* with its down would descend for a moment, touch
the red lower one at the right point and then again part
in a dazzling smile of teeth and eyes'. The princess
tells her sister-in-law, Princess Andrey's sister, Princess Maria, of her husband's departure for the war.
Princess Maria turns to her, her eyes caressing her
stomach, and asks: 'Really?' The little princess's face
changed. She sighed. 'Yes, really,' she replied, 'It's
all quite awful!' And the princess's *lip dropped.* In the
course of a hundred and fifty pages we have already seen
that upper lip four times in different expressions.
Again, two hundred pages later: 'There was a general and
lively conversation thanks to the voice and the downy *lip*
which rose above the little princess's white teeth'. In
the second part of the novel she dies in childbirth.
Prince Andrey 'entered his wife's room; she lay dead in
the same position in which he had seen her five minutes
before, and in spite of the motionless eyes and the paleness of the cheeks the same expression was on this charming childlike face with its *lip* covered in dark down.
"I love you all; I have harmed no-one. What have you done
with me?"' This takes place in 1805. 'War had broken out
and was getting closer to the Russian frontiers.' In the

midst of its dangers the author does not forget to inform
us that a marble monument had been placed over the little
princess's grave - an angel that had a slightly raised
upper lip and the expression Prince Andrey had read on the
face of his dead wife: 'Why have you done this to me?'
Years pass. Napoleon has completed his conquests in
Europe; he has already crossed the Russian frontier. In
the peace and quiet of Bald Hills the dead princess's
little son 'grew, changed, developed rosy cheeks and dark
curly hair and unconsciously, smiling and happy, raised
the *upper lip* of his charming little mouth just like the
late princess'.

Thanks to these repetitions and underlinings of the
same physical feature, first in a living person, then in a
dead, and then on the face of her monument and finally on
the face of her little son, the princess's 'upper lip' is
engraved on our memory with ineffaceable clarity so that
we cannot think of the little princess without also recalling that downy upper lip.

Princess Maria Bolkonsky has a 'heavy footstep' which
can be heard from afar. 'They were the heavy steps of
Princess Maria.' She came into the room 'with her heavy
step, walking on her heels'. Her face 'blushes in
patches'. During a delicate conversation with her brother
Prince Andrey about his wife, she 'blushed in patches'.
When they are preparing to dress her up for the arrival
of her proposed fiancé she feels herself insulted: 'she
made an angry outburst and her face was covered in red
patches'. In the following volume in a conversation with
Pierre about his old priests and religious pilgrims, his
'holy men', she becomes confused and 'blushes in patches'.
Between these last two reminders of Princess Maria's red
patches we have had the description of the battle of
Austerlitz, Napoleon's victory, the titanic struggle between nations, and events which have decided the fate of
the world, but the writer has not forgotten and nor will
he ever forget this physical feature which he finds so
interesting. He forces us willy-nilly to remember Princess Maria's shining eyes, heavy footsteps and red
patches. It is true that these features, however much
they may appear external and insignificant, are actually
connected with extremely profound and important psychological facets of the characters: thus the upper lip, now
gaily raised, now plaintively lowered, expresses the
childlike lack of concern and helplessness of the little
princess, the clumsy gait of Princess Maria expresses a
complete lack of external feminine charm, while the shining eyes and the fact that she blushes in patches are
connected with her inner feminine charm and chaste

spiritual purity. Sometimes these individual characteristics suddenly illumine a complete, complicated and vast
picture and give it a striking clarity and relief.

During the popular uprising in deserted Moscow just
before Napoleon's entry into the city when Count Rostopchin, wishing to assuage the crowd's animal fury, points
to the political criminal Vereshchagin, who is completely
innocent and just happened to be there, as a spy and
'scoundrel' because of whom 'Moscow had fallen', the long
thin neck and the general thinness, weakness and frailness
of his whole body express the defencelessness of the
sacrifice to the crude animal force of the crowd.

'"Where is he?" said the Count and at the very moment
he was saying it he saw a young man with a *long thin neck*
coming round the corner between two dragoons.' He had
'dirty, worn out, *thin* boots. The fetters hung heavily on
his *thin* legs'. '"Bring him here," said Rostopchin,
pointing to the lower step of the perron. The young man,
walking heavily to the indicated step, sighed and with a
submissive gesture folded his *thin* hands, unused to heavy
work, over his stomach. "Ladies and gentlemen", said
Rostopchin in a ringing metallic voice, "This is Vereshchagin - the same young man who caused Moscow to fall"'.
Vereshchagin looks up and tries to catch Rostopchin's
eye. But he was not looking at him. On the young man's
long thin neck a vein stood out behind his ear like a
piece of blue string. The crowd fell silent and pressed
more and more closely together. '"Kill him! Let the
traitor perish. Save the name of Russia from shame,"
shouted Rostopchin. "Count," said the timid yet theatrical voice of Vereshchagin in the renewed silence, "God
alone is above us."' And again the thick vein on his *thin
neck* filled with blood. One of the soldiers hit him over
the head with the flat of his sword. With a cry of terror
Vereshchagin plunged towards the crowd with outstretched
arms. A tall youth on whom he fell grasped his *thin neck*
in his hands and with a wild cry fell together with
Vereshchagin beneath the feet of the crowd which was
roaring and pressing forward. After the crime the same
people who had committed it gazed with a morbidly mournful
expression at the dead body with its face which was turning blue and covered in blood and dust and at the mangled
long thin neck.

There is not a word about the inner spiritual state of
the victim but in five pages the word *thin* is repeated
eight times in various connections - a thin neck, thin
legs, thin boots, thin hands - and this external feature
fully depicts Vereshchagin's inner state and his relation
to the crowd.

Such is Tolstoy's usual artistic device: from the visible to the invisible, from the exterior to the interior, from the physical to the spiritual (or at least the psycological).

Sometimes these recurring features of the characters' exteriors are connected with the most profound basic idea, the moving force of the whole work. For example the weight of Kutuzov's flabby body and the lazy old man's flabbiness and lack of mobility express the impassive, contemplative immobility of his mind, the Christian or rather Buddhist renunciation of his own will, the submission to fate or God in this primeval hero - in Tolstoy's eyes pre-eminently Russian and national - a hero of inaction or inertia as opposed to the fruitlessly active, light, and self-confident hero of Western culture - Napoleon.

Prince Andrey observes the Commander-in-Chief at the first review of the armies at Tsarevo-Zaymishche: 'During the time since Prince Andrey had last seen him Kutuzov had grown even stouter, even more flabby. An expression of tiredness was on his face; his whole body seemed weary. 'He sat on his fine horse *heavily, flabbily*; he seemed *to be overflowing* the saddle.' When the review was over he rode into the courtyard and there was expressed on his face 'the joy of a man at peace who intended to rest after a performance. He moved his left leg out of the stirrup and *rolling his whole body over while frowning from the effort lifted it with difficulty over the saddle* and he rested his elbows on his knees, wheezed and fell into the arms of the Cossacks and adjutants who supported him... he strode forward with his *plunging gait and walked heavily up the steps which creaked under his weight*.' When he hears from Prince Andrey of the death of the latter's father he 'sighed *heavily*, with his whole chest and fell silent.' Then he 'embraced Prince Andrey, pressing him to his *fat* chest and did not release him for a long time.' When he did release him Prince Andrey saw Kutuzov's *flabby* lips quiver and there were tears in his eyes. 'He sighed and leant both his hands on the bench to stand up.' And in the next chapter Kutuzov 'got up *heavily* and *the folds in his neck disappeared*'.

No less a profound and as it were mysterious meaning lies in the impression of 'roundness' in another Russian hero - Platon Karataev. This roundness personified the eternal unchanging sphere of everything simple, natural and in accord with nature, a sphere enclosed, complete in itself and self-sufficient which the author sees as the primary element in the Russian national spirit. 'Platon Karataev remained for ever in Pierre's mind as the

strongest and dearest memory and the personification of
everything Russian, good and *rounded off*.' When Pierre
saw his neighbour on the following day at dawn the impression of something *round* was fully confirmed; the whole
figure of Platon in his French greatcoat with a piece of
string as a belt, in a forage cap and bast shoes was
round, his head was completely *round*, his back, chest,
shoulders and even his arms which he always carried as if
on the point of embracing something were all *round*; his
kindly smile and his big soft brown eyes were *round*.
Pierre felt 'something *round* even in the man's smell'.
Here in one exterior *physical* trait taken to the last
degree of, as it were, geometrical simplicity and clarity
a vast and most abstract generalization is expressed, and
it is connected with the most basic, inner foundations of
everything not only artistic but also metaphysical and
religious in Tolstoy's works.

A similarly unforgettable, generalizing expressiveness
is also seen in various parts of the human body - for
example Napoleon's and Speransky's hands, hands of people
exercising power. During the meeting of the two emperors before the assembled armies when Napoleon presents a
Russian soldier with the Legion of Honour 'he removes a
glove with his *small white hand* and tearing it throws it
away'. A few lines further on 'Napoleon moves his *small
plump hand* back'. Nikolay Rostov recalls 'the self-
satisfied Bonaparte with *his white hand*'. In the next
volume during his conversation with the Russian diplomat
Balashov he makes an energetic, inquiring gesture with
'*his small, plump white hand*'.

Not satisfied with just the hand the writer shows us
the whole naked body of the hero, stripping him of the
empty insignia of human power and grandeur and returning
him to our first basic origins - animal nature - and convinces us that this demi-god has the same impotent flesh
as we all have, the same mortal body, in the words of the
apostle Paul, and is the same cannon fodder as other
people whom he seems to consider just as that.

In the morning of the day before the battle of Borodino
the Emperor is completing his toilet in his tent: 'Snort-
ing and wheezing he turned first his broad back and then
his fat chest to the brush with which a valet was scrubbing his body. Another valet holding his finger over the
mouth of the bottle was sprinkling eau-de-cologne over the
Emperor's pampered body with an expression on his face
which seemed to say that he alone knew how much eau-de-
cologne to use and exactly where to sprinkle it. Napoleon's short hair was damp and stuck to his forehead. But
his face, although bloated and yellow, expressed physical

well-being. "Come on, again; come on, harder now!" he
exclaimed, hunching himself up and wheezing, to the valet
who was scrubbing him and then he arched his back and
presented his fat shoulders.'

Napoleon's fat white hand just as the whole of his
plump pampered body evidently denote in the depiction of
the writer the fact that he does no physical labour, the
fact that the upstart 'hero' belongs to the 'idle' class,
'sitting on the shoulders of the working classes' who are
people with dirty hands whom he, with a single wave of his
white hand and without a second thought, dispatches to
their deaths as 'cannon fodder'.

Speransky too has fat white hands in whose description,
in his favourite method of repetitions and underlinings,
Tolstoy seems to go too far. 'Prince Andrey observed all
of Speransky's movements; "Speransky but recently an insignificant seminarist and now holding in his hands -
those plump white hands - the fate of Russia;" mused Bolkonsky.' 'In no-one had Prince Andrey ever noticed such a
delicate paleness of face or more especially of the hands
which were somewhat large but unusually plump, delicate
and white. Prince Andrey had only seen such pale com-
plexions before on the faces of soldiers who had been in
hospital for a long time.' A little later he again 'looks
involuntarily at Speransky's white delicate hand in the
way people usually look at the hands of those holding
power. The mirror-like glance and the delicate hand somehow irritated Prince Andrey.' This one would have thought
is enough; however negligent the reader might be he can
never forget that Speransky has fat white hands. But the
writer will not give up; a few chapters later the same
detail is repeated with untiring persistence. 'Speransky
offered Prince Andrey his fat white hand.' And again:
'Speransky caressed his daughter with his white hand.' In
the end this white hand begins to follow you around like a
ghost; it is as if it has become separate from the rest of
the body in the same way as the little princess's upper
lip and that it acts independently and lives its own life,
strange and almost supernatural, reminiscent of Gogol's
'Nose'.

In comparing himself with Pushkin as an artist Tolstoy
once said to Behrs (1) that one of the differences between
them was that Pushkin in depicting an artistic detail did
it lightly and was not concerned whether or not the reader
noticed or understood its significance, while he as it
were badgered the reader with it until he had explained it
clearly. The comparison is more acute than it appears at
first glance. Tolstoy really does 'badger the reader', he
is not afraid of boring him, he drives the detail home, he

repeates it persistently, applies the colours, layer after
layer, more and more thickly, whereas Pushkin slides his
brush over the canvas, barely touching it, in light and
careless but invariably sure and faithful strokes. It has
always seemed to me that Pushkin, especially in his prose,
is miserly, even dry, that he gives little, making one
want more and more. Tolstoy gives so much that there is
nothing left for us to desire, we are satisfied, even
over-satisfied.

Pushkin's descriptions remind one of the light watery
tempera of the old Florentine masters or Pompeian murals
with their flat, pale, airily translucent colours all but
concealing the painting like an early morning mist. Tolstoy lays on his colours more heavily, crudely but also
somewhat more powerfully like the oil paintings of the
great northern masters; alongside the dense, impenetrable
yet live blacks of the shadows there are sudden blinding
flashes of light which shine through everything and
illuminate it all and remove from the shadows some individual detail, the nakedness of the body, the fold of a
dress caught in a quick movement or a part of the face
marked with passion or suffering, and give them a striking
almost repulsive and frightening vividness as if the
writer seeks, in taking the natural to its final limits,
the supernatural and, in taking the physical to its final
limits, the metaphysical.

It seems to me that in all literature there is no
writer equal to Tolstoy in the depiction of the human
body. Although he misuses repetitions he does so rarely
enough to ensure that he usually attains what he needs
from them and never suffers from the longueurs and the
piling up of different complex physical attributes so
common in other great and experienced masters when they
are describing their characters' external appearance;
he is accurate, simple and as brief as possible, he
selects only a few small, unnoticed personal and idiosyncratic features and introduces them not all at once but
gradually, one after the other, distributing them throughout the whole course of the story weaving them into the
movement of the events and the living material of the
action....

The language of the movements of a man's body if less
varied is nonetheless more immediate and expressive, has
more power to *suggest* than the language of words. It is
easier to lie in words than by the movements of the body
or the expressions on the face. They betray the real
hidden nature of a man more quickly than words. One
glance, one wrinkle, one quiver of a muscle on the face,
one movement of the body can express what can never be

expressed in words. Successive series of these unconscious involuntary movements which impress themselves and
accumulate on the face and all the external aspects of
the body form what we call the expression of the face and
what we might also call the *expression of the body*, because not only the face but also the body has its own expression, its spiritual transparency, its own face as it
were. Certain feelings arouse us to corresponding actions
and on the other hand certain habitual movements draw us
close to corresponding inner states. A man at prayer puts
his hands together and kneels down but the very action of
putting one's hands together and kneeling down draws one
close to the state of prayer. Thus there exists an uninterrupted current not only from the internal to the external but also from the external to the internal.

With inimitable art Tolstoy makes use of this *mutual
connection between the internal and the external.* According to that law of general almost mechanical sympathy
which makes a stationary string quiver in response to a
neighbouring string which has been played, according to
the law of unconscious imitation which arouses in us on
seeing someone laugh or cry the desire also to laugh or
cry, we experience when reading such descriptions of
muscles and nerves governing the expression of our own
bodies the basis of those movements which the artist describes in the external movements of his characters; and
in accord with this sympathetic experience involuntarily
happening in our own bodies, that is by the shortest and
most direct route, we enter into their inner world, we
begin to live with them, to live in them.

Note

1 Tolstoy's brother-in-law. (Ed.)

97. SOME WESTERN VIEWS OF 'RESURRECTION'

1900-2

(a) From an unsigned notice, 'Academy', 17 March 1900.

In the summer of last year we dealt fully with Count

Tolstoy's new novel as far as it had then gone in its
serial publication. And now that the complete book has
been published, and we have read it to the end, we realize
that in choosing that time for our article we acted upon
what was nothing short of an inspiration. For the melancholy truth has to be confessed that this novel, which
began so finely and of which so much was expected, declines into something very little better than a tedious
tract. At a certain stage the publication was interrupted
while the author made up his mind how to go on - or at
least that was the report. With the book before us, there
is, alas, only too much reason to believe it; for though
the story is now brought to at least one of its possible
conclusions, it is without life, tenseness, enthusiasm,
and, worse than all, it is diffuse and wayward.

[Relation of the story omitted.]

   The trial, the seduction, the dealings with lawyers and
officials, and the Prince's relations and friends are, as
we said last summer, done wonderfully. The whole thing
lives. But with the departure to Siberia the story flags,
and apparently the author's power weakens. Life stories
of other convicts are drawn across the trail, and the end,
in which Maslova, the prostitute, declines to permit
Nekhludoff to carry out his part of the expiation, is in-
conclusive. In fact, what began as a convincing and
realistic drama of awakened conscience and convict life
constructed by a great artist, terminates as if it were
part of the heavy octave of a zealous prison reformer. It
is sincere and moving in a way; but, oh, the novel that is
lost!

(b)   Unsigned review 'Bookman', April 1900.

The creator of Anna Karenina and of the teeming life of
'War and Peace' voluntarily laid aside his creative powers
before their decay to dedicate himself to another task
nobler in his eyes. His apostleship is now the breath of
his very being, and the interpreter of actual humanity has
in great part disappeared before the visionary and the
gently stubborn reformer, the publisher of peace in a
world of strife. But the earlier man has not all died.
His marvellous perceptive powers are in his latest work
still occasionally exercised in portraiture of types,
strong, truthful, and subtle, in the contrivance of scenes

of peasant life, of fashionable society in Petersburg, in
lawcourts, and prisons. These scenes, these types, are
the work of a master. But they are only survivals; they
are merely used as back-ground, setting, accessories,
chorus, to the main stream of the narrative, the main
design of the book. 'Resurrection' is propaganda as much
as 'The Kingdom of God is within you'. And while the
artist in one of his readers may declare that the pictures
of a young man's new awakened heart, and of Easter Day in
the country are those he will remember, it is very doubtful if the fact will turn out so, for the diversion of the
earlier power has not reduced the essential strength
nearly so much as the artist in us looked for. The diverted strength reappears not merely as high purpose, but as
genius in the preacher.

[Relation of the plot omitted.]

In some press notices prefixed to the book a writer is
quoted as saying: '"Resurrection" might have been written
by Zola in collaboration with the prophet Isaiah'. Nothing could be more inapt; Zola indeed could hardly surpass
in liberal horror of detail some of the descriptions of
prison life, of prisoners on the march, and a few glimpses
into the sorry life of a prostitute, but the prophet's
voice is not that of Isaiah. Indignation has no birth in
Tolstoy's soul. A deep and all-embracing pity is born
there. The world is full of misery and sin; and anger and
punishment are of no avail. Rich and poor, learned and
unlearned, are in no need of the great cleanser, the great
liberator. If once you begin to condemn, where can you
stop? The tyrants and the oppressed are alike in need of
pity and understanding. Tolstoy makes the prisoners, the
reformers, the officials, and the socially degraded all
speak, and they each blame the rest and cry out for
revenge or punishment. He blames none. All humanity is
groaning under the same yoke, the yoke of sin, and law,
and force. His delicately bred, fastidious hero keeps
strange company, and lives in unsavoury places once his
mission is begun. But scorn and loathing die. He loves
as soon as he serves. That is the great resounding cry of
the book. Gentle it sounds, and meek. There never was
anything harder, more impossible, save by grace. Service
to humanity, not by committees, or laws, or wholesale
reform, but by individual goodness. Each man owes it to
his neighbours that he himself do justly and love mercy.
The right to gratitude, the right of punishment and of
revenge, all disappear. Love is the only law that cannot
err. Only through it will dawn the Easter of the world.

Love, then, and listen to your own inner voice. No
priest or ritual or church or outer counsellor will avail.
'To thine own self be true.' This is the high and hard
individualism that sounds with a long beseeching voice
through 'Resurrection'. It presents a task that reaches
to each man's utmost limits, but maybe not altogether
transcends those of the humblest. At least, as cure and
balm for the ills of the world, this must be said of it:
It is still untried.

(c) Unsigned review, 'Athenaeum', 7 April 1900. Reprinted by permission.

In this his latest production Tolstoy shows all the vigour
of his early days. There is the same pungency of diction,
the same picturesque power. Not a person is introduced
without a touch of vigorous individuality, reminding us of
the minor characters of one of Shakespeare's plays -
James Gurney, for instance, in 'King John'. There is
something very Dickensian in the introduction of the landlady with the fat and perspiring neck, just as Dickens
talks of the mottle-faced gentleman in 'Nicholas Nickleby'
and the commercial gentleman in the 'Christmas Carol' who
had an excrescence on his nose which made him look like a
turkey. Observe how many personal touches there are of
this description when Tolstoy deals with the miserable
convicts; each seems to carry in his looks his own individual associations of crime and suffering. In such outlines we have real gleams of genius. In antithesis to
these sufferers are the pictures of luxurious life - the
languid princesses, the fat millionaires, whose portraits
are so admirably drawn by Mr Pasternak, who must be a
Slav, and evidently knows his Russians at first hand.
The picture of the diners at the Korchagins taking their
zakuska is admirable. It is only fair, however, to the
Russians to say that such figures can be found much further west. There is no need to go to Russia to meet with
self-indulgent men who very much enjoy their dinner.
Something intensely Slavonic, but of quite another kind,
is 'The Early Mass'. The book of course, is eminently
tendenziös, as the Germans say - even more so than the
earlier works of the author. We all know the Socialistic
tendencies which we are to expect from Tolstoy. He seems
to be against all coercion and prisons; but probably there
will never be a time when such places will not be found.
The picture is a terrible one, and he heightens the

contrast by the scene of the convicts starting on their
journey and the luxurious family gazing at them from their
carriage, angry that they had to stop to let them pass.
When the reader comes upon these details he is reminded of
the account of the London prisons in Fielding's 'Amelia',
or the descriptions of what he saw by the philanthropist
Howard. Many of the characters seem to start from the
canvas of one of Hogarth's pictures. What are we to say
of the Juvenalian *flagellum* which the Count holds up over
the vice triumphant? He is very literal, and some Western
delicate readers may naturally shrink from his book, which
leaves the impression of a nightmare. Nekhludoff and
Katusha perforce interest us, but the picture is over-
whelmingly painful. The author seems to lacerate the very
fibres of humanity. The translation, with the exception
of an occasional foreign touch, is well done.

(d)   From an unsigned review, 'Literature', 7 April 1900.

Certainly 'technique' is conspicuous by its absence.
There is no light and shade, no effective contrast, no
balance or reserve in 'Resurrection'. The reader plods on
his way much in the same spirit as he puts up with a
tedious friend for the sake of his sincerity. The main
plot is a powerful one. The 'resurrection' is that of a
beautiful young Russian peasant, Maslova, who is wronged
by a prince, Nekhludoff, and afterwards falling to the
lowest depths of degradation, is convicted - unjustly -
of murder, and condemned to hard labour in Siberia. She
is saved by her seducer, who frees her from her immoral
life, and finally obtains a mitigation of her sentence.
Maslova's resurrection is complete when, though she loves
Nekhludoff, she refuses to sacrifice his future by marrying him. Here is an excellent theme, a man and a woman,
once actuated by base motives, transformed by unselfish
affection into a hero and heroine of the highest order.
But how does Tolstoy work it out? In the first place it
takes him 560 pages to do it in. Then he has dealt with
it in such a plain-spoken way as to severely limit the
circle of his readers, and to confine the book to a recess
in the smoking-room, whence it cannot be carried off to
the drawing-room table. Another defect is a purely artistic one - viz., that the main business of the writer is
not to tell a good story well, but to write an indictment
of the prison system in Russia. The book is a revolutionary treatise. While the reader is on tenterhooks to know

the fate of Maslova, he is treated to chapter upon chapter
written for a purely didactic purpose. Wearied by an endless accumulation of detail, he ceases to grasp what is
important and what is not. Characters are introduced
sufficient in number to fill a whole library of novels.
For the most part they are of little human interest, being
either prosperous officials or effete aristocrats, and
therefore labelled 'bad', or else prisoners, and therefore
labelled 'wronged'. For according to the author it is an
'incomprehensible delusion that men may punish one another'. A sombre veil is drawn over the whole book.
Scarcely a detail is chosen but to heighten the general
gloom. Here is a sample: 'Nekhludoff listened, but
hardly understood what the good-looking old man was saying, because his attention was riveted to a large, dark-
grey, many-legged louse that was creeping along the good-
looking man's cheek'.

The 'good-looking man's cheek' is an example of the
bathos in which an author who adjures technique indulges.
Often these details are purposeless. Casual characters
upon whom nothing depends are brought on the scene merely,
one would think, to disgust the reader. A landlady is
mentioned only because she has an 'extraordinarily fat
neck', and an advocate's wife because she is a 'horribly
ugly, little, bony, snub-nosed, yellow-faced woman'.
'Yellow' is quite a normal colour for Tolstoy's characters. But they are as often as not green.

Yet a perusal of this ill-proportioned and often nauseating book is not entirely fruitless. The character
of Maslova is a faultless piece of work, and we would
gladly exchange much that is dull in the book for more
about the heroine. Tolstoy - himself a peasant by conversion - gives us more than one intimate study of peasant life. Some of the scenes in prison are really vivid,
and the reader follows the exiles to Siberia under the
guidance of a closely observant cicerone. But the picture
is daubed by an unsparing brush. Even the writer's habitual sincerity is sacrificed to his care to emphasize only
what heightens our view of a suffering criminal class,
oppressed by a vicious officialdom. As a special pleader
Tolstoy has weakened his case by his obvious partiality,
and as a novelist he has marred a powerful story by a
total disregard of artistic proportion.

(e) From an unsigned review, 'Nation' (New York),
3 May 1900.

Tolstoy plunges into the story with the swift, dramatic
stroke of a novelist so sure of his art that he feels no
concern about it. In the first paragraphs God's beneficent intention is symbolized by the beauty of morning and
spring, and man's stupid malevolence by the spectacle of
soldiers with drawn swords conducting Maslova, the prostitute, from prison to court, to stand her trial for
robbery and murder. Maslova's past is then sketched in a
bare, direct way, an awful presentment of the havoc
wrought by sexual passion. Society's injustice to women
is marked by the picture of Nekhludoff, who has never been
punished for the seduction of Maslova, and who, during ten
years of selfish and prosperous life, has managed to forget all about her. In describing the trial, Tolstoy
lapses into bitter satire of processes and persons peculiarly Russian, but, with the recognition by Prince Nekhludoff, the juryman, of Maslova, the criminal, he returns to
his motive. Slowly, painfully, most reluctantly Nekhludoff's atrophied soul awakes and forces him to see himself
as the author of Maslova's shame, to know that he is in
the first place responsible for all that she has suffered
from society and may yet be condemned to suffer by the
law. After the awakening comes the battle, and the soul
does not win in one dramatic moment. All the claims of
the animal, of habit, of a great artificial society, are
arrayed against it, but, in the end, the spirit does win,
and the author vindicates his assumptions of the presence
of God in man and the power of man to redeem himself.
    When Nekhludoff voluntarily departs with Maslova for
Siberia, the moral idea seems to us to have been completely expressed, and the story told. But Tolstoy has
still a great many social wrongs and abuses to condemn,
and at this point he changes his method so absolutely
that the change cannot be accidental. He may have felt
that, so far, he had been delivering his message with too
much art, too much technical skill; that, therefore, his
sincerity may be questioned, and that, instead of working
for serious moral regeneration, he has worked only for
intense and transient emotional excitement. At all
events the rest of the book is fragmentary, the work not
of a philosopher and novelist, but of a moralist and reformer seeing nothing in life but certain defined evils.
The Russian dominates the man, and discussion of the universal spiritual gives way to denunciation of Russian
class tyranny, official injustice, and very detailed

accounts of the filth of Russian prisons. Nekhludoff,
in journeying to Siberia, sharing the prisoners' hardships,
listening to their tales, retires behind race barriers.
With the destruction of artistic unity and force, the im-
pressiveness of moral idea diminishes. By localizing the
field for moral endeavor, the stimulus to that is mini-
mized. We others cannot alter Russian society and cannot
clean Russian prisons, therefore let us dismiss these
startling pictures of hopeless misery from our minds as
quickly as possible. It is true that we take leave of
Nekhludoff announcing moral principles of general application; nevertheless, we feel that their practice may not be
so imperative for salvation if we happen to have been born
something less than a Russian prince.

(f)   Le Breton compares 'Resurrection' and 'Les
Misérables'. From a review entitled Social Pity in the
Novel by A. Le Breton, 'Revue des deux mondes', 1902,
vol. 7, 15 February.

Some of Tolstoy's admirers have expressed surprise and
even a certain displeasure at the fact that there are
some rather obvious connections between 'Resurrection' and
'Les Misérables'. It was a sign of good taste for them to
disparage Victor Hugo, and 'Les Misérables' in particular
aroused only bitter contempt. That such an old-fashioned
novel could have anything in common with the writings of
Tolstoy is an idea which never occurred to them. Yet
once they had read 'Resurrection', it should have.
What in fact did they find in 'Resurrection' which was
not already in 'Les Misérables'? A fallen woman who is
raised up again, poor people, convicts, prostitutes, the
debris of humanity and all the victims of social life
gathered together on a huge canvas; hard-hearted people
from the middle classes and judges with clear consciences,
ingenuous revolutionaries who wish to change the world
and die in the attempt; scenes in hospitals, prisons and
labour camps; and over it all, across so many terrible and
desolate sights there passes a certain spirit, a spirit of
brotherly love and compassion. Such, substantially, are
the two books, and their titles are quite interchange-
able.
     The comparison between the two is clear from the very
first page of 'Resurrection'. One cannot follow Nekhlyudov into the law court where an unfortunate young girl is
about to be sentenced for something of which he is the

cause without recalling Valjean's entrance into the
audience-chamber where a poor old man is about to be
sentenced for something Valjean did; one cannot notice the
feelings which arise in Nekhlyudov at that time without
recalling Valjean's anguish and the famous chapter about
the 'storm raging in his head'. On listening to the
Moscow lawyer questioning the innocent Katya, so needlessly and in such pompous language, one involuntarily
compares him with the *avocat général* from Arras confound-
ing the good Champmathieu with his eloquence; and one
involuntarily compares the two defendants, their bewilderment, their naive replies, and their inability to clear
themselves of crimes they have not committed. There is no
doubt that Tolstoy's hero, Prince Nekhlyudov, rich, elegant and influential, scarcely resembles Hugo's, although
the story of both of them is that of a return to right-
eousness, of their 'resurrection', and that they both
employ an equal passion in their attempt to aid the unfortunate. But alongside Nekhlyudov there is Katya, who
is actually the main character in the novel and who is
'reborn' too; and the reader is not long in seeing that
Katya is just a much a sister of Valjean as Fantine. Like
Fantine she had been seduced and almost immediately abandoned and cast to the wind. Like Valjean, and with no
more justification, she is sent to a labour camp, and
despite her shame and her bitter rancour it is enough for
her, as it is for Valjean, to experience a little tender
pity for her conscience to reawake, her heart to reopen
and to become capable again of the most noble sacrifice.

    The comparison is obvious; so why be astounded by it?
'Resurrection' is not the first Tolstoy novel to seem to
trace its parentage to Hugo. It is not without significance that in 'What is Art?' - having stated that the
aesthetic value of a work is inseparable from its religious value, but that religious feelings also change from
age to age and are expressed today in the conscience man
feels for his fellows - Tolstoy cites 'Les Misérables' as
the most beautiful work of art of the nineteenth century
and the one which most conforms to his ideal.

98.   G.K. CHESTERTON ON TOLSTOY'S FANATICISM

1903

G.K. Chesterton (1874-1936), author and critic, most
remembered for his amusing essays and the 'Father Brown'
detective stories, was also a propagandist for Catholicism;
this explains his interest in Tolstoy's religious ideas.
The article from which the following extract is taken
appeared in 1903 soon after the publication in English of
'The Kreutzer Sonata' and 'Resurrection', the works in
which Tolstoy most clearly expresses in fictional form his
ideas on sexual morality and religion, respectively.

This emergence of Tolstoy, with his awful and simple
ethics, is important in more ways than one. Among other
things it is a very interesting commentary on an attitude
which has been taken up for the matter of half a century
by all the avowed opponents of religion. The secularist
and the sceptic have denounced Christianity first and
foremost because of its encouragement of fanaticism;
because religious excitement led men to burn their neighbours, and to dance naked down the street. How queer it
all sounds now. Religion can be swept out of the matter
altogether, and still there are philosophical and ethical
theories which can produce fanaticism enough to fill the
world. Fanaticism has nothing at all to do with religion.
There are grave scientific theories which, if carried out
logically, would result in the same fires in the market-
place and the same nakedness in the street. There are
modern aesthetes who would expose themselves like the
Adamites if they could do it in elegant attitudes. There
are modern scientific moralists who would burn their
opponents alive, and would be quite contented if they were
burnt by some new chemical process. And if any one doubts
this proposition — that fanaticism has nothing to do with
religion, but has only to do with human nature — let him
take this case of Tolstoy and the Doukhabors. A sect of
men start with no theology at all, but with the simple
doctrine that we ought to love our neighbour and use no
force against him, and they end in thinking it wicked to
carry a leather handbag, or to ride in a cart. A great
modern writer who erases theology altogether, denies the
validity of the Scriptures and the Churches alike, forms a
purely ethical theory that love should be the instrument

of reform, and ends by maintaining that we have no right
to strike a man if he is torturing a child before our
eyes. He goes on, he develops a theory of the mind and
the emotions, which might be held by the most rigid
atheist, and ends by maintaining that the sexual relation
out of which all humanity has come is not only not moral,
but is positively not natural. This is fanaticism as it
has been and as it will always be. Destroy the last copy
of the Bible, and the persecution and insane orgies will
be founded on Mr Herbert Spencer's 'Synthetic Philosophy'.
Some of the broadest thinkers of the Middle Ages believed
in faggots, and some of the broadest thinkers in the nineteenth century believe in dynamite.

The truth is that Tolstoy, with his immense genius,
with his colossal faith, with his vast fearlessness and
vast knowledge of life, is deficient in one faculty and
one faculty alone. He is not a mystic, and therefore he
has a tendency to go mad. Men talk of the extravagance
and frenzies that have been produced by mysticism: they
are a mere drop in the bucket. In the main, and from the
beginning of time, mysticism has kept men sane. The thing
that has driven them mad was logic. It is significant
that, with all that has been said about the excitability
of poets, only one English poet ever went mad, and he went
mad from a logical system of theology. He was Cowper, and
his poetry retarded his insanity for many years. So
poetry, in which Tolstoy is deficient, has always been a
tonic and sanative thing. The only thing that has kept
the race of men from the mad extremes of the convent and
the pirate-galley, the night-club and the lethal chamber,
has been mysticism - the belief that logic is misleading,
and that things are not what they seem.

99.   OVSYANIKO-KULIKOVSKY ON IVAN ILICH

1905

D.N. Ovsyaniko-Kulikovsky (1853-1920), professor of Russian literature at Kharkov University, was a leading
literary historian and theoretician. He wrote influential
studies of Pushkin, Gogol and Turgenev, as well as Tolstoy.
To his contemporaries he was best known for his three-
volume 'History of the Russian Intelligentsia' (1906-11).

This extract is taken from his book 'Tolstoy the Artist', 1905.

Of what particularly is Ivan Ilich guilty before Tolstoy's moral code? His sins are as numerous as they are 'terrible'. Even in his youth,

> when he was a lawyer he was just as he was later, throughout his whole life: a capable man, cheerfully good-natured and sociable, but carrying out strictly what he considered his duty; *he considered his duty everything that people from the highest social strata considered to be his duty.* He was not ingratiating either as a boy or as a grown man, *but from his earliest years he was drawn to people from the highest social standing, like a fly is drawn to a light, he adopted their habits, their outlook on life and entered into friendly relations with them.*

Later when he was a civil servant charged with special duties in the provinces, this 'defect' took the form of fawning upon his superior and even his superior's wife. Furthermore his careerism did not cross the line of generally accepted respectability, like the misdemeanours of his youth, inasmuch as Ivan Ilich had a relationship with one of the ladies who thrust themselves on dandified lawyers; there was also a milliner; he had gone drinking with newly-arrived aides-de-camp and had 'gone to a street some way away after supper'. But 'none of this could be called by anything bad' for 'everything was done with clean hands, wearing clean shirts, speaking French and, most importantly, in the highest society and consequently with the approval of high-born people'.

Ivan Ilich is also guilty of not being a stoic but an epicurean; his ideal is an easy life, decent and pleasant. From this viewpoint he looked upon family life too. His marriage to Praskovya Fyodorovna seemed to him completely compatible with his 'programme'.

> To say that Ivan Ilich married because he loved his fiancée and found in her sympathy for his outlook on life, would be as unjust as to say that he married her because people in his social milieu approved the union. He married because of both these considerations: he made life pleasant for himself by taking such a wife and also did what high-society people considered correct. And so Ivan Ilich got married.

He is also guilty of treating everything in life, including both his work and even his family life, somewhat
formally, one could say 'bureaucratically'. So, while
serving as a civil servant charged with special duties and
later as a coroner, he

> very quickly adopted the habit of keeping at a distance
> all circumstances which were not connected with his
> work and of clothing any highly complicated matter in
> such a way that it appeared on paper only in its exter-
> nal details, excluding completely his personal opinions,
> and, most importantly, observing all required formality.

It is exactly the same in his family life where Ivan Ilich
finds it most convenient and pleasant to keep to the same
system - to observe all the generally accepted 'formali-
ties' of family life without participating in the intimate
life of his family. In his family he is 'a civil servant'.
Furthermore, he did not become like this at once, but
after a year of marriage when spiritual discord developed
between the couple and Praskovya Fyodorovna adopted the
tactics of ceaselessly complaining, moaning and generally
behaving badly. Then Ivan Ilich

> understood that married life, while offering a certain
> convenience to one's life, was a very complicated and
> serious affair, to which, in order to fulfil his duty,
> i.e. to lead a respectable life of which others would
> approve, it was necessary to work out a definite
> attitude, just as to his work. And this is just what
> he did. He demanded from family life only those com-
> forts of dinner at home, of looking after the house, of
> bed, which she could give him and, most importantly,
> the proprieties of external forms which are set by
> social opinion.

Family life gave him annoyance and unpleasantness and
contradicted his 'ideal of an easy, pleasant and respectable life'. And so he spiritually deserts his family and
recognizes this desertion as something normal and even
'the object of his life'. 'His object consisted in freeing himself as much as possible from these unpleasantnesses and giving them the character of harmlessness and
respectability.' He achieved this by spending as little
time as possible in the family and also 'ensured it by
having other people present'. It is unpleasant, cold and
empty at home and he seeks some 'spiritual home' in his
work, in his civic obligations. He becomes more and more
ambitious.... But he shows himself as bankrupt in this as

he does in family life - and again he is 'guilty'.
  He is guilty in that he is incapable of introducing
any, as it were, 'breath of life' into his civic obligations, that he has no calling for his work, but merely
training, skill and official thoroughness; he only observes the rites of his work so as to receive his salary on
the twentieth of the month and works only for promotion
up the salary scale. In a word he is guilty of being a
man of office routine and making a career. When he is
unsuccessful in his work and looks for another post, he
goes to St Petersburg

> for one thing: to obtain a post at 5,000-a-year.
> He was not choosy about any Ministry or any particular
> type of work. He only wanted a post, a post with
> 5,000, in the administration, banking, with the rail-
> ways, in Empress Maria's household, even in the Cus-
> toms - but certainly with 5,000, and certainly out of
> the Ministry where no one knew how to value him.

  If we gather together all these factors of his guilt
and then add them to all those little characteristics
which Tolstoy so skilfully groups together in order to
expose as clearly as possible the spiritual emptiness and
vulgarity of Ivan Ilich, then we will have a conclusion
as follows: Ivan Ilich is brought before the moral court
because he is an average, ordinary man who has no 'divine
spark'. The moral consequence, so artistically shown by
Tolstoy, is that the defendant has no real love for his
work, has no real feelings for his family; as a citizen,
as a pillar of society he is a blank; he has no convictions that he has worked out in his own head or from his
own experience; as a moral individual he is nothing.
From this spiritual poverty he is sentenced to death, and
the heavy process of dying will be for him a kind of moral
penalty and at the same time - expiation. In dying he
will gradually come to a realization of the emptiness,
vulgarity and disorder of the life he has led, will see
its nothingness and will feel all the horror of his spiritual loneliness. And he will die, transfigured and enlightened by the consciousness of the fact 'that his life
had not been as it should' that his life had indeed been
'the most empty and commonplace' and also 'the most
terrible'.
  To discover and show this 'most terrible' in 'the most
empty and commonplace life' was the object of the artistic
experiment, carried out with such rare mastery. This is
perhaps Tolstoy's most successful experiment.
  But this 'most terrible' which Tolstoy found in the

life of Ivan Ilich can possibly appear in various different lights, dependent upon the reader's particular point
of view. One could profit from the results of Tolstoy's
artistic experience without sharing the artist's dogma
and without making such severe demands upon Ivan Ilich as
Tolstoy makes. For him Ivan Ilich is a real moral freak
who can 'be straightened out' only by death. For us this
exclusive point of view is not obligatory. We meet people
like Ivan Ilich on almost every corner but we do not at
all consider them freaks. And actually Ivan Ilich is not
a bad man, not an evil man; he is honourable, and incorruptible, etc. Although most of these characteristics
are negative in that they show not so much the presence of
good as the absence of bad, they none the less give us a
picture of a very respectable person. Knowing that Ivan
Ilich even before the Great Reforms when he served as a
civil servant showed himself a man who could not be
bought, that later in his position of coroner or procura-
tor he did not misuse his power and even tried to soften
its influence, etc., we have every right to include Ivan
Ilich among so-called 'good people'. And the name of
these good people is legion. And it seems to us that to
investigate and judge these people from the standpoint of
high religious and moral demands, as does Tolstoy, there
are insufficient grounds. I dispute in the given circumstances the 'jurisdiction' and the 'choice of instances'.
Tolstoy wants every such Ivan Ilich to be a fully developed moral and religious personality, rising above the given
level of commonplace conceptions, he wants this average,
morally insignificant man to be a participant in life, to
react critically (and in this respect from a high moral
standpoint) to established forms, morals and the accepted
proprieties in order, in the end, to avoid being a petty
egotist and not to look on life as a pleasant and orderly
passing of the time, but see its meaning and value in
serving some higher ideal. Tolstoy demands too much....
From the Ivan Iliches one can demand but one thing: that
they do not descend below the average level, in a moral
and civic sense, and do not prevent from living and acting
those who rise above it. If they satisfy this modest,
minimal requirement, we shall say to them: May health go
with you! Labour and multiply! ...
     In describing the domestic disorder, the eternal argu-
ments and disagreements between Ivan Ilich and his wife,
in showing that 'arguments were always on the point of
flaring up', Tolstoy gives us a type of abnormal family
life, when there is no real love between the couple, only
a sensual attraction in the satisfaction of which their
mutual enmity flares up even more and takes on the

explicit character of an organized loathing for each
other. There were (in between the rows) a few periods of
that mutual affection which comes over couples, but they
did not last long. These were little islands at which
they anchored for a time, but then again put out to their
sea of suppressed hatred, expressed in their alienation
one from the other. This serves as the starting-point for
another artistic experiment in which the complicated question of the ethics of sexual relations in general and those
of marriage in particular could be put point-blank. An
adept at ascetic morals, Tolstoy will come to the dubious
conclusion that sexual relations, no matter whether within
or outside marriage, contradict man's ethical nature and
that man, as a moral being, should abstain from them. The
fact that the consequences of the carrying out of this
principle would lead to the demise of the human race is of
no concern to the moralist. For him the 'moral law' is
superior to humanity and must triumph even at the price of
the destruction of humanity - a point of view that humanity itself will never accept and which science and critical philosophy will refute and disprove.

100. GEORGE SAINTSBURY ON TOLSTOY

1907

Saintsbury (1845-1933), distinguished academic critic and
historian of immense productivity, is typical of those
Victorian critics, attracted, for example, by the precise
literary technique of Flaubert, who were overwhelmed by
the vast scale of Tolstoy's novels. This extract appeared
in vol. XII, 'The Later Nineteenth Century', of 'Periods
of European Literature', 1907. Reprinted by permission.

Count Tolstoi's work is extensive. As he says in his
peculiar way, 'I write books, and therefore know all the
evil they produce'; and the present writer is not
acquainted with the whole of it, even so far as it has
been translated. But the early Cossack stories, the two
great novels of 'War and Peace' and 'Anna Karenina', 'Ivan
Ilyitch' and some other short stories, 'The Kreutzer
Sonata' itself and the long recent novel of

'Resurrection', should give fair texts for judgment on
those points that can be judged from translation. One
thing strikes us in all, as it struck even a critic so
favourably disposed as the late Mr Matthew Arnold, — that
the novels are hardly works of art at all. It is, however, pleaded for them that they are 'pieces of life';
and so perhaps they are, but in a strangely unlicked and
unfinished condition. One constantly finds touches, not
of talent so much as of genius. But these touches are
hardly ever worked even into complete studies; while the
studies, complete or incomplete, are still less often
worked into pictures. It is almost startlingly exemplary
and symptomatic, for instance, to find, in the early,
vivid, but emphatically local studies of the Cossacks,
that the best of all Olyenin's moods and manners is a
study of Incompleteness itself. The greatest and most
powerful thing, in the writer's humble judgment, that
Tolstoi has ever done, — 'Ivan Ilyitch', that terrible and
wonderful picture of the *affres* of death and the prelimin-
ary gloom of hopeless disease, — however marvellously
observed and imagined, *has* to be incomplete, and so
escapes the fault found elsewhere.

Again, Count Tolstoi owes nothing to deliberate
Impressionism, yet he is the head malefactor of the
Impression itself. Even Mr Arnold himself gently complained of the irrelevances of 'Anna Karenina', and these
are multipled ten times in 'Resurrection'. Yet more,
there is in him, and in fact in most of the authors of
these younger literatures, — the absence of it was the
reason of the special praise given to Señor Valera in the
last chapter, — a singular particularist parochialism.
They are so constantly absorbed in special things that
they cannot bring them *sub specie aeternitatis*. They do
not see, as their literary elders, by no merit of their
own, have been brought to see, that things are merely
parts of life, — that you must rise and 'find the whole';
while of course in books like 'Resurrection', the purpose, the *tendenz*, entirely blinds them to proportion,
art, and everything else. They seem — at least this
greatest of them seems — to be constantly duped by single
observations or sets of observations, just as they are by
individual writers: not merely, in Tolstoi's case, serious
if faulty thinkers like Herbert Spencer and Karl Marx,
but mere blatant quacks like Henry George. So that the
great war scenes of 'War and Peace', the sketches of
society and the autobiographical study of Levine in 'Anna
Karenina', the 'crimes and punishments' of 'Resurrection',
leave us — all of them, if not all of us — with a sense of
the half-digested, the crude.

This crudity comes no doubt from more causes than one;
but one of the causes from which it comes is very note-
worthy.   Soon after 'The Kreutzer Sonata' became known
among us, an English critic admiringly observed that when
you compared 'Tom Jones' with it you saw 'what a simple,
toy-like structure had served Fielding for a human world.'
It was rather unlucky for this critic that Count Tolstoi
very shortly afterwards explained, in the remarkable paper
referred to above, to what the complexity of 'The Kreutzer
Sonata' was due.   It was due (*habemus confitentem*) to the
existence of a large number of crotchets and fads, most,
if not all, of which Fielding undoubtedly would not have
admitted to his simple, toy-like structure.   And these
crotchets group themselves round a central one — the doctrine that marriage, and love itself, are bad things *per
se*.   There is no need, if there were room, to discuss
this crotchet here.   But it cannot be improper to say, at
the end of a survey of European literature, that almost
all the greatest things in that, and in all literature
most probably, — that an enormous proportion of these
things to a mathematical certainty, — have been dictated,
directly or indirectly, by the inspiration of Love — physical Love in the end, though sublimated more or less now
and then.   The man who denies himself this inspiration is
in effect a member of the sect, in Russia itself, of whom
most tolerably well-informed people must think when they
read some of Count Tolstoi's writings.   He condemns himself to sterility and impotence.

This particular craze, though it had not developed
itself explicitly at the time of the writing of 'Anna
Karenina', explains why the heroine of that book and the
book itself, interesting as they seem to be to some
people, are almost absolutely uninteresting to others.
Anna has no more real love for Wronsky than for her husband; and her false love is infinitely less interesting
than that of Emma Bovary, with whom Mr Arnold very rashly
compares her, to her and her creator's advantage.   But we
must not digress into particulars.   The point is that a
man who sets his face, as Tolstoi does, against both Love
and War (though he had really utilised the latter in 'War
and Peace', and had tried to utilise the former in 'Anna
Karenina'), deprives himself of the two great reagents,
solvents, harmonising and unifying *catholica* of his art.
There remains Death, and he has, as we saw, got a wonderful success out of that; but even in days that like to
deal with gloom and grime, Death is not a card that you
can play very often.   He may by sheer *tours de force* —
and again in a time which likes *tours de force* — utilise
exceptional and minor motives to some extent.   But he cuts

himself off from the real and principal things. Add to
this that Tolstoi, though not exactly destitute of humour,
— he has not a few quaint and interesting touches of it,
— possesses it in nothing like the abounding and universal
supply which makes it almost a sufficient solvent or *men-
struum* of itself. Add once more that in him — as in all
his three compeers — we never get rid of the passing hour:
and it will be of little need or use to say more. Ladies
who are not prepared to wear their garments for a day and
then to cast them to the winds or the waiting-maids, have
a well-grounded objection to things that 'date themselves'
— that are *merely* fashionable. In literature nothing that
is merely fit to be cast to the winds, and the readers in
circulating libraries, is of any value at all; and here
too the fact of 'dating itself' too much is a serious drawback to any work. That there is much in Count Tolstoi
which is not merely fashionable may be and has been freely
granted. But there is a great deal too much that is.
'What does it matter to me,' Prince Posterity will say,
'that this was the way they crotcheted then? Art is long,
and the crotchet, thank Heaven! is short. Give me Art and
give me Nature, which is long likewise.' Now, the Prince
will not find very much art in the Count, and the nature
which he *will* find is too often unnatural.

101. PLEKHANOV ON TOLSTOY AND NATURE

1908

G.V. Plekhanov (1857-1918) was 'the father of Russian
social democracy' and a leading marxist politician and
theoretician of extreme orthodoxy. Because of his opposition to the Bolsheviks in 1917 his position in the Soviet
pantheon has been insecure. This is a pity for he was a
much better literary critic than Lenin and it is the
latter's opinions which have influenced much subsequent
Soviet criticism.
    This article, written in 1908, was first published in
the 'Star', 1924, no. 4.

Everyone who has read Tolstoy's works knows that he loves
nature and depicts it with a mastery that no one else has

apparently ever attained. Nature is not *described* in the
works of our great artist, it *lives*. Sometimes it appears,
as it were, as a character in the story: remember the incomparable scene of the Rostovs' Christmas sleigh-ride in
'War and Peace'.

The beauty of nature finds in Tolstoy a most responsive
connoisseur. In his travel notes on Switzerland .... one
comes across the following expressive lines:

> It is an amazing thing that I lived in Clarens for
> two months and whenever in the morning or more
> particularly before evening after dinner I opened the
> shutters on which the shadows had already fallen and
> glanced at the lake and beyond it to the blue mountains
> which were reflected in it, the beauty blinded me and
> for a moment unexpectedly affected me with its force...
> Sometimes, even sitting by myself in the shaded little
> garden and gazing and gazing at these shores and this
> lake, I felt, as it were, the physical impression of
> beauty pouring through my eyes into my soul.

But this extremely sensitive man who feels the beauty
of nature *pouring through his eyes and into his soul* goes
into raptures over by no means every beautiful scene.
Thus, having climbed to the top of one of the hills near
Montreux (the Roches de Naye, if I am not mistaken), he
notes: 'I don't like these so-called magnificent and famous
views; they're somehow cold.' *Tolstoy likes only those
views of nature which arouse in him a consciousness of his
oneness with it.* He himself says in the same travel notes:

> I love nature when it surrounds me on all sides and
> then expands into the endless distance, yet I am still
> in it. I love it where *the hot air surrounds me on all
> sides* and this same air rolls away into the endless
> distance, when those same succulent blades of grass,
> which I have squashed by sitting on them, form the
> green of the endless meadows, when those same leaves
> which, rustling in the breeze, move their shadow
> across my face and form the blue of the endless forest,
> when the same air that you breathe makes the deep blue
> of the endless sky, when you are not alone in exulting
> and rejoicing in nature, when near you miriads of
> insects buzz and couple, ladybirds crawl and everywhere
> around is inundated with birds.

Those who have been to Clarens will remember that the
view there over the lake to the mountain, in all its rare
beauty, has nothing magnificent or cold about it; on the

contrary it is marked by an attractive gentleness. This
is exactly why our Tolstoy loved nature at Clarens; this
is exactly why it filled his heart with the living joy of
being. 'I immediately wanted to love,' he says, 'I even
felt I loved myself; I regretted the past and held hopes
for the future; living became a joy for me, I wanted to
live for a long, long time and the thought of death took
on a childlike poetic terror.'

This terror at the thought of death is very characteristic of Tolstoy.

It is well known that this feeling played a large part
in the process of the working out of those views, the
totality of which form what in common parlance is called
Tolstoyism. But I do not intend to comment on that here.
I am concerned here only with the interesting fact that -
at least at a certain time in his life - *Tolstoy experienced most strongly the feeling of a horror of death at
the very time he was enjoying most the consciousness of
his oneness with nature*.

It is by no means like this with everybody. There are
people who see nothing particularly frightening in the
fact that in time they will have to merge completely with
nature, to dissolve finally into it. And the more
clearly they recognize under one impression or another
their oneness with nature the less frightening for them
becomes the thought of death. Shelley was probably like
this; Shelley, to whom belong the profoundly poetic words,
spoken on the death of Keats: 'He is made one with Nature.'
So was Ludwig Feuerbach who said in one of his distichs:

Fear you not death; you will remain for ever in your
                                              homeland
On the familiar ground which takes you lovingly into
                                           its embrace.

I am sure that nature, similar to that at Clarens,
would have particularly strengthened in Feuerbach's heart
the feeling which dictated to him this distich. It was
not, as we know, like this with Tolstoy. In him the views
at Clarens intensified his terror of death. Enjoying the
consciousness of his oneness with nature, he shakes with
terror at the thought that the time when the antithesis
between the 'I' and the beautiful 'non-I' of the nature
surrounding him will have disappeared. Feuerbach in his
'Thoughts on Death' showed with real German thoroughness
the groundlessness of the idea of personal immortality
from four points of view. Over a long period of time, if
not always, it appeared to Tolstoy (see his 'Confession')
that if there is no immortality then life is not worth

living. Tolstoy felt quite differently from Feuerbach and
Shelley. This is, of course, a matter of 'character'.
But it is remarkable that at different historical epochs
people have reacted differently to the thought of death.
St Augustine said that to the Romans the glory of Rome was
a substitute for immortality. And it was to this side of
the question that Feuerbach directed his readers' attention when he said that aspiration towards personal immortality was confirmed in the souls of Europeans only from
the time of the Reformation which was the religious expression of the individualism of the new age. Finally the
justice of this same thought is shown in his own way, that
is by the help of vivid artistic images, by Tolstoy himself in his well-known story 'Three Deaths'. There the
dying noblewoman displays a great horror of death, while
the incurably sick coachman, Fyodor, remains as it were
completely impervious to this feeling. This expresses a
difference not of *historical* but of *social* status. In
modern Europe the upper classes have always had a much
more marked individualism than the lower classes. And the
deeper individualism penetrates the human soul the more
firmly the horror of death becomes fixed in it.
    Tolstoy is one of those who with genius and in the
most extreme way represent individualism in modern times.
Individualism has left a strong imprint on both his artistic works and in particular on his views as a publicist.
It is not surprising that it is also reflected in his
views on nature. However much Tolstoy loved nature he
could find nothing convincing in Feuerbach's arguments
against the idea of personal immortality. This idea was
for him a psychological necessity. And if together with a
thirst for immortality there lived in his soul, one might
say, a pagan consciousness of his oneness with nature then
this consciousness led him only to being unable, like the
ancient Christians, to find consolation in the idea of an
immortality beyond the grave. No, an immortality *of that
sort* had too little appeal for him. He needed an immortality in which the antithesis between his personal 'I' and
the beautiful 'non-I' of nature would continue to exist
for ever. He needed an immortality in which he would not
cease feeling all around him the hot air 'rolling away
into the endless distance' and 'making the deep blue of
the endless sky'. He needed an immortality in which
'miriads of insects' would continue to 'buzz and weave
about, ladybirds crawl and everywhere around would be
inundated with birds'. In short there could be no consolation for him in the Christian idea of the immortality
of the soul; *he needed the immortality of the body*. And
perhaps the greatest tragedy of his life was the clear

truth that such an immortality was impossible.

This, of course, is not to praise him; nor is it, of course, a reproach. It is simply an indication of the fact which has to be taken into account by anyone who wishes to understand the psychology of the great writer of the Russian land.

102.   LENIN: TOLSTOY AS THE MIRROR OF THE RUSSIAN REVOLUTION

1908

Published in 'Proletarian', 1908, no. 35. This article was one of hundreds of comments on the occasion of Tolstoy's eightieth birthday. V.I. Lenin (real name Ulyanov), 1870-1924, was the founder and leader of the Soviet Communist Party and the Communist International, founder of the Soviet Union and the first head of the Soviet Government. He was a brilliant theorist of politics, less so of economics and philosophy. Perhaps the best that could be said of his general ideas on literature is that they have been remarkably influential on those open to such influences.

The introduction to this piece, on the generally hypocritical praise for Tolstoy on his anniversay, is here omitted.

The contradictions in Tolstoy's works, ideas, teachings and his school are really glaring. On the one hand there is the artist of genius who has given us incomparable pictures of Russian life and also given first-class works of literature to the world; while on the other hand there is the landowner obsessed with Christ. On the one hand there is the remarkably powerful, direct and sincere protest against social falsehood and hypocrisy, while on the other the 'Tolstoyan', i.e. the worn-out, hysterical sniveller of a Russian intellectual who publicly beats his breast and declares: 'I am bad, I am vile, but I am engaged in moral self-perfection. I no longer eat meat, I now live on rice cutlets.' On the one hand there is the pitiless criticism of capitalist exploitation, the exposure of violence perpetrated by the government, the

revelation of all the profound contradictions between the
growth of wealth and the achievements of civilization and
the spread of poverty, the degradations and sufferings of
the working masses; and on the other the 'holy fool'
preaching 'non-violent resistance to evil'. On the one
hand there is that absolutely sober realism and the
stripping-off of each and every mask, while on the other
the preaching of one of the vilest things in the world,
namely religion, the attempt to replace priests who are
but state bureaucrats by those who have moral convictions,
i.e. the cultivation of the most refined and consequently
particularly revolting clericalism. In truth (1)

> Thou art destitute, yet thou art rich,
> Thou art mighty, yet thou art powerless
> - Mother Russia.

It is obvious that Tolstoy, with all these contradictions, could not conceivably understand either the working-
class movement and its role in the struggle for socialism
or the Russian revolution. But the contradictions in Tolstoy's ideas and teachings are not accidental, they are the
expression of the contradictory conditions in which Russian
life was set in the last third of the nineteenth century.
The patriarchal countryside, only yesterday liberated from
serfdom, was literally given over to the wholesale pillage
of capitalist and tax collector. The old foundations of
peasant economy and peasant life, foundations that had held
really firm for centuries, were scrapped with unusual rapidity. And the contradictions in Tolstoy's views must be
evaluated not from the point of view of the contemporary
working-class movement and contemporary socialism (such an
evaluation is, of course, necessary, but it is not sufficient by itself) but from the point of view of the protest against advancing capitalism, against the ruination
of the masses and their dispossession of land, a protest
which had to be born of the patriarchal Russian countryside. Tolstoy is ridiculous as a prophet who has discovered new prescriptions for the salvation of mankind....
Tolstoy is great as the spokesman for those ideas and
feelings which took shape in millions of Russian peasants.
Tolstoy is original, for the totality of his views, taken
as a whole, express the very originality of our revolution
as a *peasant* bourgeois revolution. The contradictions in
Tolstoy's ideas, seen from this point of view, are a real
mirror of those contradictory conditions in which the
historical activity of the peasantry in our revolution was
set.

Note

1 From Nekrasov's 'Who Can Live Happily in Russia?' (Ed.)

103. HENRY JAMES ON TOLSTOY

1897 1909

Henry James (1843-1916), novelist, playwright and eminent
man of letters, was a writer of immense art and technique;
he could never come to terms with the vast scope of the
two greatest Russian novelists (on 19 May 1912, in a
letter to Hugh Walpole, he called Tolstoy and Dostoevsky
'fluid pudding') and was more at home with the rather more
'European' Turgenev, whom he knew in Paris in 1875. The
first of the two passages which follow is taken from 'Turgenev' which appeared in 1897 in volume XXV of 'A Library
of the World's Best Literature', and the second from the
preface to 'The Tragic Muse', 1907-9.

Turgenev is in a peculiar degree what I may call the
novelist's novelist - an artistic influence extraordinarily valuable and ineradicably established. The perusal
of Tolstoy - a wonderful mass of life - is an immense
event, a kind of special accident, for each of us; his
name represents nevertheless no such eternal spell of
method, no such quiet irresistibility of presentation, as
shines, close to us and lighting our possible steps, in
that of his precursor. Tolstoy is a reflector as vast as
a natural lake; a monster harnessed to his great subject -
all human life! - as an elephant might be harnessed, for
purposes of traction, not to a carriage, but to a coach-
house. His own case is prodigious, but his example for
others is dire: Disciples not elephantine he can only
mislead and betray.

A picture without composition slights its most precious
chance of beauty, and is, moreover, not composed at all
unless the painter knows *how* that principle of health and
safety, working as an absolutely premeditated art, has
prevailed. There may in its absence be life, incontest-
ably, as 'The Newcomes' has life, as 'Les Trois

Mousquetaires', as Tolstoy's 'War and Peace' have it;
but what do such large, loose, baggy monsters, with their
queer elements of the accidental and the arbitrary, artistically *mean*? We have heard it maintained, we well remember, that such things are 'superior to art'; but we understand least of all what *that* may mean, and we look in vain
for the artist, the divine explanatory genius, who will
come to our aid and tell us.

104. HERFORD ON TOLSTOY AFTER 'ANNA KARENINA'

1910

From an obituary notice in the 'Manchester Guardian', 17
November 1910, by C.H. Herford entitled Leo Tolstoy: His
Life and Work. Reprinted by permission.

The publication of 'Anna Karenina' gave Tolstoy a pre-
eminence among living Russian men of letters which only
Turgenjef, far away in Paris, and perhaps Dostojevsky,
still struggling with poverty in the capital after years
of exile could contest. With fame and wealth, abounding
health and strength, an unclouded home life, and genius
hardly surpassed among living men, Tolstoy might seem
possessed of all that makes for sane and rational happiness. But precisely at this point there emerged decisively that profound, revolutionary simplicity of the man
which had from the first disturbed the even tenour of his
course through the intricacies of modern society, but was
also one of the hidden sources of his power. Something of
the savage and something of the child, such as is in most
men swiftly lulled or permitted only momentary accesses of
fugitive and harmless eloquence, had in Tolstoy never
ceased to trouble his content, precisely when he was most
contented, with estranging doubts and tormenting problems.
Now, when he had attained the summit of his ambitions, it
woke to full activity, mastered his whole being, and for a
time changed the whole tenour and aspect of his life.
With the frank simplicity, the untamed directness of
childhood, but at the same time with the anguish of the
mature and responsible man who is bound to find some
answer to the problems he raises, he asked: 'What is the

meaning of my life? Why am I here? What am I working for?
What is life itself?' The very amplitude of his means for
living made more inscrutable the enigma of their purpose
and their end. His existence seemed to be a horrible joke
played upon him by some unknown power, and the temptation
to put an abrupt and decisive end to the game became so
dangerously urgent that he hid away a cord lest he should
be tempted to use it and ceased to carry a gun. He turned
with wonder to observe how other men escaped from the
perplexities which baffled himself. In his own class he
found nowhere any satisfactory solution. Some escaped it
by ignorance, some by drowning thought in pleasure, some
by weak acquiescence, some by the resolute yet desperate
resource which he with difficulty put aside. The kings
of modern thought were dumb; culture was bankrupt.

It was not merely a natural sequence but the inevitable
prompting of deeply ingrained habits of mind and heart
that led the quondam devotee of Cossack village folks, the
landowner who had laboured to educate his peasants by
emancipating them from all that was called education, to
turn for help, in the helplessness of wisdom, to the
'unwise' millions whose labour enables the cultured world
to live. 'So I watched the life common to such enormous
numbers of the dead and the living, the life of simple,
unlearned, and poor men, and found something quite different.' They, at any rate, had no doubt of the meaning of
life. He began to draw nearer to them, in a sense in
which even the genial story-teller who held entranced the
children of Yasnaya school, even the 'squire' making hay
all day with his men and sharing their midday mess of
bilberry-water and bread, had never drawn near to them
before. At one point of his line of advance he made a
prompt and final retreat. The Orthodox Christianity of
the peasantry and of the ignorant priesthood who ministered to them could never be his. A single experiment
with the Communion, involving a compulsory declaration by
the communicant that he believed he was swallowing 'the
real body and blood', sufficed, and he never went again.
But if he revolted from Orthodoxy it was not in order to
return to the barren scepticism he had left, but to reach
a simple and spiritual Christianity far more in keeping
with the humble and homely life which was now becoming the
source and feeding-ground of his ideals. In a series of
unique pamphlets he laid before the astonished world an
account, calm and closely reasoned but informed with the
passionate conviction of the 'conversion' of the author of
'Anna Karenina'. 'My Confession', 1879-82, was followed
by 'A Criticism of Greek Orthodox Theology' (published at
Geneva) 1880-1, 'The Gospels Translated, Compared and

Harmonized', 1882, 'My Religion', 1884, and the stern and
searching summons to the sleeping conscience of his contemporaries, 'What, then, is to be done?' The glaring
economic disparities of society, if they were not the root
of its disease, yet loomed largest in his eyes, and economic remedies took at the outset an even disproportionate
place in his scheme of reform. He preached 'work' in
language which, in a context of utterly un-Carlylean political and ethical conceptions, continually recalls
Carlyle. Labour for him was primarily 'bread labour', by
which the labourer earned his own living instead of being
fed by others; and 'bread labour' he proclaimed to be 'the
remedy which will save the human race'. But he repudiated
the mechanical worship of 'work' as such; and he recognized as legitimate and desirable forms of activity among
which every man should ideally divide his day - together
with hard physical toil and manual arts - science, art,
and intercourse with friends.

On its positive side Tolstoy's teaching was profoundly
salutary at almost every point. On its negative side its
healthful elements were mingled with perversities of conception which from the first impaired their effect. In
the Rousseauesque negation of society in the name of
Nature he went far beyond Rousseau; if he resembles in
some degree the Rousseau of the early essays, he stands
almost in antithesis to the Rousseau of the 'Contrat
Social'. Rousseau sought to frame a Constitution which
should make the State truly the expression of the general
will; Tolstoy repudiated the State and every other agency
which exercises forcible control. Primitive society, with
its rigid system of custom and taboo, gave no warrant for
the absolute individualism which Tolstoy, like Rousseau,
but without his excuse, preached in its name. Still gra-
ver perversities resulted from his rejection, in the
sphere of art and letters, of all other criteria than the
satisfaction of the simple hearer whose bodily industry
and believing heart had provided his ideal of humanity.
In 'What is Art?' (1898) he rode roughshod over the convictions of the whole cultivated world by a very incomplete and partial application of this in itself inadequate
theory. Herein his canon of judgment was sound and potent
where it affirmed but fallacious where it rejected and
denied. We may be grateful, where so much artistic and
literary work went by the board, that Molière and Cer-
vantes, 'David Copperfield' and 'Adam Bede' were saved;
but it was at the heavy price of consigning not merely
Wagner, upon whose enduring quality Europe is not yet at
one, but Beethoven, Dante, Goethe and Shakspere to limbo.
Eight years later (1906) this grand work received its

appropriate completion in the famous Shakspere Study - a
critical flagellation such as has probably never before
been administered in cold blood and with profound conviction from one supreme artist to another; for even Aristo-
phanes's chastisement of Euripedes owes much of its animation to exuberant humour and sheer joy of the game.
Throughout this, however, there ran a vein of thinking and
feeling about art which, within its proper limits, was
altogether salutary; a protest against the divorce of art
from life which only missed its mark because Tolstoy
refused to reckon with any other kind of beneficent union
between them than that which he found in regions where the
social needs of life and the sensibilities of art were
alike elementary.

In the meantime a long series of new artistic productions of his own testified to the sincerity of his teaching
about Art and also to its incomplete psychological base
and also to an expression of his own artistic needs. From
1885 onward he issued a series of tales for the people
which for fertility - of unpretentious narrative power and
striking appeal - have no equals in modern literature.
Such were, among a host of others, 'The Two Pilgrims',
'The Candle', and 'Ivan the Fool'. In 1886 he entered
the field of drama with the terrible village tragedy 'The
Power of Darkness' written for the People's Theatre. In
1889 for a very different audience - his own children and
their friends - he wrote the genial and humorous comedy
'The Fruits of Culture'. And to the educated Russian
Public as well as to the folk, he was still willing to
speak through his proper instrument, the tale. Two considerable narrative works belong to these later years -
'The Death of Ivan Ilich' (1884-6) and 'Resurrection'
(1899) - the first a concentrated study of physical
suffering almost unbearable in its remorseless power, and
the second, like all Tolstoy's later writing, injured by
the over-indulgence of an inexhaustible descriptive bent,
and by the too uniform gloom of its presentment of Russian
society, but when all deductions have been made, one of
the great books of the century.

During the early years of the twentieth century the
veteran man of letters continued to lead a life of singular activity, interrupted only by a severe illness in
1902. He projected tales and plays, poured forth pamphlets, open letters, prefaces to translations of cognate
foreign writers (Amiel, Maupassant, Edward Carpenter), and
a mass of private correspondence, in swift succession.
None of his later work, perhaps, created a more powerful
impression in this country than his 'I Cannot be Silent'
(1908) - a magnificent protest against the wholesale

hangings ordered by the Russian Government even after the
Revolution had been suppressed. In Russia he held a
position of unapproached authority and prestige, and after
the death of Ibsen no living man of letters could vie with
him in European fame. Outside Russia at any rate his
prestige was enhanced by the formal decree of excommunication at length pronounced upon him by the long-suffering
Holy Synod of the Orthodox Church, whose fundamental
tenets he had denounced for twenty years (1901). His
reply to the decree dated April 4 (o.s.) is a powerful
restatement of his convictions. Ousted from his church
he remained the more securely and visibly the head of a
spiritual community dispersed throughout the civilized
world, which revered him as a great social teacher, the
prophet of a gospel of abstinence, non-resistance and
simple religion, 'plain living and high thinking', inter-
preted with a severity of which Wordsworth never dreamed,
and applied (as in 'The Kreutzer Sonata') to regions of
life which he would have shrunk with horror from subjecting
to discussion at all. However inadequate his principles,
and however perversely extravagant, or incomplete, his
practice of them, his will remain one of the most imposing
figures in the line of those who from Rienzi and More to
Rousseau and Shelley, and onwards, have sought to cure the
diseases of modern society by a radical simplification of
its structure, its organization, and its aims. The memory
of the indefatigable teacher will perhaps survive his
teaching. The fame of the great artist in story is in any
case secure.

105. GORKY RECOMMENDS A YOUNG ACQUAINTANCE TO READ
TOLSTOY

1910

Maxim Gorky (1868-1936), real name Peshkov, novelist,
playwright and publicist, first met Tolstoy in the Crimea
in 1900 (when he was shocked by the great man's bad
language). Tolstoy's opinion of him was that he was
'better than his writings'. However, Gorky's 'Recollections', first composed in 1919, is still one of the best
things ever written on Tolstoy. This letter was written
to L.L. Frenkel at the end of 1910.

Yes, Tolstoy the man is dead, but the great writer is
alive; he will be with us for ever. In a few years' time,
when you are a little older and begin to read Tolstoy's
wonderful books, you will feel a deep joy, you will feel
that he is immortal, that he is there with you, giving
you hours of enjoyment through his art.

Appendix

Listed below are brief notes on Russian literary and historical references made in the text.

Aksakov, S.T. (1791-1859), father of Konstantin (see No. 7) and Ivan; writer; his best-known works are 'Family Chronicle' (1856) and 'The Childhood Years of Bagrov's Grandson' (1858).

Aleko, hero of A.S. Pushkin's narrative poem 'The Gypsies' (1824, published 1827).

'Andrey Kolosov', short story by I.S. Turgenev (1844).

'Arabesques', collection of prose works (including 'Nevsky Prospect', 'The Memoirs of a Madman', and 'The Portrait') by N.V. Gogol (1835).

Arakcheev, Count A.A. (1769-1834), first minister during the second half of the reign of Alexander I.

Bagration, Prince P.I. (1765-1812), commander of the second Russian army during Napoleon's invasion of Russia, mortally wounded at the battle of Borodino.

Bakhtyarov, character in 'The Simpleton' by A.F. Pisemsky (1850).

Belinsky, V.G. (1811-48), Russia's first notable literary critic; see Introduction.

Belkin, see 'Tales of Belkin, The'.

Beshmetev, hero of 'The Simpleton' by A.F. Pisemsky (1850).

Bestuzhev-Marlinsky, A.A. (1797-1837), poet and novelist of the Romantic school.

Bobchinsky, character in N.V. Gogol's comedy 'The Inspector General' (1836).

Boborykin, P.D. (1836-1921), novelist and journalist.

'Bronze Horseman, The' (1833, published 1841), the greatest of A.S. Pushkin's narrative poems.

'Captain's Daughter, The', historical novel by A.S. Push-
kin (1836), set in the times of the Pugachov Uprising
(1773-5).
Catherine II, the Great, born 1729 in Prussia, Empress
1762-96.
Chatsky, hero of the play 'Woe from Wit' (1823), a social
satire by A.S. Griboedov. Chatsky is usually seen as
the first of Russian literature's 'superfluous men'.
Chichikov, hero of N.V. Gogol's 'Dead Souls' (1842).
'Correspondence with Friends' (full title 'Selected
Passages from a Correspondence with Friends') by N.V.
Gogol, a collection of reactionary preachings, published in 1847. Tolstoy called it 'horribly revolting
rubbish'.

Danilevsky, G.P. (1829-90), minor historical novelist.
Danilevsky, N.Ya. (1822-85), thinker, scientist, historian
and leading Pan-Slavist. His 'Russia and Europe'
(1869) develops a theory of history based on individual
civilizations.
Davydov, D.V. (1784-1839), soldier and poet.
'Dead Souls', novel by N.V. Gogol (1842), one of the first
of the great Russian nineteenth-century novels.
Decembrists, the first revolutionary movement in Russia in
the nineteenth century. The revolt took place on the
accession of Nicholas I in December 1825 but was poorly
organized and easily put down.
'Demon', narrative poem by M.Yu. Lermontov (1839).
'Diary of a Madman' ('Memoirs of a Madman'), short story
by N.V. Gogol (1835).
'Diary of a Sportsman', see 'Hunter's Notebook, A'.
Doukhabors (more usually Dukhobors), a peasant sect of
Christian Communists much persecuted by the tsarist
government. Tolstoy gave the royalties from 'Resurrection' to enable many of them to emigrate to Canada.
'Dubrovsky', unfinished novel by A.S. Pushkin.
Durnopechin, hero of 'The Hypochondriac' by A.F. Pisemsky
(1852).

Elchaninov, hero of 'Boyarshchina' by A.F. Pisemsky (1858).
Emancipation of the Peasants (or Serfs), first (1861) of
the Great Reforms carried out during the reign of
Alexander II (1855-81).
'Evgeniy Onegin', novel in verse by A.S. Pushkin (1823-31).

Famusov, character in 'Woe from Wit' by A.S. Griboedov
(1823); he typifies reactionary conservatism.
'Fathers and Sons', novel by I.S. Turgenev (1862).

Glinka, S.N. (1776-1847), writer, journalist and historian.
His 'Memoirs of 1812' was published in 1836.
Gogol, N.V. (1809-52), novelist, playwright and short-
story writer, author of, among others, 'Dead Souls',
'The Government Inspector', 'The Overcoat', 'The Nose'
and 'Taras Bulba'.
Goncharov, I.A. (1812-91), novelist; his best-known work
is 'Oblomov' (1859).
'Government Inspector, The', comedy by N.V. Gogol (1836).
Griboedov, A.S. (1795-1829), writer, remembered for his
social satire 'Woe from Wit' (1823); murdered in Persia
during anti-Russian riots.
Grigorovich, D.V. (1822-99), novelist ('The Village',
1846, 'Anton Goremyka', 1847) and man of letters.
Grushnitsky, character in M.Yu. Lermontov's novel 'A Hero
of our Times' (1840).
'Gypsies, The', narrative poem by A.S. Pushkin (1824,
published 1827). See also under Aleko.

'Hamlet of Shchigrov Province', one of the stories in 'A
Hunter's Notebook' by I.S. Turgenev (1852).
'Hero of our Times, A', novel by M.Yu. Lermontov (1840).
Herzen, A.I. (1812-70), thinker, publicist, and founder
of Russian Populism.
'House of Gentlefolk, A' (or 'A Nobleman's Nest', or 'A
Nest of Gentlefolk'), novel by I.S. Turgenev (1859).
'House of the Dead', novel by F.M. Dostoevsky (1861)
based on his experiences while in exile in Siberia.
'Humiliated and Insulted, The' (or 'Injury and Insult'),
novel by F.M. Dostoevsky (1861).
'Hunter's Notebook, A' (or 'The Diary of a Sportsman'),
series of short stories of peasant life by I.S.
Turgenev (1852).

'Injury and Insult', see 'Humiliated and Insulted, The'.
Irene (or Irina), heroine of 'Smoke' by I.S. Turgenev
(1867).
'Ivanov', first play by A.P. Chekhov (produced 1887).

Kaydanov, I.K. (?1790-1843), writer and pedagogue of
conservative persuasion; many of the textbooks he wrote
on history and politics were adopted in contemporary
educational establishments.
Khlestakov, hero of 'The Government Inspector' by N.V.
Gogol (1836).
'Khor and Kalinich', short story by I.S. Turgenev (1847)
included in 'A Hunter's Notebook' (1852).
'King Lear of the Steppes, A', short story by I.S.
Turgenev (1870).

Kutuzov, M.I. (1745-1813), field marshal and commander-
in-chief of the Russian forces against Napoleon at the
end of the 1812 campaign.

Lavretsky (-tzky), hero of 'A House of Gentlefolk' by
I.S. Turgenev (1859).
Lermontov, M.Yu. (1814-41), poet, novelist and playwright;
author of 'Demon' (1839), 'A Hero of our Times' (1840),
'Masquerade' (1835) and many others.
Litvinov (-off), character in 'Smoke', by I.S. Turgenev
(1867).
Liza, heroine of 'A House of Gentlefolk' by I.S. Turgenev
(1859).

'Madman', possibly mistaken for 'The Diary of a Super-
fluous Man' by I.S. Turgenev (1850).
Maksim Maksimych, character in 'A Hero of our Times' by
M.Yu. Lermontov (1840).
Manilov, character in 'Dead Souls' by N.V. Gogol (1842).
Markevich, B.M. (1822-84), minor writer and novelist.
Marlinsky, see Bestuzhev-Marlinsky.
Mary, Princess, character in 'A Hero of our Times' by
M.Yu. Lermontov (1840).
Mikhaylovsky-Danilevsky, A.I. (1790-1848), soldier and
notable military historian; adjutant to Kutuzov in
1812.
'Mirgorod', collection of short stories by N.V. Gogol
(1835) containing 'Viy', 'Taras Bulba', 'Old-World
Landowners' and 'How the Two Ivans Quarrelled'.
Mironov, Captain, character in 'The Captain's Daughter'
by A.S. Pushkin (1836).
'Mulla-Nur', novel by A.A. Bestuzhev-Marlinsky (1836).
Muravyov-Karsky, N.N. (1794-1866), Russian soldier,
later general; received his name for capturing the
fortress of Kars in Armenia during the Crimean War.

Natalya Alekseevna, heroine of 'Rudin' by I.S. Turgenev
(1856).
'Negro of Peter the Great, The', unfinished historical
novel by A.S. Pushkin (1828).
'Nest of Gentlefolk, A', see 'House of Gentlefolk, A'.
'Ninth Wave, The', novel by G.P. Danilevsky (1874).
'Nobleman's Nest, A', see 'House of Gentlefolk, A'.
'Nose, The', short story by N.V. Gogol (1836).
Novikov, N.I. (1744-1818), leading journalist, publisher
and philanthropist, imprisoned during the last years
of the reign of Catherine the Great.
Nozdryov, character in 'Dead Souls' by N.V. Gogol (1842).

Oblomov, eponymous hero of the novel by I.A. Goncharov (1859); see also under Goncharov.

Old Believers, large sect who broke away from the Russian Orthodox Church in the seventeenth century because they refused to recognize the changes introduced by Patriarch Nikon in the sacred texts and church ritual; some small groups still exist.

Onegin, Evgeniy, hero of the novel of the same name by A.S. Pushkin (1823-31).

'On the Eve', novel by I.S. Turgenev (1860).

Ostrovsky, A.N. (1823-86), playwright ('The Poor Bride', 1852, 'Poverty is no Crime', 1854, 'The Storm', 1860, etc.).

Pechorin, hero of 'A Hero of our Times' by M.Yu. Lermontov (1840).

Peter I, the Great, born 1682, reigned 1696-1725, reforming tsar.

Pigasoff (-ov), character in 'Rudin' by I.S. Turgenev (1856).

Pisemsky, A.F. (1820-81), novelist ('A Thousand Souls', 1858, etc.) and playwright ('A Hard Lot', 1859, etc.).

Plyushkin, character in 'Dead Souls' by N.V. Gogol (1842).

Pochvennik, name for a follower of the ideas on literary criticism originated by A.A. Grigoriev; see headnote to No. 11.

'Polinka Sachs', novel by A.V. Druzhinin (1847).

Poprishchin, hero of 'The Diary of a Madman' by N.V. Gogol (1835).

Potugin, character in 'Smoke' by I.S. Turgenev (1867).

Preobrazhensky Hospital, a hospital for the poor in Moscow.

'Prisoner of the Caucasus, The', 'Byronic' poem by A.S. Pushkin (1822).

Pugachov, E.I. (1726-75), Cossack leader of a popular revolt during the reign of Catherine the Great.

Pushkin, A.S. (1799-1837), generally regarded by Russians as their greatest writer, author of 'Ruslan and Lyudmila' (1820), 'Evgeniy Onegin' (1823-31), 'The Gypsies' (1824), 'Boris Godunov' (1825), 'The Bronze Horseman' (1833) and 'The Captain's Daughter' (1836) among many others.

'Quarter of a Century' (actually 'A Quarter of a Century Ago'), novel by B.M. Markevich (1878).

'Queen of Spades, The', short story by A.S. Pushkin (1834).

Radishchev, A.N. (1749-1802), writer and thinker,

generally regarded as the first Russian radical.   In
  his 'Journey from St Petersburg to Moscow' (1790) he
  depicts the evil conditions of serfdom.
Rudin, hero of the novel of the same name by I.S. Turgenev
  (1856).
'Rusalka', unfinished play by A.S. Pushkin.
'Ruslan and Lyudmilla', one of A.S. Pushkin's earliest
  poems (1820).

Saltychikhla, mistress of Arakcheev (q.v.) whose serfs
  killed her after years of tyranny and cruelty.
(Saltykov-) Shchedrin, M.E. (1826-89), writer and novel-
  ist, most remembered for his novel 'The Golovlyov
  Family' (1872-6) and his many satirical writings.
Silvio, hero of 'The Shot', one of 'The Tales of Belkin'
  (q.v.).
'Smoke', novel by I.S. Turgenev (1867).
'Solid Virtues, The', novel by P.D. Boborykin (1871).
Solomonida, character in 'The Hypochondriac' by A.F. Pis-
  emsky (1852).
Speransky, M.M. (1772-1839), chief minister during the
  first half of the reign of Alexander I.
Stolz, character in 'Oblomov' by I.A. Goncharov (1859).
Sukhovo-Kobylin, A.V. (1817-1903), playwright.
'Superfluous Man', persistent type of hero in nineteenth-
  century Russian literature, intelligent, idealistic,
  but for a variety of reasons ineffectual. The most
  enduring examples are Griboedov's Chatsky, Pushkin's
  Evgeniy Onegin, Lermontov's Pechorin, Turgenev's
  Rudin and Goncharov's Oblomov.
Suvorov, A.V. (1730-1800), Russia's greatest military
  commander.

'Tales of Belkin, The', series of narrative tales by A.S.
  Pushkin (1831), containing 'The Shot', 'The Blizzard',
  'The Undertaker', 'The Postmaster' and 'The Squire's
  Daughter'.
Tania (-nya), character in 'Smoke' by I.S. Turgenev
  (1867).
'Taras Bulba', short story by N.V. Gogol, published as
  one of the collection entitled 'Mirgorod' (1835).
Terek, river in the Caucasus.
'Turning Point', novel by B.M. Markevich (1880).

Uvar Ivanych (Stakhov), character in 'On the Eve' by
  I.S. Turgenev (1860).

Varvara, character in 'A House of Gentlefolk' by I.S.
  Turgenev (1859).

446   Tolstoy: The Critical Heritage

'Virgin Soil', novel by I.S. Turgenev (1877).
Voroshilov, character in 'Smoke' by I.S. Turgenev (1867).

'What is to be Done?', poor but very influential radical
   novel by N.G. Chernyshevsky (1864).
'Who Can Live Happily in Russia?', epic poem on Russian
   peasant life by N.A. Nekrasov (1870-4).

Yasnaya Polyana, Tolstoy's estate and his home for all his
   adult life; it is near Tula, to the south of Moscow.
'Yasnaya Polyana', name Tolstoy gave to his educational
   journal.

Zador-Manovsky, character in 'Boyarshchina' by A.F. Pisemsky (1858).
Zagoskin, M.N. (1789-1852), writer and novelist, best
   remembered for his historical novel 'Yuriy Miloslavsky'
   (1829).

Bibliography

This short bibliography does not aim to be at all comprehensive; it lists a selection of the main works concerned
with criticism of Tolstoy.

(a) TOLSTOY'S WORKS

The definitive edition of Tolstoy's works in Russian is
the 'Polnoye sobraniye sochineniy' ('Complete Collected
Works'), 90 vols, Moscow, 1928-58; each work has a critical essay appended. Translations of Tolstoy's works into
English are numerous and variable in quality. 'The Complete Works of Count Tolstoy', translated and edited by
Leo Wiener, 24 vols, Boston, 1904-5 (not complete and the
translations leave something to be desired), and 'Tolstoy
Centenary Edition', translated by Louise and Aylmer Maude,
21 vols, London, 1928-37 (fairly complete and still probably the best English versions), are the two most ambitious. Much of the major fiction has been published in
English by, particularly, Penguin Classics and Modern
Library.

(b) BIBLIOGRAPHIES OF TOLSTOY CRITICISM

BITOVT, YU., 'Graf L. Tolstoy v literature i iskusstve'
('Count L. Tolstoy in Literature and Art'), Moscow, 1903.
SHELYAPINA, N.G., et al., 'Bibliografiya literatury o
Tolstom, 1917-58, ('Bibliography of Literature on Tolstoy,
1917-58'), Moscow, 1960.
SHELYAPINA, N.G., et al., 'Bibliografiya literatury o
Tolstom, 1959-61' ('Bibliography of Literature on Tolstoy,
1959-61'), Moscow, 1965.
SHELYAPINA, N.G., et al., 'Bibliografiya literatury o L.N.

Tolstom, 1962-7' ('Bibliography of Literature on L.N. Tol-
stoy, 1962-7'), Moscow, 1972.
ZHILINA, E.N., 'L.N. Tolstoy, 1828-1910', Leningrad, 1960.
   There are no comparable editions in English.

(c)   COLLECTIONS OF CRITICAL COMMENT ON TOLSTOY

BULGAKOV, F.I., 'Graf L.N. Tolstoy i kritika ego proiz-
vedeniy' ('Count L.N. Tolstoy and Criticism of his Works'),
3rd edition, Moscow/St Petersburg, 1899.
BYCHKOV, S.P., 'L.N. Tolstoy v russkoy kritike' ('L.N. Tol-
stoy in Russian Criticism'), 3rd edition, Moscow, 1960.
GIFFORD, H., 'Leo Tolstoy', Penguin Critical Anthologies,
Harmondsworth, 1971.
MATTLAW, R.E. 'Tolstoy, A Collection of Critical Essays',
New Jersey, 1967.
ZELINSKY, V., 'Russkaya kriticheskaya literatura o proiz-
vedeniyakh L.N. Tolstogo' ('Russian Critical Writings on
the Works of L.N. Tolstoy'), 8 vols, 2nd edition, Moscow,
1898.
   There are also various articles on Tolstoy in
DAVIE, D., 'Russian Literature and Modern English
Fiction', Chicago, 1965.
ROBERTS, S.E., 'Essays in Russian Literature', Ohio, 1968.

(d)   OTHER WORKS

DECKER, C., Victorian Comment on Russian Realism, 'Papers
of the Modern Language Association of America', 1937,
no. 52.
GRINYOVA, I.E., Russkaya zhurnal'naya kritika 70-kh godov
XIX veka o romane L.N. Tolstogo 'Anna Karenina', 'Uchoniye
zapiski moskovskogo oblastnogo pedagogicheskogo instituta
imeni N.K. Krupskoy' (Criticism of Tolstoy's Novel 'Anna
Karenina' in the Russian Journals in the 1870s, 'Papers of
the N.K. Krupskaya Moscow Regional Pedagogical Institute'),
vol. CXXII, 1963.
HEMMINGS, F.W.J., 'The Russian Novel in France 1884-1914',
Oxford, 1950.
LEDNICKI, W., Tolstoy through American Eyes, 'Slavonic
Review', vol. 25, April 1947.
LEVIN, Yu.D., Tolstoy, Shakespeare and Russian Writers of
the 1860s, 'Oxford Slavonic Papers', new series, vol. 1,
1968.
MOTYLEVA, T.L., 'O mirovom znachenii L.N. Tolstogo' ('On
Tolstoy's World Significance'), Moscow, 1957.
PHELPS, G., 'The Russian Novel in English Fiction', London,
1956.

SHKLOVSKY, V.B., 'Voyna i mir' v zhurnalistike 60-kh
godov, 'Chitatel' i pisatel'' ('War and Peace' and the
Journals in the 1860s, 'Reader and Writer'), 1928, no. 36.
SLONIM, M., Four Western Writers on Tolstoy, 'Russian
Review', April, 1960.
SMITH, J.A., Tolstoy's Fiction in England and America,
PhD thesis, University of Illinois, 1939.
STRUVE, G., Tolstoy in Soviet Criticism, 'Russian Review',
April, 1960.

Select Index

The index is in four sections: I Periodicals mentioned and/or from which material has been quoted; II Those who passed comment; III Tolstoy's works discussed or mentioned; and IV Other writers discussed or mentioned.

I PERIODICALS MENTIONED AND/OR FROM WHICH MATERIAL HAS BEEN QUOTED

III   TOLSTOY'S WORKS DISCUSSED OR MENTIONED

IV   OTHER WRITERS DISCUSSED OR MENTIONED

THE CRITICAL HERITAGE SERIES

GENERAL EDITOR: B. C. SOUTHAM

Volumes published and forthcoming

MATTHEW ARNOLD:	
THE POETRY	Carl Dawson
JANE AUSTEN	B. C. Southam
SAMUEL BECKETT	L. Graver and R. Federman
WILLIAM BLAKE	G. E. Bentley Jr
THE BRONTËS	Miriam Allott
BROWNING	Boyd Litzinger and Donald Smalley
ROBERT BURNS	Donald A. Low
BYRON	Andrew Rutherford
THOMAS CARLYLE	Jules Paul Seigel
CHAUCER 1385–1837	Derek Brewer
CHAUCER 1837–1933	Derek Brewer
CLARE	Mark Storey
CLOUGH	Michael Thorpe
COLERIDGE	J. R. de J. Jackson
WILKIE COLLINS	Norman Page
CONRAD	Norman Sherry
FENIMORE COOPER	George Dekker and John P. McWilliams
CRABBE	Arthur Pollard
STEPHEN CRANE	Richard M. Weatherford
DEFOE	Pat Rogers
DICKENS	Philip Collins
JOHN DONNE	A. J. Smith
DRYDEN	James and Helen Kinsley
GEORGE ELIOT	David Carroll
WILLIAM FAULKNER	John Bassett
HENRY FIELDING	Ronald Paulson and Thomas Lockwood
FORD MADOX FORD	Frank MacShane
E. M. FORSTER	Philip Gardner
GEORGIAN POETRY 1911–1922	Timothy Rogers
GISSING	Pierre Coustillas and Colin Partridge
GOLDSMITH	G. S. Rousseau
THOMAS HARDY	R. G. Cox
HAWTHORNE	J. Donald Crowley
ALDOUS HUXLEY	Donald Watt
IBSEN	Michael Egan